C.R.W. Nevinson

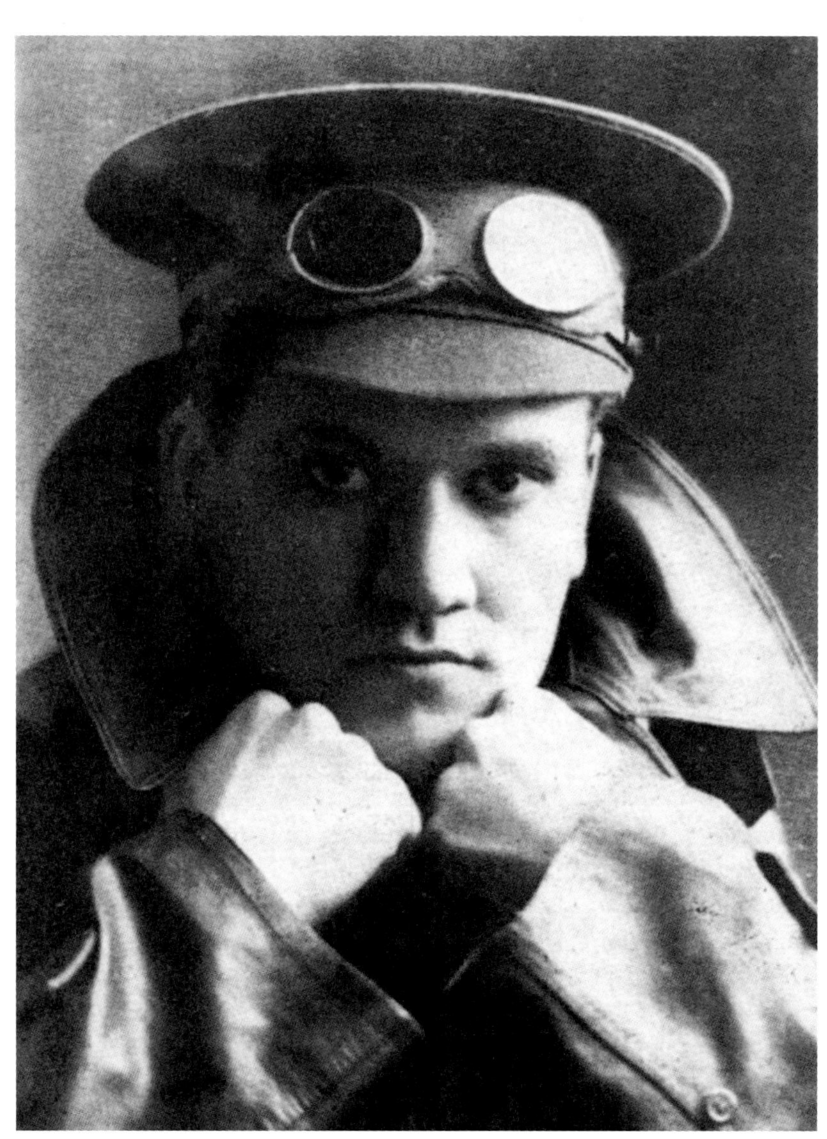

C.R.W. Nevinson

This Cult of Violence

Michael J. K. Walsh

Published for the Paul Mellon Centre for Studies in British Art by
Yale University Press New Haven and London

Library of Congress Cataloging-in-Publication data
Walsh, Michael J. K., 1968–
C.R.W. Nevinson : this cult of violence / Michael J. K. Walsh.
p. cm.
Includes bibliographical references and index.
ISBN 0-300-09507-4
1. Nevinson, C.R.W. (Christopher Richard Wynne),
1889–1946—Criticism and interpretation. I. Title.
ND497.N4 W35 2002
759.2—dc21

20020054 64

Typeset in Walbaum and Futura; typesetting and design by Kate Gallimore
Printed in Italy

Frontispiece: Photographic portrait of C. R.W. Nevinson by Malcolm Arbuthnot, March 1917.

For Mum, Dad and Cathy

CONTENTS

ACKNOWLEDGEMENTS

In writing this book I have incurred a large number of debts to a great many people, all of whom have assisted in one way or another. I have been overwhelmed by the patience, professionalism and assistance offered by the keepers of the archives listed.

It all began with tea and cakes with Charlotte Hallyday at the New English Art Club in 1998, and ended three years later with an apartment full of photocopies, newspapers, letters and photographs from universities, institutions and individuals all over the world. Special mention should go to Hannah Frost at the University of Texas; Gillian Forrester at Yale University; J. Rudman at Uppingham School; the staff at the Tate Archive; Roger Tolson and Michael Moody at the Imperial War Museum; the staff at the Bodleian Library, Oxford University; Lisa Messinger at the Metropolitan Museum of Art in New York; and the staff at Cornell University, Harvard University, Friends House Library, the Slade School of Fine Art and the Museo di Arti Moderna, Italy.

The staff at TASIS Hellenic International School deserve a thank you – especially Julia Langley, Polly Kaldelli, Aline Boundy, and George and Jane Salimbene. Also, at Francis Holland School, Chelsea: Michael Hill, Lyn Jones Parry, Sally Bassington, Ruth Bramley and Katrine Collins. At Rochester Independent College Brian Pain gets a big vote of thanks for funding my studies and granting me sabbatical leave in which to work on the book. Also, Simon de Belder, Sue Cooper, Meg Chapman, Pauline Bailey, Liz Harding, Dorcas Pettit, Jackie Clarke, Alistair Brownlow, Michael Flavin, Steve Medhurst and Pete Gowers. What a decent bunch of people to work with.

Other friends who have contributed and whom I would like to thank in particular are: Dave and Karen (Perkins) Bellamy (Bonhams and the British Museum), Bill and Catherine Cleveland (Tilbury Manor), the Reverend Wealands Bell, Damien Kinvig, Gareth Joel, Jules Wilson, Jenny Cussack, Bobby Tzakpinis (fharisto file mou), Emma Joynes (Cyprus), Mick Smith (for the 'up-grade'), Dave McGee (Antwerp), Tom and Anita O'Shea, Rowan 'Ted' and Lucy MacNeary (Millfield), Niall and Tracy Mills (and all those at Sweet Cheater), Ryan 'Razza' Owen and Kari Vestreng (101st Street, Texas and Norway), Rich Tomes (Brussels), Luisa Tanzi (Milan), James 'Magoo' Muncie and his wife, Ana (Japan and Portugal), Dave Butcher (Brazil), Christie Priode (Atlanta), Jo

Birch, Steve and Rose Anne Mahorney (N. Carolina), Bobby and Dave Kennedy (Pennsylvania), Dougie Hutton (Portora Royal School), Bill Davies (Paris, Athens and Milan), Blakes of the Hollow, Sally Low, Despina Pangalos, James 'Rafter' Binns and everyone in 'Skid Row' (St Andrews), Sarah Draper (Hong Kong), Roy 'Boy' Skanes (Nova Scotia), Toby Gane (Rad Mobile), Michael 'Hobbo' Hobson and Becky (Trinity Hall, Cambridge), Professor Janet Myles, John Rimmer (De Montfort University), Sian Finch, Becky Wigmore, Alice Sage, Michael 'Thatch' Clack (Jesus College, Cambridge), Steve Butler and Steve Howard of the 'Sokhovs', Terry Kavanagh, Pete McCanny (LLT), Charlie Gillam, Conor Hillen (Athens), Olivia Hill, Millie Blundell, Helen and Greg Wearne (British Columbia), Lee Wortman and Woodie (N. Carolina), Bill Wortman (Indiana), Marilyn Griffin, Clint Orr, Ben Nuttall, Oleg Roslak, Serge Bhachy (Kentucky), Sean Savage (New York), Mary Blake, Don and Barbara Schullian, Dennis Forbes (Jesus College, Cambridge), Mark Audley-Thewles, Angheliki and Nassita Petropolou (Athens), Mark Taylor, Andy Morris, Thomas 'T' Eaton, Rod 'Rodders' Jones, Ma Belles, Tony 'Scanners' Scanlan, Zarir 'Z' Bharucha, Jane de Rome, Mary and Marty Connelly (Enniskillen), Dr Robert Chaplin (FHS), Penny Paparunas (Switzerland), Jason Egan (Australia), Chris Entwhistle, Alan Slade, Jackie Ingham, Mikey Hume, Natalie Gouaze, Ian Young, the Greene family (Enniskillen), the Patterson family, Fred Clough, Andy Hale, Major Jack Doonan, MBE, Mark Hallett, and Frances Spalding.

For being my special partner in Greece and England and for putting up with me for four years, I thank Anna Rogakou.

There have also been many useful discussions and an exchange of information with Jonathan Black and Christopher Martin, both of whom, through our mutual interest in Nevinson, have become friends.

Professor Angela V. John has been more than helpful, reading the early drafts of this book and also sharing her expertise on the Nevinson family. Her book on C.R.W. Nevinson's father, Henry, is nearing completion. Dr Andrew Gray also made an enormous contribution with his comments and corrections concerning the more advanced stages of the text. Dr David Peters Corbett at the University of York deserves thanks for his guidance and contributions from the very beginning.

Amazingly, at the outset of my research, following my return from Greece, I was offered an apartment in Chelsea by a philanthropic family who wished to assist me as best they could. To Nancy, Anthony, Catherine and Christopher Sykes I offer my heartfelt thanks.

My everlasting thanks go to Grant Carder who never knew how much he meant to me, nor ever appreciated how much he taught me. Eleven years on, I miss him every single day, and know now I always shall. Rest in Peace.

Pride of place goes to my mother, father and sister. My debt to you is incalculable but never think that I don't appreciate it. None of this would have happened had it not been for your academic, emotional and financial support. It is a mere token then that I should dedicate this study to you. I love you.

This war did not take the modern artist by surprise. I think it can be said that modern artists have been at war since 1912. Everything in art was in turmoil – everything was bursting – the whole talk among artists was of war. They were in love with the glory of violence. They were dynamic, Bolshevistic, chaotic. Not only European artists but Americans as well were bitten with this cult of violence.

C.R.W. Nevinson, 1919

INTRODUCTION

When the *New York Times* reported the death of a 'genius, playboy and war hero' on 8 October 1946, they were bringing down the curtain on the career of one of the most glamorous and high profile English artists of the early twentieth century. However, the obituary did not fail to mention that he had also been 'a bundle of admitted complexes' whilst conceding that 'at bottom [he had been] a sensitive neurotic'.[2] The British press might have been reporting the death of a different person entirely in an obituary entitled 'Stricken artist dies in his native Hampstead.'[3] Even in the death of C.R.W. Nevinson, a complex and contradictory set of standards emerged, typical and reminiscent of those he had generated and played upon in his own lifetime. Remembered as a rebel, a Futurist, a soldier of the Great War and an outspoken critic of so much and so many within the art world, both in Britain and in the United States of America, the charismatic Nevinson, and his carefully crafted persona, was being laid to rest.

Importantly, this reputation, and artistic momentum, had been built during a surprisingly short period in the artist's career, over a quarter of a century earlier, principally between the years 1912 and 1919. John Rothenstein claimed that this was a misfortune and that his subsequent relative obscurity was due to the fact that 'his finest pictures had for their subject something that everyone was under an almost irresistible compulsion to expel from their memory'.[4] The remainder of his life and work, therefore, was to be eclipsed by the events and artistic achievements of these formative years. The era of the *bon viveur* of London, Paris and New York, however, had only just begun.

As his own record he left behind the aptly named and highly subjective autobiography *Paint and Prejudice*, and this has formed the basis of our understanding of his life and work for over half a century. This account however has to be treated with caution and has been described as 'one of the least trustworthy documents in 20th Century British art history'.[5] In acknowledging these inconsistencies, whether accidental or deliberate, this new study has been undertaken leaning heavily on recently uncovered archival sources. Therefore, by questioning Nevinson's own accounts, and those that have subsequently been ingrained into art history, an alternative history of this crucial period in both the life of the artist, and in modern English painting, can now be presented.

The year 1920 is a logical point at which to conclude as, under examination, the majority of Nevinson's post-war painting fails (in my opinion) to attain the status of artistic value, integrity and intelligibility of the pre-war and war years. One critic summed this up neatly by saying, 'His brush with war was his brush with fame',[6] while another went so far as to suggest that 'had Nevinson been killed at the Front in 1916 his reputation could only have been of the young genius cut short, his few pictures treasured for what might have been; instead we have what was.'[7]

But Nevinson loathed critics and would certainly have taken umbrage at these comments, which he would have attacked as entirely fallacious. Undeniably though, when it came to making a very public record of his own life, he dedicated almost two thirds of his autobiography to this early period, the latter years being swept over quickly and without the mention of a single painting. It seems logical, therefore, even by Nevinson's own admission, that this book should look at the student, rebel, celebrity, soldier and artist in these halcyon days in the second decade of the twentieth century.

That no independent study of Nevinson and his art has been conducted until now is surprising considering his undoubted celebrity in, and importance to, the period in question. Perhaps now he can begin to re-emerge from the art-historical obscurity into which his name has inexplicably retreated over the last eighty years to take his rightful place beside his student peers, Percy Wyndham Lewis, David Bomberg, Edward Wadsworth, Mark Gertler, Dora Carrington and Stanley Spencer, to whom history has been more accommodating.

Lastly, it is significant to note that Nevinson has always been seen as one of the very few Britons to benefit directly from the turmoil and upheavals of the period 1912–19. Instead, as the convalescent post-war period began, this book demonstrates that Nevinson, like so many others of his generation, was a victim of what he himself had called 'this cult of violence'.

1

Family and Early Education 1889–1909

He is the son of H. W. Nevinson, the war correspondent, who also has a rebellious temperament. The father, however, confines his violent revolutionism to politics and journalism, while the son finds more colour for his views in the paint-box.[1]

There can be little doubt that the family into which Christopher Richard Wynne Nevinson was born, on 13 August 1889, was both as dynamic and as unusual as his autobiography suggests.[2] The family home was in John Street, Hampstead, and was described as being an 'old, white, Hampsteadean monument of stucco, dampness, bad plumbing, and immense kitchens, set in a garden of lilac and may'.[3] In 1896 the family moved to 44 Savernake Road, off Parliament Hill,[4] and again, in 1901, to 4 Downside Crescent, Hampstead. Richard's father, Henry Woodd Nevinson (1856–1941), was a famous war correspondent, social and political reformer and a high-profile member of Victorian and Edwardian London society (fig. 1). His mother, Margaret Wynne Nevinson (née Jones) (1858–1932), was an active liberal, a suffragette campaigner and one of London's first female Justices of the Peace. Richard only briefly mentioned in his autobiography that he had a sister, Philippa (1885–1950), who trained at the Royal College of Music and who played piano duets with Margaret. The Nevinson household, therefore, at whatever address, was a centre of enlightened, intellectual and international thought and cultured activity. Richard recorded: 'I was born into the most exquisite and intellectual ambience, and in the early years at home I was surrounded by scholarship and all the brilliance and wit of the nineties.'[5] The legacy of the liberal and philanthropic family was obvious and he wrote: 'Although both my Father and my Mother came from old English families, I was brought up in a spirit of internationalism. My father had only lately given up a post he had held as professor at Jena.'[6] He added: 'Both my parents were as much at home in Europe as they were in London',[7] and then went on to explain that even when they were in London they employed foreign servants. By his own account it was this that gave him his ability to communicate in French and German with the same ease as he did in English.[8] He claimed also that he had been familiar with the theories of Wilde and Whistler from childhood and that he had been no stranger to enlightened thinking in Britain, or to the European avant-garde, from an early age.

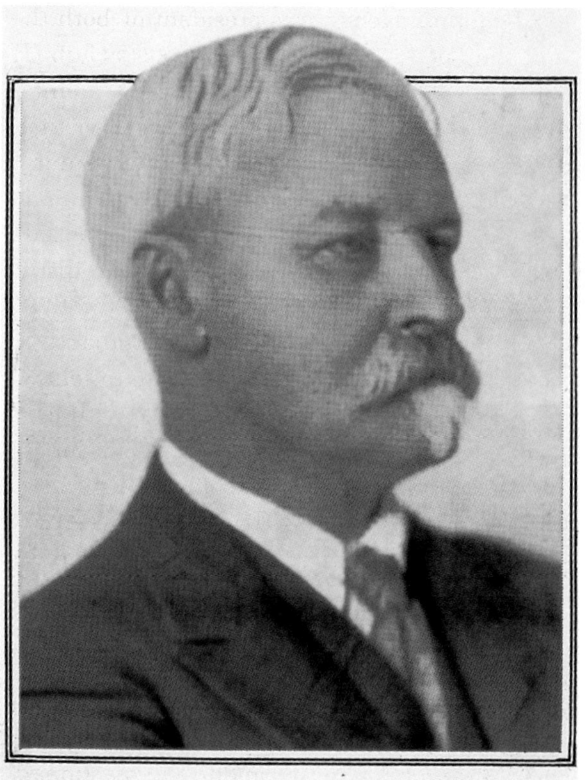

1. H.W. Nevinson. Private collection.

Several years later, in 1913, as a student, he recorded frustration with the highly charged intellectual atmosphere at home when he wrote privately, 'If my mother does happen to be in for a meal she is so engrossed in other things that she hardly hears & certainly never takes in a word I say.'[9] In his autobiography, however, he glossed over this and flamboyantly reminisced about his francophile mother, claiming:

> In the art colonies at Pont-Aven, Concarneau, Quimper, St. Pol, Cauelebec, and St. Michel we always associated with the painters. The name of Monet had been familiar to me for some time. As my mother had been in Paris from about 1870 she was particularly versed in the Impressionist school; and I had already devoured, by the age of fifteen, the books of Camille Mauclair on Renoir, Monet, Degas, Sisley and Pissarro, and had heard of Gauguin and Cezanne. I had even heard of the 'mad' painting of Van Gogh some five years before their 'discovery' by Roger Fry and the dealers.[10]

His grandfather on his mother's side, the rector of St Margaret's in Leicester, had also been influential and had had a house hung with Italian art and Constable landscapes. Richard reminisced that these were amongst his earliest memories and that this surely had nurtured in him a very early love of art. An ambiguity in this account stems from the fact that Margaret's father died before he was born.[11]

His father, Henry, was president of both the National Council for Civil Liberties and the Poets, Essayists and Novelists Club (P.E.N.),[12] he was the vice-president of the Anti-Slavery Society, a founding member of the Men's Political Union for Women's Enfranchisement, while still writing and speaking on the subject of Irish nationalism and the disgrace of slavery in Portuguese Angola. Both of Richard's parents were champions of polemic and 'underdog' causes and as a result Richard could recall that 'My father had been chucked out of more meetings than any other man in London and had achieved the distinction of being publicly rebuked by Lloyd George at the Albert Hall'.[13] His mother kept an open-door policy at home for 'French, Germans, Finns, Russians, Indians, "Colonials", Professional Irishmen and Suffragettes'.[14] In July 1912 he wrote to fellow Slade student, Dora Carrington, displaying, once again, some frustration with his parents: 'I have seldom met such egoists as either my father or mother. On Sunday instead of you we had two Indian revolutionists, a fellow of some college at Cambridge & the other a Black, an authority on economics. They had dinner & went up to William Rothenstein's to hear Yeats read his poems.'[15] Both father and mother, on the other hand, were also accredited by their son with a tolerance of the lower classes as the former was secretary to the London Playing Fields Association and the latter taught French in the slums of the East End of London. Utilizing this unusual attribute, and immune to what he considered the English fear of the poor and the uneducated, he was led, he recounted, to men like Mark Gertler at the Slade. Through his father too came the early introduction to war and to the reactionary nature of strong opinions surrounding it. Retrospectively Richard mused: 'I was trained in war long before my doomed generation.'[16] His father, as well as constantly being away in Africa or the Balkans, was seen at pro-Boer meetings and demonstrations in and around London, particularly at Parliament Hill. This, it is recorded, guaranteed that the son found himself 'thrown into handy ponds by patriots'.[17] Far from being sad at his father's frequent absences he wrote: 'Fortunately my father soon left for South Africa.'[18] Another characteristic of Henry's, which filtered down to the son, was that of nocturnal living. He recalled that his father would scarcely ever arrive home before three or four in the morning, waking him up in the process. Rather bitterly he stated that during the day 'I was driven out so that my father could sleep.'[19] Generally though, his father's legacy was positive and Richard claimed that 'I of course have freedom bred all over me thanks to my father.'[20] Though the relationship between father and son could be trying Richard did acknowledge him as a brilliant man and professed an admiration for both his career and his 'man of action' profession. The recollections say nothing however of affection or warmth. It is known that Henry and Margaret became informally estranged when Richard was a boy.[21]

Little wonder then that Richard could muse in his autobiography, 'By upbringing I could never accept the established.'[22] Frank Rutter's reminiscences followed the same lines when he wrote that Richard was 'the child of parents who had singularly noble ideas, who were markedly progressive and humane in their habit of thought'. He went on to add 'Nevinson started life with a pre-natal tendency to revolt against injustice, cruelty and oppression.'[23] But if, as it was to prove in later life, he was temperamental, outspoken and argumentative, he was also deeply sensitive and this had been observed by his mother from early childhood. She recorded the very diverse nature of her young son who would 'throw himself on the floor and roll over and over, not crying, but roaring softly and holding his breath till he was black in the face',[24] and then contrasted this with the observation that stories, pictures and music could lead the child to tears. If intellectualism, liberalism, internationalism and revolutionary opinions were what really moulded the youth then, the stage set in Hampstead was precisely the sort on which a great artist might appear.

Uppingham: 'A Necessary Unhappiness'[25]

Education proved traumatic for Richard and in his autobiography he was not slow to castigate his parents for the painful course upon which he was now to embark. Firstly they had sent him to a large (unnamed) school at the age of seven from which he had to be removed following a public flogging.[26] The transfer to University College School, under Charles Simmons, was a successful one, and there he recorded a normal development, even winning prizes for painting. His father didn't agree however, and wrote in his private diary in 1901 that his eleven-year-old son 'Rich [was] growing up all wrong.'[27] Despite private tuition at home in Greek and Latin, the father was to learn from Simmons that his son had 'no exceptional talent',[28] and so turned his attention to applying for a place at a public school, notably at Haileybury, Clifton or Uppingham.[29] The whole business of being extracted, once again, from a happy environment, and from his circle of friends (known as the Manboya Gang[30]), was recorded rather coldly in the following way:

> Before that, when Ladysmith was relieved, my Father had returned on short leave before going to Pretoria, and there is no doubt he was impressed by the charm and brilliance of the Army staff, and the nobility and altruism that seemed to be founded on the public-school spirit. It was much later on in life that he became a Socialist. In those days he was a polished Englishman of culture, and said he wanted me to go to Shrewsbury, his old school, and on to Balliol, if not into the Army itself.[31]

In his father's absence, he recorded, his mother chose Uppingham instead of Shrewsbury, taking him away from University College School[32] and from the private tutorship of John Fulleylove[33] in 1903 (fig. 2). 'No qualms of mine gave me an inkling of the horrors I was to undergo', he mused, over thirty years later.[34] While his father was abroad, 'chiefly in India, in Central Africa, or in Spain, reporting the Spanish–American War',[35] Richard was miserable, at the mercy of the institution, the masters and pupils, suffering not only patriotic indoctrination, mental and physical bullying, but also sexual abuse. 'I learned nothing: I did nothing. I was kicked, hounded, caned, flogged, hairbrushed, morning, noon and night. The more I suffered the less I cared.'[36] Illness, induced by a particularly harsh beating at the hands of the cricket eleven, coupled with the suggestion of the headmaster, that he should go into fruit farming in California, was enough, according to his recollections, to

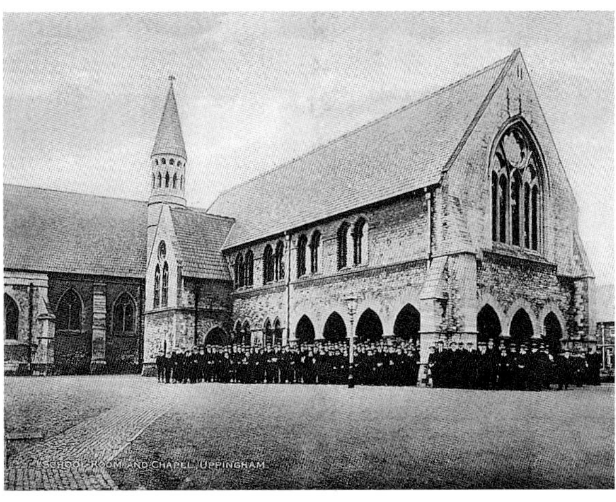

2. Uppingham School, *c.* 1903. Uppingham School Archive.

persuade his father that it was time to withdraw his son.[37] Uppingham had fostered no love of the classics in the boy, rather an interest in art and modern mechanics. More than anything it created the loathing of institutions that was to be so recurrent throughout his life. But his unhappiness, he believed, during the three-year stay had not been sufficient to make his father withdraw him, neither had his illnesses, and rather, the father had left him alone to face the overwhelming odds of the establishment. He had sent him to school, then gone away again to report on some foreign conflict, rarely been in touch and certainly shown no concern, let alone remorse, at his decision to send him to board. Such self-proclaimed victimization at the hands of family, friends and institutions, is simply part of Richard's complex character, so prevalent throughout his lifetime (and his autobiography), and the case of Uppingham merely an early example of this.

Archival research finds many of these claims unsubstantiated or simply untrue. Henry's journals show that he had applied for Uppingham two years in advance, and that six months before his son took his place there, father and mother (separately) had travelled to Leicestershire to meet the headmaster, Selwyn, but had not been particularly impressed.[38] The father actually took his son to school personally, and, far from being thousands of miles away and uncaring, had felt the emotion of the parting very closely, describing it as 'a day of choking sadness to me & us all'.[39] The same diary entry reads: 'I never felt such sorrow as when the train whistled & the boy had to turn back alone to go to his lonely place, unknowing what to do & alone for the first time. He tried to be brave and that made it the harder. It was worse than going to school again myself. Came home in extreme misery.'[40] Neither did the sadness pass quickly as his entries for the following weeks are full of references such as 'Full of grief & yearning about poor Rich',[41] 'Missed poor Rich very much'[42] and 'Unhappy all day at Rich's unhappiness.'[43] Conditions were poor, that much is substantiated by a letter he received from his son, which he then subsequently described in his journal as follows: 'Usual work & all the time my poor Rich is suffering horrible misery, – bullying, filth, thieving, underfeeding and every torment. I can hardly live for sorrow.'[44] From the very beginning, as was to happen so many times in the future, his father intervened to fight his son's battles for him, sending a copy of his son's letter, which had been 'full of terror and rage', to Selwyn, whilst sending his son a note 'to hold out in hope'.[45] An appointment was arranged for a trip to Leicestershire and it was carried out on 10 October 1903.[46] When he met Richard the boy 'cried terribly at first', then 'poured out all his griefs & miseries quite frankly and pathetically'. Soon he regained his composure and became 'manly & capable & resolute' by the end of the meeting. He also tried to take his father to see his paintings, though the particular building in question was locked up.[47] When Henry left he was convinced that the problem was homesickness and wrote to Selwyn on 11 October saying, 'the boy will pull through & be a good sort of man', requesting also that he not change house as the headmaster had suggested.[48] By the Christmas holidays his father could report: 'Rich came home with great joy and success.'[49] The problem by now had shifted, it appears, to Selwyn himself who was finding Richard not only sickly and proud but also, he complained to his father, displaying a 'want of manners & brusqueness'.[50]

By 1905 Henry could record that his son was 'much advanced in freedom and manner',[51] though continually suffering from illness, which a certain Dr Williams was attempting to deal with. Indeed, the headmaster had kindly let Margaret come and share his house as she nursed her son back to health over a three-week period. This illness was not specified but had allegedly led to sleeplessness and delirious fits, and eventually to his being removed for an entire term. The father believed that his son was playing upon the illness to elicit sympathy and reported that Richard would hide his happiness during visits to look sulky and unwell, presumably in a desire to be removed from the school.[52] In April 1906 it was proved that the illnesses had been genuine as he was operated upon for appendicitis.[53] Eventually Henry began to agree that it had all been a mistake, and that the school, focussing on sports and on the Cadet Corps, was displaying little encouragement or enthusiasm for the one talent which his son was showing, art. He wrote privately: 'Came away with some sense of failure & loss at the wasted years in the boy's life there, just through the bad choice of school.'[54] Nevertheless he did not withdraw him. Instead, on termly visits home, he and his son would visit art galleries, in particular admiring the works of Stanhope Forbes, John Lavery, Muirhead Bone and James Jebusa Shannon.[55] In term time, his father would keep his distance, communicating only by letter.[56] Eventually, in late 1907 Richard was removed from Uppingham, though in a later publication Henry instigated speculation that this may have been for financial reasons. It was recorded that 'The expenses for my daughter's excellent musical education, and for my son's continuance in ignorance at a great public school, were heavy, and the future of both was dubious.'[57] He later observed in *Changes and Chances* his son's hatred for the establishment and his discovery of a new interest which was to be his future:

> For myself, by far the most vital external event in those years was the discovery of my son Richard's love of drawing and capacity for imagining scenes in uncommon forms. He was then about thirteen and I recognised with apprehension that he would become an artist or nothing. Soon afterwards, most unhappily, I was

> induced to send him to a public school for three years, and I might just as well have sent him for three years to hell. Once or twice I went down to play the unpleasing part of the indignant parent, but it is useless to try changing the tone of a school from the outside. I offered to remove him to Shrewsbury, where my old friends among the masters would have helped him, but he preferred to 'stick it', and very likely the school was not in itself much worse than the average public school for a boy whose main interest lay in art. Indeed, one can imagine no more fatal characteristic for ensuring the contempt or detestation of boys and our ordinary masters alike. And it seems to me a terrible thing that any boy, however unusual and incomprehensible his inclination, should look back upon his school days with horror, and only wish to blot them out of his memory, after having in three years, at great expense, learnt nothing.[58]

Interestingly, his father and mother maintained that it was their son's decision to stay despite everything. Henry also implied, though perhaps unintentionally, that his son may have been unusual, and that the source of the problem was the school's inability to deal with that. His tone verged on apologetic and there seemed to be a greater empathy with the school and 'our masters' than with the misfit son. Richard had no such doubt, however, about the legacy of the establishment when he claimed: 'It has made me aggressive on one hand and too shy on the other hand, and both states are opposites of the same thing. The only things that I ever learned as a youth are those I have spent years trying to forget.'[59] Ironically, he was happy to promote himself as a public school man several years later when it came to getting a position in the army.

Not for the last time Richard saw himself in the role of the victim and victimized, helpless at the hands of a greater institution. He depicted himself, as he would do so often in the future, as the outsider. He portrayed himself as striving for his destiny as an artist despite hindrances, both mental and physical, all around him.

Between Uppingham and the Slade

It was his mother, according to *Paint and Prejudice*, who rallied round after his withdrawal from Uppingham to take him on a 'Grand Tour' of Spain, Northern Africa, the Italian Lakes and Venice. It is difficult to substantiate this claim as the only record of his departing for anywhere with his mother was on brief trips to France and to the south coast of England. Throughout late 1907 and 1908, following his return to London, it was his father who nurtured his love for art and together they went to exhibitions, such as that of the work of Max Beerbohm at the Carfax Galleries, which they attended with Robert 'Robbie' Ross.[60] Likewise, Henry began taking his son's pictures to influential people and possible patrons, even while his son was a teenager and before he formally attended an art school.[61] Meanwhile at home the political, artistic, progressive and musical atmosphere led the confused youth to the realization that his future lay with painting. Fired by his intellectual and international upbringing, by visits to Venice and other European capitals with his mother, and by his revulsion of all that established English society had offered him, he proclaimed that it was impossible for him to do anything else. Richard made the decision to distance himself from his unhappy past and to turn to art school. Retrospectively he could therefore record that 'From Uppingham I went straight to heaven.'[62]

St John's Wood School of Art

St John's Wood School of Art was located at Elm Tree Road and had been founded by A. A. Calderon in 1878 as a form of nursery school for the Royal Academy Schools.[63] The principal in Richard's time, 1907–8, was a Mr Ward. A later prospectus, from 1912, gives us an idea of the priorities of the establishment, stating that 'The advanced student is fitted to take his place in the art world, thoroughly equipped in technical training and with his personality unscathed.'[64] Richard himself appears to have been extremely happy there with little to suggest the turbulent and polemic nature of the years to come. Later, however, he would write privately that the school was full of either 'fools or gentlemen'.[65] Nevertheless, he wrote that 'within half an hour, [I was] almost unrecognizable as the same character that had been at Uppingham'.[66] There was a celebration of youth and an excitement for art that manifested itself not only in 'my craze' [67] for Messina, Holbein and Dürer, but, more importantly in 'the music hall habit'[68] the latter of which, in years to come, may have directed him towards Sickert[69] and colleagues at Fitzroy Street. He expressed a profound admiration for De Wint, Monet and Turner, but claimed that when an unnamed elderly turor introduced him to the works of Augustus John it was this which 'upset my apple cart'.[70] Contradictory, and as profoundly English as these influences may seem, they indicated to Richard that he should reconsider where his mature formal art training was to take place after the apprenticeship at St John's Wood was complete. Paris, he believed, would have to wait until he was ready to appreciate it and maximize the time he might spend there, while the Royal Academy was becoming daily less and less appealing. Meanwhile, working in life classes and sketching classical casts, he developed the ability to create tonal effects and tightness of technique which he believed were essential prerequisites before dabbling in the more avant-garde ideas coming from France. He also participated in a sketching club, working on landscapes daily and life drawings with the son of the artist William Orchardson. It was at St John's Wood too that he first started to enjoy the company of female students, in particular one called Philippa Preston,[71] whom Henry would describe as 'wildly impossible & irrepressible in charm, with a touch of Ibsenite daring'.[72] Richard wrote nostalgically of the student dances and visits to the bohemian Café Royal, the Tivoli, the Pavilion, the Alhambra and the Empire. Artistic recognition also began, according to his own recollections, at this time with a prize from Sir David Murray and encouraging words from Charles Syms, Sir James Lynton and Sir John Clausen. *Paint and Prejudice* goes on to record that at this time, at about the age of seventeen, his first commission came in from none other than Ramsay MacDonald, who had visited the Nevinson household to discuss certain contemporary issues with Margaret and Henry. Lunch at the House of Commons, followed by an introduction to Keir Hardie, the Independent Labour

Party pioneer, seems a rather grand start to a teenage artist's career if not prompted by influential contacts. In the end, however, the commission was rejected. Further trips with his mother kept the admiration of continental art prominent, especially in the light of the material vulgarity of the *nouveaux riches* English patrons which he identified as being mostly merchants from the north. In a society where 'money was rapidly taking the place of breeding, birth and culture'[73] art had been dragged down to 'Darbies and Joans, deeds of daring-do or of sacrifice, or perhaps young girls praying while dogs looked on with human eyes expressing reverence mixed with envy'.[74] He even claimed to have met Toulouse-Lautrec, 'a dwarf in a frock-coat',[75] at this time when he was becoming as at home in the French capital as ever he was in London.

Certainly, as can be expected, he displayed a disorientation artistically which is recorded when Henry wrote of going to see 'that queer kind of work that seems so unlike work'[76] only to be told that 'he has no true style yet but tries every way'. Orchardson apparently lectured him on his son's 'want of concentration', and led the former to conclude that 'he has no true line yet'.[77] Richard had gone to some length in *Paint and Prejudice* to depict this as the era of the Café Royal, of the Music Hall, of winning prizes and of making a living by selling landscapes, often of foreign subjects, necessitating the opening of his own bank account at the age of seventeen. He also recorded that these were perhaps the happiest of all his student days. Then, following an observation by Sargent, and on seeing a copy of the *Studio*,[78] he came to the realization that the path to the Royal Academy seemed the wrong one to pursue and that perhaps the more liberal, and European, Slade ought to be thought of more seriously.[79] Here, the 'method of draughtsmanship had a liveliness and intention unknown in the misapplied energy of the old-fashioned dogmas that came to England through the salons of 1870.'[80] The result was clean cut. 'I left for the Slade and abandoned any attempt to get into the Royal Academy Schools, a grave step which I took lightly.' [81]

2

The Slade: Friendships and the Developing Artist 1909–1912

It was an exciting age in which to be young.[1]

Nevinson at the Slade

Richard wrote that the Slade in 1909 'was full with a crowd of men such as I have never seen before or since'.[2] Paul Nash described it in a similar fashion saying that it 'was in one of its periodical triumphal flows'.[3] But Chaplin has also highlighted a gulf between tutors and students, stating 'Indeed with the student generation of 1908–1912, it was unbridgeable. Nevinson and Wadsworth were within, Roger Fry within and without; and both Cezanne and Picasso announced.'[4] Richard's own first impressions certainly did not bode well for the future when he recorded: 'Immediately I was aware again of that terrible disapproving atmosphere of the public school. Once more shyness and uncertainty came back to me.'[5] Nash too recorded the phenomenon saying the Slade was 'more like a typical English Public School seen in a nightmare' comparing it to 'St. Paul's at its chilliest'.[6] The parental atmosphere of St John's Wood had been replaced with the more sinister tutorship of Professor Brown[7] and Henry Tonks[8] and Richard remembered an early brush with the latter which 'managed to shatter my self confidence'.[9] Stanley Spencer also recalled the former's 'ruthless and withering criticism'.[10] The unity between student artists may not have been immediate either and Richard declared himself unhappy and lonely throughout his first year, though this possibly could be because he enrolled late in January 1909, despite having left St John's Wood in the summer of 1908.[11] To add to everything else he also felt unfulfilled as an artist and bolstered his lessons with additional studies privately at Heatherly's.[12] It is probably in relation to this early period that he was described as 'a lone wolf'.[13]

The friendship of Wadsworth[14], Gertler[15] and Allinson[16], in his second year, soon led him to the social circle of what was know as the Coster Gang, which also included of Ihlee,[17] Lightfoot,[18] Claus,[19] Currie[20] and Spencer.[21] Together, they began to show some of the youthful exuberance and rebellious tendencies that would, for Richard at least, find ultimate expression with the activities of Futurism and the rebel coteries of which he would soon be part. Already a radical change in direction was observed when he declared that 'We represented a reaction against

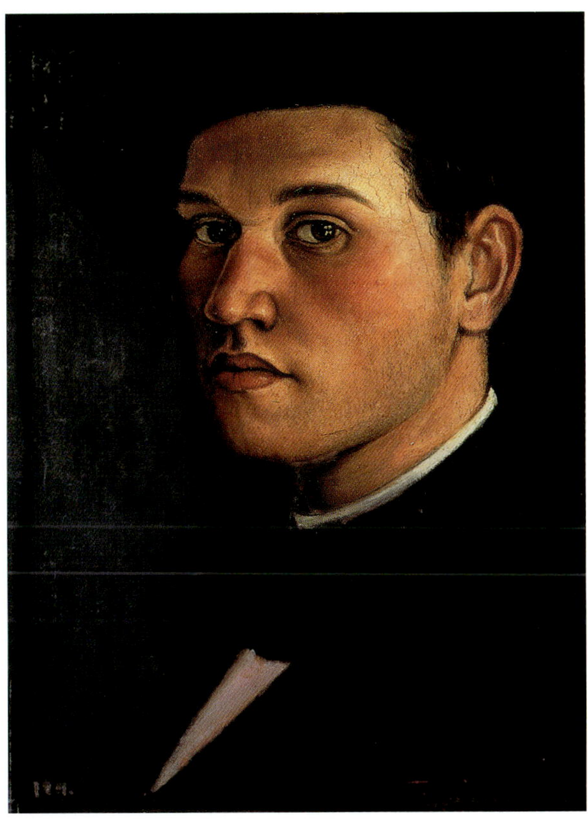

3. *Self-Portrait*, 1911. Oil on panel, 31.1 x 23.2 cm. Tate Gallery, London.

the priggishness, posturing and posing, which had been left as a legacy to the Slade from John's generation.'[22] He was probably quite right in saying that 'we must have been a sore trial for poor virgin Tonks'.[23] Conversely Tonks would later ponder 'What a brood I have raised.'[24]

On a personal level Richard's confidence grew to the point that Nash remembered him at the Slade as being the school bully, reminiscing that 'He invented the tortures for the self-conscious new boys. I came in for sarcasm because of my rather neat appearance.'[25] Stanley Spencer was victim too of his taunts, though was not so passive in accepting them. His biographer described the scene as follows: 'His dedicated nature had little patience with the public-school-type humour prevalent among some of the well-heeled young bloods there. Goaded on one occasion beyond endurance, he silenced one tormentor by pouring white paint over his new suit.'[26] The tormentor, of course, was Richard. Also recorded, in the Nash text, was the rather cosmopolitan appearance of the student Nevinson 'with his Quartier Latin tie and naïve hat'.[27] This was further described by Richard himself when he reminisced about how fellow students gathered around to see the work of 'this old hand with the large bow-tie, bewaisted coat, socks and hankerchiefs of a delicate peacock blue, and a slight growth of whiskers *à la* Rapin about his ears'.[28] His *Self-Portrait* of 1911 (fig. 3) would certainly support the description of the artist's bohemian appearance. To iron out any ambiguity he stressed that 'In those days it was possible to be a dandy without being thought a pansy as well.'[29] Rather less kindly Allinson recorded that 'Because of his bulbous forehead, high cheek-bones, flat nose and crinkly hair, Richard received the nickname "Bucknigger"'.[30] To fellow student Dora Carrington[31] he was just 'Chips'.[32]

Richard nostalgically recorded that with his colleagues he had been 'the terror of Soho and violent participants, for the mere love of a row, at such places as the anti-vivisectionists'.[33] The police stations and courtrooms of Bow Street and Vine Street were allegedly familiar to the members of 'the gang'. More often they were all regulars at the Café Royal on Regent Street and the Petit Savoyard on Greek Street, behind Shaftesbury Avenue, the latter of which was decorated by the group.[34] Allinson recorded: 'We formed a quintet that became inseparable in work and play. Nevinson and Wadsworth as first and second violins, led, Gertler and I followed as viola and 'cello, with Sassoon occasionally audible in the background in the part of the double bass.'[35] Later, in 1911 and 1912, the gang also travelled to Paris together.

Richard also observed that his early passion for the music hall was being nurtured and was developing to the point that 'The Bedford Music Hall was our Mecca.'[36] This passion led him, inevitably, to Sickert, Pissarro, Gore, Gilman, Ginner and in turn to Lewis, with whom his post-Slade reputation would be so closely linked. He suggested too that it was at this stage that he was beginning to get noticed through exhibitions at the Friday Club and to come in for special comment by Robert Ross and Frank Rutter.[37] As parting advice from the Slade in 1912, however, Tonks advised him to give up art as a career altogether. This was advice that Richard was happy to ignore from a man he had come to loathe.

His memoirs therefore portray him as the rebel, the anti-establishment standard bearer of intellectualism and internationalism in a stifling environment of shallow standards and myopic vision, and this is how existing published sources continue to treat his period of study at the Slade. Recent research shows this to be inaccurate at best, if not entirely false.

Nevinson, Gertler and Carrington at the Slade

The photograph of the Slade outing and picnic from the summer of 1912 (fig. 4) acts as a useful introduction to the key personages associated with the 'rebel generation' at the art school. Seated in the front row and on the extreme left is Dora Carrington with her characteristically cropped hair. Beside her and wearing a bow-tie is Richard with his arm draped over the leg of third friend, Mark Gertler.[38] In parallel to this, and useful in any introduction to these artists, and the period in question, is the novel *Mendel*, by Gilbert Cannan, written in 1920.[39] Though written as a portrait of Mark Gertler (Mendel), it relates the story of the Slade (Detmold), and the friends therein, like Carrington (Morrison), Currie (Logan), John (Calthrop) and Nevinson (Mitchell). It affords us an interesting insight into the interrelationships from Gertler's perspective, and to the life at the Slade of the friends in the photograph.

Carrington, as she insisted on being called, was the focus of attention from her arrival at the college in 1910. She experimented with hairstyles and clothes '*à la* Augustus John' and, together with Barbara Hiles, Ruth Humphreys and Dorothy

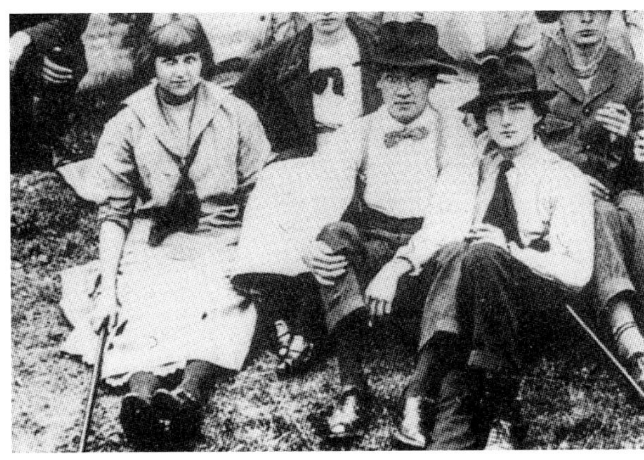

4. Photograph of the Slade picnic (detail). Tate Gallery Archive.

Brett,[40] was often to be seen in their equivalent of the high profile Café Royal, the rather run-down Café Eiffel Tower. As with Richard, it took time for her to feel comfortable at the Slade but as soon as she did her true adventurous personality came out. Paul Nash recorded: 'I got an introduction to her and eventually won her regard by lending her my braces for a fancy-dress party. We were on the top of a bus and she wanted them then and there.'[41]

Though he denied it both then and later, Richard's infatuation with Dora Carrington became progressively more acute. In Carrington he had met his match, not only in intellect and in personality, but also in that she could be as obtuse as he could. Perhaps it was the intellectual stimulation that he valued the most and the relief that he had found a partner in his 'graphomania' who could actually respond intelligently.[42] Glibly he told her of the refreshing change this made and remarked that in his previous experience 'girls' letter[s] consist of four sheets of prosaic ball-dadash [*sic*] of unemotional fatuity without one original or intimate thought or phrase, a mere cold formality that needs answering.'[43] The friendship was always confused, faltering between brotherly affection and unfulfilled love affair, rooted in Richard's reluctance to trust strangers and her notorious desire to remain 'unattached'. In *Mendel*, even the father of Mitchell (Nevinson) approved of the platonic relationship, saying that it was 'The first sensible thing you've done, my boy. A pure relationship between a boy and a girl has a most ennobling influence – most ennobling.' Mitchell's mother commented: 'She is truly spiritual, the type who justifies the independence of the modern girl, whatever the Prime Minister might say.'[44] For Richard she could be everything from 'an ill-bred shop-girl', in moments of temper, frustration and rejection, to a 'gorgeously egotistical, impulsive, unsettled youth'.[45] At first his entire attitude to her was paternal and that of the Slade mentor keeping an eye on the immature female in case she might falter artistically or socially. But as the year advanced the friendship intensified and the two exchanged trust, advice, celebrations, worries and ambitions as two best friends might be expected to do. Having sworn off the Coster Gang by writing to her 'I am not going to waste your time next term with riotous living',[46] Richard turned his attention to their futures as artists and to the Slade scholarships she would need to win in order to stay there. He lived in fear that if funding failed she might be withdrawn and with her would go one of the most solid friendships he had yet experienced. His vested interest could be felt when he wrote to her 'I will really turn my face to the wall & die if you miss it.'[47] Though a sense of humour could be traced in his letters to her concerning this very grave issue, the undertones were more than apparent: 'I am not after your money, my honey, but I simply want you, for don't yer see if yer dinna get this scholarship, you are going home & I am lonely, way down here & the rain coming down.'[48]

The two were spending a lot of time together and records exist of them attending dances, going to the music halls, and generally living the 'student life'. It seems quite natural that the feelings should have intensified and this too became apparent on Richard's behalf, though to what extent it was encouraged by Carrington is unknown. Having recorded in March that 'I am leading the most profoundly dull life',[49] his entire mood had been transformed by the following month when he could write: 'I have risen early in the morning before the day was dawning in order to await the post which comes about eight o'clock! I do not recall ever having been in such an exotic condition.'[50] The reason for this transformation was in the belief that he had met the perfect partner in Carrington and that his sentiment was being reciprocated. Having written disparagingly of his one and only previous love affair, he now believed, that unlike that occasion, a happy and worthwhile relationship was being instigated and one which he very much wished to encourage. He wrote again to Carrington: 'I am flattered, I believe you really love me. If I should happen to be in a fools' paradise don't tell me. I infinitely prefer it to a wise man's purgatory.'[51] Similarly he wrote from the Café Royal suggestively that 'we need not strain ourselves by exerting self control'.[52] What he was not aware of was that Carrington was also conversing, writing and meeting with Gertler in a similar fashion, and the latter was beginning to want to rid himself of competition for her affections. For Gertler the friendship would be complicated by sexual frustration, while Carrington had no particular desire to become romantically involved with either man. By early summer the entire business of the scholarship was very much more of a concern for Richard and Carrington than the Gertler situation, and he, at least through this, was beginning to express his feelings openly for her. In May Richard wrote 'I do believe I will be more relieved than you to know the result'. This comment was made within the context of a letter which opened with 'My Cherubim' and finished with 'I do so love you Carrington & I am absolutely yours.'[53] He did worry, however, about the friendship and the effect it might have on her schooling and her chances of winning the scholarship, when he informed her 'I do not think my friendship with you is exactly popular especially as I am supposed to be leading you to the dogs.'[54] He had no doubt at all, however, about her ability to wake 'old Brown out of his senile sleep'.[55] If he was charitable to Carrington as an artist, and he was, it was not a sentiment he extended to all females at the college. In *Mendel* Mitchell exclaims 'Gawd! It makes me sick to see all the fools and the women wasting their time, scratching away, while those of us who have any talent and could learn anything are left to flounder along as best we may.'[56]

Despite his ardour he was curiously concerned to conceal their relationship from others. He sent his letters to her direct to the Slade and with instructions not to leave them lying around. An explanation for this was offered in one communication when he wrote 'I am not ashamed of really liking you (I have even carried that basket of yours) but I am rather secretive not by nature but experience. You must remember I am now middle aged.'[57] Likewise he refrained from sending letters to her home address in holiday times and so, barring the accepted social conventions of the day, there was a form of secrecy, which extended to her family, surrounding the friendship. Regardless of its nature, Richard's friendship with Carrington was one of the most vital elements of his entire time at the Slade. This, combined with his admiration and friendship with Gertler, made the Slade days what they were, and the friendships of both were precious to him.

Of all of Richard's male peers at the Slade, Mark Gertler was by far the most important, influential and reciprocal in friendship. Gertler entered the Slade in 1908, one term before Richard, and yet ironically it is generally recorded by Gertler's biographers that it was Richard who took him under his wing. This is also suggested in *Mendel*, where Mitchell (Nevinson) introduces Mendel Kuhler (Gertler) to the rest of the gang, saying 'He is a genius.'[58] Gertler was an intelligent and extremely talented student, from a working-class immigrant family; his aura of mystery appealed to his new found middle-class friends. He was remembered as being very intense and quite lacking in basic formal education. With growing confidence at the Slade he developed both socially and artistically and, as Carrington cropped her hair, so Gertler let his grow. Certainly Richard recorded then, and in subsequent years, that it was to Gertler that so much of his artistic and personal development was indebted. Little is known of the nature of the friendship between 1909 and 1911, but certainly by their final year at the college they were inseparable. Together they studied at the British Museum, met at the Café Royal, dined at the Nevinson household, went on short holidays and discussed art at length. Independently of each other too, they wrote of the value of their friendship and of the mutual respect they held for each other as artists. The latter, Richard said, was 'the genius of the place…and the most serious, single-minded artist I have ever come across'.[59] He was also the key to the *terra incognita* of Whitechapel, home of Russian, Polish and central-European Jews, which Richard was to find so refreshing in comparison to his own middle-class and intellectual upbringing in Hampstead. This was not exactly the tone of Mitchell, in *Mendel*, when he dismissed the up and coming artist, and the East End, by saying 'Rubbish! You'll soon be getting commissions, and you can't ask people who can afford to pay for portraits to a hole like that.'[60] In return Richard too was of use to the student Gertler, so much so that in a letter to William Rothenstein, the latter remarked: 'My chief friend and pal is young Nevinson, a very, very nice chap. I am awfully fond of him. I am so happy when I am out with him. He invites me down to dinners and then we go on Hampstead Heath talking of the future. Oh! So enthusiastically!'[61] But together they recognized each other's talents and Cannan again implied the paternal role of Richard's character saying 'Mitchell at last took up a protective attitude towards him and defended him from the detestation which he aroused in the majority of his fellow students'.[62] A little later Mitchell exclaimed: 'Well I'm jolly glad to know you. I'm not much of a fellow, but I'd like you to know my people. My father's a great man. He'll stir you up.'[63] Gertler accordingly, and in real life as opposed to the novel, was a regular diner at the Nevinson household and a further letter shows Henry helping 'the Whitechapel jew Goertler [*sic*]' by introducing him, on personal recommendation, to Professor Sadler.[64] The Nevinsons were Gertler's introduction to middle class and intellectual English society. Richard recorded in his autobiography: 'I am proud and glad to say that both my parents were extremely fond of him.'[65] Certainly Henry enjoyed Gertler's stories, and recalled: 'Gertler came to supper, very successful, with admirable naïve stories of his behaviour in rich houses & at a dinner given him by a portrait club, how he asked to begin because he was hungry.'[66] As a final comment on his Slade days and on Tonks's advice to give up art, Richard said 'Had Gertler, for instance, told me seriously that I was wasting my time I should have been heart-broken, but as things were I managed to bear up.'[67]

Father, Son and the Slade

For all the emphasis that has been placed on the role of the new friendships Richard made at college, he still had his very influential and supportive family behind him throughout these years. In fact, when the decision was taken to send his son to the Slade, Henry, after a brief skiing holiday with Richard in Champéry, stepped up his artistic activities and networking around the capital.[68] His personal journals record, for example, that he, Henry, was a visitor and a diner at the home of Walter Sickert, and it is possible that is was through this connection that Richard was introduced to the Camden Town Group.[69] The friendship with C.F.G. Masterman, a vital contact during the war years, was also being developed, though it was momentarily at a nadir over the question of women's suffrage. The father too was a regular visitor at his son's studio in 1909 and he could record 'Went to see Rich's pictures, wh. are good but still uncertain.'[70] Certainly he was giving his son the support he required though the father, like the son, still doubted the entire choice of career when he wrote 'Cycled early to Hendon & met Rich going drawing: felt very sad about it, perhaps without reason.'[71] Later, Muirhead Bone came round to look at his paintings on his father's request. They did not realize then how their paths would cross again during and after the war years and how the relationship would fluctuate, resulting, ultimately, in Richard referring to the latter as 'Bonehead Muir'. Later in the month father and son went together with college friend Gertler to the Post-Impressionist show[72] in the company of Charles Lewis-Hind,[73] a friend of Henry's and a critic of extreme future importance to Richard's career. It is clear that Henry had more than a passing interest in art, the avant-garde in Europe and consequently in his son's progress. Indeed, Tonks was an admirer of Henry, the latter returning the compliment by recording that he was a 'remarkable man with wide sympathies & knowledge'.[74] It is no coincidence that other friends' names, as recorded in his personal diaries, were later to become much more closely associated with his son's work. For example, throughout 1911 the entries talk about social visits paid to Charles Lewis-

Hind,[75] letters of thanks and personal visits paid to Frank Rutter following favourable reviews,[76] and dinners and introductions to influential people such as the Rothensteins.[77] Likewise, it is recorded that father and son went together to effect an introduction to Roger Fry,[78] which was followed up by a visit together to the latter's show on 3 January 1912. Clive Bell was also visited in Gordon Square by father, and possibly son, in July 1912, and was described by the former as a 'long-haired, exuberant man, like an artistic Winston Churchill'.[79] However interested Henry may have been in the intellects of Fry and Bell he could not appreciate the aesthetic they propounded, and described the decorations for Crosby Hall which he had been shown, as 'perfectly ludicrous and unmeaning'. In the same recollections he conceded that Rothenstein believed Roger Fry to be 'a bit crazy'.[80] Frederick Etchells and Duncan Grant too were singled out by the bewildered Henry for being beyond the pale and were thus described as being 'conspicuous by absurdity' when they exhibited at the Friday Club.[81] Regardless, Henry seemed very willing to meet the new artist friends of his son and to assist them in any way he could. Edward Wadsworth and Mark Gertler were, therefore, regular diners at the Nevinson household, though again, Henry had difficulty in appreciating their works. If Margaret Nevinson's account is to be believed, the household was open to, and visited by, the majority of the avant-garde student artists of the day, including Lightfoot, Allinson, Currie, Lewis, Ethelbert White, the Nash brothers, the Carlines, McKnight Kauffer, Gaudier-Brzeska, John, Sickert, Epstein, Ginner, Bevan, Gilman and Odle.[82]

It emerges also that the father/son relationship was deeply personal too, and this is something Henry, not Richard, fully acknowledged. Simple family pleasures were apparent when he went with Richard, and his friends from the Slade, to a Guy Fawkes procession and bonfire at which he observed their innocence, chasing and tickling the girls.[83] Previously he had also been skating with his son and friends, and playing soccer, to say nothing of giving them camping lessons. This gives us a more human insight into the young student, his life and relationship with his father, than perhaps the artist himself would ever have cared to do.[84] On 27 August 1911 Henry went for a walk with Richard before going to Albania to report on the crisis there, and wrote in his diary 'Parted in great friendship.'[85] Even in the middle of preparations for his departure he took time to go and look at his son's pictures and recorded that, on the whole, 'about half [were] good'.[86] Immediately on his arrival home from the Balkans, six weeks later, he went to inspect his son's work and could observe that it showed 'a great advance'.[87] Whether busy or not, and he almost always was, Henry would also check his son's essays before they were submitted, in much the way he would do in years to come with the various manifestos and catalogue prefaces. By late summer, 1911, he was correcting his son's final essay, on the Mona Lisa,[88] and fostering the Nevinson family tradition for politics and protest in the young man by going 'with Rich to very large meet of Dock strikers in Trafalgar Square.'[89]

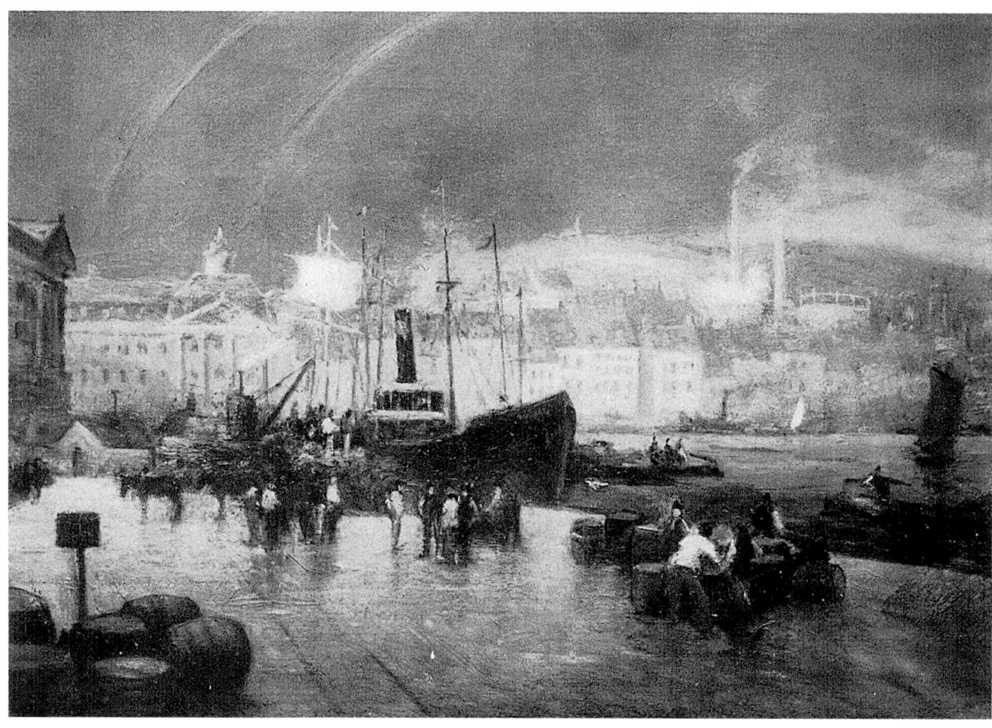

5. *The Port*, 1909. Oil on canvas. Private Collection.

The Developing Artist at the Slade

Crucially, however, it is the development of Richard as an artist at the Slade that must be understood in order to comprehend the subsequent rebel in the pre-war years. Ironically, his autobiography does not put much emphasis on this element of his student days at all, though Cannan observed the admiration, by the entire group, for Calthrop (Augustus John) in *Mendel*. 'Calthrop dressed extravagantly: so did the four. Calthrop smashed furniture: so did the four. And as Calthrop drank, embraced women, and sometimes painted outrageously, the four did all these things.'[90] The focal point for all of this in the novel was the fictional Paris Café, which can easily be identified as the Café Royal, and it was here that the great artist advised them 'You've got life to paint from – real, stinking life.'[91]

Richard, at the outset of his studies at the Slade, classified his work as being in the 'impressionist style'[92] and examples of his painting tend to support this description. Very few of his paintings from this period have been located, though there are some photographic reproductions. Many are simply lost while others will certainly have perished at the hands of his wife, Kathleen, in carrying out the directions of his last will and testament.[93] *The Port* (fig. 5) painted in 1909[94] has, both in subject matter and technique, clearly been executed in a manner that might closely be associated with the French Impressionists. The 'snapshot' composition is of an everyday, contemporary scene, with the sensation being that of a composition conducted *en plein air*. The handling of paint and the impastoed surface demand parallels with Impressionism, though only with an awareness of their debt to Constable and Turner.[95] These apparent influences are certainly in keeping with his writing of the time which suggested that his artistic eclecticism was the result of merging both the English and French traditions in painting.

The First Post-Impressionist Show

It is known that Richard attended the *Manet and the Post-Impressionists* exhibition in 1910 with his father, Lewis-Hind and Gertler.[96] Tonks could do little to contain this generation of students, describing how he 'could not . . . prevent our visiting the Grafton Galleries; he could only warn us and say how very much better pleased he would be if we did not risk contamination but stayed away'.[97] The exhibition had made quite an impact as it provided a survey of late nineteenth- and early twentieth-century painting from France.[98] The emphasis had been on Cézanne, Van Gogh, Gauguin, the Fauves and Picasso and so this exhibition exposed the English art world, albeit rather suddenly, to the latest developments in France. Perhaps more interestingly, it led to an entirely new set of questions being asked as to how exactly one defines the parameters of art and art criticism.[99] Sargent claimed that it had no right to claim itself as art at all,[100] while Robert Ross said that the exhibition should be burned in its entirety before the infectious virus spread.[101] Perhaps Wilfrid Blunt spoke for the majority when he wrote

> The exhibition is either an extremely bad joke or a swindle. I am inclined to think the latter, for there is no trace of humour in it. Still less is there a trace of sense of taste, good or bad, or art or cleverness. Nothing but the gross puerility which scrawls indecencies on the walls of a privy. The drawing is on the level of that of an untaught child of seven or eight years old, the sense of colour that of a tea-tray painter, the method that of a schoolboy who wipes his fingers on a slate after spitting on them...Apart from the frames, the whole collection should be worth £5, and then only for the pleasure of making a bonfire of them.[102]

History records how Richard, Wadsworth, Lewis, Roberts, Bomberg, Gertler and Paul Nash, upon whom the English avant-garde was soon to depend, attended, learned from and emulated these foreign masters. The emergent polemicism of the era was lapped up by the youthful students and was epitomized by the pamphlet that Frank Rutter wrote and distributed there, entitled 'Revolution in Art' in which he declared: 'To the rebels of either sex all the world over who in any way are fighting for freedom of any kind, I dedicate this study of their painter comrades.'[103]

In practice however, Richard seemed to have been rather slower to adapt and learn than has hitherto been suggested. The earliest written critiques of his Slade paintings date from his penultimate year of study and tend to suggest that the impact of this landmark show had not necessarily been felt. The reviewer from the *Sunday Times*[104] was remarkably prophetic when writing about *Liverpool Street* and *Gasometers* (both lost), exhibited with the Friday Club[105] at the Alpine Galleries in 1911. Though acknowledging that the works were remarkably 'complete in achievement' he believed that he had not yet found a style of his own, nor one with which he felt comfortable. He did, however, optimistically predict that there was ample time in which to experiment and that inevitably 'if he is true to himself and keeps his head cool he will in his own time work out his own way of delivering that message'.[106] Concerning *Gasometers*, Richard had written 'I think it is the best thing I have done so far'[107] and as such it must have embodied all the basic theories and criteria as set forward by, and for, himself at this time.[108] Certainly there seemed to be an interest in the modern, the city and the un-picturesque, and perhaps that could be seen as a link between his early works and a degree of avant-garde thinking. In technique, however, he lagged behind the artists of the 1910 show and this is seen when the same review went on to say 'Mr. Nevinson, obviously in love with his selected subjects, feeling the charm of form and colour in unexpected industrial situations, finds a half-way house of his very own between the colour and technique of Boudin and Claude Monet.'[109] The same could be said of the next exhibition of his works, also in 1911, at Frank Rutter's Allied Artists' Association (AAA) in the Albert Hall, where the chosen scenes were *Carting Manure* and *Cement Works* (both lost). Richard claimed: 'I, who was born for Oxford and the army in a hotbed of intellectualism, religion and the classics, found refreshment in ugliness and the uncouth.'[110] The *Sunday Times* observed this too when referring to him as 'a painter who sees beauty in what the crowd condemns as ugly'.[111] Richard seemed to be turning his attention to 'real, stinking life' as John had suggested. Disaffection with the New English Art Club (NEAC) and disagreement with Bloomsbury formalism within the members of the Fitzroy Street Group, and amongst students at the Slade, had led to the proposition of a rival exhibiting society. Sickert himself observed that a 'glance around the walls of any NEAC exhibition does certainly not give us the sensation of a page torn from the book of life'.[112] The result was the establishing of the socially engaged Camden Town Group, which was to exhibit three times together and which Harrison described as a 'sheer weight of talent [which]...has remained unmatched to this day'. Though Richard was never a member he was associated with the group who were painting in a style loosely equated to Impressionism, Post-Impressionism and perhaps even Fauvism. More importantly they had 'a respect for the appearance of otherwise uncelebrated people; and an aspiration faithfully to record the conditions and surroundings in which unglamorous lives were lived'.[113] Perhaps then it was in subject matter that the young artist moved away from the dictates of national perceptions of etiquette, though not all scenes chosen were uncouth and this is seen in his description of a painting, now lost, of the Oxford and Cambridge boat race. Here, he said, 'I have done a little panel of the crowds & river & pubs & Flags & blue & white skies.'[114] There seems a distinct overlap here, in terms of subject matter, with many of Monet's depictions of Argenteuil or with the boating parties of Renoir. So too he exhibited a panel entitled *Spring* at the restaurant Petit Savoyard, which both father and Frank Rutter admired in early 1912.[115]

Far from being inspired and in awe of the new wave of continental abstraction coming from France he was suspicious of it. Describing the situation as both 'anarchic & egotistical'[116] he warned Carrington not to be distracted by these apparently liberal standards, and far from encouraging her to become part of the avant-garde wave sweeping its way across the channel from Paris, he advised her 'above all don't get into this post-impressionist cleverness of pretending to be a great[er] fool than

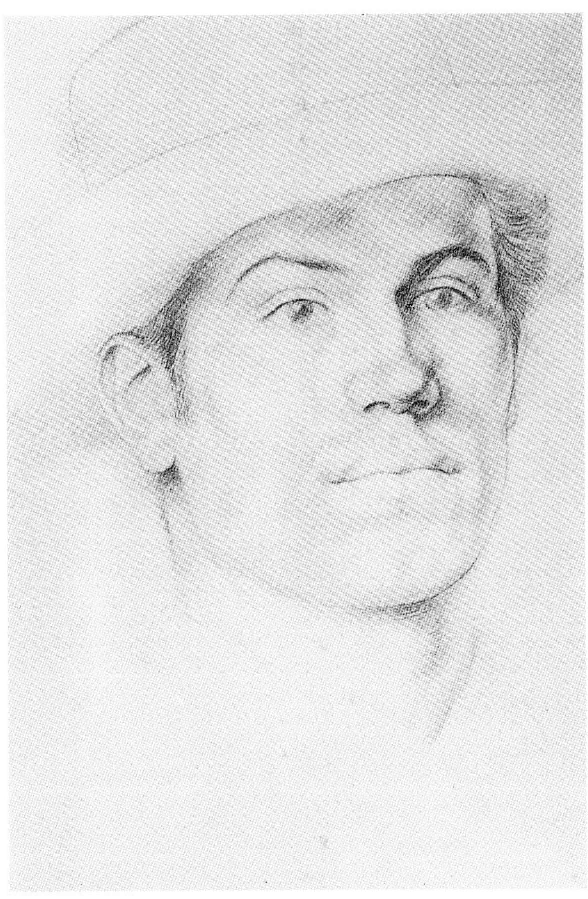

6. *Self-Portrait,* 1911/12. Graphite, 27.1 x 22.2 cm. British Museum, London.

you are'. His ambitions seemed to be very much more conservative and really quite modest:

> You cannot think how frightfully keen I am to get on & be appreciated sometimes, yet my brain always is telling me how silly and futile it is of me as I know only to [*sic*] well I have not a single touch of genius, yet I still have this mania to do at least one really good picture in [the] course of my lifetime & as a secondary ambition I would love someday to get hung in the new English...I will never get in to the New English & Allinson always will.[117]

He was prepared to work hard to conquer his own lack of ability and this can be seen in an early communication, which read: 'I have been working like Satan drawing my own and my mother's head...I am really improving in my drawing. If only I could feel some hope that I might someday do a fairly good drawing I think my life would be more tolerable. Even if I lost everything and gained some hope' (fig. 6). Later, in the same letter he claimed: 'I can warn you it is quite the lowest ebb of misery to become always a passive onlooker of your own incompetence or to be fatuous, hopeless.'[118] In the same letter he advised her 'Get your work as solid & as simple & as strong as you can, avoid superfluous ornimentation [*sic*] & remember all

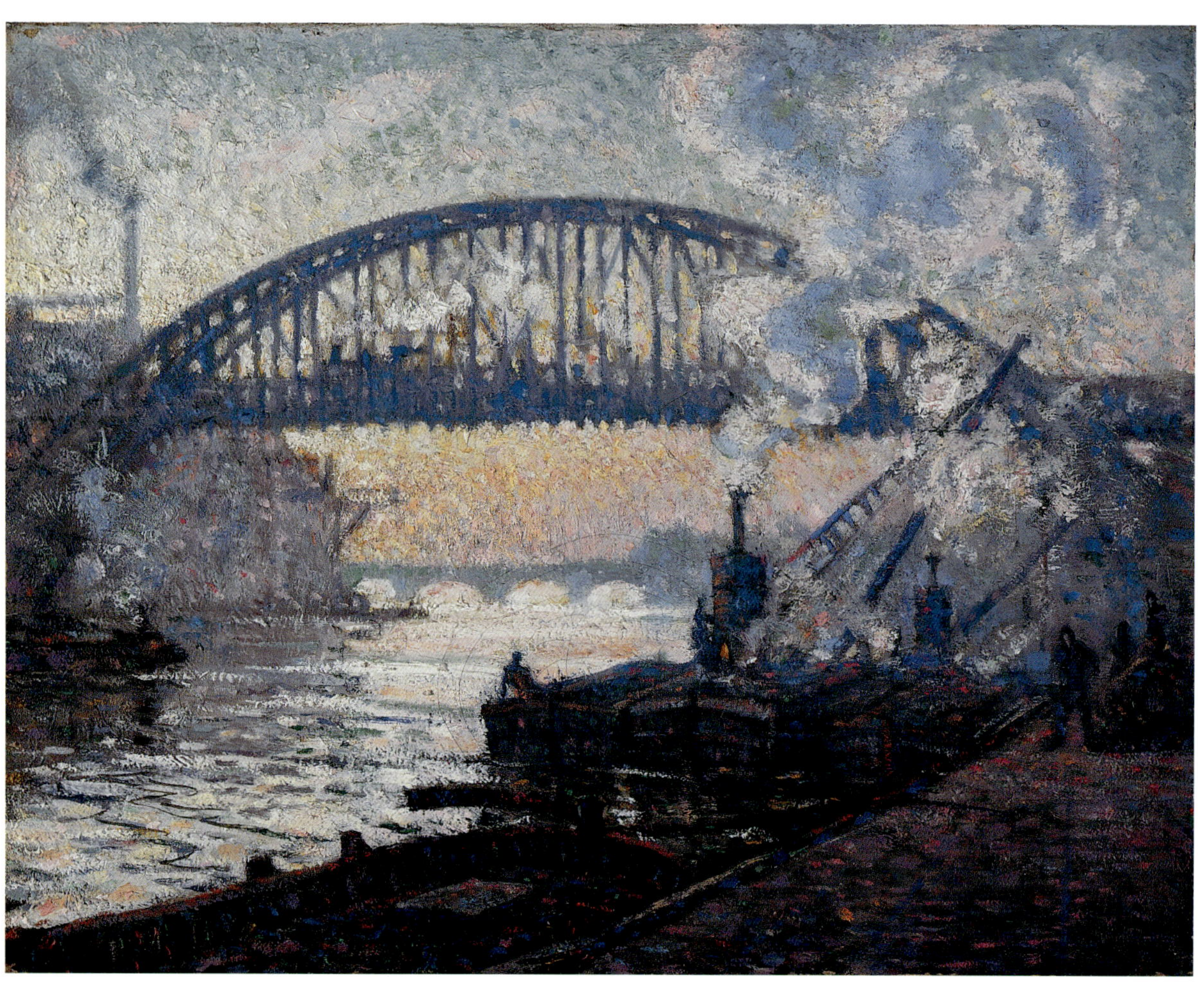

7. The Railway Bridge, Charenton, 1911. Oil on canvas, 40.9 x 51.5 cm. Manchester City Galleries.

useless things are ugly, all useful things beautiful.'[119] A serious-minded approach to composition and technique would inevitably lead to desirable results, he believed, and so 'the greatest difficulties in all arts is to keep spontaneity & completeness together, it is really a matter of concentration, but so is the greatest art from Michael Angelo downwards & particularly in the primitives & Early Greeks'.[120]

Surviving paintings such as *The Railway Bridge, Charenton* (fig. 7), and *The Towing Path, Camden Town* (fig. 8), confirm this Impressionist leaning and suggest, in essence, that he was far from an artistic rebel as a student. Of *The Towing Path, Camden Town* there are written records of the work in progress. On 28 March 1912 he wrote to Carrington exclaiming 'I am just completing my Camden Town love drama. I rather think it is going to come off but at present it seems rather dull, but it may be because I am sick of it.'[121] Later he would pessimistically report 'My Camden Town is a failure I think.'[122] The essence of the painting is not the dynamism or glorification of the city, rather the survival of human sentiment in that apparently hostile environment.[123] The surface of the canvas and the subject matter depicted does not experience the fragmentation or the semi-abstractions of

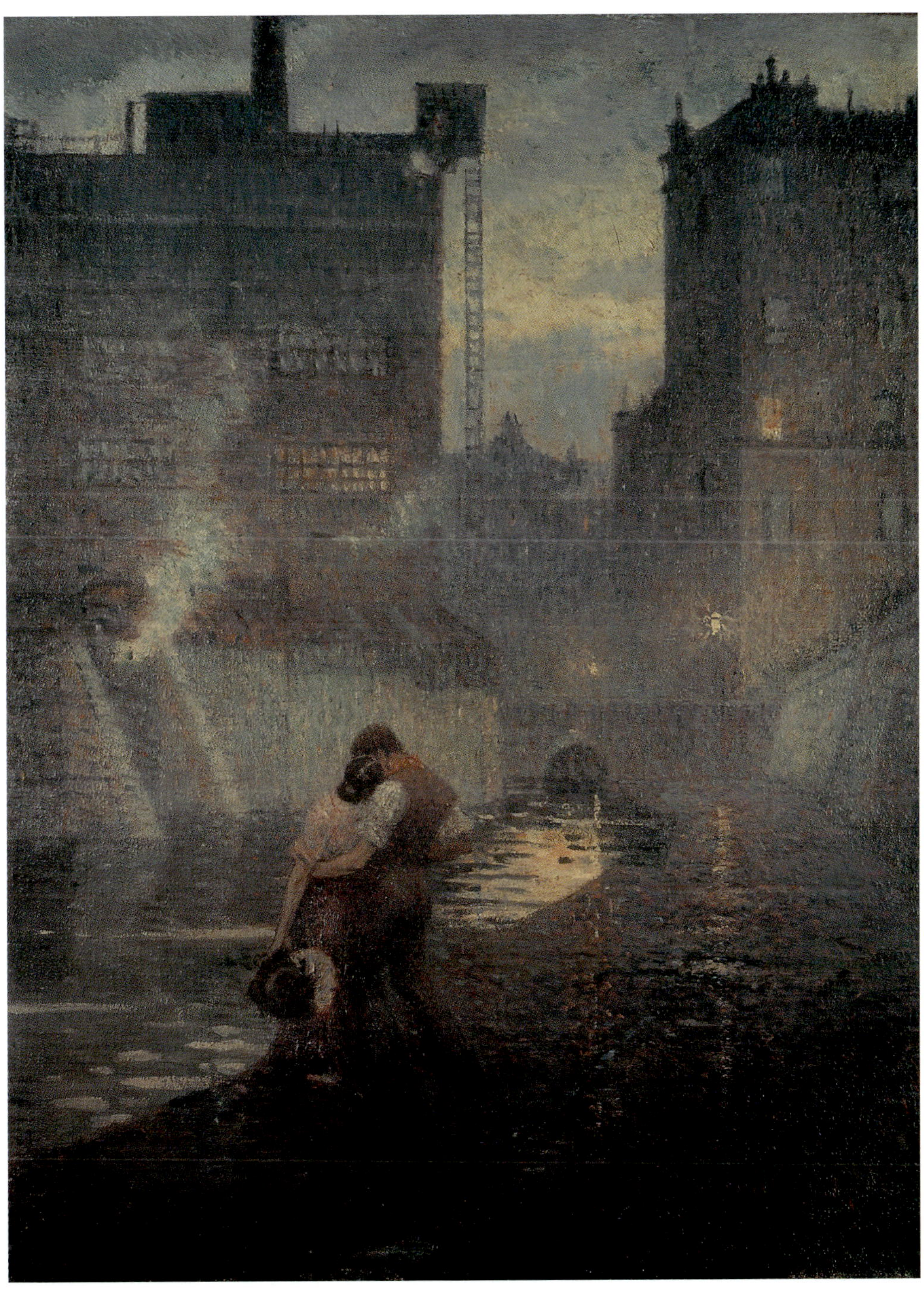

8. *The Towing Path, Camden Town*, 1912. Oil on canvas. Ashmolean Museum, Oxford.

the European avant-garde of the time, nor does the scene require any interpretation or comprehension beyond the visual and therefore immediate. Colour is representational, as is form. Pictorially the composition reflects what was seen, it supports the narrative, as opposed to being an epitome of any other theory or expression. One way or another it seemed to affiliate itself to the standards established by the NEAC for painting in terms both of subject matter and technique. In the light of what was happening in Paris at the time, and indeed just outside the walls of the Slade, it was hardly an avant-garde painting.

Other works such as *Self-Portrait* (fig. 3) from the same year, show little leaning even towards Impressionism. Cork has described the picture as having a greater affinity with realist painting,[124] as well as seeing a perhaps more conventional, if flattering, connection with Botticelli.[125] Richard himself seemed happy with the spoils of his labour saying 'I think it has come off rather well as far as I can judge.'[126]

By the time of the exhibition of the Friday Club in 1912, also in the Alpine Galleries, Richard had settled into the style of painting most closely associated with the Camden Town Group.[127] In fact critics could observe that the Friday Club 'appear to be unconscionably proud of having got about ten years ahead of the Camden Town Group and being only fifteen years behind the latest Paris fashions'. The *Sunday Times* singled out, in particular, *Railway Bridge, Charenton* for particular praise, claiming that it was one of the few exhibits to 'linger pleasantly in [my] memory'. This, the critic claimed, was because 'instead of trying to be clever and original, we feel that Mr. Nevinson has put every ounce of his knowledge of paint and colour into the endeavour to give a true impression of what he saw'.[128] Certainly in subject matter, technique, colour and finish the composition bore many similarities to the *plein-air* compositions of the French Impressionists and perhaps more specifically to Monet and his studies conducted at the Gare Saint-Lazare in Paris in the 1870s. The 'fleeting moment', the play of light on moving surfaces, contemporary society, the absence of a specific narrative function and the snapshot composition, secured the affiliation to France, albeit three decades retrospectively.

However favourable and encouraging some of the early reviews may have been, Richard was also exposed to failure and rejection at this time. Throughout his lifetime he was apt to suffer from depression at the rejection or criticism of his works and this could often turn to anger and vitriol. Both can clearly be seen at this early stage in his career and the culprits for the early disenchantment were the Friday Club and the New English Art Club. With regard to the former, Henry had recorded on his return from Belfast 'Rich much depressed because 2 (best) pictures were rejected for Friday Club & his other two taken.'[129] Having said that, when he visited the show three days later he recorded: 'Gertler, Allinson and Rich were excellent; and a few more, Rich's *Suicide* his best for emotion.'[130] The father, though concerned at his son's despair, was quietly confident that he was making progress and simply taking the blows alongside the accolades, which were beginning to flow from the pens of his literary colleagues. He was jubilant too to see that the show produced the first sale of his son's work and he recorded with delight the excitement and the euphoria surrounding the purchase of the 'Bridge on the Seine' (*The Railway Bridge, Charenton*) by an anonymous buyer on behalf of Manchester City Art Galleries. The father's delight was soon to pass when he wrote in his diary the next day, 'Was unhappy all day from suspicion that M. has caused Rich's picture to be bought & is placing him in a Fools' Paradise.'[131]

Richard wrote to Carrington concerning the NEAC, expressing the impact the rejection had upon him by saying 'today I am cursing the New English &...am praying that Tonks may soon be called upon to make his ascent to Heaven.' In the same letter he displayed the shattered confidence that the rejection had left him with and the sense of conspiracy that was to be an ever-present feature of his personality from here on. 'I shall not probably try to exhibit there for another 2 years by then I hope to have improved somewhat...& possibly some will have died off'.[132] Clearly he took rejection as a personal defect and wrote imploringly 'I am chucked from the New English, I am ashamed to say...please don't despise me.'[133] This was compounded when he actually visited the show at the NEAC and found the whole affair profoundly dull. His father, always a source of comfort, offered him solace saying 'I am in good company & Millet & most good men have their failures early in life.'[134] Always prone to the dramatic he pondered 'I don't know whether God is trying to speak to me & telling me to give up Art if so I wish He would convey his meaning more clearly.'[135]

By his final month at the Slade he had established the priorities that he carried into the London art world after graduation, and these he condensed into three basic criteria: 'First I wish to paint this present age above all, secondly to combine it with the pattern of form besides colour as the primitives did, third to keep realism predominant in spite of it[s] decorative qualities or shortly to combine Atmospheric effects & design.' There was also a clear emphasis on technical virtuosity as an underlying prerequisite, having been achieved, in his opinion, for the last time in Britain by Whistler. His analogy, though crude, was straightforward when he wrote 'A man with an impediment in his speech can't talk well, I don't care what he's got to say, nor will I read a badly printed book.'[136] There was no need, either, to be scared by the inclusion of sentiment in a painting, and he wrote of this too saying that to ignore it would be the act of a 'Futurist Shavian'.[137] It is ironic to observe that the first ever recorded reference to Futurism is in a negative tone and as a source of derision, and this at a time when Futurism (in which his parents were showing a considerable interest) had arrived in England in full force.

Turbulent Friendships

At this early stage his budding hatred for artists and critics which he carried throughout his life, began to emerge. For example, when, at a dance at St John's Wood, he met a girl for whom he clearly had an interest, he observed: 'best of everything [she] knows & cares nothing of pictures! Never even heard of John'. In the same correspondence he advised Carrington 'keep away from all artists, of course Wadsworth is different he is better bred, & better read & big minded & larger outlook on life generally'.[138] There was some room however for youthful exuberance and in a charming note, hastily scribbled by Richard in the company of Currie, Gertler, Allinson and a few others at the Café Royal, we are left with a commentary which captures the excitement at the entrance of Augustus John. 'John has just arrived wild excitement at our table keen competition whether he will sit at our table or the Camden Town lads.' Later he added, flattered, 'John did after all come & sit with us and was most pleasant & affable, he actually knew my name and all about me.'[139] But this was the exception, not the rule, in the life of a young artist who was plagued with insecurities and was prone, alongside physical illness, to severe bouts of melancholia. The latter was an illness that was to stay with him all his life, intensifying especially in times of loneliness, stress and rejection, and often developing into a form of intense paranoia. At the Slade it was in its early stages, but present nonetheless, and can be found in his letters to Carrington. In a self-diagnosis he wrote 'I try to kid myself that I am misunderstood instead of being too well understood.'[140] Later he tried to tackle the problem and wrote from Falmouth 'I wish to preserve my sanity & throw off this melancholia. I think by meeting people & talking & having to put on a cheerful face I may get myself out of the vile introspection which my absolutely lonely life leads me to.'[141] The hint to Carrington that they ought to go to more 'Red Revels', 'Artist's Revels', 'Gorgonzolas' and 'Circuses' together, seems to have gone unheeded and in a later communication he complained again 'I am dreading a fearfully lonely life…no-one comes to see me now & I am alone with my Chinese pots. I really deserve sympathy.'[142]

And yet it was she, he felt, who was to be his saviour when he told her 'I owe you everything. I have no doubt but for the sudden appearance of you, I would now be a dissipated criminal of the most carnal description. I would [have] lost money, reputation & my very soul.'[143] He alluded here to the support she had given when he had become involved in a scandal involving a model at the Slade who had given birth to a child who, it was believed, could have been his. This too was recorded in *Mendel* when Mitchell (Nevinson) received a letter whilst in Brighton with Mendel (Gertler) instructing him to come back to the Pot-au-Feu café in London to meet Mendel's model friend, Hetty Finch. She was pregnant by Mitchell who offered her money and marriage, both of which she rejected. Richard's nervous state was more accurately recorded in a letter to Carrington when he wrote retrospectively, 'I was always alert for a telegram announcing a death & birth with a child left for me to look after or every letter I was terrified might be from that busybody Tonks or some blackmailer.'[144] For all that he claimed: 'Women have always proved the triumph of matter over mind',[145] it was clear that he had become almost dependent upon this woman for support.

Nothing could have aggravated this Achilles' heel more than the rift that was to occur in his final days at the Slade, which would cost him his two most precious friendships. The problem appeared quite suddenly on 21 June 1912, when a letter arrived from Carrington. The letter has not survived, but his response to it has. It starts 'Your note came as a horrible surprise to me. I cannot guess what has happened to make you wish to do without me as a friend next term.' Obviously Gertler's name had not come up in the original letter, but nonetheless Richard was in a panic. Perplexed at what might have caused the rift he guessed that perhaps it had been the increasingly intimate tone which he had been adopting with her and promised 'I swear I will never speak a word to you as your lover.' He went on to reiterate the point claiming 'I promise you I will be a great friend of yours nothing more & nothing less & if you want to get simple again I am only too willing to do the same.' He opened up to her emotionally and appealed to her sense of pity saying 'you & Gertler & Wadsworth & mother are the only friends I have ever known', before satisfying himself with the explanation that the problem must be her great desire to study and to remove all other distractions. He finished his reply by writing

> if you still find it absolutely necessary to chuck me, remember should you ever need any help or companion[ship] do please come back to me as I know I shall always like and respect you for the rest [of] my life. I most admire your self-control & grit to throw away a great deal of your happiness for your work even though I consider you are horribly wrong in doing so.[146]

As awful as this all may have seemed he was as yet unaware that worse was to come and that the real cause of the problem involved his other best friend, Gertler, who had written to Carrington two days earlier, on 19 June 1912. This letter had been a final admission of his love in which he had clearly outlined, in five points, why Carrington should marry him. Although he admitted in the letter that he expected she would reject his proposal, he also requested that, this being the case, the friendship should end there.[147] On 2 July Gertler wrote a further letter in which he identified the problem, observing, 'Your affections are completely given to Nevinson. I must have been a fool to stand it as long as I have, without seeing through you. I have written to Nevinson telling him that we, he and I, are no longer friends.'[148] This letter also survives as Richard, on receiving it, sent it directly on to Carrington with his own distraught observations. It began

> Dear Nevinson, I am writing here to tell you that our friendship must end from now, my sole reason being that I am in love with Carrington and I have reason to believe that you are so too. Therefore, much as I have tried to overlook it, I have come to the conclusion that rivals, and rivals in love, cannot be friends.
>
> You must know that ever since you brought Carrington to my studio my love for her has been steadily increasing. You might also remember that many times, when you asked me down to dinner, I refused to come. *Jealousy* was the cause of it. Whenever you told me that you had been kissing her, you could have knocked me down with a feather, so faint was I. Whenever you saw me depressed of late, when we were all out together, it wasn't boredom as I pretended but *love*.[149]

The letter finished by blocking all prospects of reconciliation. Quite simply Gertler had put their friendship to an end and in doing so had torn Carrington away from Richard too. The blow, as sudden and severe as it was, placed an enormous burden on him, and his response to Carrington expressed desperation as opposed to anger, and exasperation at the thought of becoming friendless again through no fault of his own. Had he known the contents of a further letter from Gertler to Carrington he would have been even more hurt when it stated: 'As regards Nevinson, I am afraid I cannot go back to being his friend. It is not jealousy at all. You see I have lost interest in him . . . why should I be with a person for whose company I do not care'.[150] The competitive edge was still present when Gertler wrote 'Nevinson was once my friend, but now my greatest friend is Currie, and Currie would consider it rather funny if I said tomorrow night I shall go out with Nevinson.'[151] This too was suggested in *Mendel* when Mitchell (Nevinson) had taken Mendel (Gertler) to meet Logan (Currie) and almost instantly the latter two had conspired against him. Logan said the following about Mitchell: 'He is a liar and a coward, and he will never be an artist because he is too weak. He is not true. He is not good. I have trusted him with my secrets and he tells. I wanted him to be my friend, but it is impossible.'[152] In despair Richard, though probably ignorant of the depth of Currie's feeling for him, wrote to Carrington 'I am now without a friend in the whole world except you.' He went on 'I cannot give you up, you have put a reason into my life & I am through you slowly winning back my self-respect. I did feel so useless so futile before I devoted my life to you.' He tried to reason and assured her that he was perfectly calm and collected 'as fortunately I have been able to weep hard', going on to say that he would not stand in their way if she and Gertler wished to love each other openly. He claimed that he would be fine taking second or even third place in a group friendship and assured her that 'I am not so exotically in love with you as Gertler.'[153] The letter does not come across as a plea to get her back as a lover, but rather as a friend, and also to win back Gertler's friendship. He obviously had felt the loss of both profoundly and wrote of how he was 'aching for the companionship of Gertler, our talks on Art, on my work, his work & our life in general, God how fond of him I am, I never realised it so thoroughly till now.'[154]

Of course with time came acceptance and cynicism. In a later letter Richard could write to Carrington 'I am distinctly amused at you two. I congratulate Gertler on his delightful ease and facility he is able to change from the role of a passionate and over-jealous lover to that of a philanthropic platonic friend.' The trouble he said had left him, as a result of his 'abnormally affectionate temperament', with an enlarged liver, which accompanied the sense of betrayal, disappointment, disillusionment and everything else that had been thrust upon him. In finishing he (mis)quoted Oscar Wilde saying 'All men kill the thing they love, a brave man with a sword, the coward with a kiss.'[155]

Shortly before departing for Paris with Allinson, where they would meet up with Wadsworth,[156] Richard went to Gertler's house and some sort of reconciliation was effected. This is confirmed in another letter from Gertler to Carrington which informed her that 'I shall have to do my best to be friends with him too.'[157] Richard wrote to Carrington, believing that the situation was now resolved 'I do earnestly beg you: may I, in the future be kept absolutely outside all your future lapses and quarrels & depressions'.[158]

Richard left the Slade in the summer of 1912 on a turbulent note, unsure of his destination, career, friendships, or indeed his artistic orientation. At the time of graduation he could simply muse on the time that had been. In summing up his final year he talked about 'these horrible wild nine months of births, scandals, police courts, Slade dances, Friday Clubs & Chenils, of hopes . . . my complete disillusionment of some of my "friends", then getting more and more mad on you & now complete boredom'.[159] Instead of leaving the Slade hungry for his chance as an artist in the outside world, as we are led to believe in his autobiography, he recorded: 'I am now unfitted for everything else & so I must stick to painting as my only possible means of livelihood.'[160] By 1912 he was by no means at the forefront of any avant-garde, though he had established very solid connections in the art world through his father. He remained unconfident about his work and, it appears, immune to the radical movements which had already arrived and created a stir in London by that year. Without a clear path to follow he wallowed in his own loneliness and artistic disorientation. And yet, to put the artist in his context, he graduated into a London already familiar with Post-Impressionism, and moreover, Marinetti's Futurism. Richard was either unaware, or unimpressed, as neither his writings nor his paintings show the slightest influence, affiliation or attraction, to either.

3

From the Slade to Paris 1912

My clearing away to this God forsaken hole has been quite useless.[1]

Paint and Prejudice makes only a light-hearted reference to the days that immediately followed the Slade. It is mentioned in passing that his work was being exhibited, selling and receiving the praise of critics such as Robert Ross and Frank Rutter who appreciated the Impressionist vein in which it was done. It is suggested too that he was moving in very progressive circles such as the Camden Town Group, with Sickert, Gore and Gilman, and not least Percy Wyndham Lewis. This, apparently, was not enough to contain the young and ambitious artist seeking inspiration outside of England and the English tradition. And so with an old friend from St John's Wood, named Rudhall, he went to Paris to live and, he recorded, 'I could have had no better companion.'[2]

Richard suggested that it was in Paris, immediately after graduation, and due to the friendships which evolved there with Modigliani and Severini, that a more focussed orientation began. Here he was exposed to the full avant-garde in European painting, as opposed to the selected examples that Rutter and Fry had been bringing to London. Far from feeling that his education was now complete, he immersed himself in further learning, both formal and informal, at the Salon des Independents, the Saturday salons of Gertrude Stein (where he almost certainly met Picasso), at the Académie Julian, both in rue du Dragon and in Montmartre, and in Matisse's school, the 'Circle Russe'. According to his autobiography he was now ripe for Paris, sufficiently grounded in the arts to plunge himself into the essential bohemia of internationalism at the cutting edge of the avant-garde. 'Obsessed' with Goya, Daumier and Toulouse-Lautrec he became absorbed in the seedy life of Paris going by the acquired name of 'Nevinski'. 'The bleak poverty of Paris and the desperados were mere colourful grist for my mill',[3] he reminisced, and delight could be found in the brothel/café areas around rue de la Gaite. Dining regularly at the Eléphant on rue Blanche among the artists, actors, actresses and musicians, evenings normally continued with drinks at Medrano's Circus with the clowns and the performers, then finished off, with Severini, whom he had met through a clown named Titi, at the Monaco or the Tabarin. The days, apparently, were spent rubbing shoulders with Picasso and Matisse at the Louvre or visiting haunts made famous by Degas. The evenings, always alive and vibrant, could even be spent, according to the artist, in conversation with Lenin, Apollinaire, Fry, Bell, Derain, Modigliani, Soficci and Boccioni, where 'we used to hammer out the solution of things in those days!'[4] Attending the Moulin Rouge he said the list of his acquaintances were too numerous to attempt to recall in any detail, though he did emphasize a prevalence of Austrian and Russian aristocrats. Finally, he recorded, his direction began to turn towards the influence of Italy, albeit in France, and away from the stifling limitations of his formal English education. After a short return to London, in which time he purchased a motor bike, and had Whistlerian-type breakfasts with Albert Rothenstein, Richard returned to Paris. Not before the dynamic young rebel had upset many of the members of the NEAC by turning up to a meeting on his motor bike, and having almost exhausted himself with dances and 'revels' at Covent Garden, the Botanical Gardens and the Assembly Rooms of the Eyre Arms at St John's Wood. In rue Lepic, he was led to 'the strangest epoch of my life' in which he declared he 'was dissatisfied with representational painting'.[5] He also stated: 'Like many others I was attracted by abstract art, and the colour harmonies of Kandinsky.'[6] He was also greatly taken by the work of the Fauves, most particularly Vlaminck, Derain and Matisse. So too came the inevitable impact of an even more modern form of representation, and Richard recorded: 'I felt the power of this first phase of Cubism and there was a desire in me to reach that dignity which can be conveyed pictorially by the abstract rather than by the particular.'[7] He went on, in his autobiography, to emphasize the level of this Parisian revelation, saying 'I was like a man in any other walk of life who is struck suddenly by a truth which he has always known to be at the back of his mind, and I was altering my standards accordingly.'[8] Together with Severini, Derain and especially Modigliani, he could dismiss the apparent avant-garde back in England and express his contempt for the Bloomsbury Group. He could also categorically state that earning money from painting was perfectly acceptable, finding the blurred parameters of professionalism and prostitution bewildering and yet so typical of the London art tradition from which he had emerged.

The period 1912–13 was spent either in Paris or London, according to the artist, or, during the remainder of that time, between Belgium and Holland. Though dogged with poor health, following pericarditis and rheumatic fever, he continued to study, and to learn from the dynamic environment around him, in whichever European capital he found himself.[9] After all, if Malcolm Bradbury's description of London at that time is to be believed, Richard was missing nothing, in 'one of the dullest and most deadening of capital cities, one with no real artistic community, no true centres, no coteries, no cafes, a metropolis given to commerce and an insular middle-class life-style either indifferent or implacably hostile to the new arts'.[10] Alternatively, Paris was turning out to be a glittering, crucial, developmental venue in the emergence of the artist and of the artistic legacy he would bring back, in his opinion, to the aforementioned uninspiring and uninspired English avant-garde.

In Search of Artistic Orientation

More penetrating research, however, reveals that Richard's time in Paris was, in fact, extremely unhappy, uninspiring and was substantially shorter than he had suggested. It was in fact a series of short visits rather than a residential stay. Once again it is through the personal letters that a true image of this period can be recreated, backed up by his father's journals, which, if nothing else, give us an exact location for his son at any given time. For example on 22 July 1912, it is recorded that 'Rich went away to Havre and Paris.'[11] This seems to have been done, as with the second residential period, in the wake of great unhappiness and an argument with Carrington. Later, he met up with his mother in Rouen and several letters originate there. One such letter, dated 24 July 1912 confirms his arrival in Paris and sets to work to display his prejudice and disappointment from the outset. Having gone straight to the Louvre and been surrounded by Americans he wrote to Carrington, 'I heard nothing but nasal banjo-strings twanging out puritanical Anglo-Saxon sentences of crass vulgarity & tedious appreciations of well-known hackneyed but bad work of which the Louvre is crammed'.[12] Having said all that, and having once again placed himself in a position of superiority to 'the mob', he did go on to comment 'My God, there are some pearls among the swine', though he professed to be 'losing my vocation as a swineherd'.[13] His lack of true international spirit was also immediately apparent when he wrote 'Little is more repulsive than a modern French woman' and talked of its 'diseased men'. He was at least comfortably accommodated at the Hôtel de la place de L'Odéon, where he, his friend Sassoon, and Allinson had stayed the previous year on their student visit. Artistic priority was still given to visiting the Impressionist Room at the Luxembourg Gardens where he felt he could learn the most. Searching for inspiration in landscape painting and in working from nature he was aware of a restlessness within himself that demanded a totally new artistic direction. The problem was that he simply did not know in which direction to turn. He wrote 'I am displeased in every way with the work I have done up to now and I don't want to merely improve on the sort of stuff I have done . . . but what am I to do if I *can't* find out how to do it. I am quite in the dark and completely lost.'[14]

The direction of Richard's development paralleled the work of the Impressionists in France, some three decades earlier. This is confirmed, specifically concerning Pierre-Albert Marquet, Signac and Monet, when he remarked: 'What a pity I was not born fifty years earlier . . . I would have been considered quite good & even revolutionary'.[15] These artists then, at this stage in his career, epitomized his concept of 'modern'. His search for an artistic identity had by then reached the stage where he at least knew what he wanted to avoid even if he was not entirely sure what the alternative might be. He could look retrospectively at England, the Slade and previous experiments of his own, and see how they might be deemed unoriginal. Indeed, he expressed himself clearly on this matter saying 'The New English falls back on the 18TH C, the Academy on the Medieval times, Howard Thomas tries to be Greek, Epstein Egyptian, & I now see a danger amongst Currie &

Gertler to be early Italian & costumy. We must guard against raking up the past.'[16] There was a new hatred appearing too for the 'loathsome rich' and also for the decaying population of 'Chinamen', 'niggers' and 'Germans', all of whom suffered from 'poverty of the imagination'.[17] At least he could be sure that the way forward lay in the depiction of modern times and civilizations, and not in this permanent reverence for the past. The latter he described as a 'stomach cancer', so typical in the work of the watercolourist Samuel Prout and Albert Rothenstein, and the solution for him lay in 'the triumph of man over nature'.[18] These sentiments and radical descriptions would create the basis for the modernism that Richard was looking for, though it would remain elusive for perhaps a further year to come.

Renewed Friendships

He was also convinced that the argument with Carrington was over. His letters present evidence of a crisis past and a friendship resumed, for example when he wrote 'Oh, I am so fond of you today. I already long for the sight of you after these wibble-wobbling French women.' She was reprimanded jokingly for her 'rather bad-mannered & deplorable habit of answering back' by Richard who identified himself, in relation to Carrington, as her Sir Launcelot.[19] But this closeness was still upsetting Gertler and would lead subsequently to a further break in the three-way friendship.

It was in a letter from France too that the details of the 'scandal' in which he had become involved in his dying days at the Slade finally became clearer. It appears, as confirmed in *Paint and Prejudice*, that a model had become pregnant and that the identity of the father had been a mystery. Richard joked in the autobiography that it could have been any one of seventeen men, including Tonks himself, but that when the child was born it had looked just like him. Subsequently he had offered to marry the girl and received quite a rude rebuttal. The letters to Carrington tend to imply that he felt the whole affair deeply and remarked 'This affair has blighted the whole of my life.' It seems also that Tonks had collected money for the girl but that Richard could not afford to make his contribution. He explained this to Carrington as follows:

> Tonks has been saying about me that he has never in all his life heard of any man behaving wors[t]e than I have done, he little knows how I loathe not being able to pay for my own misfortune (if it is mine) but as it is by the girl's particular wish not to tell my people I do not see how I can pay Tonks the beastly £10 or whatever it is he gave the girl.[20]

He pleaded to Carrington to keep the whole shameful affair quiet for the sake of his own good name, but more importantly to protect his sister and mother. It seems possible then that he had a son or daughter sometime in early 1912. In *Mendel* the illegitimate baby of Mitchell and Hetty Finch died shortly after its birth.

By 16 August, Henry recorded that he was having dinner with his son in the family home, and so we must assume that this first period overseas was, in total, about three weeks. At this dinner, coincidentally, Richard told his father of 'his woes &

quarrel with Goertler [*sic*] over the girl Carrington, whom both prefer now to hate'.[21] This was a simplistic version of events that were daily becoming more complicated. Richard, who had just had his twenty-third birthday, and received 'fags' from Carrington as a present, had written to Gertler explaining to him that there need be no rivalry between them. He explained to Carrington that he had told Gertler that he would be 'perfectly willing to play second fiddle to him' so long as he did not object to the continuance of the friendship.[22] Within a week, however, he was observing cynically that Gertler 'has simply used me as a stepping stone & now that in his estimation I am no more use he is no longer interested in me'.[23] Worse still, Gertler seemed to have convinced the rest of the old Slade boys that he was the victim of the situation and that Richard had been the perpetrator of cruel and unsporting actions. The result was 'now I am cut dead in the street by Currie', and Gertler, who was 'almost a gentleman' in the midst of 'cads', had caused him to be ostracized from the company which had been so important to him throughout his student days.[24] In short, there was very little left for him in London, and that, not the lure of fine art, was the starting point for the idea of returning to Paris on a more permanent basis.

Bradford

Artistically, if Richard was making progress, it was slow. There was talk of going up to Bradford with Allinson and perhaps some others, prompting him to comment 'I think a studio for finishing off Slade students should be started there without delay.'[25] The lack of artistic confidence was still prevalent but now it was something that he was setting out to overcome. Writing of 'the revolting horrors & disappointments of a painter' he attempted a self-diagnosis of what had been going wrong so far and concluded: 'I have been misunderstood a bit in my life & too well understood in my work.'[26] To counteract this he wrote to Carrington saying 'I am now working all day really trying to do some justice to myself & trying to get back some hopes and beliefs in myself.' Never one to understate his case he went on 'I then do really think I might feel not so hopelessly empty & at war with myself & as far as [I] know my only salvation will come not through Christ but draughtsmanship.' The alternative to success and triumph in this goal was unthinkable and he summed up saying 'Oh I would love to prove I could draw; I think I would shoot myself to prevent any deterioration.'[27] Neither was he convinced that exhibiting at this stage was the tonic that was required for his lack of confidence. This is clearly seen when he wrote 'I think it is better to make a fool of myself in private than public, though I suppose the "moderns" would laugh at me for this.'[28] It is interesting to record the distance Richard put between himself and the 'moderns', in no way considering himself one of them in late 1912: neither respected nor even known by the leading figures of the day. This again is a very different picture to the one painted in *Paint and Prejudice.* He did, however, seem to have outgrown the Slade and in particular his old mentor, Augustus John. He wrote 'I am not very fond of John's work. It strikes me as being by a symbolic Slade man who is a marvellous exponent of Slade teaching, conventions and eccentricities, but somehow not quite art.'[29]

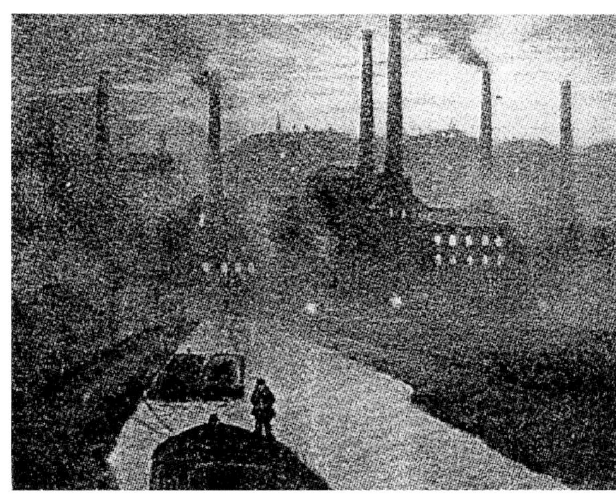

9. *A View of Bradford*, 1911/12. Oil on canvas. Private collection.

His removal to Bradford on 29 August 1912 seems to have been a good decision and archival sources show a young man, very relieved to be getting out of London. His father, for example, recorded on 3 September: 'The one comfort is that Rich is happy at Bradford.'[30] He presumably did not know of an incident that Richard had written about in a letter to Carrington the previous week. In it he told of a fit of fury which had overcome him for two days and which had led to 'a dreary street at midnight' where he found himself 'in order to administer a thrashing on the offender's doorstep with my stick'. Richard appeared to feel no remorse; quite the contrary, he wrote: 'How superb is physical violence if you happen to be the stronger.'[31] In a later undated letter he even joked about it saying 'in future if I ever get violent insane or melancholic I will go & knock about a bit. Tonks for preference.'[32] Though he was in Bradford only for a short time, and despite the fact that 'Allinson blights the place',[33] he got the breathing space, socially and artistically, that he had been seeking. As a pleasant surprise Ruth Humphreys, an old Slade colleague and friend of Carrington's, seems to have been living there at the same time. To begin with he could pinpoint his happiness to having 'cut entirely away from all artists and the Slade clique' and went on to say that 'my work does not want criticism, it wants doing'.[34] The only work identified from this early visit is *A View of Bradford* (fig. 9), a painting done very much in the mode of *The Railway Bridge, Charenton*, and still firmly rooted in the NEAC tradition. Strangely he also commented, in the same letter, that 'I hope my interest in landscape will revive' – an unusual sentiment for someone on the brink of breaking into the ultra-modernist coteries of Paris and London.

Regardless, upon his return, there was an evident change in attitude and tempo and now he could write 'I am now horribly & deliriously happy.' It appears that Wadsworth had come round to see the paintings he had done in Bradford and had been very enthusiastic indeed about them. This had been reciprocated with a visit to Wadsworth's studio and the conclusion that what he had seen there had been 'bloody good'. Wadsworth he described as having 'healthy strength & vigour & modern feeling & independence';[35] qualities that Richard, himself, was soon to hold up as essential in 'vital art'. Wadsworth was now the artist to be admired, perhaps even more so than Gertler. The good news continued when he learned that he had sold a painting, via the dealer Cupid, and so could turn his attention to real, undoubted progress and perhaps for the first time, with real enthusiasm, to Paris. Here he would attempt, one more time, to find himself artistically, perhaps somewhere along the lines of what Wadsworth might do, were he to be taken out of England. He would also do what he could to forget his Slade training where he felt he had been allowed to continue in the production of 'art', even though he had not sufficiently grounded his knowledge in technique and draughtsmanship. He warned Carrington against the 'Albertian Slade' and cited himself as an example of someone who has had 'to go right back & begin fresh & think only of the fees I have wasted'. In prefixing the Slade with the word 'Albertian', Richard referred to Albert Rothenstein of whom he had the following to say: 'If this day I commit murder I am sure Albert R. will be the victim. He is to me all that is symbolic of all that is useless, futile, civilised, beautiful, soft . . . [which] leads to exactly what Art should not do or be'.[36]

Return to Paris

The first serious reference to a long residential period in Paris appears in a letter to Carrington when Richard, in the wake of yet more problems with her and Gertler, said that two months away would help to 'get out of London & forget all this trouble'.[37] The letter goes on to say 'I am rather dreading it' and makes it clear that he felt he was being pushed out of London as opposed to being irresistibly attracted to Paris. By way of an explanation he told Carrington that 'I was practically compelled to make a choice between losing one of you & naturally I preferred a man.' The bungled diplomacy continued when he informed her that 'There was one person I liked better than you & that was Gertler, but now that's over you have the privilege of being the "favourite".'[38] Though probably not approaching the task in the best manner, he was in fact trying to encourage Carrington to wait for him while he was gone. He told her one last time that he actually still loved her but that he had become proficient at suppressing it, and told her that he would delay his departure to Paris until after the next Slade term started. Perhaps seeing him before his departure might encourage her to look no further and in return he promised her 'I am also going to be as pious as possible.' The rooming arrangements, sharing with Rudhall, he said would keep him in line, even if his willpower was weak, and this would prevent him from 'bringing women in at night'.[39] If he anticipated having to restrain himself in Paris it would at least make a pleasant change from his post-Slade life in London. By September he seemed to have given up and wrote: 'I am now getting quite used to seeing no-one all day or night. I hope by degrees to be able to get rid of all desire for people's company & get quite self-contained & happy without them.'[40] When his loneliness was broken it simply led to confrontation so that he also observed, just prior to his departure, 'I have practically quarrelled with everyone.'[41] The one event that set him on his way in more positive spirits was finding out that Carrington had rejected Gertler's advances and told him to expect nothing. Indeed there are the undertones of conspiracy when, jubilant, he wrote to Carrington 'for heaven's sake & mine don't go & write to him *at all* or see him alone, do please promise me this if you are my friend & don't breath [*sic*] [a] word to anyone that I helped you to come to the conclusion that you ought to give him up'. Far from harbouring hostility and being unsure of what to do next, he could quite categorically state 'Gertler must become my friend again, I can't do without him even if he can do without me.'[42]

In the days immediately before his departure Richard worked on a painting of a span of Southwark Bridge. He had managed to secure two more sales through Cupid and once again had submitted work at the NEAC. Concerning the latter he took comfort in leaving England by saying 'I shall be in a far country when the judging goes on. If I get rejected again it will not be quite so terrible.'[43] But socially and artistically the sincerity could be felt in his sentiment when he wrote 'I do hope Paris puts me right.'[44]

It is profoundly surprising, and contrary to the account in *Paint and Prejudice*, to find that Richard loathed his time in Paris. Departing on 8 October 1912, the first correspondence was dated only four days later. Addressed from 120 boulevard Raspail, the letter opens 'I am very wretched indeed I simply cannot find any work & the fellow I am living with is a frightful slacker with no energy whatever.' The bonus, he claimed, was that Paris had helped him to find his soul, the problem being that he now realized that that was actually back in London. Even at this very early stage he was planning his return and could tentatively predict 10 November as that was the end of the length of time for which he had taken his room. He did concede that 'Paris is artistically perfect' but saw no role for himself there. The reason, despite all earlier claims to internationalism, was 'After all I am not Parisian but a Londoner.' He went on to say that he could not change his skin and so every artist should paint his own era and country. To clarify his point he ridiculed the idea of Rembrandt painting in Florence. As to the artistic, intellectual and enlightened friends which he was reported to have made there, he recorded: 'The artists here are swine either Bohemians who slack about all day sitting in the Luxembourg Gardens talking to sluts . . . The rest are Americans who are worse . . . or doodaas from the Slade'. And as to the cutting edge of modernism the bewildered artist commented that they all were 'endeavouring to be more incompetent than [their] neighbour in treatment & more eccentric in outlook'. Even the nightlife was second rate: 'I went to a Cours de Croquis to-night at Colorossi's, it wasn't bad but London is better.'[45] Perhaps if Carrington could have come to Paris to share it with him then the whole city and experience would have been seen in a different light. Accordingly, in Richard's mind at least, plans were afoot to get her away from Gertler for a short period and over to France to stay with him, though this never happened. Interestingly, in a letter giving her directions to his lodgings, he casually mentioned the Nord-Sud without displaying any of the Futurist enthusiasm for the modern electrical railway service that would later lead directly to a composition of the same name. The modernist sensibility, it is obvious, had not as yet matured.

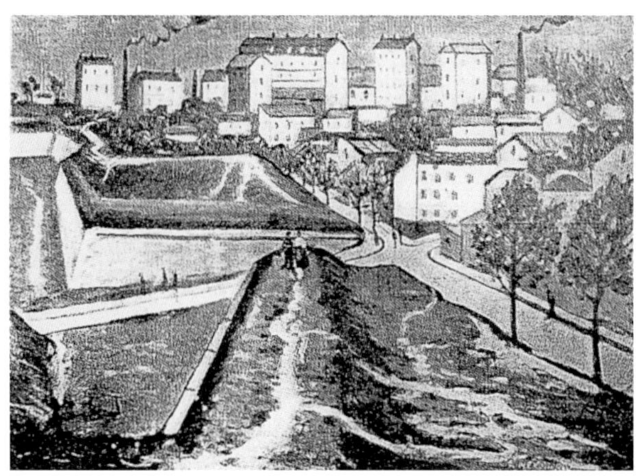

10. *Fortifications of Paris.* Whereabouts unknown.

A second letter, from the same address, dated 13 October 1912, shows no improvement or any sense of benefit from being in the French capital. It opens with the sentence 'My clearing away to this godforsaken hole has been quite useless.' The source of the dissatisfaction was firmly placed on Carrington and her continued complications with Gertler rather than on Paris itself. The fact that business at home had not been concluded, indeed run away from, was making the stay in Paris even more difficult to appreciate. Richard was unhappy and miles away from the problem, which was making the situation worse. Patience, even with Carrington, was wearing thin, and this could be felt when he told her 'To be quite frank I do this time feel very annoyed with you.' Losing any pretence at reconciliation he continued 'if you intend to be "just friends" with Gertler you may as well know you are his worst enemy'. If anything Richard was beginning to take his former friend's side in this argument and Carrington must have been aware of it when she read 'I do hope you will let Gertler either win or lose you & finish this dangling about as he can't stand it.'[46] This outspoken letter led to a silence from Carrington, which in turn led him to write to her again pleading to open up the lines of communication one more time – if only to tell him that 'Tottenham Court Road runs into Oxford Street'. He apologized and said that really his outburst was the fault of his environment as 'I am morbidly bored & uninspired in this "gay city".'[47] After that there is no further communication from Paris. It is also possible that he wrote these letters in a pessimistic tone to gain sympathy from Carrington, and this suspicion is highlighted when we read his mother's account of her son's 'bohemian days', as she, for a time, shared his rooms there. She, too, wrote of meeting a wonderful group of intellectuals at the Closerie des Lilas and La Rotonde, which included Picasso, Boccioni, Modigliani, Apollinaire, Marinetti and Severini, though she seems to have stayed long after her son had returned to London.[48] The period of residence, for Richard, appears to have been one month in 1912, and a very unhappy and uninspiring one at that.

Though presumably benefiting from the enlightened and bohemian atmosphere that Paris provided, as suggested in *Paint and Prejudice*, his works from this period show no dynamic shift towards the style and ethos of the company he was allegedly

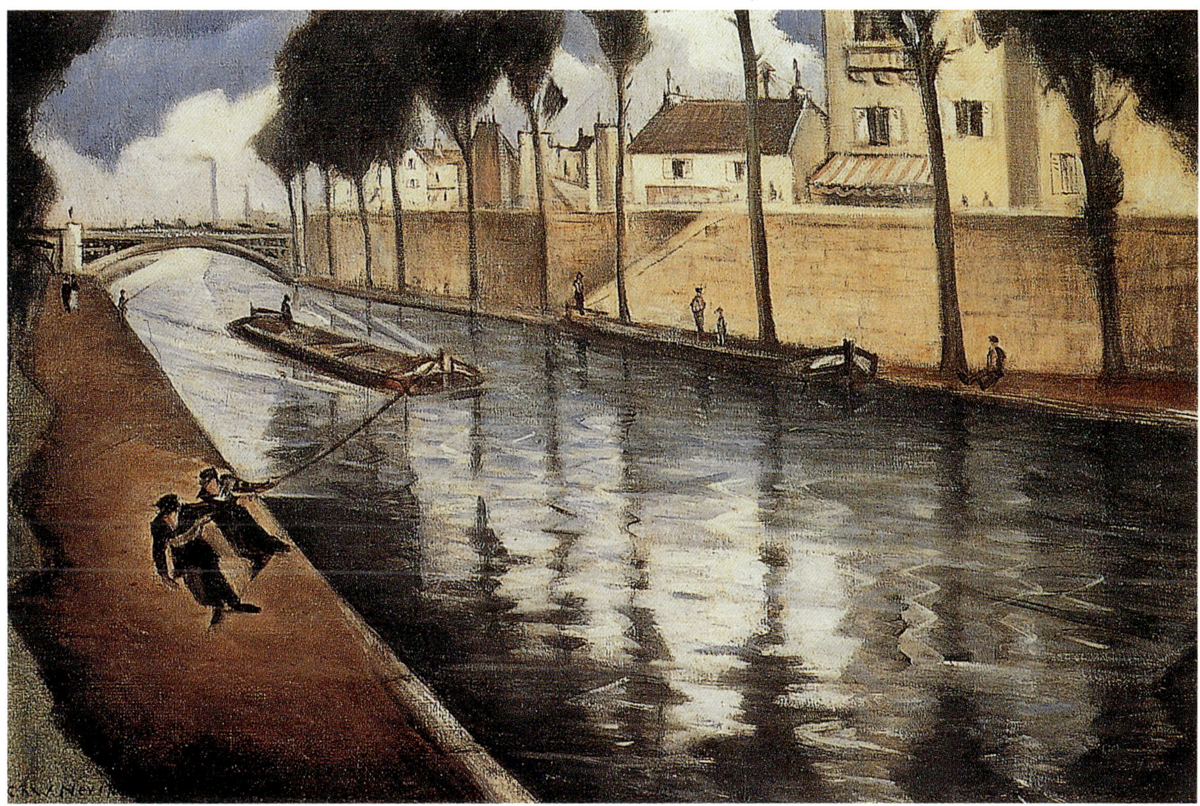

11. *Canal at Charenton*, 1912. Oil on canvas, 51 x 76.2 cm. Private Collection.

keeping. The series of paintings he did of the fortifications of Paris if anything tend to indicate an ignorance of the progress being made around him, and rather witnessed him shedding the affiliation with Impressionism for a more simplified, geometric and sterile representation of the city. Works such as *Les Fortifications de Paris* (fig. 10) and *Canal at Charenton* (fig. 11) illustrate a change in direction, away from an Impressionist style, towards a form of naïvity, with structural rather than tonal emphasis, and certainly not as yet showing any hint of the oncoming vitality and priorities of Futurism.

The variety of interests and influences tend only to point to the general dissatisfaction and artistic disorientation of the artist up to and including the year 1912. Richard was failing in his attempt to create his own unique, individual and vital identity, confused by the many and conflicting influences he had allowed to act upon him. Though open to ideologies from other artists in other countries, particularly France and the European artists resident there, and certainly willing to experiment, an artistic foundation remained to be laid that could be attributed to the artist himself. Though as yet without a style he exuded youthful exuberance for innovation and foreign influences, claiming 'Abroad I had been fired with an enthusiasm which precluded any other consideration. I was a modernist.'[49] Perhaps an involvement, or at least an association, with an already recognized movement, gaining in momentum, but devoid of a national sympathizer, might help traverse the seemingly unbridgeable gulf between promising young graduate and potential figurehead of the country's avant-garde.

That opportunity would come the following year, not from Paris but from Milan, and would be felt at home, in London. Perhaps this early metamorphosis had been hinted at as early as August when he had made his frustrations clear about the worship of the past and the contempt for today so prevalent in artistic circles. So too traces were detected when he had written of the triumph of man over nature and of the stifling nature of art institutions.

Meanwhile, 1912 finished back in London, on the same solitary note that had been so characteristic of his time since leaving the Slade. Alone he attended Christmas services at Westminster Cathedral and at Brompton Oratory,[50] and in desperation he pleaded: 'Come back to me, Carrington, as soon as Gertler lets you.'[51] There is very little to suggest, at the close of 1912, that the following year would see him thrust to the centre, and perhaps even the forefront, of the English avant-garde in London. Little, too, to suggest that he would become, to the public and press at least, the dynamic, vital, Futurist.

4

Creating the Rebel and the Alignment with Futurism 1913

You have to remember that by 1913 Futurism was really a world movement...[it] did not leave anyone time or breath to squeal with. Marinetti made such a noise...the walls of Jericho fell down.[1]

London in the years immediately prior to the Great War was the perfect destination for Futurism. Socially and politically a new ideological climate existed in Britain, which rejected the strictures of its Victorian inheritance. If anything, the radicalism in the arts was eclipsed by the newsworthy momentum attained by the Suffragette movement, Carson's Ulstermen, the rising power of the Trade Unions and the decline of the Liberal Party. This shift was specifically identified, by Virginia Woolf, as dating from December 1910.[2] Petrie observed also that 'The year 1910 . . . does seem to associate itself with an unwelcome change in the country's state of mind.'[3] Dangerfield went on to add that 'violence made a stronger appeal to the public than any other form of speech and action'[4] and observed the change that was to become typical of the four years leading up to the war when he assessed that 'the old order, the old bland order, was dying fast'.[5] Sir Osbert Sitwell recalled that 'A ferment such as I have never since felt in this country prevailed over the world of art. It seemed as if at last we were on the verge of a great movement.'[6]

Whatever the cause, 1910 to 1914 were years of change, and a period in which foreign innovations were welcomed and admired by a few, then accepted and grafted onto English culture more generally. The centre and focus of this activity was the capital city and Ezra Pound observed accordingly 'new masses of unexplored arts and facts are pouring into the vortex of London'.[7] But the change was not to be peaceful, with the need felt not only for the adaptation and modernization of what had gone before but also, in a Nietzschean way, for the destruction of the past to make way for this new generation. Sinclair captured this feeling declaring that 'Art has got to be made young and new and clean'[8] then added that 'If you had youth and life in you, you were in revolt.'[9] Marinetti's cry of 'Voliamo liberare questo paese dalla sua fetida cancrena di professori, d'archeologhi, di ciceroni e d'antiquarii'[10] seemed almost as relevant to this country as the one in which it had actually been born, and was adapted by Richard into a contempt for England's 'canker of professors, connoisseurs, archaeologists, cicerones, antiquaries, effiminacy, old fogyism and snobbery'.[11] The vitriolic attack launched against the establishment, and even the newly acquired orthodoxy of Post-Impressionism, by the alternative and energetic rebel factions of the avant-garde, heralded in the new age of Cubism, Vorticism and Futurism in England. For the aforementioned the technological achievements of the male intellect would be celebrated in an abstract manner, which T. E. Hulme would describe as being symptomatic of a society taking no pleasure from its mirror image.[12]

Futurism

The extravagant rhetoric of the manifesto set the philosophical tone of the movement, albeit for poetry, and propounded the concepts of danger, energy, fearlessness, courage, audacity, speed (the newest form of beauty in the world), war (the world's only hygiene), militarism, patriotism, scorn for women and an absolute contempt for the past. It was this last point that came across most ferociously in passages such as

> So let them come, the gay incendiaries with charred fingers! Here they are! Come on! Set fire to the library shelves! Turn aside the canals to flood the museums! Oh the joy of seeing the glorious old canvases bobbing adrift on those waters, discoloured and shredded!...Take up your pickaxes, your axes and hammers and wreck, wreck the venerable cities, pitilessly.[13]

Founding father and chief theorist of the movement, Filippo Marinetti aimed to manipulate mass culture, almost in a political fashion, and through the related publications *Poesia* and *Lacerba*, aimed at the mass audience of the working classes as opposed to the socially élite. Its philosophical basis lay in revolt, in the rejection of the past, and in accepting and celebrating the today in which they lived. In keeping with the theories of Sorel[14] they promoted violence to a form of political doctrine, or Machiavellian necessity, equating it with freedom. Inspired by Nietzsche[15] they propounded the theory of war as an art, an aesthetic and purifying force in a heightened patriotic and nationalist fervour, where violence was a necessary precondition in the preparation for social, political or aesthetic change. Like fellow Italian, Gabriele D'Annunzio,[16] Marinetti also propounded the glory of the machine, the triumph of technology, the 'man of action', and the evolution and celebration of the city. The depiction of the modern city, however important, was not the dominant objective. Rather, in keeping with the ideology of French philosopher Henri Bergson,[17] the intuitive capturing and depiction of a 'vital life force' or impulse, seeking freedom in the face of the resistance of matter, was the goal. A new understanding was being demanded whereby the medium became the message, not simply the vehicle of it. This was interpreted by the Futurists to mean 'The gesture which we would reproduce on canvas shall no longer be a fixed moment in universal dynamism. It shall simply be the dynamic sensation itself made eternal.'[18] In short, an amalgamation of what was outside, concrete and therefore real, had to be combined with an interior, abstract emotion. Futurist painting, accordingly, abounds in interpenetration, simultaneity, synthesis, force lines and dynamism, whilst demanding subject matter that is both dramatic and engaged in the modern adventure. Perhaps this is why, for some, it was deemed to be Cubism in motion. This was the era of Einstein, Morse, Bell and Edison and as such it was also the era of the factory, the high-rise, the aeroplane, the ocean liner, the car and a host of other technical triumphs which demanded appreciation and acknowledgement. More than anything Futurism was dynamic and vital, abhorring the retrospective obedience Italy, and fellow European nations, had to their heritage and cultures. Marinetti, described as 'The Caffeine of Europe',[19] was setting out to rid European art of its lethargy and its worship of the past, this being done in the most high-profile and controversial ways possible. The press was utilized to the full, speeches were given, arrests effected and the case overstated, when stated at all, in a tirade of inflammatory language and antagonistic actions. With regard to painting in particular, the same destruction was to take place and was to be replaced with an art altogether more relevant to the twentieth century. The specifications for this change were outlined in two particular manifestos. 'The Technical Manifesto of Futurist Painting', launched on 18 March 1910, in *Poesia*, outlined the concept of Bergsonian flux as adapted to art, declared its loathing of the past, then in two lists defined precisely what 'We Declare' and what 'We Fight'.[20] The past, good taste, art critics, the nude, amongst many other elements of painting, were violently rejected once and for all in the search for a new and dynamic art form. From this point on the viewer was not to be a passive participant, but instead was to be thrust to the centre of the canvas to become an active part in the experience of speed, dynamism and movement in the urban and industrial environment. In painting, as in performances, Futurism would require a high degree of audience participation. The 'Manifesto of the Futurist Painters' signed by Boccioni, Carra, Russolo, Balla and Severini, had previously been published in *Poesia* in February 1910 and in it ambiguity was swept away with statements such as

> We will fight with all our might the fanatical, senseless and snobbish religion of the past, a religion encouraged by the vicious existence of museums. We rebel against the spineless worshipping of old canvases, old statues and old bric-a-brac, against everything which is filthy and worm-ridden and corroded by time. We consider the habitual contempt for everything which is young, new and burning with life to be unjust and even criminal.

In conclusion it stated

> The dead shall be buried in the earth's deepest bowels! The threshold of the future will be swept free of mummies! Make room for youth, violence and daring.

London, Futurism and the Nevinsons

D'Harcourt has claimed 'The Futurists were fascinated by London, a modern metropolis which took them to its heart with a warmth that Paris never displayed,'[21] and that 'Between 1910–1914 the English received the full force of the Futurist campaign'[22] and indeed Marinetti was already a household name in London by the time of Richard's return from Paris at the end of 1912. Futurism had been known throughout Europe from the publication by Marinetti of 'The Founding and Manifesto of Futurism' in *Le Figaro* on 20 February 1909, and from the dynamic and polemic actions and publications of the developing group in the ensuing years. The manifesto had been widely translated, appearing for the first time in Britain in the low-key publication *Tramp*, in August 1910.[23]

As early as 1910 Richard's mother, Margaret, had reported on an evening Marinetti had given at the Lyceum Club, at 138 Piccadilly, when he had delivered a lecture in French entitled 'Un Discours Futuriste aux Anglais'.[24] He praised certain elements of Englishness, most specifically Ernest Shackleton, Charles Rolls, the Dreadnought and the courage and fighting spirit of the English soldier in the Boer War. He then went on to attack

> your deplorable Ruskin, whom I intend to make utterly ridiculous in your eyes ... With his sick dream of a primitive pastoral life, with his hatred of the machine, of steam and electricity, this maniac for antique simplicity resembles a man who, in full maturity, wants to sleep in his cot again and drink at the breasts of a nurse now grown old[25]

The attack on Ruskin complete, he went on to vilify English tourists in his country, the class system, traditions of etiquette, and the English male of whom he said 'almost all are homo-sexual for a time'.[26] In true Futurist manner he was not trying to make friends, but rouse people from their lethargy. In fact he even goaded them into starting right away, saying 'you who are among the many who disapprove of ... Futurist convictions ... but who nevertheless force yourselves to applaud me because of the duty of hospitality, go ahead and brutally break the block of your beautiful English courtesy and hoot lengthily at me, at your pleasure and freely'.[27] Whether or not this actually happened is unknown, but Margaret wrote the following in the *Vote*: 'The members of the society are young men in revolt at the worship of the past. They are determined to destroy it, and erect upon its ashes the Temple of the future. War seems to be the chief tenet in the gospel of Futurism: war upon the classical in art, literature, music'.[28] War was 'the hygiene of the world' and the Futurist was to 'admire today the dreadful symphonies of the shrapnels and the mad sculptures that our inspired artillery moulds among the masses of the enemy'.[29] Though she found Marinetti a 'very stimulating companion' and a 'brilliant conversationalist',[30] she found Futurism, on the whole, a 'shallow and insubstantial piece of Latin bombast and exuberance'.[31] But for Marinetti in 1910, and again on his second visit two years later, London was '*the* Futurist city par excellence'.[32]

In this second visit, which began in March 1912, Marinetti openly spoke of his admiration and excitement in London at the experience of the underground, the bright red double-decker buses, the electric lighting in the Mall, the music halls, and the 600,000 registered motor vehicles now present in the capital city. He rapidly became a society novelty and was entertained by Viscountess Warwick and Lady Cunard, the latter whom he described as having the 'wit of an aviary'.[33] Cricket bored him, though watching Chelsea play soccer was better, warm beer repulsed him and the London fog irritated his throat. But this was a working trip, and so, accompanied by Russolo, Boccioni and Carra, the lectures and Futurist activities, both official and unofficial, began. As a consequence, and entirely according to plan, it was not long before they were in the news and generating the attention they so desired. This was exemplified, for example, by Boccioni when he joined a suffragette demonstration in London. Though totally unsympathetic to the cause, he admired the radical and violent means of the women protestors. Boccioni wrote to Vico Baer 'In London I went with Marinetti to insult a journalist at his home. What a wonderful car trip, sixty kilometres out of London! I witnessed all the riots of the suffragettes, encouraging and cheering them on when I saw them being arrested . . . I fought with fists and elbows.'[34] In the middle of this fracas was Margaret Nevinson. Marinetti and Boccioni, in the same trip, tracked down journalist Frank McCullagh to his Surrey home and challenged him to a duel for an unfavourable report he had written concerning the Italian army in the 1911 Tripoli campaign.[35] To their frustration he refused the duel but invited them instead for afternoon tea. Nonetheless, Futurism was rapidly becoming a novel movement, heard of by almost everybody, but not always being treated with the seriousness that the protagonists desired. Cork has observed this phenomenon: 'Almost overnight, anything new and shocking was saddled with the nickname of "Futurist": men's pyjamas, lampshades, cravats, silk purses, quilts and bathing suits.' He went on to reiterate the point claiming 'The movement had become so much a part of the nation's consciousness that its name was bandied about indiscriminately to describe any new developments in the arts.'[36] Regardless of the nature of the 'success', Futurism had started to put down roots in London. Marinetti then turned his attention to what might even have eclipsed London as the world's ultimate Futurist city, New York. He decided that the Futurists should make a grand entrance there on board the epitome of man's engineering achievement to date. Perhaps the White Star Line would allow a Futurist Salon in the engine room, and certainly the press would be ready to greet both them and the celebrated *Titanic* when it arrived on its maiden voyage in New York harbour from Southampton.[37] Due to a variety of unforeseen circumstances this plan was not put into action and so Futurism lived to fight another day, literally.

This was obviously not a passive movement concerned only with the minutiae of aesthetic principles of art, a fact that was confirmed in a key lecture, entitled 'Futurism in Literature and Art', delivered by Marinetti at the Bechstein Hall on 19 March 1912. Here he found his stride and turned on the English whom, though he admired their 'brutality and arrogance', he described as 'a nation of sycophants and snobs, enslaved by old worm-eaten traditions, social conventions and romanticism.'[38] In a letter to a Milanese friend he went further in his description of the English describing them as 'beautiful, monstrous, elegant, well-fed, well-dressed, but with brains as heavy as steaks. Inside the houses are magnificent: cleanliness, honesty, calm, order, but fundamentally these people are idiots, or semi-idiots.'[39] The Turners and Pre-Raphaelites of the National Gallery, he advised, should be piled up in Trafalgar Square and set alight.

In the midst of this high-profile publicity and exposure, the Sackville Gallery show, *Exhibition of Works by the Italian Futurist Painters*, opened on 1 March 1912, having travelled from the Galleries Bernheim in Paris.[40] The exhibition introduced the theories, and over forty paintings, of Marinetti, Boccioni, Carra, Russolo, Balla and Severini, to a public who, unprepared for the impact of the ideology, were soon as outraged as Marinetti could have hoped. The catalogue carried the 'Initial Manifesto of Futurism' and the 'Manifesto of Futurist Painters' and so the academic principles of the movement were introduced in tandem with the actual images. The critical response was perfect, if not predictable. To Rutter, their works were 'the pictorial rendering of confused nightmares',[41] while Charles Lewis-Hind felt confident that 'England as a whole will laugh at or loathe these works.'[42] *The Times* could categorically state that 'The anarchical extravagance of the Futurists must deprive the movement of the sympathy of all reasonable men.'[43] For Marinetti, however, it was an unmitigated success. He wrote: 'The colossal success of London increases in a fantastic fashion. More than 350 critical reviews in a *month and four days*, because the galleries did not want the paintings to depart, given the crowds of paying visitors. Sales to date are more than 11,000 francs!'[44] He went on to note that Boccioni, Severini, Carra and Russolo had also sold works for substantial sums. In reality only Boccioni and Carra made sales from the show.[45] Likewise, of the hundreds of claimed reports of the show, perhaps only a dozen were truly critical pieces. Behind the façade of success, the reality was somewhat different and this can be seen in a letter from Severini to Boccioni. In this he agreed that the 'moral' success of Futurism was undoubted, but mourned the fact that there had not been 'even a sign of a sale'. He also needed Marinetti to send him 150 *lire* in order to get home.[46]

Whether or not Richard, in his final year at the Slade, attended either the exhibition or the Bechstein Hall lecture, is not known, but he had to be aware of the existence of Futurism in London. In very much the same way that the *Second Post-Impressionist Exhibition*, of the same year, caused a stir, fundamentally amongst the students at the Slade, so too the Futurist exhibition, attracting record crowds for the gallery, could not have gone unnoticed. The impact, it has been suggested, was widespread and almost unavoidable: 'Most young English artists were caught up in this enthusiastic and vigorous approach to life, art and science. Despite their surface reservations, they rarely resisted the opportunity to see, hear or read the Futurists.'[47]

Futurism may not actually have brought these radical ideologies to Britain but certainly the movement embodied the values more concisely and definitively than ever before. Hamilton put this beyond debate claiming 'there is no credit nor understanding to be gained by refusing to face the obvious welcome and rapid assimilation of the Futurist credo in that London vortex of 1912–1914. The future, like the traveller, does eventually arrive.'[48]

The connection between Futurism and the Nevinson family, before 1913, does not end with Margaret Nevinson's report on the 1910 lecture. Henry had attended the Sackville Gallery show on 3 March 1912.[49] He had also come to know and admire some aspects of Marinetti's work before his son, following

> a never-to-be-forgotten occasion in the Balkan Wars, when the Italian had found himself cooped up in a train full of journalists for a whole day, a golden opportunity for him. He made the most of it by reciting for hours on end various Italian poems and expounding the theory of Italian Futurism to an audience which could not get away.[50]

Henry himself wrote about the experience at the Bulgarian frontier town of Stara Gora, in October 1912, where 'in a dirty little restaurant . . . Marinetti conceived his finest and wildest poem . . . a pathetic description of Turkish wounded going home in a train attacked by Bulgarian cavalry.'[51] Henry's close connection with Futurism had already begun, and his son's was just about to.

The Futurists in England, if there were to be any, would have to have a strong, virile, modern, patriotic and masculine character. Perhaps Richard desired to attribute such qualities to himself, living in the shadow of his war correspondent father, possible sexual abuse at Uppingham, his indecision at the Slade and artistic failure in Paris. The resultant art would have to display the primacy of instinct and imagination over reason, energy over tradition, primitivism over civilization, and anarchy over peace. This would be a strong and direct alternative to the dissatisfaction he had been feeling concerning his painting up to this point. In short, the combination that attracted him was to be that of the primitive and the scientist in the modern environment. Futurism, alongside everything else, was a male-dominated philosophy in an environment that has been described as homo-social and in turn anti-homosexual.[52] The man would replace the dilettante, masculinity would replace effeminacy and strength would replace the weak and indecisive.

Creating the Rebel and the Futurist: 1913

Following his return from Buxton, where he had been undergoing treatment for pericarditis and rheumatic fever, and where he had met his wife-to-be, Kathleen Knowlman, Richard could record that the change he had been looking for had, almost effortlessly, arrived. He wrote 'Now began my life as a rebel artist, discussed everywhere, laughed at and reviled by all contemporary critics, with the exception of P. G. Konody,[53] Robert Ross, and Frank Rutter.'[54] He was exhibiting, by his own admission, at the Salon des Independents in Paris and also with the London equivalent, the Allied Artists Association, organized by Frank Rutter. In the latter he listed himself alongside Lavery, Sickert, Gore, Ginner, Gilman, Pissarro, Manson and Lewis. This then had led to an introduction to the Dore Gallery where he placed himself amongst Signac, Cezanne, Picasso, Derain, Soffici, Balla, Severini, Matisse and Vlaminck, in other words, the Who's Who of European modern painting at the time. The evening lectures given there by Rutter facilitated introductions to society hostesses like Lady Paget and Lady Lavery, and this provided the social bridge to pre-war London society, the equivalent of which Modigliani had provided in Paris. He had also accepted Lewis's invitation to join the Rebel Arts Centre (RAC),[55] in its opposition to the Fry-run Omega Workshop, and found his new companion 'the most brilliant theorist I had ever met'.[56] And then, quite suddenly and without introduction, in *Paint and Prejudice*, he declares 'Marinetti, the Italian Futurist, thought of coming to England and told Severini, who wrote to me about him. I asked Severini to persuade him to come.'[57] Accordingly, he and Lewis organized a dinner for Marinetti at The Florence, and, amidst about sixty of London's intelligentsia, Richard gave his first public speech, which ensured much press coverage in the ensuing months. He described the evening as 'grand, if incoherent'[58] and recollected the humour of the entire situation. He also observed that here the very early sign of a split between himself and Lewis might have started to appear. According to his recollections then Futurism arrived in England and he, if not the actual person responsible for this arrival, became the young rebel artist most closely, indeed inextricably, associated with the movement. This is a misleading interpretation of the year 1913 and an over-simplification of the sequence and nature of events.

The transition was not fast and 1913 began in very much the same vein as 1912 had ended. On 3 January Richard and his father went to Muirhead Bone's studio to see the drawings he had made on a recent trip to Italy, and the following day father and son visited the Grafton Galleries to see *The Second Post-Impressionist Exhibition of English, French and Russian Artists*, though Richard, unlike some of his English colleagues, did not exhibit there. The 'Old Masters of the Modern Movement' were exhibited, with pride of place going to Matisse, Kandinsky, Picasso, Vlaminck and others associated with the Cubist and Fauve ilk. If Cézanne had been difficult to comprehend, let alone appreciate, then this abstraction, with its musical references and its claim to reality in place of illusion, was to be an impossibility. What was being asked of the public was not only to observe what was happening in the art world in France, but to question completely what the aims and objectives of art in the modern period were in their entirety. In doing so they were being made to reassess and re-evaluate the means by which they viewed art and by which it justified its existence at all. Clive Bell's introduction in the catalogue optimistically assumed that the basic tenets in art criticism were now accepted:

> The Battle is won. We all agree, now, that any form in which an artist can express himself is legitimate, and the more sensitive perceive that there are things worth expressing that could never have been expressed in traditional forms. We have ceased to ask, 'What does this picture represent?' and ask instead, 'What does it make us feel?' We expect a work of plastic art to have more in common with a piece of music than with a coloured photograph.[59]

To all but a few the exhibition was anathema, more so even than the first one. Not so for the students and ex-students of the Slade. Nash emphasized this point:

> The Slade was then seething under the influence of Post-Impressionism. Roger Fry had brought about the second exhibition of Modern continental art in London and now all the cats were out of the bag...It seemed literally to bring about a national upheaval . . . All this had a disturbing effect at the Slade. The professors did not like it at all. The students were by no means a docile crowd and the virus of the new art was working in them uncomfortably. [60]

Henry, however, recorded his difficulty in appreciating what was being exhibited saying 'about 10 were comprehensible: or fine: the rest were insanity to me, espec. a man W. Lewis who paints everything including women as though made of plate armour. But Roger Fry who was there admires him.' At the same exhibition they met Gertler who 'came in quite friendly again'.[61] What Richard thought of the show is not recorded, though certainly he would not immediately have been attracted to the anti-impressionist sentiment which was so prevalent there.[62] Four days later, on 8 January, Wadsworth dined at the Nevinson household, and this, Richard wrote in a letter to Carrington, had alleviated some of the misery attached to his solitude. Prior to this he had seen no one since Currie on Christmas Eve.[63]

He was now painting again and aiming to exhibit with the Friday Club. For this he did a charcoal version of one of his Paris panels of the fortifications there. He then worked on a painting of the same theme and described it as follows:

> I have painted the sky a flat deep blue, ultramarine and Prussian blue & very little white on a clean canvas. Against this I have silhoutted [*sic*] the white and yellow houses with black and scarlet roofs & the grass on the battlements I have made a deep green pure viridan (?) & black & cadmium deep & vivid cadmium green in foreground & all the little patches drab yellow, orange or white. The whole is very full of colour but low in tone as I believe the best of modern work will not be violent or vivid in colour.[64]

It is interesting to observe here what Richard's concept of 'modern' was, not least because he went on to say with relief how much he felt that the composition, on the whole, had succeeded. Declaring that it 'smells strongly of Cézanne' he had clearly hit a formula with which he was more satisfied. Better still, all of his paintings were accepted a fortnight later for the Friday Club show,[65] though they were still a very long way from anything which could be described as being sympathetic to the basic tenets of Futurism. On the contrary, out of sheer hopelessness, and blind to Futurism and its presence in England, he had the idea of turning his attention once again to Paris to 'try & raise some interest in something'. His work, like his friendships had 'fizzled' and this he attributed to trying 'every conceivable medium' since Christmas, the result being that he had 'run dry'.[66] This condition led, in May, to a 'morbid state of terror' when his pictures went before the selection committee of the NEAC. Prepared for rejection he had sworn off drinking as a means of dulling the terror but reported: '[I] am saturating myself with sanatogen.'[67] By 22 May Henry recorded that all his son's pictures had been rejected and commented 'so another artist's life goes miserably on'.[68] But the fact that he was still submitting pictures to the NEAC, a soon to be sworn enemy, shows his mindset still trapped in the Impressionist/Post-Impressionist era of late 1912. Other sources, however, show undercurrents of progress in these early months of 1913. Henry, for example, recorded that Richard had exhibited at Roger Fry's Post-Impressionist show at the Alpine Club, and that he had gone to see it on 15 March 1913. His comments, always favourable to his son, reported that 'Richard's two of a Paris suburb . . . much the most beautiful there'. He also commented that the accompanying work of Duncan

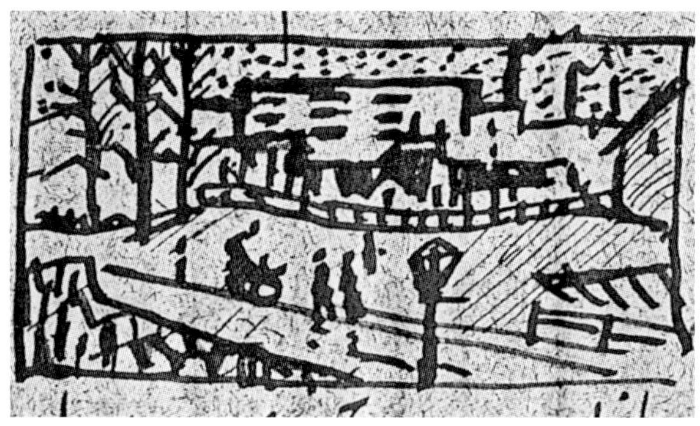

12. (above) *Port de Montmartre*. Sketch, Department of Rare Books, Wyndham Lewis Collection, Karl A. Kroch Library, Cornell University.

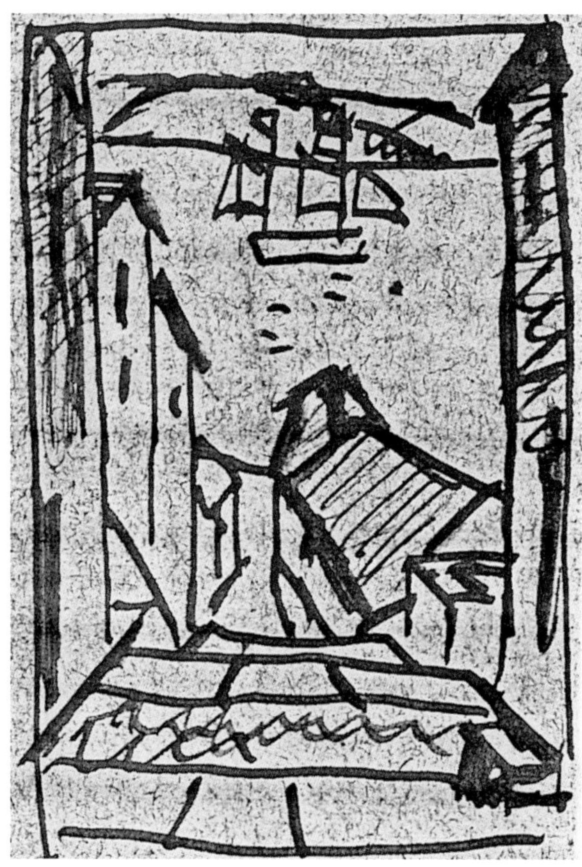

13. (right) *Falmouth*. Sketch. Department of Rare Books, Wyndham Lewis Collection, Karl A. Kroch Library, Cornell University.

Grant, Max Wilber, Wyndham Lewis and Frederick Etchells was 'just insane'. Acknowledging that his 'old age' may be the problem he concluded his comments on the latter artists by entering in his journal 'What a lot!'[69] A brief glimpse at Richard's picture is possible through a sketch drawn on a letter from him to Lewis (fig. 12), in response to Lewis's invitation to exhibit. This was accompanied by descriptions of what the finished composition would have looked like. There is also a view from a window in Falmouth (fig. 13) with which Richard was pleased by the simplicity and experimentation in the piece. It was 'dark in colour, [with] dull reds, ochres, Prussian blues & black greens'.[70] In a minimalist way, scenes were stripped to their structural basics in a process of reduction, which almost eliminated the tonal and *chiaroscuro* considerations of previous Impressionist affiliations. This orientation was reiterated in the same letter when he wrote 'I cannot get that self-portrait of Rousseau out of my head.'[71]

Enter Lewis and Severini

But if things were stabilizing artistically, they were rapidly declining in the ongoing saga of the Gertler–Carrington–Nevinson triangle. Patience had clearly run out on Richard's part and he wrote furiously to Carrington saying 'Does Gertler own you? If so *it is final*. If not I *am* damned why I should not see you. I don't care if

Gertler can't stand it, I can't stand this frightful lonely life that *he* has compelled me to live. Why should I not have friends? He is not God Almighty.' Any attempt at reconciliation or mediation had disappeared in a poorly written, punctuated and presented letter, which ranged from rage against the 'little bounder', criticism of Carrington for putting up with his abuse, to a final outburst of self-pity at his own lonely state. Once again his temper lead him to the melodramatic in which he expressed the desire to murder Gertler, or if not, to kill himself as life was growing daily more vile. Only Wadsworth now was his companion and he mourned this saying 'Everybody's dropped me.'[72] Later letters adopted a superior tone and talked about Gertler being 'the produce of Petticoat Lane', criticizing his over-jealous state, his abusive comments about Carrington, and his lack of manners in breaking appointments and his word.[73] The latter trait, he warned, was rubbing off on Carrington and this, alongside everything else, was giving him grave concern. Still he did not give up. Two days later, for example, he called three times at her house on Fitzroy Street, though she was out on every occasion. Apparently she had stopped writing too and Richard could only observe in bewilderment what was going on. He had ruled out a formal relationship a long time ago and he reiterated the point in a letter, which implored 'I like you for *other* reasons besides your sex.' He went on to say 'naturally being a man I should have liked more' but clarified, once again, that he was perfectly content with the role of 'second fiddle'.[74] He reminded her of how his stay in Paris was on her account, trying to make life easier for someone he cared about, and that his thanks was this. Loneliness was now becoming obsessive and he played on her conscience by reporting 'you are my only friend. I see no-one week in week out except once or twice my mother at breakfast & weekends & my father on Sunday'.[75] He made it clear that he was not going to consider Gertler's feelings as he had not respected his, and that, like it or not, he would continue writing, at least to her. He declared: 'it will do no harm to you & a lot of good and happiness to me'. His last letter that month reverted to the apologies and low self-esteem, characteristic of the artist who had lost his temper so often in the past, and who now had to resign himself to his lonely fate. Taking the blame away from her, he wrote: 'I have lost all control of myself & my nervous state makes me think all sorts [of] delusions against people & imagine everyone my bitter enemy . . . no wonder every one else has dropped me'. Going on to call himself 'a little spiteful beast' and 'such a cad', he left the decision with her as to the future of their friendship, and signed off by saying that he felt burning shame and remorse over the entire situation.[76] No response came and he therefore left for Falmouth. A letter he sent from there also went unanswered and so, on his return, he reopened the lines of communication, but this time in a very different tone. Enclosing a stamped, addressed envelope, to assist her return letter, he began formally with 'Dear Miss Carrington'. As if having one final purge of emotions he got to work calling her friends 'scum' and claiming that 'they make a whore of you'. Ironically he signed off telling her that, young and naïve as she was, he was still her best friend.[77] Carrington now appeared to wash her hands of him entirely despite his pleas that he was 'insane with misery' and his protestations that 'everybody has kicked me down'.[78] When the letters started again on 26 March it was only another attempt on his behalf to clear his name and to elicit pity one more time. He wrote of his solitary life, his going to dances alone and his disappointment that his new motor bike was not the solution to his problems. There is a heavily disguised compliment deep in the letter too when he wrote 'I admit the only happy times of my life were spent with you, but how you have blighted my life since.' He did, however, make a point of saying that having given his trust once, and having it abused like this, he would never be such a fool as to do it again. And then there is the return to the manic depression and to the thoughts of suicide in the lines 'I have spent hours trying to pluck up the necessary half second to kill myself but I only sweat and tremble.'[79] He signed off by saying that he saw himself as the protagonist in Maxim Gorky's *Man That Was Afraid*, to the point that he could not finish reading it.

Just as Richard was observing the death throes of the friendships and artistic ideas which had developed at the Slade, so too he was fostering and nurturing friendships in a different, and ultimately more beneficial, direction. Henry's journals record that his son and Wyndham Lewis had met as early as the end of January 1913.[80] A letter from Richard, dated 18 February 1913, rather formally invited Lewis to his studio to look at two or three new canvases with which he was pleased. It was clear that the latter's opinion would be important for him. For Henry, Lewis was simply known as 'the queer artist'[81] and Wadsworth was seen to be virtually as incomprehensible, though both were admirable in many ways for their new ideas and original approach to composition. For Richard, however, the friendship was a whole new lease of life, which placed him in the more central flow of the English avant-garde. He was therefore replacing Gertler and Wadsworth with Lewis and new arrival, Gino Severini, as the new artists to admire and emulate.[82] By late 1913, Rutter could retrospectively comment that it was through Severini that the young Englishman 'had become thoroughly impregnated with the principles of Futurism'.[83] How and when he met Severini remains open to speculation. There is an entry, dated 21 April 1913, in Henry's journals which reads 'Severini came to dinner and talked Futurism in French.'[84] It is not known whether the Italian was the guest of Richard or of his parents, both of whom were conversant with Futurism. The connection might also have been through Charles Lewis-Hind who supported the Futurist in London and, in addition to introducing him to Epstein, might also have provided the introduction to any of the Nevinsons. In trying to piece together the exact sequence of events we may observe that Henry's journals record that Severini arrived in London on 6 April, that they first met on the 13th and that he dined in the Nevinson household on both the 18th and 21 April. In any case, it seems less likely now that the friendship had been made in Paris in the bohemian nightlife of the Tabarin and the Monico and through the Italian-cockney clown, Titi, as Richard had suggested in his autobiography.[85] Other theories suggest that they had met the previous year at the Futurist exhibition at the Marlborough Galleries while Rothenstein claimed that the friendship was made over lunch at the invitation of Clive Bell and Roger Fry.[86] Nonetheless, we might conjecture that this friendship was the definitive turning point in his career, and almost certainly turned his attention to the images, theories and proponents of the Italian movement. It would be Severini who would introduce the young Englishman to other protagonists of the group and get him exhibited in Paris and Berlin (according to *Paint and Prejudice*). He would also be responsible for forming the link with Marinetti and, to a very large extent, would act as the pathfinder for Richard's emerging artistic style. It is known that Richard attended Severini's one-man show at the Marlborough Galleries, 23 Duke Street, in 1913, *The Futurist Painter Severini Exhibits His Latest Works*. Severini, who, like Marinetti, was fascinated by London, praised the city and the inhabitants for their spirit, strength and energy, whilst in a familiar way declared that the National Gallery was full of 'dead things' and ought to be turned into a crematorium.[87] The emphasis of his comments fell on the same areas as before with statements such as 'Motor-omnibuses passing and re-passing rapidly in the crowded streets, covered with letters, red, green, white, are far more beautiful than the canvases of Leonardo or Titian.'[88] Severini must also have been delighted that Richard took him out for rides on his motor bike around the Edgware Road and also on Haverstock Hill and Camden High Street.[89] But more importantly, through the exhibition and the catalogue that accompanied it, a very straightforward, yet dynamic set of theories were being put forward. A balance between the plastic and the abstract was being attempted in a celebration of the modernity of the contemporary urban scene, and this undoubtedly was attractive to Richard. Severini's explanation is evident and relevant when he wrote 'One object does not leave off where another begins but the lines and planes which constitute the one influence the lines and planes of the other. The desire to regard things as entirely isolated from one another belongs to analysis. We remain thereby within the realm of the relative, in the domain of scientific experience.'[90] Even a glance at the names of the paintings exhibited demonstrates a brand-new excitement, which, for Richard at least, must have offered a tempting alternative to compositions he had attempted, unsuccessfully, for the NEAC. Amongst Severini's titles were *The Motor Bus*, *The Nord-Sud Railway*, *A Dancer at Pigal's*, *Spanish Dancers at the Monico* and *A Spanish Dancer at the Tabarin*. Richard, if he too was to pursue Futurism, would have to make the transition from his adoption of the visual and representative ideologies associated with Impressionism/Post-Impressionism, which had served him reasonably well for several years, to those of intuition, dynamism, and the synthesis of abstraction inherent in all objects. Certainly, from this time forward he could be seen to experiment both in subject matter and technique in a similar way to his new Italian counterpart.

Shortly after this Richard became ill with a liver complaint, possibly, he suggested, inflamed by the blow he felt at being rejected by the NEAC and the stress built up over the Carrington dilemma, which kept him housebound for several months. His father, on returning from Albania, recorded the seriousness of the ailment, and stated that it had effectively prevented his son from doing any further painting. The transition to Futurism then was neither immediate nor complete and he, even in restored health, did not assume that he would automatically head the English branch of the movement. In fact, if anything, he rather encouraged Lewis to take the helm. This is substantiated, over six months later, by a letter from

Richard to Lewis, dated 5 November in which he declared: 'it will need the combined effort of Etchells, Hamilton & Wadsworth & myself under your command'.[91]

As yet, however, there was no direct association between Richard and Marinetti, though it seemed that a return at this time might be more fruitful than any of the previous visits, as now there was some native interest in, and perhaps sympathy for, the movement. Severini wrote to Marinetti on 3 November to tell him just this and to urge him to return quickly.[92] He appears to have been actively sought by the English artists as well, as a letter from Richard to Lewis states with relief: 'I have at last run Marinetti to earth. He is in Brussels! & has just wired me from there & fixed an appointment with me at the Savoy tomorrow (Sat) at 6 o'clock.'[93]

The Post-Impressionist and Futurist Exhibition

By this time, however, a band of rebel artists had already linked themselves closely to the movement via the exhibition of the previous month at the Dore Gallery, entitled *The Post-Impressionist and Futurist Exhibition*. For this Frank Rutter had written a foreword, in an attempt to introduce 'schools of painting which have made some noise in the world during the last quarter of a century'.[94] He also used Richard's *Gare Saint-Lazare* for the invitation card.[95] The show did not contain any works by the Bloomsbury artists, nor, ironically, any by the Italian Futurists. Instead, the emphasis went on Post-Impressionism, Fauvism, Neo-Impressionism and Intimism. Importantly, however, there were many contributions by the 'rebel' English artists, amongst whom were Sickert, Lewis, Wadsworth, Etchells and Nevinson, representing the ill-defined Cubo-Futurist 'school'. These were exhibited together in the prestigious continental company of Cézanne, Van Gogh, Matisse, Delaunay, Picasso and Franz Marc. In all, 213 works were presented, including the following six by Richard: *Waiting for the Robert E. Lee* (fig. 14), *The Departure of the Train de Luxe* (fig. 15), *The Circular Railway* (lost), *The Iron Bridge* (*The Railway Bridge, Charenton*) (fig. 7), *Portrait of the Artist* (fig. 3) and *Issy-les-Moulineaux* (fig. 16).

One of the texts which had accompanied the Sackville show of the previous year, entitled 'The Exhibitors to the Public', declared 'there can be no modern painting without the starting point of an absolutely modern sensation'.[96] Here, meaning and the relationship of art to society, ethically, socially, politically and aesthetically justified the defined demarcation between Futurism and Post-Impressionism, and perhaps even Cubism, and went some way to understanding the exclusion of Futurism from Fry's 1912 *Second Post-Impressionist Exhibition*. By 1913, however, Rutter was able to introduce the alternative modernity of the key rebel English artists saying 'That "Cubism" and "Futurism" have already stirred English artists is shown by the contributions of Mr. Wyndham Lewis, Mr. Nevinson and others.'[97]

The Departure of the Train de Luxe and *At the Dance Hall*

Though not listed in the catalogue for the exhibition, Richard's *The Departure of the Train de Luxe* (fig. 15) was by far the most modern interpretation of an industrial

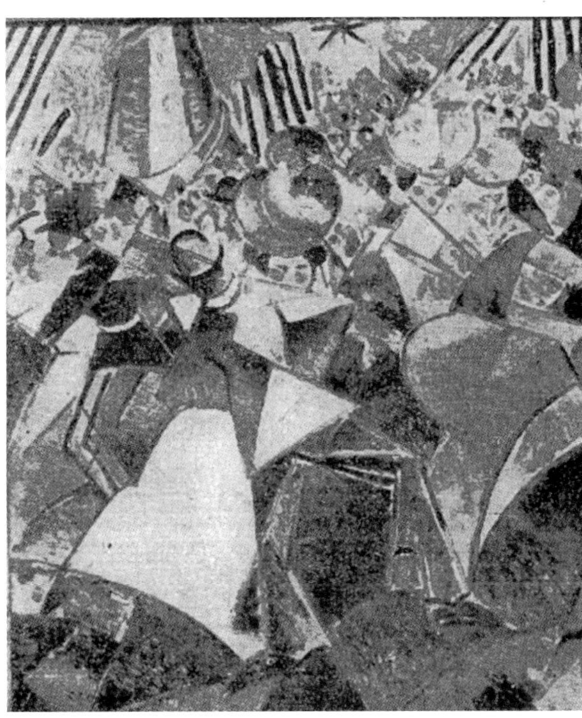

14. *Waiting for the Robert E. Lee*, 1913. Oil on canvas. Whereabouts unknown.

urban scene yet undertaken by the artist. Frank Rutter went so far as to call it 'the first English Futurist picture'.[98] It certainly was a watershed composition, starkly and suddenly contrasting with the techniques he had employed before. The artist was now, in homage to Severini and Boccioni,[99] turning to embrace the concept of multiple exposure through the fractured picture plane in a manner associated more closely with Analytical Cubism, and in turn, Futurism.[100] An early attempt at this had been seen in another, more moderate, depiction of Matisse's home town, exhibited at this show and entitled *Viaduct, Issy-les-Moulineaux* (fig. 16).[101] Regardless of teething troubles there was a definite move towards modernizing the presentation of the modern theme. Now, industrial and urban scenes were executed using a more modern technique than any compositions undertaken by Richard in the previous year, which moved towards what Frances Spalding has referred to as 'brittle images that rested firmly on the picture surface'.[102] But more specifically it is the debt to Severini which remains obvious, and direct parallels can be drawn between *The Departure of the Train de Luxe*, and the Severini's *Nord-Sud* of 1912. Severini described his painting in the catalogue for the Marlborough exhibition thus:

> The idea of the speed with which a lighted body spins through dark or lighted tunnels, is conveyed by means of colours, tones and forms. The great notice boards placarded in the stations enter the compartments in motion. The letters written on the placards act upon the memory through their literary significance at the same time as they act upon the eyes by means of their colour.[103]

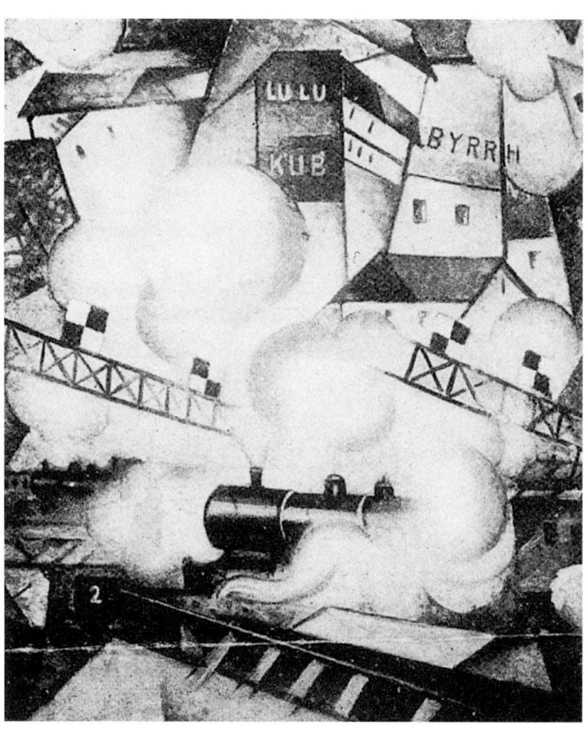

15. *The Departure of the Train de Luxe*, 1913. Oil on canvas. Whereabouts unknown.

The scenes depicted are similar, both artists attempting to capture the sensation of motion in a modern, mechanical and urban context, thus introducing a kinetic element to the painting.[104] In doing so they employed similar techniques, such as the inclusion of truncated words and interlocking planes, thus rendering the composition not immediately visually comprehensible, but more importantly creating a fourth dimension, which is movement, in space and time.[105] The concept of simultaneity was created by the superimposition of multiple viewpoints of the object, as the Cubists would have done, but then, in a more complex manner attempting to capture the movement of the object itself by depicting multiple versions of the same event in sequence. A further element is attempted in the depiction of multiple events, simultaneously, from multiple viewpoints, but superimposed onto the canvas in one frozen moment. What was being sought then was much more than the creation of a likeness, rather it was the pursuit of rendering a sensation, though in this composition, as in *The Arrival* (fig. 19), the actual subject is not fragmented, only its environment, and is treated from a single perspective point. This may be interpreted as displaying a lack of commitment or courage, or it may be symptomatic of the 'compromise' that was soon to be so prevalent in Richard's work. Perhaps the legacy of the 1912 *Second Post-Impressionist Exhibition*, or his possible friendship with Picasso,[106] can also be seen as the composition contains the truncated word 'KUB', which is identical, and hardly coincidental, to the latter's composition, *Le Bouillon Kub*.[107]

For Richard at least this was the point of departure into what would dominate his art stylistically and topically for the following two years. We know that he had

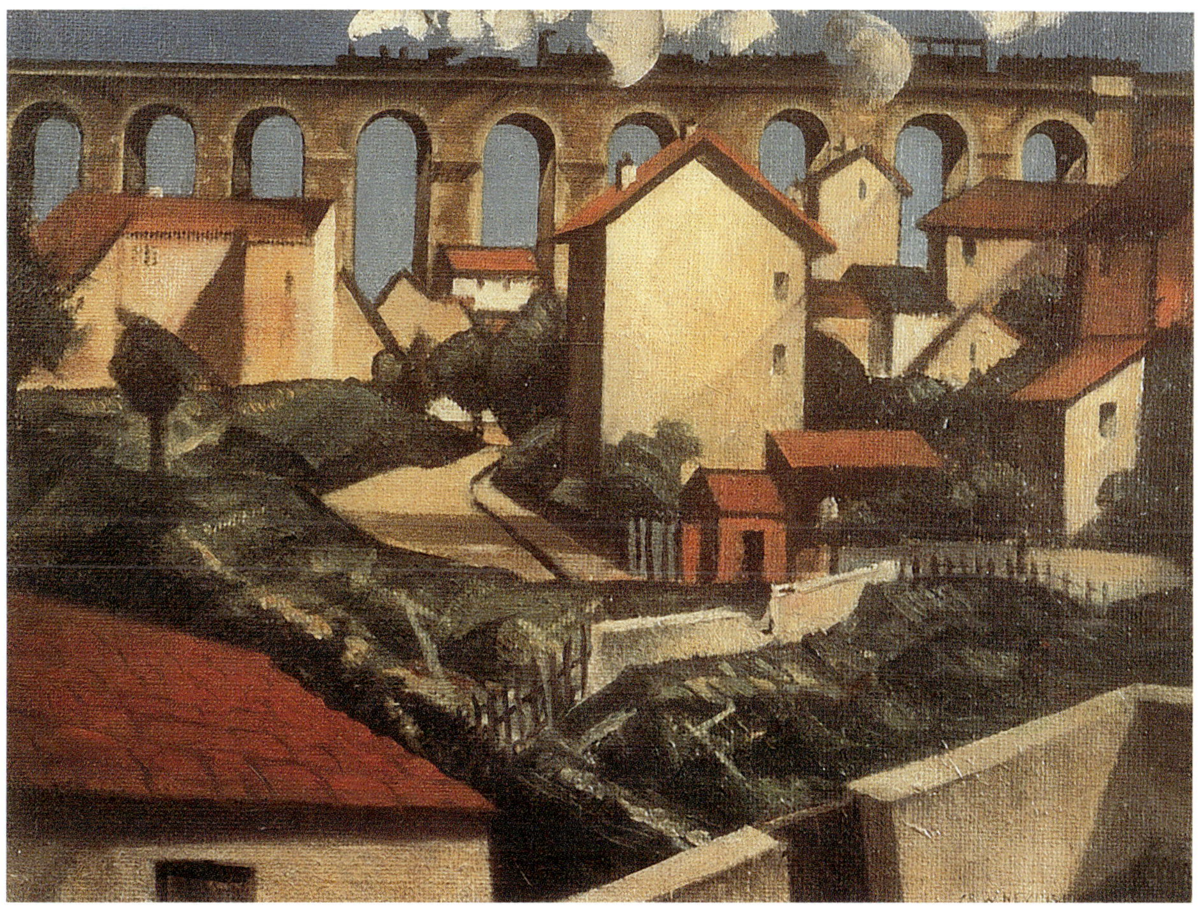

16. *Issy-les-Moulineux*, 1913. Oil on canvas, 45.7 x 61cm. Private collection.

also been particularly taken by another painting, the highlight of Severini's at the Marlborough and Sackville shows, *Pan Pan at the Monico*. This composition would later form the foundation for Richard's *At the Dance Hall* (fig. 17). Severini's goals were clearly defined in the catalogue of his 1913 exhibition at the Marlborough Galleries when he declared that the image was trying to capture 'Light and ambience [which] act simultaneously on the forms in movement.' Both the scenes, by Severini and his English friend, revel in the noise and movement of modern music, fashion and dance as seen in two of the main capital cities of Europe. Stylized figures, forms and colour convey the sensation of the experience, as opposed to creating an accurate visual representation of it. Both seemed to be pursuing the goal of 'Displacement of bodies in atmosphere. Two persons form but one plastic unity, rhythmically balanced.'[108] Severini too tried to recreate the rhythm of the evening in his use of forms and in the harmony of colours used on the canvas. Severini's own description says 'Musical rhythm accompanies the arabesque of lines and plains, the harmony of tones and values. Lights translated through abstract forms, now and then breaks into the rhythm.'[109] The composition by Severini was enormous, three by four metres, a trait that would also be echoed in Richard's work, as he recorded

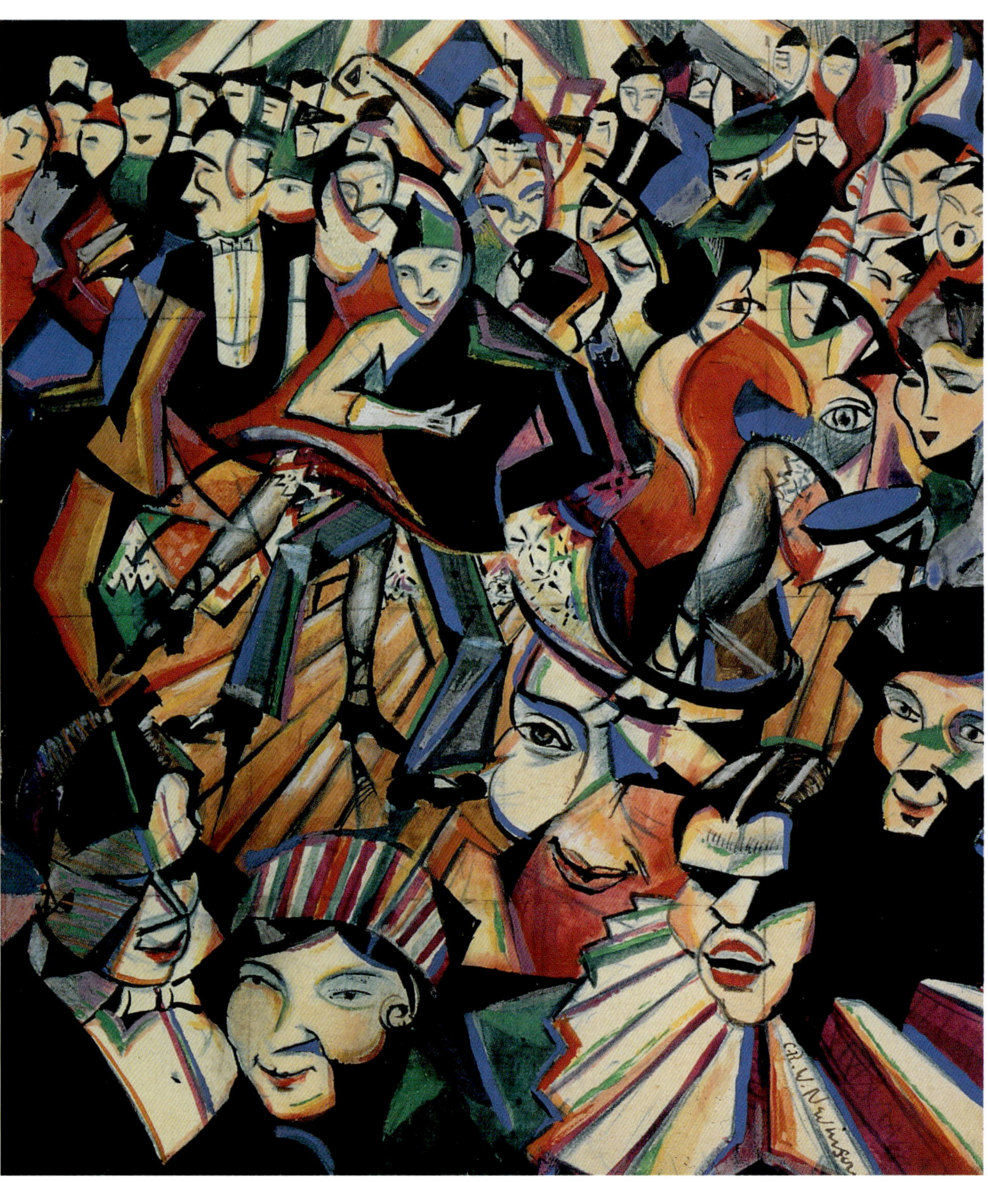

17. *At the Dance Hall*, 1913. Chalk, gouache and watercolour, 20.5 x 17cm. Tate Gallery, London.

the impression, or the 'state of mind' created by the nightclub.[110] The combination of internal and external visions here were combining to create the plastic synthesis so central to Severini's Futurist compositions, and was dubbed by Apollinaire 'the most important work painted up to now by a Futurist brush'.[111]

In accepting this, we observe the continuing, and now definitive, shift in Richard's painting away from the influence of turn-of-the-century French art. The difficulty for both him and Severini lay more in the counter-productive method in which they believed the work was presented. Severini recorded in his autobiography, 'each time the Parisian art world had contact with the activities of the Italian Futurists, I always deeply regretted the erroneous Futurist feeling of antagonism, of competing with Paris and Cubism: it would have been more advantageous for them to function harmoniously.'[112]

Richard, it appears, had set out to contemplate the same artistic challenges. Critically this met with a mixed response: his period of transition, for some, representing the visual development of ideas and techniques in a logical progression towards an ultimate goal. He escaped the worst of the critical backlash that the Dore Gallery show provoked, though the *Daily Sketch* did publish one of his paintings upside down, along with Delaunay's *The Football Team* and Wadsworth's *The Omnibus*, under the scathing banner 'You wouldn't think that these were paintings, Would you?'[113] The *Daily Mirror* also published the same painting, and so, for the first time, his works were reaching a wide audience, albeit as the source of ridicule. Though the *Daily Telegraph* referred to *The Departure of the Train de Luxe* as 'an uncalled revelation of semi-sanity',[114] other 'English Cubists'[115], as they were crudely called, such as Lewis and Etchells, drew the more biting reviews. To the reviewers these artists and works were mere imitations of a more legitimate European equivalent. 'We have learned to measure the facts in better perspective, and can admire Van Gogh or Paul Cézanne for the original artists they were, but we have no laugh left for the cranks and notoriety hunters that follow in their train.'[116] In fact, if anything, the press in the confusion which surrounded the terminology of modern painting, tended to refer to Richard as a Post-Impressionist whilst isolating Robert Delaunay as the Futurist. Regardless of this attention to detail, Clive Bell was scathing in his condescending review which stated that 'Futurism is a negligible accident' which 'is sqeaking, "I am advanced – I am advanced."' One artist, however, was pardoned by Bell: 'Yet Nevinson bears the Briton's burden more lightly than his fellows; probably because he is cleverer than most of them. He is clever enough to pick up someone else's style with fatal ease; is he not clever enough to diagnose the malady and discover a cure.'[117] In short, Bell believed that after this brief flirtation with a plagiarized style, Richard would see the error of his ways and probably be a fine painter in time, unlike the others. Bell finished with some advice for the rebel artists in search of the spotlight: 'I would advise Nevinson and the more intelligent of his company to shut themselves up for six months, and paint pictures that no-one is ever going to see. They might catch themselves doing something more personal if less astonishing than what they are showing at the Dore Galleries.'[118] Not least, criticism was reserved for the Futurist use of the 'style' more essentially associated with Cubism. Clive Bell, proponent of 'significant form', relegated this to the status of 'simplifications, schematizations and tricks of drawing'[119] while other reviews cynically observed that 'the Futurists stole the Cubists' clothes and have put them on the wrong way'.[120] Finally, Richard did not entirely evade cynicism when one article summed up 'The squares and angles school is well represented. Mr. C.R.W. Nevinson precipitates himself on public notice with his *Departure of the Train de Luxe* a glaring defect of which is the close resemblance that a splash in the middle of the canvas bears to a railway engine.'[121] Another reviewer commented that the young artist had 'taken his father's "Essays in Freedom" a little too seriously' and praised the *Departure of the Train de Luxe*, but said that *Waiting for the Robert E.*

Lee 'perfectly expresses the feeling aroused by five barrel organs in succession playing that inescapable tune under one's windows'.[122]

On a more personal and intimate level, Henry's journal for 16 October 1913 reads 'Went to the Futurist show at the Dore Gallery: some strange things there, but I feel the whole fashion for Post-Impressionism is becoming stiff: It is already imitative and doesn't grow. Rich's 3 pictures & 3 drawings were well liked. To me both Wadsworth and Wyndham Lewis were horrible: really hideous and I was sorry, for I like the two men.'[123]

Severini, talking of the 1912 Futurist exhibition, summed up well the same ideas, which could be applied to this exhibition and to Richard in particular, when he said 'The truth of the matter is that, at a time when the quality of art in Italy was at a particular all time low, these young artists used every possible means to up date their knowledge of European artistic activity as it was manifested in Paris. That endeavour in itself deserved praise, not criticism.'[124] The accusation that Richard was constantly in pusuit of notoriety at any price was one that he never entirely rid himself of throughout his lifetime. Nonetheless, the publicity, the accolades and the recognition of being a dynamic, young English artist, were welcome and long overdue as far as he was concerned.

Socially and artistically Severini and Richard were now on a parallel, if not converging, course, which would see them travelling to Paris, studying and even living together from time to time up to, during and after the war years. The extent of the impact of Severini's ideologies on Richard were beginning to be felt and were to come to fruition especially in late 1913 and throughout 1914. Artistically, however, Severini made no record of the influence that his English counterpart might have had on him. He did, however, remember him affectionately in his autobiography saying 'the person with whom I became closest was the painter Nevinson. He was a reserved man like many of the English, but very sensitive and intelligent.'[125] It is also recorded in Severini's autobiography that Richard, Roger Fry and the English rebels were the only artists to send him money, £10, when he was desperate and when his Futurist colleagues refused to help.[126] A letter housed in the archives at Trentino Rovereto, from Richard to Severini, shows that more funds were being collected by the English artists to help the Italian and that Roger Fry, ironically, was happy to contribute.[127]

Marinetti Returns to London

Whether Richard was the source of Marinetti's invitation, as he claimed in *Paint and Prejudice*, or not, a renewed lecture tour by the latter began in November 1913, which involved presentations at the Cave of the Golden Calf's cabaret, the Poet's Club, the Poetry Bookshop, Clifford Inn Hall and the Dore Gallery on New Bond Street. Henry, amongst others, reported enthusiastically declaring that 'no-one could escape the spell of listening'[128] as he attended recital after recital. Imagist poet Richard Aldington also recorded in the *New Freewoman*: 'Mr. Marinetti has been reading his new poems in London . . . London is vaguely alarmed and wondering whether it ought to laugh or not . . . It is amazing and amusing to a glum Anglo-Saxon to watch Mr. Marinetti's prodigious gestures . . . a better man than the bourgeois men and women who grin at him when he reads.'[129] Lewis too wrote enthusiastically of these performances telling Mrs Percy Harris that 'Marinetti declaimed some peculiarly blood-thirsty concoctions with great dramatic force . . . He will be lecturing again soon . . . and will no doubt be well worth hearing'.[130] If anything the reputation of Futurist evenings preceded the events and Fishburn, the proprietor of the Dore Gallery was reported to be 'most nervous of any of the pictures getting injured, especially Delaunay's but I don't suppose they will chuck anything even if the fools come'.[131] So far as Marinetti was concerned things could not have been progressing better and a letter to Severini, in the same month, shows that already he had committed himself to a return to the Dore Gallery in early 1914.[132]

Accordingly, and in response to this new wave of notoriety, a committee of rebel artists including Etchells, Roberts, Lewis and Richard, organized a dinner in Marinetti's honour at the Florence Restaurant on Rupert Street on 18 November 1913. The fact that Richard took a leading role in this, if not the leading role, is confirmed in a letter from Fanny Wadsworth to Lewis which says 'Nevinson wants to get up a dinner for Marinetti who is coming to London [on] November 14th for six days.'[133] The idea was a popular one and was well supported. Futurism, its audience and associated artists, was strengthening not only in interest but also in numbers. Henry's journal provides us with a further insight into the evening, though contradicts the figure of sixty people given in *Paint and Prejudice*: 'About 25 men came & one woman appeared for a short time. Rich and Wyndham Lewis gave the toast in French. Marinetti spoke & recited in French with extreme vigour & eloquence & apparently could have continued all night. He gave his Adrianople & the train of wounded.'[134] Six months later, Lewis would call Marinetti 'the intellectual Cromwell of our time' and acknowledge that 'England has need of these foreign auxiliaries to put her energies to rights and restore order'.[135] But Lewis, however glad of the vitality of the inspirational voice of Marinetti, did not wish to see the Italian dominate the emergent English avant-garde. Richard too, at this stage, saw the dangers, or at least wanted to appear aware of them, and wrote to Lewis the day after the dinner saying 'I had quite a great deal of difficulty in preventing Marinetti from again expounding and proposing his philanthropic desire to present us to Europe and be our continental guide.'[136] The relationship between Marinetti, Lewis, Nevinson and the other English avant-garde artists however, had a long and controversial course yet to run, but for the moment it was still, on the whole, positive.[137] What is obvious from existing letters from Richard to Lewis is that their partnership was now attracting attention and commissions from the wealthy art patrons in London. For example on 4 November he wrote of a visit to the Dore Galleries at which Fishburn told him of 'a certain Lady Muriel Paget' who, when they met, was 'astonished to find me not absolutely insane nor some form of clown'. As an admirer of Cuthbert Hamilton's work and as a well-known buyer, Richard encouraged Lewis not to take her offer for work lightly.[138] In fact, on the 13 November he wrote to him again reminding him of his appointment to visit her at 2 Norfolk Crescent.[139] The same week he received, and forwarded to Lewis, a letter from Lady Drogheda and another from 'The old Bitch of the Cave' (possibly Kate Latchmere, the owner of the Cave of the Golden Calf), again, concerning commissions and the upcoming lecture that was being organized for the Dore Gallery. The former was developing an idea concerning a 'Futurist Frieze' which Richard was happy to pass on to Lewis on account of his rapidly declining health.[140] There was a further commission from Lady Cunard for Lewis, Wadsworth, Hamilton and him to design small gifts for the 'rich & influential' at a dinner to honour the American millionaire George Moore. Taking them away from easel painting all together the request was for handkerchiefs, scarves, fans, and in his case, candle shades, each of which would command ten shillings. Futurism, or Cubism, or simply the avant-garde, was indeed becoming fashionable amongst the society set and Richard was quick to recognize the value of this, writing: 'It seems an excellent opportunity for you to get in touch with her & others.'[141]

Perhaps the last major artistically significant event of 1913 for Richard and his cohorts was the *Camden Town Group and Others* exhibition in Brighton from 16 December 1913 to 14 January 1914.[142] Though this essentially represented the future members of the London Group, one faction of artists, including Nevinson, Etchells, Lewis, Wadsworth and Hamilton chose to separate themselves from within, distinguishing their exhibit as the 'Cubist Room'.[143] Lewis wrote of their unity and compared them to an island in the otherwise tranquil and respectable archipelago of English art.[144] This complete segregation was indicative of the emergent diverging courses within the English avant-garde.[145] Here Richard exhibited two paintings, both now lost, of the Gare Saint-Lazare, and this further enhances the Monet, Severini, Marinetti and Carra connection. Perhaps this is one of the last occasions when the group of young rebel artists in England were moderately homogenous, prior to the discordant events of 1914. A further letter to Lewis, before the show even opened, revealed that his health was poor by December 1913, saying 'I am so unwell & I am going away to try & get right.'[146] On 10 December he left with his mother for Boulogne and then travelled on to Paris. The following day, a letter to Severini, from Boulogne-sur-Mer, saw Richard, retrospectively, giving himself much of the credit for the success of the previous few months, and also witnessed him beginning to assume that Futurism and the avant-garde in England were synonymous. It was precisely this sort of assumption that was going to lead to turbulent times, and the fragmentation of the avant-garde group, in 1914.

> Quand Marinetti été à Londres j'ai vu beaucoup de lui et j'ai organisé un diner en son honneur des jeunes peintres de l'avant-garde, c'était un grand sucès et je crois que Marinetti ete tres content de voir qu'en Angleterre une movement assez fort et avec un grand sympathetic pour Futurism a commence et qu'une groupe d'artistes anglais se sont bandis en cause d'un art avance que nous nous ferrons sentir dans le monde intellectuel et internationale comme vous Futurists Italiens.[147]

Not content to sit back and enjoy the momentum of this recent success, he was already planning on how to get Severini to London for the exhibition which was almost certain to run the following March. Aware of the Italian's financial difficulties he invited him to stay at Downside Crescent for the duration of the show but warned that due to serious strikes London was not, as yet, spending money on art.[148] Nonetheless, further plans were being made for the future.

From Paris, in the sixth *arrondissement*, Richard sent a postcard to Edward Marsh on Christmas Day in which he recommended visiting Kahnweiler's for Picasso's work, and Sagot's for the paintings of Severini, Boccioni, Metzinger, Marchand and Picasso. It is interesting that this was now what he considered to be 'modern' and to be the epitome of the European avant-garde. It is also interesting that he spelled Boccioni's name incorrectly on the card and so, despite the sequence of events depicted in *Paint and Prejudice*, it seems possible that the two artists might not, as yet, have become friends, or, indeed, met.[149] The following day he wrote again to Severini confirming his debt to the Italian's work and saying 'I am delighted that you will write soon about your latest ideas, because they interest me enormously.'[150]

Despite the constant decline in physical health throughout the year, 1913 had witnessed a very welcome break in Richard's fortunes. From his disorientation at the beginning of the year, through his new associations made in the latter half of the year, he had found direction and legitimate, original artistic goals which he now endeavoured to follow. Shaking off the legacy of the Slade, both in friendships and in ideals concerning painting, he embarked on an altogether more dynamic and exciting route as a rebel painter closely associated with the Futurist movement. To say that Wadsworth, Lewis, Etchells or Nevinson were actually Futurists at this stage would be a sweeping statement, difficult to defend. It would also be difficult to argue convincingly that they had created, or even attempted to create, an identifiable 'English Futurism'. They did, however, seem to be advancing with a degree of unity towards something altogether more dynamic and exciting, under the guise, for the moment, of Italian Futurism. That they were impressed by the movement is beyond doubt, but not all to the same degree. Regardless, 1914, in the remaining eight months of peace before the outbreak of war, it was certain, would be an interesting year in London for the avant-garde, for Futurism and for Richard.

5

Nevinson the Futurist 1914

One evening I strolled into the Dore Galleries, in Bond Street, because a meeting of art extremists had been announced, and because I like wild words...Richard was on his legs, talking to beat the band, slashing out, but sanely...and there was papa in the chair, smiling.[1]

Richard's ill health bridged the years 1913 and 1914 and shortly after his return from France, Henry recorded: 'Helped Rich to wheel his motorcycle to be sold owing to his wretched illness. All very sad.'[2] Together they looked at a studio at Hillfield Garden, though it is not known whether they took it.[3] Regardless, father and son embarked on a year that for both would gravitate towards Futurism and its chief protagonists.[4] Though neither mentioned nor even hinted at in *Paint and Prejudice*, it was not only the son who took an active interest in the movement and lectured and performed in its name. Instead, father and son together affiliated themselves to the movement, using their different media and different strengths to observe, then participate. Indeed, it was the father's name that was first linked to the movement in the press in 1914 when, on 17 January the *Evening News* published a long article entitled 'Some of the Manifestoes of "Futurism;" Amazing, Absurd, Amusing – As You Like.' In it an understanding was attempted which observed that the movement 'deliberately defied every known canon, not merely of art but of eyesight'. Henry was quoted at length in an article which, instead of ridiculing the movement, attempted to come to terms with it. The passage, about Marinetti, read:

> Into our ancient life of precedents and perpetual repetition he burst like a shell. Antiquity exploded. Tradition ceased to breathe. Those who heard him in the last few days know what vitality means. He over-runs with it. There is no stinting or sparing. He pours out life like ungrudging nature. Like all true hearted fanatics he lives only for his cause and never counts the cost. I have heard many recitations, and have tried to describe many battles. But listen to Marinetti's recitations of one of his battle scenes – a train of wounded stopped by the enemy, or the destruction of a bridge under fire. I may very well have witnessed both the events he describes for he was with us in the Bulgarian Second Army a year ago. But I have never conceived such descriptions as these nor heard such recitations. The noise, the confusion, the surprise of death, the terror and courage, the

> grandeur and the appalling littleness, the doom and chance, the shouting, curses, blood and agony – all were recalled by that amazing succession of words, performed or enacted by the poet with such passion of abandonment that no-one could escape the spell of listening.

The article finished on an upbeat note by observing that 'At any rate, Signor Marinetti has performed a service in stirring people up.'[5]

The work requested by Lady Cunard in late 1913, which was possibly the only commission the Rebel Art Centre ever received,[6] seems to have been completed satisfactorily as Richard wrote to Lewis, 'As I arrived home to-night, an American with an extremely rude manner and a pimply face came with the £50 cheque & much bluster. My joy is unbounded.'[7] The actual finances of the centre seemed to be rather shakier and he suggested that 'the artist ought to pay his expenses for materials etc & and the Rebel Art Centre take 25% of the article he succeeded getting'.[8] Likewise, he divided equally the profits of the Marinetti lecture at the Dore Gallery between the five members of 'the "Blast" Group'. Each member's share was £1 19s 4d from the total takings of £9 17s 0d.[9]

By March Richard was taking the Futurist experiment into the galleries with the London Group, and together with his rebel peers, was attracting the critical and press response that any Futurist, or rebel of any nature, would have desired. Described as 'The Camden Town Group, the seceders from Mr Roger Fry's Omega Workshops, and other English Post-Impressionists, Cubists and Futurists',[10] the exhibition at the Goupil Galleries became the focus of the critical debate surrounding most avant-garde painting of the day. Many articles were written and a lively discussion instigated, while several newspapers reproduced his painting, *The Strand* (fig. 18), though somewhat cynically under the title 'The London streets are indeed perilous.'[11] Certainly the works Richard exhibited there: *The Arrival* (fig. 23), *Tum-Tiddly-Um-Tum-Pom-Pom* (fig. 20), *The Strand* (fig. 18), *The Chauffeur* (fig. 21) and one sculpture, *Automobilist (Machine Slave)* (fig. 22) marked his closest association yet with Futurism. It was at this exhibition too that he exhibited *Non-Stop* (lost), a depiction derived from the sensations experienced whilst travelling on the London underground. This, once again, makes a direct reference to Marinetti and to the interview he had previously given to the English press in which he had professed that the underground had given him what he had wanted. It also made direct reference to the Futurist dictum in painting, which declared that

> To paint a human figure you must not paint it; you must render the whole of its surrounding atmosphere. Our bodies penetrate the sofas upon which we sit, and the sofas penetrate our bodies. The motor bus rushes into the houses it passes and in their turn the houses throw themselves upon the motor bus and are blended with it.[12]

This theory of dislocation and dismemberment, of fused simultaneous details and liberty from accepted logic, did not meet with universal approval. 'Mr. Nevinson's picture does produce the effect of a journey in the tube upon jaded senses very clev-

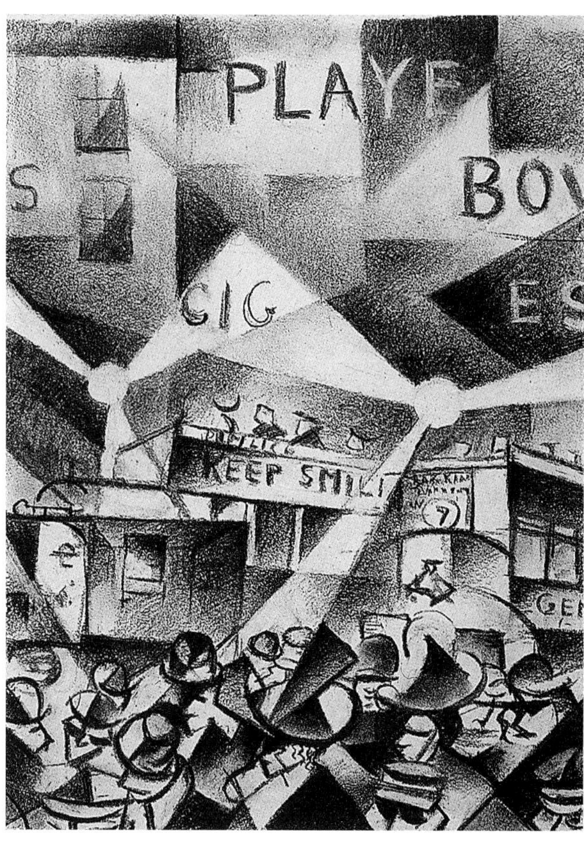

18. *The Strand*, 1913/14. Conte, 36.5 x 26.5 cm. Private collection.

erly. It is, that is to say, a kind of realism as much calculated to kill any talent as the realism of the lion on a Victorian hearth rug.'[13] Other reviews were more perceptive and claimed: 'That mixture of streaks of light, and fragments of advertisements, and curves, and colour, with lines that suggest straphangers here and there, is quite obviously an impression of a compartment on the Underground. This exhibition is certainly a success of curiosity; and it proves, at any rate, that the young London artists are not deficient in daring.'[14] Once again Severini's eloquence is useful in describing Richard's intentions. For a similar composition the former had explained: 'It has been my endeavour to produce by means of lines and planes the rhythmic sensation of speed, of spasmodic motion, and of deafening noises.'[15] The *Observer* review noted also that had this sort of work been exhibited three years ago it would have 'provoked unmeasured hilarity or furious indignation',[16] suggesting that by 1914 the efforts of the Slade generation of artists were having some impact on critical opinion in pre-war London. Other reviewers remained bewildered, claiming that there was still 'truth in Whistler's contention that only the artist is capable of understanding his art'.[17] The press, on the whole, however, once again spared Richard. The *Observer* pointed out that 'Mr. Nevinson more than ever proclaims himself an English disciple of Severini and the other Italians of the memorable Sackville show.'[18] It was also quick to praise experimentation, when it was done by a competent and talented artist, and praised the legitimacy of his experiments, while finding

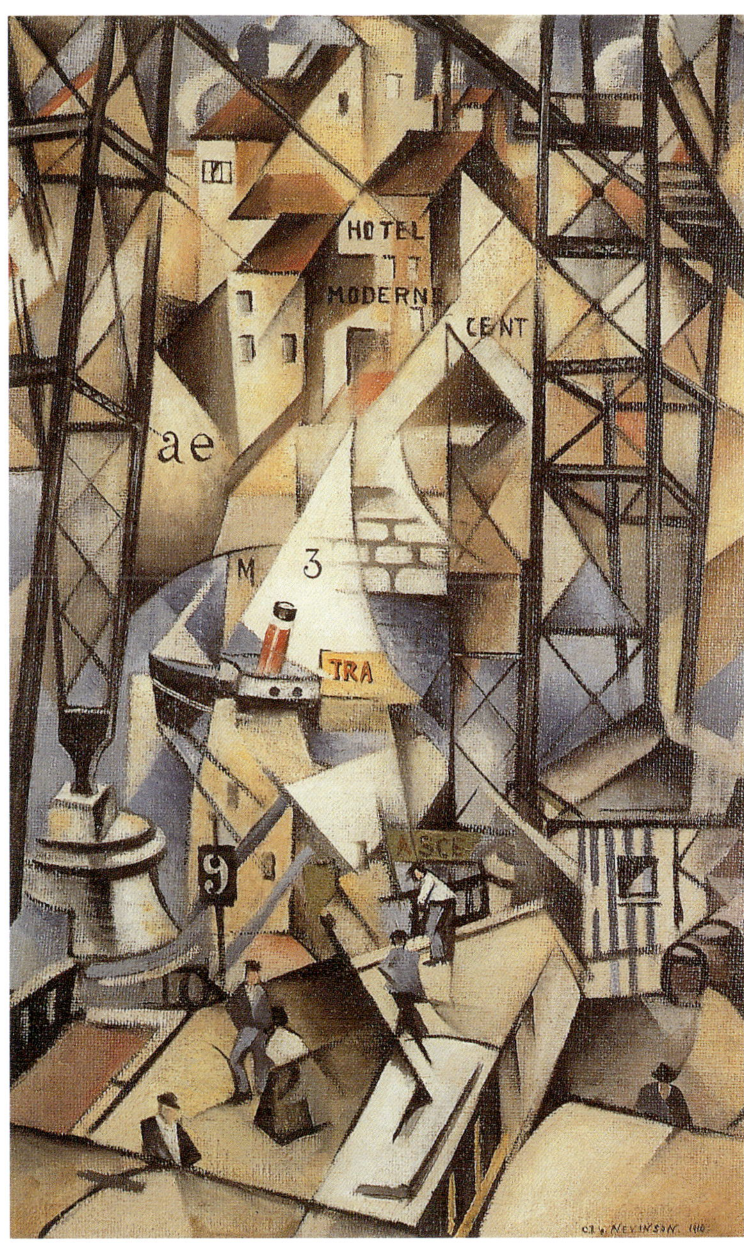

19. *Le Vieux Port,* 1913/1914. Oil on canvas, 91.5 x 56 cm. Government Art Collection of the United Kingdom.

no such sympathy for the majority of the other exhibiting artists. The affiliation to Severini, as opposed to Futurism in general, was an interesting point to have been made, and did not go unnoticed by the more perceptive critics at the time.[19]

Criticism was not confined to the newspaper and journal critics and one of the most direct attacks came from an extremely unlikely source. In a letter to the press, Sickert directly singled out Richard and accused the young artist of 'Resting on your oars.' He went on to say 'If these meaningless patterns are all they have to show for the time that has passed since their scholarships, they will have considerable leeway to make up to convince neutrals that they take their own talents seriously.'[20] This

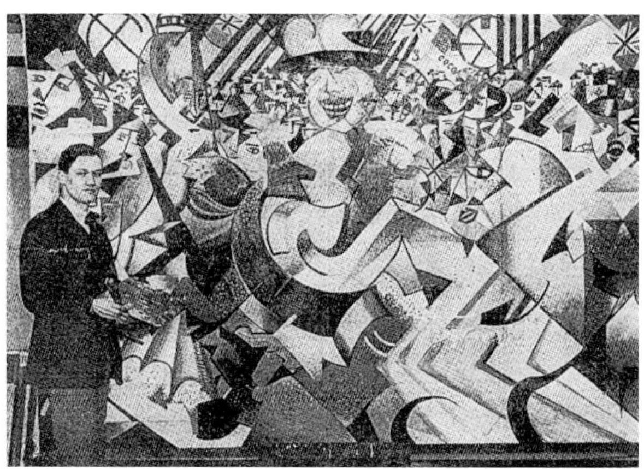

20. *Tum-Tiddly-Um-Tum-Pom-Pom*, 1914. Oil and confetti on canvas. Whereabouts unknown, reproduced in *The Western Mail*, 15 May 1914.

came as a particularly harsh criticism from an established artist who had been one of the few noted figures to speak positively about the March 1912 exhibition. This he had called 'Austere, bracing, patriotic, nationalistic, positive, anti-archaistic, anti-sentimental, anti-feminist', and had gone on to say that the movement 'is one from which we in England have a good deal to learn'.[21]

In his first recorded letter to the press, Richard responded, not to Sickert's comments, but to those made by 'G.R.H.' on 7 March in the *Pall Mall Gazette*. His letter

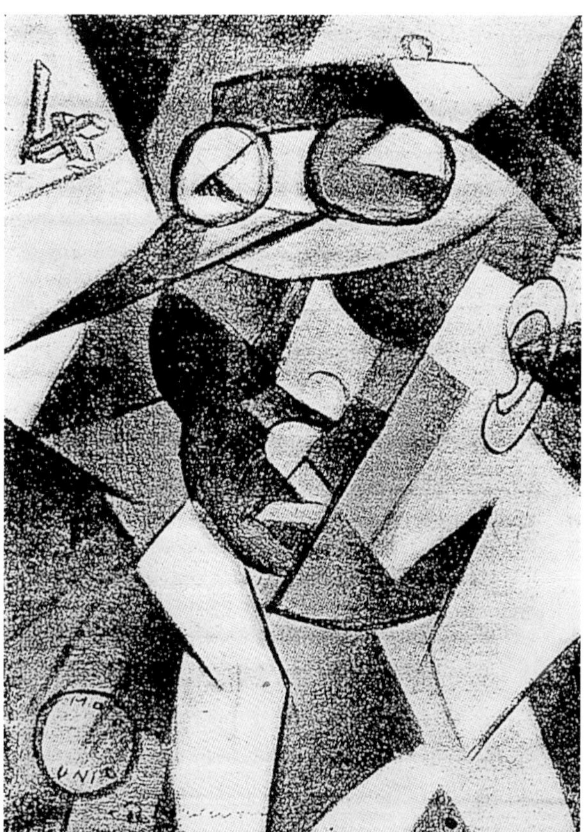

21. *The Chauffeur*, 1914. Chalk. Whereabouts unknown.

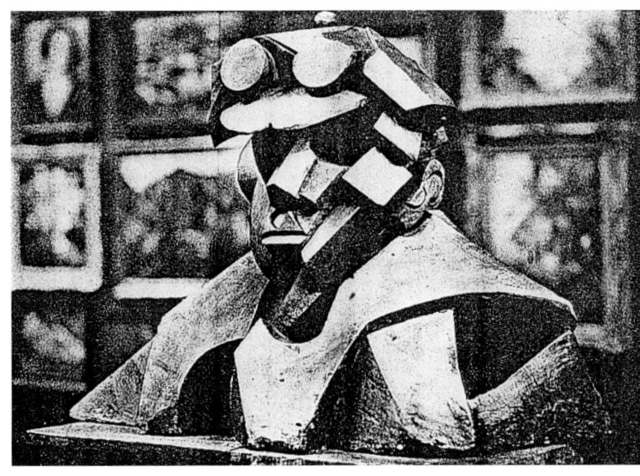

22. *Automobilist (Machine Slave)*, 1914. Bronze or stone. Whereabouts unknown.

concluded 'I can well afford to do without notoriety. I prefer something not quite so useless.'[22] In so doing he made clear from the outset that he was a legitimate artist, in pursuit of legitimate goals and was not a fraud in search of the spotlight. He had also launched what was to be a long and turbulent relationship with the press.

The press was also spotting splits within the ranks of the rebel artists and creating a hierarchy in assessing the value of their output, a hierarchy that was witnessing Richard's shift to a central position. A review from March 1914 observed: 'Mr. Nevinson and, perhaps, Mr. Bomberg, show that they can be the medium of both beauty and thought. But the pictures of Mr. Wyndham Lewis, Mr. Etchells, and Mr. Wadsworth can, surely, only be the work of men who know that there is a buying public that cannot distinguish the real thing from third-rate imitation.'[23] The *Daily Herald* too was beginning to refer to Nevinson, Wadsworth and Phelan Gibb as 'out-and-out Futurists',[24] relegating all others to a peripheral, and less genuine and legitimate, role. Sir Claude Phillips, a more conservative commentator, drew little distinction between the rival factions and showed little tolerance of any of the new movements when he wrote 'for he, a Cubist, shows himself a partial convert, or pervert, to Italian Futurism'.[25]

The Dore Gallery *Conferenza*

Richard and Marinetti finally came together publicly at the Dore Gallery for their first joint public performances on 28, 29 and 30 April 1914.[26] This was part of an overall Futurist show, which had opened its doors on 23 April, exhibiting eighty works by Boccioni, Balla, Carra, Severini, Soffici and Russolo. Naturally the exhibition became the focus of press attention and articles appeared which asked typically 'Would You Allow A Futurist To Marry Your Daughter?'[27] and 'How Would a Futurist Die?'[28] Marinetti predictably moved to centre stage and became a keystone in the Futurist 'fashion' which was about to sweep over London. He declared 'I like London very much because it is the most Futurist city in Europe [however] it is not yet completely Futurist . . . the traffic is too slow. You should have more electric light, more noise . . . light, noise, speed, you can never have too much of these'.[29]

Cementing the association between Richard, in particular, and Futurism, the evenings were planned as typical *conferenze*, giving Marinetti, and his new-found English disciple the opportunity to deliver their theories on the nature of painting, sculpture, poetry and music. Already other rebel artists, however, were starting to distance themselves from the movement, such as Lewis who was claiming 'Futurism is largely the product of Anglo-Saxon civilization.'[30] Modern life, he felt, was the invention of the English and so, he was starting to imply that Marinetti, to some extent, was both a plagiarist and outdated in what he was saying. By proclaiming him 'Man of the Week' he seems to have been suggesting that he would be gone and forgotten again soon. The evening was noted particularly for the recitation of Marinetti's poems *The Siege of Adrianople* and *Dynamic & Synoptic Declamation*, which, typically, were light on syntax but rich in onomatopoeia.[31] *The Siege of Adrianople* was enhanced by his striking wood with a hammer, echoed by the beating of 'two big drums in a distant room from which the painter Nevinson, my colleague, produced a boom of cannon fire when I told him to do so over the telephone'. Marinetti went on to further describe the evening: 'Blackboards had been set up in three parts of the hall, to which in succession I either ran or walked, to sketch rapidly an analogy with chalk. My listeners as they turned to follow me in all my evolutions, participated, their entire bodies inflamed with emotion, in the violent effects of the battle described by my words-in-freedom.'[32] Though the audience reaction to the work was essentially positive, this infuriated Marinetti who announced at the end of the reading: 'This was a very imperfect rendering. There should be no passive listeners. Everyone should take part and act the poem.'[33] Even Lewis, recalling the evening in his autobiography, could not help but profess some admiration for the combined efforts of the protagonists when he recorded: 'A day of attack on the Western Front, with all the "heavies" hammering…was nothing to it'.[34] He consequently extended an invitation to Marinetti to perform at the Rebel Art Centre, shortly afterwards on 6 and 8 May, where the latter made 'loud puffing noises pretending he was a train'.[35] Henry, who had been reading pamphlets sent from Milan and visiting the 'Futurist School' on Great Ormond Street,[36] recorded in his journal his admiration for the Italian once again. 'Gould and I went to Marinetti at the Dore Gallery. He was superb on new & old poetry. Recited his Automobile and the Bombardment of Adrianople with effects of hammering for machine guns.' Henry believed also that 'No Englishman could have touched it. It overwhelmed me. It was so terrific.'[37] The passion felt by Marinetti and Henry was not as obviously shared or understood by Richard who, in his autobiography, recorded simply that 'I made a good deal of noise and enjoyed myself'.[38] The symbolic gesture of Richard beating someone else's drum was not lost on the more cynical of his peers.

Meanwhile Marinetti went on with his publicity campaign, turning now to writers of the day, performing most notably in the home of W. B. Yeats. Here Aldington recorded that a 'bewildered Yeats begged him to stop as his neighbours were banging in protest at the row on the floor, ceiling and on the front door'.[39] He and Richard were introduced to London society by Ford Madox Ford through gatherings at his home, South Lodge in Campden Hill.[40] Though it is not known whether it was at Richard's invitation or that of his father, Marinetti dined at the Nevinson household on 3 May, where Henry recorded he was 'quite tame and sensible'.[41] He also recorded his son's 'Englishness' by writing, 'We entertained Marinetti, and listened to his fervid speech and recitation of his poems – the Italian Futurist declaiming in sharp contrast to the English manner of my son, Richard, in those days the Futurist of London.'[42] Marinetti is also believed to have seen, and approved of, Richard's most daring Futurist composition to date. A large photograph of the artist standing in front of this Futurist 'masterpiece', *Tum-Tiddly-Um-Tum-Pom-Pom* appeared in the press ten days later.[43]

Tum-Tiddly-Um-Tum-Pom-Pom

Tum-Tiddly-Um-Tum-Pom-Pom (fig. 20)[44] was his self-professed Futurist masterpiece and was a composition that had been on his mind for over two years, as a letter to Carrington testifies. In this he had written

> Last Friday nineteen hundred and twelve years ago Christ was crucified therefore Christian London went up to Hampstead Heath in its thousands to celebrate the occasion amid blaring ... bands & booths of bright and brilliant colour. Really you must next whitsun bank-holiday come up with me to see sweating democracy heeding not the rumble of the distant drum it is a glorious sight, the gipsies, the cocoanut shies, all men, bright purple factory girls, old women, fat & thin, all yelling, song-sellers singing, barrel organs grinding . . . jew boys auctioneering, women washing & cooking & feeding infants, some eating, most drinking...& all happy. Oh Baby dear why aren't you here to revel in it, it's wonderful, & why is a crowd always happy & individuals always unhappy.[45]

The name has inherent similarities to Marinetti's publication *Zang-Tumb-Tumb*, but that association remains superficial, perhaps even comical. Hampstead Heath on a Bank Holiday, it could be argued, was a tame theme for a Futurist composition, though it is clear at least that the artist attempted to capture the dynamism of the atmosphere rather than making a static recording of the day, place and time. It is however, on the surface, an immediately recognizable and popular theme, and to a very large extent the treatment of the subject and the means of its depiction had much in common with the theoretical Futurist handling of paint (and confetti) on canvas. Cork is scathing about the painting however, criticizing the 'obvious vulgarity of the formal arrangement', and describing it as 'hopelessly disorganised and ineloquent'. He summed up by claiming 'It hits out at the sensibilities of the aesthetes with all the boorish conviction of a fist, and the force of the blow was all that the artist really cared about.'[46] At the time, however, T. E. Hulme had been able to declare it Richard's 'best picture', praising it particularly for its 'interesting contrasts of round and angular forms'.[47] Gaudier-Brzeska had not shared the enthusiasm, and had rather shared the idea of vulgarity when he called it 'union jacks, lace stockings and other tommy rot'.[48]

The stylistic references are once again to Severini, and in particular to *Dynamic Hieroglyph of the Bal Tabarin*, but also to *The Laugh*, by Boccioni. In these works the artists are recalling the sensation of their experiences, not creating visual records of them. Severini had made this objective clear when he wrote that 'Art is now, before everything else, perception and expression.'[49] In both paintings truncated figures appear in the form of words and numbers, and the sequins added in Severini's composition, are echoed by the confetti on Richard's. In both there is a reference to music, in Richard's title and in the inclusion of the words 'POLKA' and 'VALSE' in Severini's. Both compositions represent a semi-abstraction of movement and dynamism on a large scale.

Severini had attempted a definition, which may usefully be applied here:

> This, in short, is the conception of Futurist painting.
> Painting will no longer translate some spectacle (*Anecdote*) or the outward semblance of some person who has given an expression either of gaiety or sadness (*Literature or Psychology*), and will no longer limit itself to the simple pursuit of arabesques upon a plane (*Matisse*), or of mass (*the Cubists*), but by means of abstract forms will give the pictorial rhythm of an ideal world.[50]

The same work, with the addition of *Aerroplane* (lost), Futurist at least for its onomatopoeic title and its mixed media of wood carving and painting, appeared at the London Salon held by the AAA at the Holland Park skating rink. This latter work is adequately described, albeit unintentionally, by Severini when he explained that

> We choose to concentrate our attention on things in motion because our modern sensibility is particularly qualified to grasp the idea of speed. Heavy powerful motor cars rushing through the crowded streets of our cities, dancers reflected in the fairy ambience of light and colour, aeroplanes above the heads of the excited throng . . . These sources of emotion satisfy our sense of the lyric and dramatic universe, better than do two pears and an apple.[51]

Then came the real focus of the critical attention, most of which ridiculed Richard's work. *The Times* in its article 'Rebels in Art' singled him out:

> But Mr. Nevinson . . . is a rebel in execution. He used to be a painter with a modest talent; but now he is like a singer with a small voice who has taken to shouting. Futurism, we are sure, is merely poison to him; and, if he has not lost his talent altogether, it will take him some time to recover it.[52]

The distinction between Post-Impressionism, Cubism and Futurism was, once again, extremely unclear, and this was something the artist had done little to define with a letter to the press which had stated 'I believe Cubism finds out the incompetent, the feeble and the slovenly minded quicker than any other "ism" by its very sterness and severity of expression, its accentuation of forms defined with knife-like hardness.'[53] If anything he was advocating the merits of an 'ism', other than Futurism, and one with which confusion often occurred. In the end critics simply referred to the 'Cubo-Futurist School' as a compromise.[54] It was still unclear whom the press believed to be Futurists as the word now was virtually interchangeable with 'rebel' or even 'modern'. Lewis, Wadsworth, Gibb and others were constantly enclosed within the same bracket.

The press did not have long to dwell on the show as events of equal note, happening simultaneously, were leading up to the rupture of the 'Blast Group', an event which would occupy the headlines for some time. There can be little doubt that the *Zeitgeist* had become controversial, topical and even fun.[55] Caricatures of Marinetti were easily recognized in the London press, and the name 'Futurist' became synonymous with anything new or shocking. Nothing could undermine more the tenets of Futurism than widespread acceptance by the very establishment that it had set out to destroy. Rebel artists concerned with individuality and seriousness of purpose may at this stage have felt it wise to put some distance between themselves and the 'fad' of Italian Futurism in London, though the impetus for the breakaway was as yet lacking.

A Futurist Manifesto for England

The most distinctive and significant alliance of Marinetti and Nevinson was in the joint declaration of 'A Futurist Manifesto: Vital English Art', in early June 1914.[56] Though the document bears all the hallmarks of its predecessors it also raises questions concerning the nature and degree of Richard's control over the direction of Futurism in England. John Rothenstein has suggested that had it simply been presented by Marinetti, and Marinetti alone, it would merely have been seen as 'a spirited display of fireworks'.[57] The fact that the English artist co-signed it, and thus elbowed his way to the forefront of the avant-garde, was, in Rothenstein's view, the true problem, rather than the content of the document. It had been designed to unite the rebel artists of the day, but it was to have precisely the opposite effect. Ingleby has summed up concisely, saying 'In one stroke Nevinson had succeeded in alienating himself from his contemporaries: once again he had become the outsider.'[58] Certainly, it was a clumsy piece of political manoeuvring which alienated both himself, and Futurism in general, from the rest of the British avant-garde. This happened not only as a result of using the Rebel Art Centre address on the manifesto, as if it were the London branch of Futurism, but also in naming, as signatories, individual artists, none of whom had given their consent, or been consulted about what the document contained.[59] Ironically Henry had referred to the Rebel Art Centre as 'the new Futurist school in Great Ormond Street' in his journal on 4 April 1914, implying that the mistake, in terms of definition of the institution, was there to be made.[60] He had also read the manifesto and seen no cause for alarm.[61] The name 'Futurist' had also appeared in the prospectus of the RAC, but nonetheless, the inclusion of members' names on the manifesto was an assumption that was intolerable. The document is reproduced here in full.

A FUTURIST MANIFESTO
Vital English Art

F.T. Marinetti
C.R.W. Nevinson.

I am an Italian Futurist poet, and a passionate admirer of England. I wish however, to cure English Art of that most grave of all maladies – passé-ism. I have the right to speak plainly and without compromise, and together with my friend Nevinson, an English Futurist painter, to give the signal for battle.

AGAINST:

1. The worship of tradition and the conservatism of Academies, the commercial acquiescence of English artists, the effeminacy of their art and their complete absorption towards a purely decorative sense.

2. The pessimistic, sceptical and narrow views of the English public, who stupidly adore the pretty-pretty, the commonplace, the soft, sweet, and mediocre, the sickly revivals of mediaevalism, the Garden Cities and their curfews and artificial battlements, the Maypole Morris dances, Aestheticism, Oscar Wilde, the Pre-Raphaelites, Neo-Primitives and Paris.

3. The perverted snob who ignores or despises all English daring, originality and invention, but welcomes eagerly all foreign originality and daring. After all, England can boast of Pioneers of Poetry, such as Shakespeare and Swinburne; in Art, Turner and Constable (the original founders of the Impressionist and Barbizon School); in Science, Watts, Stephenson, Darwin, etc etc.

4. The sham revolutionaries of the New English Art Club, who, having destroyed the prestige of the Royal Academy, now show themselves grossly hostile to the latter movements of the advance guard.

5. The indifference of the King, the State, and the politicians towards all arts.

6. The English notion that art is a useless pass time, only fit for women and schoolgirls, that artists are poor deluded fools to be pitied and protected, and Art a ridiculous complaint, a mere topic for table talk.

7. The universal right of the ignorant to discuss and decide upon all questions of Art.

8. The old grotesque idea of genius – drunken, filthy, ragged, outcast; drunkenness the synonym of Art, Chelsea the Montmartre of London; the post Rossettis with long hair under the sombrero, and other passéist filth.

9. The sentimentality with which you load your pictures – to compensate, perhaps, for your praiseworthy utter lack of sentimentality in life.

10. Pioneers suffering from arrested development, from success or from despair, pioneers sitting snug on their tight little islands, or vegetating in their oases

refusing to resume the march, the pioneers who say: 'We love progress, but not yours'; the wearied pioneers who say: 'Post-Impressionism is all right, but it must not go further than deliberate naïveté'. (Gauguin). These pioneers show that not only has their development stopped, but that they have never really understood the evolution of Art. If it has been necessary in painting and sculpture to have naïveté, deformation and archaism, it was only because it was essential to break away violently from the academic and the graceful before going further towards the plastic dynamism of painting.

11. The mania for immortality. A masterpiece must disappear with its author. Immortality in Art is a disgrace. The ancestors of our Italian Art, by their constructive power and their ideal of immortality, have built for us a prison of timidity, of imitation and of plagiarism. They sit their on grandfather chairs and for ever dominate our creative agonies with their marble frowns; 'Take care, children. Mind the motors. Don't go too quick. Wrap yourselves up well. Mind the draughts. Be careful of the lightening'. 'Forward! HURRAH for motors! HURRAH for speed! HURRAH for draughts! HURRAH for lightening!'

WE WANT:

1. To have an English Art that is strong, virile and anti-sentimental.

2. That English artists strengthen their Art by a recuperative optimism, a fearless desire of adventure, a heroic instinct of discovery, a worship of strength and a physical and moral courage, all sturdy virtues of the English race.

3. Sport to be considered an essential element in Art.

4. To create a powerful advance guard, which alone can save English Art, now threatened by the traditional conservatism of Academics and the habitual indifference of the public. This will be an exciting stimulant, a violent incentive for creative genius, a constant inducement to keep alive the fires of invention and of Art, so as to obviate the monotonous labour and expense of perpetual raking out a re-lighting of the furnace.

5. A rich and powerful country like England ought without question to support, defend and glorify its advance guard of artists, no matter how advanced or how extreme, if it intends to deliver its Art from inevitable death.

F.T. MARINETTI.
C.R.W. NEVINSON. [62]

[This is the reproduction of the manifesto from *Paint and Prejudice*. It is interesting that it leaves out all of the sixth clause which, in the original read as follows:]

6. So we call upon the English public to support, defend, and glorify the genius of the great Futurist painters or pioneers and advance forces of Vital English Art – ATKINSON, BOMBERG, EPSTEIN, ETCHELLS, HAMILTON, NEVINSON, ROBERTS, WADSWORTH, WYNDHAM LEWIS.

Also, the original document was signed: 'F.T. Marinetti – Italian Futurist Movement (Milan)' and 'C.R.W. Nevinson – Art Rebel Centre (London)'.

The document begins in the first person, Marinetti speaking, and so it is obvious from the outset who is setting the direction and the pace of the attack, in very much the same format as had been witnessed in *Lacerba*. Marinetti, in the introduction, referred to the co-operation of 'my friend Nevinson, an English Futurist painter', then had gone on to echo many of the original statements and sentiments from the initial Futurist manifestos, which were now five years old. Importantly, he involved only one other English artist in the manifesto, not the wider range of rebels that Richard himself brought in. In so doing, the *Daily Express* was inaccurate when it reported 'Signor Marinetti…has put his hand into a wasps nest',[63] when in fact the problem, as we shall see, was caused by his colleague. Nevertheless, the polemic tone remained dominant, though was not quite so blunt as previously, calling for the rejection, above all else, of passéism. The analogies chosen were those of English art being a sick patient, and he, or they, providing the antidotes which would bring to it, in addition to revolution, both hygiene and purity.[64] Richard's voice, acting perhaps for the first time in the place of Marinetti's, could be witnessed in the rejection of a variety of considerations and institutions specific to England, most notably the Royal Academy. Inconsistent, however, is the fact that at St John's Wood School of Art he had originally trained for the Academy Schools, and later in life he was to become an Associate of the Royal Academy (ARA). In rejecting the taste of the English public there were further inconsistencies in that the manifesto specifically isolated Neo-Primitives (his own group of only eighteen months previously) for condemnation. The influence of Paris, where his artistic homage had been paid (by his own account only), and where, ironically he had met, and become influenced by the Futurist painters, was attacked. Paradoxically it was in Paris that one of his most successful pre-war Futurist compositions, *The Departure of the Train de Luxe*, had been set. The manifesto criticized England for not making more of its own heritage, constantly looking abroad for leadership, though this is precisely how he had lived his life, and developed as an artist, up to this point. It attacked the NEAC by name, yet he, in the same year, had allowed his name to be put forward for membership, had already exhibited there and would continue to do so for the rest of his life, becoming a full member in 1929.[65] There were further attacks on sentimentality, another accusation of which he was not guiltless, but as the monologue continued it became less and less credible and more and more impetuous, declaring, as if defiantly, 'Hurrah for draughts!' Following the eleven-point list of complaints there were five itemized alternatives proposed. Legitimate were the calls for a virile, strong, anti-sentimental art, optimistic and heroic, violent and in the domain of the genius, but again questions must be asked concerning points such as 'Sport to be considered an essential element in art.' Richard had loathed sport, and sportsmen, at school and suffered from ill health all his life, which prevented him from participation, even if he had been inclined to do so.[66] At no stage in any of the Italian manifestos is this specification ever mentioned. The document also expressly attacks Oscar Wilde, the previous loyal friend of his own friend and supporter, Robert Ross.

Ironically, Marinetti had also earlier condemned the English public for their treatment of Wilde.

Not only did the press, *The Times*, the *Observer* and the *Daily Mail*, print the original manifesto, but they also acted as the stage on which the whole inevitable Futurist debate would now be played out. Marinetti was a master of manipulating the press and in England, no less than abroad this had the desired impact for the movement. The *Daily Express*, however, made a valid observation when it highlighted the fact that the manifesto had not offended or alienated the passéists for whom it had been intended, rather the other progressive artists with whom there should have been an alliance.[67] The *Sketch* also made a good point when it commented that the Futurists had turned on, and criticized, things that 'are as dead as mutton', implying that it is hardly modern, or revolutionary, to attack something which already belongs to the past.[68] G. K. Chesterton advised against this dismissive approach when he wrote 'But there is no light touch about the English Futurists, and one must deal with Mr C.R.W. Nevinson as with a professor.'[69] Years later, the same writer, was less sympathetic when he wrote 'But Mr Nevinson and the Futurists...rush after the car of progress like poor baby-laden charwomen after a motor bus'.[70]

Lewis, in the first issue of *Blast*, had recognized the value of Futurism and also the emerging difficulties in definition stating that 'Of all the tags going, "Futurist", for general application, serves as well as any for the active painters of today.' Though this is vague he went on to attempt a semi-cynical definition when he declared that 'Futurism as preached by Marinetti, is largely Impressionism up to date. To this is added his Automobilism and Nietzsche stunt.'[71] Pound too had acknowledged the influence of the 'ism' by saying that they were all Futurists in a way, insofar as they all followed the dictum of Apollinaire: ' On ne peut pas porter partout avec soi le cadavre de son père' though he too went on to describe it artistically as 'a sort of accelerated Impressionism'.[72] What the majority of the English avant-garde did not want now, however, was to be seen as a regional branch of Italian Futurism, nor indeed for their ideas to be seen as Futurism in English dress. The named artists, therefore, accordingly counter-parried with a letter to *New Weekly* on 13 June 1914 and stated:

> Dear Sir,
> To read or hear the praises of oneself or one's friends is always pleasant. There are forms of praise, however, which are so compounded with innuendo as to be most embarrassing. One may find oneself, for instance, so praised as to make it appear that one's opinions coincide with those of the person who praises, in which case one finds oneself in the difficult position of disclaiming the laudation or of even slightly resenting it.
>
> There are certain artists in England who do not belong to the Royal Academy nor to any of the passeist groups, and who do not on that account agree with the Futurism of Signor Marinetti. An assumption of such agreement either by Signor or by his followers is an impertinence. We, the undersigned, whose

ideals were mentioned or implied, or who might, by the opinions of others, be implicated, beg to dissociate ourselves from the 'Futurist' manifesto which appeared in the pages of the *Observer* of Sunday, June 1.

Signed

Richard Aldington, Lawrence Aldington, David Bomberg, Gaudier-Brzeska, Frederick Etchells, Cuthbert Hamilton, Ezra Pound, William Roberts, Edward Wadsworth, Wyndham Lewis. [73]

By mentioning Richard, not by name, but as a 'follower', a condescending glance had been cast in his direction and the split became progressively more inevitable. Ironically Roberts's recollection is that though his signature was used on the counter-attacking letter, he had not given permission for it to be used this second time either, claiming 'When this repudiation took place I had not yet met Lewis.'[74]

A letter by Richard to *New Weekly* outlined both his mistake and its innocent nature, describing in four clear points how the error had happened. Indeed he claimed it was a simple misunderstanding as he had used the RAC address in the same way that any gentleman would use the address of the club to which he belonged. The letter was neither angry nor offensive, rather an attempt to put the record straight. It went unanswered.

Were we to follow the chronological progression as presented in *Paint and Prejudice* we would believe that Wyndham Lewis and Richard now collaborated on the forthcoming publication to which the latter would give the name *Blast*. Certainly their association had been definite on the project, designed as a quarterly, and happy to incorporate the name 'Futurism' into it, prior to the manifesto. The venture was supported by Henry who had provided the two artists with a letter of introduction, dated 28 January 1914, to a publishers called Bliss, in which he referred to his son and Lewis as 'both revolutionary artists of futurist fame'.[75] Richard's participation in this project, in actuality, probably ceased in February 1914, as a letter from Wadsworth to Lewis, dated to that month, suggests.[76]

Mutiny at the Dore *Conferenza*

In *Paint and Prejudice* no hint is made at the magnitude of the consequences of the manifesto which became apparent in the mutiny at the Dore Galleries, on 12 June 1914. Henry recorded 'The Whites & Rich's gold-haired girl to dinner. Then all to the Dore Gallery where Rich read good papers on Futurist painting: very strong style & thought: too quickly given. Marinetti then spoke: superb: partly in answer to Wyndham Lewis and others who denounced the new manifesto.'[77] Richard, stepping out from behind Marinetti's proverbial shadow, had delivered a lecture on the disgrace of immortality in art and of how the United States viewed England as 'a little old woman with a past' and read out a list of enemies of progressive art, which included the King.[78] Henry reported further on his son's lecture

No one could live with a singer incessantly and constantly singing in a room. So it is impossible to live with a picture. This applies to all pictures past, present and future. Why is it that no-one would take the *Mona Lisa* as a gift ? . . . Nothing can be done twice. That is why my son is right in saying that only bad work goes on forever.[79]

The *New Age* offered a transcript of the evening's proceedings, six days later, in an article entitled 'Futile-ism' by Charles Brookfarmer.[80] Through it we see that Richard's attack had extended to the 'backwoods of Chelsea' the 'barbarians of the West End' and those who painted in the style of Blake, Constable and Turner. Having read the Futurist Manifesto in its entirety he sat down and Marinetti stepped in to attack the rich for not buying Futurist pictures and to give another of his typically energetic performances. Disappointingly, the noise tuners, which had been advertised, never arrived.

But the evening had its detractors too, whose denunciation of Futurism and of the manifesto was led by Lewis. He recorded: 'I assembled in Greek Street a determined band of miscellaneous anti-Futurists. There were about ten of us.'[81] The artists whose names had been used on the document, with Hulme and Gaudier-Brzeska in addition, heckled the speakers, let off fireworks and generally disrupted the evening. Richard particularly recalled the heckling by Gaudier-Brzeska in his autobiography, not least when he got the new group name wrong and referred to them as 'Vorti-kists'. Jacob Epstein also added to the tirade of abuse before trouble erupted, resulting in chairs being overturned, the fire brigade and the constabulary being called and the violence spilling out onto New Bond Street. Marinetti is recorded as having gone for Gaudier-Brzeska whilst Richard's attack was on Ezra Pound in retaliation for having being called a 'negroid jew'.[82] Though this is a pleasing report of a successful Futurist evening, disappointingly, the *Manchester Guardian* offered a different version of events. Here it was reported that the antagonists had 'promised at the beginning to provide a belligerent opinion' but had 'dwindled into silence very early in the evening'.[83] One way or another, however, the avant-garde in Britain was now openly and clearly split, denouncing this southern European phenomenon, Futurism, and uniting in an expression of the modern age, unique to the north and to Britain for whom the machine was no novelty. The split, as reported in the *Yorkshire Observer*, can be dated accurately to the first fortnight in June, 1914.[84]

Undeterred, in fact positively delighted with the turmoil, Marinetti immediately continued with Futurist events in London. Richard, as a Futurist, attended, though did not participate in, Marinetti's first performance of Futurist music at the Coliseum. The latter exposed his audience to the Grand Futurist Concert of Noises, including *Awakening a Great City* and *A Meeting of Motor Cars and Aeroplanes*, coming from twenty-three of the newly invented *intonarumori*. The poster advertising the event promised 'The Performance of Two Noise Spirals . . . composed and conducted by Luigi Russolo [with]: Buzzers; Exploders; Thunderers; Whistlers; Murmerers; Gurglers; Rattlers; Cracklers and Roarers . . . Electrical Instruments invented and constructed by Luigi Russolo and Ugo Piatti.'[85] The reaction was predictable both from audience and press alike. Richard's reactions though were, once again, apparently naïve for someone affiliated closely to the movement. In his autobiography he referred to the evening as 'one of the funniest shows ever put on in

London',[86] which seems a shallow interpretation for what was ultimately an intellectual exercise, attended by musical notables such as Stravinsky.[87] Secondly, when the audience became hostile in reaction to the performance, Richard seemed shocked that Marinetti would have deemed this as the ultimate success of the work. He described the evening in *Paint and Prejudice*

> Marinetti swaggered onto the vast stage looking about the size of a housefly and bowed. As he spoke no English there was no time wasted with explanations or in the preparation of his audience. Had they understood Italian, I do believe Marinetti could have magnetised them as he did everybody else. There was nothing for it, however, but to call upon his ten noise-tuners to play, so they turned handles like those of a hurdy-gurdy. It must have sounded magnificent to him for he beamed, but a little way back in the audience, all one could hear was the faintest of buzzes. At first the audience did not understand that this was the performance offered them in return for their hard-earned cash, but when they did there was one vast, deep and long sustained 'Boo!'[88]

The entire nature of Futurism and Futurist Evenings was to invoke such reactions, since polite response or passive acceptance was the ultimate sign of failure. Marinetti, in a letter to Severini, pronounced the entire project 'trionfali'.[89] The work was performed twelve times to London audiences who were coming rapidly to regard Futurism as a fad, and quite an amusing one at that. The addition of an Elgar gramophone record to play over the top of the Futurist piece in the remainder of the shows promoted the audience response to stony silence. *The Times* simply reported that 'the audience seem to be of the opinion that Futurist music had better be kept for the Future. At all events, they show an earnest desire not to have it at present.'[90] Henry, who also attended the show, simply recorded that it was 'queer and full of interest'.[91] Five months later he wrote: 'At the Coliseum in London we have lately seen and heard what the Futurist can do with sound. The first and most beautiful composition or combination aroused the emotion we feel at the "Awakening of a great city".'[92] The experiment, he argued, was both as legitimate and as adventurous as anything Wagner had attempted in his lifetime.

Henry continued his writing and lecturing on Futurism, often carrying his son's pictures with him to illustrate his talks,[93] from this point until well after the war had begun.

The 'Laughter Show'

The first exhibition of the London Group at the Goupil Gallery had been 'magnificent in its failure, nobody came'.[94] So too the exhibition of the AAA, or the 'laughter show'[95] as it became known, at the Holland Park skating rink, was 'needless to say . . . a fiasco, though a splendid one'.[96] *Town Topics* set the tone, writing that 'The Futurist is the super-joke of the century'[97] before levelling individual attacks at specific artists and their work. Certain paintings by Richard again attracted a lot of comment. *The Non-Stop* caused Konody to report accurately that 'he is obsessed with the idea of speed, devotes himself to conveying by pictorial means the sensation of speed in railway trams and other means of locomotion, and gives the idea of movement by displacing objects, making them penetrate each other in fact, making several successive moments simultaneous'.[98] This criticism openly acknowledged that the work had Futurist leanings, both in subject matter and technique. Fry, however, was more specific claiming once again that his painting was 'almost a copy of a work by Severini'.[99] Interestingly, *Syncopation* drew some positive reviews, which, while acknowledging its Italian roots, actually praised the composition for being a very improved version of similar attempts by Severini,[100] though they did refer to it as Futurism at second hand. The *Standard* reported that it was a 'rag-time subject of many figures, cubistically treated, but with just enough reference to reality to make the picture intelligible'.[101] Rutter seemed to believe in the quality of the work and in doing so secured some critical credibility to Richard's own Futurist claims. He said 'I well remember one of [Nevinson's] paintings of this period, a circular picture of the interior of a compartment in a "Tube" in which the vibration of seated figures and strap hangers was kaleidoscopically expressed in vivid bright colours.'[102] Conversely, it was also described thus 'Others like C.R.W. Nevinson's "Syncopation" are hideous suggestions of all that is most objectionable in modern life. It is like a subtle distillation of the noises in the streets and the smell of motor cars on a hot day. It reminds us of everything in modern life that most of us are anxious to forget.'[103] Also exhibited here, and catching the attention of the press, was *The Strand*, similar in appearance to Wadsworth's *Radiation* of the previous year. The reproduction in the *Manchester Guardian* came under the banner 'A Futurist's Conception of a London Street.'[104] More importantly it represented a Futurist adaptation of an essentially figurative and representational scene that could easily be related to, especially in comparison to the extremism on display at the hands of Lewis and Bomberg. Confusingly, the latter commanded his own headline in the *Pall Mall Gazette* which read simply 'Mr. Bomberg's Futurist Bombshells.'[105] On the whole though the press was quick to pick up on signalling a differentiation between the kaleidoscopic, though illustrative, paintings of Richard, and the impenetrable abstraction of Lewis and Wadsworth.

The Arrival

The canvas that possibly epitomizes the zenith of Richard's peacetime Futurist painting is *The Arrival* (fig. 23).[106] Associations concerning the source of the subject have been made with the French Futurist painter Felix Delmarle who, while sharing a studio with Severini in Paris, painted two depictions of a similar theme, both called *The Port*.[107] Agnese also claimed that Boccioni had recorded: 'Nevinson fu cosi colpito da *Souvenir de Voyage* di Severini e da *Ricordi di Una Notte* di Russolo, che di questi due quadri innovatori riverso lo spirito nel suo dipinto *The Arrival*, del 1913, sintesi delle esperienze, della sensazioni e dei ricordi che giungono assieme a un piroscafo in un porto.'[108] Certainly, in subject matter, the arrival in port of a transatlantic steamer would meet the criteria set forward by Futurist ideology,

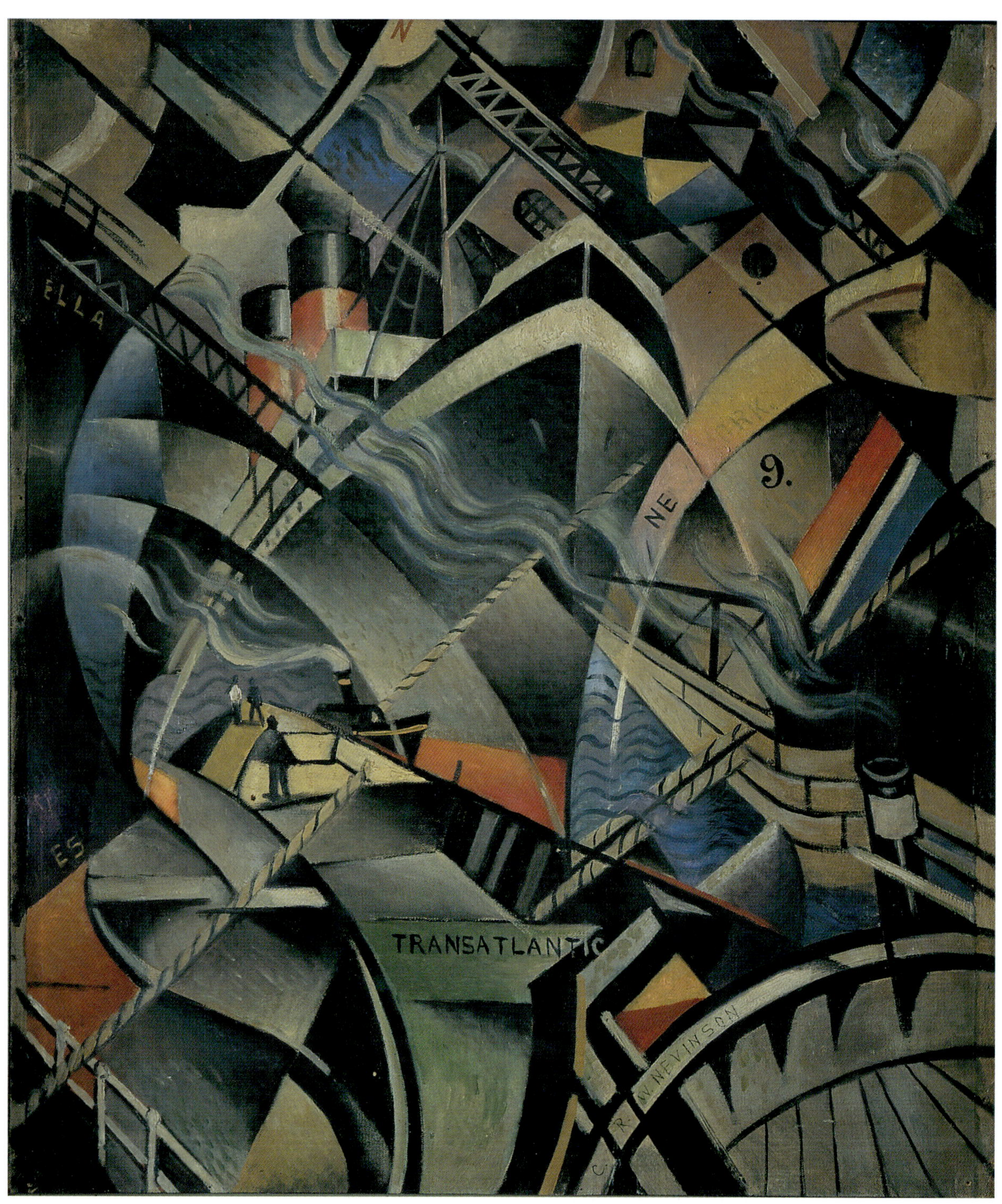
ELLA
NE
9.
ES
TRANSATLANTIC
C R W NEVINSON

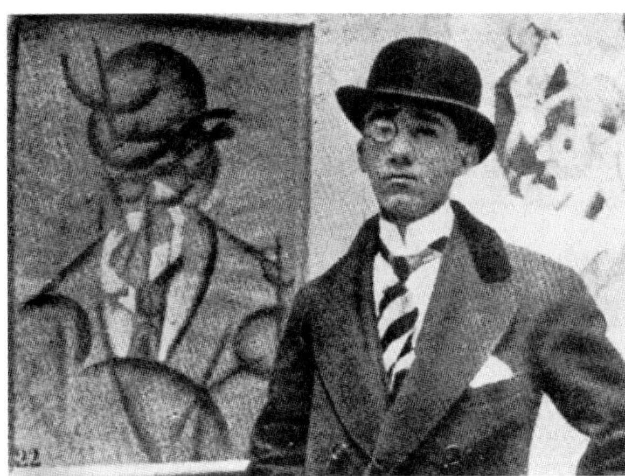

24. 'Severini in front of his paintings in London, 1913'.

whilst the technique employed of fragmenting the picture plane into a simultaneity of time and movement would also be deemed sufficiently modern. In this, and also in the inaccurately dated *Le Vieux Port* (fig. 19),[109] there is an attempted form of 'universal dynamism', escaping from the frozen moment on the static canvas. Certainly, an association can be made with the idea that 'all subjects previously used must be swept aside in order to express our whirling life of steel, of pride of fever and of speed'.[110] The steamer creates a space/time compression, an interaction with its surroundings in magnitude, sound, smell, movement and colour and it is this which Richard, as a Futurist, was trying to capture.[111] There is still a strong representational element within the picture, however, it being a shattered abstraction of a recognizable theme as opposed to a non-subjective painting in its entirety. The artist was clearly trying to capture events surrounding the arrival of the ship, from the cacophony of noises, to the cranes and notices of the dock side, all eclipsed by the towering hull of the vessel. The interlocking planes, the inclusion of truncated words, and the kaleidoscopic overall effect is reminiscent of earlier more basic experiments, such as in *The Non-Stop*. The attempt once again is to hurl the spectator to the centre of the composition, to be in the midst of the subject, not an impartial observer of it. The conventional sense of space and time, however, is distorted, not to say confounded, in a single vision of the event in its entirety. For some critics it was the moderation and restraint exercised by the artist which made the painting unsuccessful, the diluted Futurism of an artist not willing to alienate the public totally, in pursuit of pure radical principles. At the time, however, it was well received, though the *Star* jokingly observed that 'It resembles a Channel steamer after a violent collision with the pier.'[112]

To the press Richard was now 'the eminent English Futurist',[113] though the real affiliation was specifically born out of the bombast of Marinetti and the artistic orientation of Severini, as even the briefest comparison of Richard's *The Chauffeur* and Severini's *Self-portrait* (fig. 24, see painting behind artist), will further verify. In comparing these two works we observe not only the standard fragmentation of the picture plane, but a depiction of dehumanized, mechanized forms, appropriate for

23. (facing page) *The Arrival*, 1914. Oil on canvas, 76.2 x 63.5 cm. Tate Gallery, London.

the age of industry and speed for which they were intended. A three-dimensional version was attempted by Richard and was called *Automobilist (Machine Slave)*, but this is now lost.[114] Certainly he could evoke public and critical responses from the bland and dismissive, to the furious. *T.P.'s Weekly* at least gave credit to the theory (concerning, motion, colour and music) that the English rebel had been interested in; even if his actual paintings were not seen as successes: 'they are bad pictures when they are pictures at all. But a serious theory has a right to be considered on its merits, apart from the crimes that are committed in its name.' [115] Pessimistically the same lengthy article, entitled 'The Asceticism of the Futurists', went on to say that the paradox of Futurism was that it had no future due to its sterile and suicidal nature. Such was the furore it created, the AAA show was also reported on as far away as India.[116]

Nevinson and the Futurist/Vorticist Divide

Meanwhile, the public debate between Futurism and the newly formed Vorticism was taking centre stage in a press hungry to report all the latest developments. Lewis was now doing everything possible, not only to disassociate himself and his peers from the Futurist title, but also to compete against them, promoting what was now his own individual cause. In *Blast* No.1 Lewis observed: 'The Latins are at present . . . in their "discovery" of sport, their Futuristic gush over machines, aeroplanes, etc., the most romantic and sentimental "moderns" to be found.' He went on, in the same 'manifesto', to clarify the second-rate nature of Futurism by saying 'Machinery, trains, steam-ships, all that distinguishes externally our time, came far more from here than anywhere else.'[117] The Italian rail network had been constructed principally by British engineers, and even the inventor of the wireless, Marconi, though Italian, was based in London and had sent the first message from Cornwall. And in terms of military prowess, the Italians, following costly struggles in Eritrea and Libya, could hardly compete with the famous British redcoat. Lewis, therefore, laid national claim to the origins of Futurism: 'you wops insist too much on the machine. You are always on about these driving belts, you are always exploding about internal combustion. We've had machines here in England for donkey's years. They're no novelty to us.'[118]

This dissatisfaction had been building for a while and the manifesto was simply the opportunity to break away from Futurism in as determined and high-profile a way as possible. The declaration of 'Vital English Art' was not the beginning, end and sole reason for the fission of the English avant-garde into two further subsections. Even before the 'putsch', as Lewis described it, differences had occurred concerning speed, movement and machinery, away from the romanticizing of the modern era and the representation of the *élan vital* of Bergsonian flux, towards solidity, rigidity and geometric interpretation. Lewis and his cohorts wanted to exercise a classical control over the phenomenon of modernity in a structural, geometric and precise way, which would imply a reverence to, but not a novel fascination with, the modern industrial era. This would now be realized in the pursuits of the Vorticist group. And yet Hamilton identified much common ground between the two divergent factions when he wrote

> There was behind the Futurist project, and in the art of the Vorticists, where this tendency was especially welcomed, a movement towards a new Platonism, an abstract beauty now to be realised in forms of geometrical perfection – machinery and weapons – beyond any forms conceived by Plato himself. A concern for the eternal Romanticism . . . inasmuch that man is no longer the measure (Da Divina Proportione), nor intellect the acknowledged creator, nor life and living things – nature – the subject.[119]

The conflict now developed into a weekly occurrence in the national press, even becoming the source of satire as seen in the *Observer* where 'Marionetti Bomblewis' wrote on the merits of Infinitism from 'The Only Art Centre'.[120] Directly parodying 'Vital English Art' the original manifesto was trivialized to the point of being humorously absurd and in doing so publicly mocked Futurism in England. The *Nottingham Guardian* noted in accordance that 'All this is sufficiently volcanic and at any rate, temporarily exciting.'[121] Later, the nature of the debate decreased the chance of reconciliation between the two groups as relations deteriorated into a complex and highly publicized game of art politics. The attacks became more personalized and in the end Lewis wrote openly of the puerility of the Latin temperament claiming that for them 'the machine has come as an immense toy'. Besides, he claimed, what could a nation that had H. G. Wells learn from these Italians?[122] Undeterred, Marinetti carried on from London to Cambridge University, without Richard this time, and a further riot occurred on Magdelene Bridge, ensuring the name of Futurism remained in the headlines.[123] Marinetti returned to Italy in July, convinced that Futurism had now rooted itself sufficiently deeply in England. He felt no immediate threat from the Vorticists and this was echoed in the *New York Times*, which talked of the latter's *reductio ad absurdam* being 'a rather dull imitation of Signor Marinetti and his Futurists'.[124]

Although Richard had initially presented an explanation for his actions in the press, and in private to Lewis personally, and in a way tried to explain that his actions were not inflammatory, the tone between the two men soon became much more hostile. On 13 June Richard wrote ' I regret having been the cause of so much trouble & expense to the "Rebel" Art Centre on account of my "irresponsibility" regarding the Manifesto that Marinetti & myself drew up.' He went on to say that he had not meant to imply that the named artists were Futurists, or even endorsed the movement. Rather, he had included them as 'advanced forces of English Art'. This list had not included Pound, Aldington and Gaudier-Brzeska, and so why they were involved in the counter-attack perplexed him. Why would he have written about them in the context of Vital English Art, as they were as unrepresentative as 'the Pope, the King, the Tsar, the Kaiser, Rosevelt [*sic*]' and a long list of others, being foreigners. He also expressed his bewilderment at why the other rebel artists would want to dissociate themselves so definitively from Futurism as previously they had been happy to be associated with the movement. This lack of comprehension is understandable as the origins of Vorticism and Futurism have significant common ground. The attack became more personal as the letter progressed, to the point where Richard said that the problems are 'entirely and absolutely the Delusions of your highly suspicious NEURESTHENIC mind'. In his opinion, Lewis believed that he was using dirty tactics to foul relations between himself (Lewis) and Marinetti. Conversely he again felt a little bewildered that Marinetti 'does not seem to care in the slightest of your attitude'.[125] He went on to say that it was his right to praise whomsoever he pleased though conceded that he had made a mistake in using the address of the Rebel Art Centre. This, he said, was 'through thoughtlessness, not evil intent as *you* naturally suppose'. Richard got to the bottom of the problem, in his opinion, in the same letter, where he concluded that jealousy had to be the problem: 'Also, neither you nor the others have in the past objected to your names being used by Marinetti, but when my name appears also then you adopt your narrow minded and pompous tone. *There lies the cause of the trouble.*'[126]

As had been seen before in the Carrington/Gertler débâcle, he now envisaged himself as 'the outsider' and the victim. The tone of this letter was personal, especially when he wrote: 'in your desire to abuse me you have accused me of being a very clever knave & a very great fool'. The break in the rebel ranks seemed final when he concluded the letter with 'I am utterly indifferent whether they (RAC) endorse my opinions or not.' The letter finished with a comment scrawled in the margin 'Beyond pointing out two or three inaccuracies I shall ignore your letter.'[127] In short, as Lewis decreed, 'It is time for definition',[128] though the differences appeared to be becoming more personal than ideological. The private nature of the attack also detracts from accusations that the high-profile conflict was staged for publicity reasons.

In a hand-written letter to the editor of the *Observer*, published on 12 July, Richard pondered further in amusement at the 'ex-Futurist professors . . . performing intellectual contortions within the centre of a whirlpool that the strong swift flowing stream of Futurism is bound to cause'.[129] In it he also made it very clear that there was a 'vast distinction' between Futurism and Vorticism. The duel was now being fought on a public stage, not in private as it had been up to this point.

In a further letter dated 14 July, written on board the ship S.S. *Maria* in the Bay of Biscay, Richard wrote of how Lewis might attack him using specific labels but that how 'I naturally prefer to be attacked for the opinions I happen to possess and not the ones you would like me to have.'[130] There was now little hope of, or attempt at, reconciliation: 'As a Futurist and not a Vorticist I have no doubt I shall change and evolve what ideas I possess. I know this to be a great source of trouble to you as I notice a continuous complaint in your articles on "automobilism" that the Futurists are not doing exactly what they were doing two years ago.'[131]

Evidently Richard now identified himself completely with the movement, to the point that he was becoming its defender in the face of contemporary hostility and in the absence of his Italian mentors. It may also be speculated that the manifesto, and the resultant divergence of groups within the avant-garde, had not only pushed his ex-rebel peers further away from him, but had also forced his defensive stance based around the tenets of the movement. Previously, he had associated with the movement, even promoted it, but now he was having to defend it, and, it could be argued, that it was at this point only, that he, and Futurism became irrevocably intertwined.

A further consideration should be noted when he recorded in *Paint and Prejudice* that 'I was still busy experimenting on, but not exhibiting, many pictures of a purely abstract nature.'[132] In *New Age*, on 18 June, Richard also highly praised three paintings by Kandinsky, calling them 'the finest modern paintings I have ever seen'.[133] These ideologies are not wholly in keeping with the tenets of Futurism, and so he was careful not to exhibit his experiments, and so dilute or confuse his public's perception of him. Was he afraid of alienating himself from the Futurist bandwagon and the public, on which his notoriety was now dependent? Moreover, was he afraid that this might expose a lack of depth of understanding or commitment to Futurism? Certainly his spoken replies of the time bore many characteristics of pure Futurist rhetoric, not least when he was asked 'Will your movement last?' To this he replied in textbook Futurist manner, 'No good movement lasts; only bad work goes on forever.' The report also quoted him as declaring that art must be a 'Plastic abstraction of emotion, seen, smelt, or heard; an intensification of life', saying also that 'Pictures are no longer to be static: that condition has been killed by photography. They must become dynamic.'[134] The *Manchester Guardian*, while not arguing that point, did, however, start to muse as to whether, by Futurist evolution, the 'cinematograph, thirsting for blood, will not follow on to the slaughter of Futurism'.[135] Richard's commitment to Futurism at this stage can hardly be questioned though he did not yet stand as a Futurist in his own right, rather as an associate, or disciple, of Marinetti. The *Yorkshire Observer* was unhesitant in calling him 'the best believed and most devoted of his disciples'. In the same article the critic observed that Marinetti and Nevinson had now absolutely alienated themselves and remained 'the only orthodox Futurists left in England'.[136] The division, they reported, had happened in the opening fortnight of June, though, according to Sickert, it was only a temporary mishap before returning to 'as you was'.[137]

When Marinetti left to agitate for Italy's involvement in the Great War, it would be difficult to claim that he had achieved his Futurist ambitions in England, at least on anything other than a short-term and limited scale. Futurism had not won over the rebel English artists *en masse*, though it had caused a counter reaction away from Futurism and in doing so gelled a faction of the previously disparate English avant-garde. Hamilton sums up boldly saying that Marinetti, 'Arriving in London in 1912, found the most industrially and scientifically advanced nation in the world, the country of H. G. Wells, overrun with some of its most backward and house trained poets and painters. Two years later they were breaking up his lectures on a British Futurist programme they claimed more futuristic than the Futurists.'[138] Also, despite the open denial and rejection of Marinetti and the Futurists, the connections with Vorticism are too many to be coincidental. True, Lewis and the avant-garde artists of the era had welcomed Futurism, but their enthusiasm had waned for a variety of reasons. The debt of Vorticism to Futurism, however, remains undeniable. The links between *Blast* and *Lacerba* are obvious, not only in content but in typographical style, while the polemic tone is familiar in two lists of 'Blasted' and 'Blessed'. Likewise, the first issue of *Blast* promised 'Discussion of Cubism, Futurism, Imagisme and all Vital Forms of Modern Art.'[139] Vorticism was not mentioned. Even the name that the rebel artists chose for their group, the Vorticists, finds its origins in a manifesto by Carlo Carra entitled *La Pittura dei suoni, rumori e odori* ('The Painting of Sounds, Noises and Smells') from March 1913, where he talked of 'boiling vortexes of forms and light' where the artist himself 'must offer a vortex – must be a vortex – of sensations'. It is believed that Pound did not use the term until September 1913. Vorticism appears also to be a direct consequence of the English Futurist Manifesto which is not an insubstantial fact. Both Futurism and Vorticism concentrated on the modern, industrial and mechanical age, albeit from different viewpoints. Both rejected the art of their predecessors as decadent, feminine and passive and both spoke of the value of destruction in creating a rootless art form, devoid of tradition and self-originating. Certainly the *Observer* had little doubt as to the debt when it declared: 'And yet, without Marinetti "Blast" would have been inconceivable. The manifestos are based on those of the Italian Futurists, but lag far behind them as regards force, literary form, wit and original thought.'[140] Both groups epitomized the pre-war capitalist societies' most militarist, nationalist, patriotic and misogynist tendencies.[141] In searching for differences one must firstly acknowledge the difference in appearance of the resultant compositions, the Vorticists with their straight, geometric and mechanical lines, the Futurists with fluidity and linear effects associated with motion and flux, and the preoccupation with the space/time compression. Pound went on to highlight a further difference in radicalism by stating that the Futurists wanted to destroy the academy while the Vorticists only wanted to replace its current membership.[142] Also, the Vorticists did not share the view that art should die with its generation; rather Lewis, Pound, Gaudier-Brzeska and others planned to set up a 'College of Arts' to perpetuate their ideas. Farrell argues that if anything, Vorticism was trying to preserve autonomous high art in a rapidly modernising mass culture.[143] In short, the Futurists tried to destroy the institution of art, the Vorticists did not. Richard himself, in a letter to the editor of the *Observer* cynically suggested that Konody, the critic in question, had 'failed to apply enough ice to his head in order to grasp the vast distinction between Vorticism and Futurism'.[144] Lewis too responded with an article in *T.P.'s Weekly* though even in this he was introduced as 'Mr. Wyndham Lewis, one of the foremost Futurists and the Editor of "Blast."'[145] Ultimately there was still confusion at grass-roots level as to what Futurism actually was and there was even a lack of fundamental understanding as to exactly who was a Futurist and who was not. By now it was clear, as Wees observed, that 'Of the English avant-garde painters, only C.R.W. Nevinson unmistakably deserved the label "Futurist".'[146] The *Yorkshire Observer* identified the same and projected that 'When Signor Marinetti leaves us, Mr Nevinson will have the distinction of Abdiel – "Faithful among the faithless, only he."'[147]

Futurism, by the summer of 1914, according to some press reports, was losing momentum. The *English Review* reported that 'the hideous Futurist craze for sensationalism is happily passing',[148] while the *Poetry Review* declared: 'Futurism, even with a big drum, has ceased to draw and . . . no longer the latest thing . . . these desperate iconoclasts [are] in danger of being tagged "Passeists".'[149] The *Illustrated London News* declared: 'Let them paint whatever they do not dislike, and welcome; but one still wonders against whom they desire defence; for as far as one can see, they have no enemies.'[150] Another article in the same publication opened by saying 'I should have thought it was now a thing of the past, exploded by its own silly gun powder train of progressive theory.'[151] The theories had all been propounded; they had not, in the eyes of the critics, been matched in practice in the confusion as to what exactly Futurism was, and so patience and tolerance for the group was wearing thin. The Futurist picture, it was concluded, was not a picture as it failed to depict and the Futurists themselves had done little to assist in this understanding. Indeed, such was the lack of impact that one Italian newspaper, *Il Piccolo della Sera*, recorded the eclipse of the movement and announced that 'Vorticists surpass Futurists in Audacity.'[152]

It would, however, be erroneous to say that Futurism had had its day. By August and September 1914 the main protagonists of Futurism were back in Italy. Demonstrations, flag burning and similar high-profile statements such as the creation of the 'Political Action Theatre', led to prison sentences for Marinetti, Boccioni, Carra, Russolo and Piatti, yet even from there they issued one further manifesto, *The Futurist Synthesis of War*. Though politics, prior to the summer of 1914, had played a relatively minor part in Futurist functions now anti-Austrian sentiment and agitation to break with neutralism became prevalent. Here too the roots of the association of Futurism and Fascism began with the first co-operation of Marinetti and Mussolini, the latter of whom was converted, according to the former, to the philosophy. War, the catalyst for fighting spirit, creative and active lives and the agent of change, had arrived. There was a whole new Futurist impetus which had to be harnessed. Even if the impact and influence of Marinetti was now doomed to obscurity the legacy of the 'second rate symbolist', with his 'coterie of largely decorative artists' was enormous, and was to survive beyond many of the Futurists themselves.[153]

Richard, meanwhile, had set sail with his mother for the South of France where he was residing when the news of the outbreak of war came. Perhaps this alone hints at the difference in conviction, extent and implementation of Futurist principles between himself and his Italian counterparts.

Whilst it would be difficult to argue that Richard had been responsible for creating a definitive English Futurism, he did contribute substantially to establishing Italian Futurism in England, giving it the foothold that Marinetti had been hoping for. Futurism, as Richard understood it, had come to England and taken root, before his own involvement. It then, following the ideologies of Marinetti and Severini, took on a superficial English identity, being conducted by himself and other English artists, using English scenes, people, fashions, flags and sentiments as the subject of its work. But Futurism, whether in England or in Italy, did not have a unified, concrete and constant philosophy to which an artist could adhere, and so there is no watertight definition of the 'ism' against which the rebel artist can usefully be compared. A similarly close scrutiny of Severini, Balla, Boccioni and Carra might lead to the same accusations of inconsistency that have been levelled at Richard. But Marinetti was happy to associate with him and have him act as his right-hand man, in turn being the voice of Futurism in England. This too must add credence to the association between the artist and the philosophy. The manifesto that they jointly issued crucially made no reference to war and to hygiene. This separates Futurism in England from that of Italy and also may account for England's tolerance of the movement after the outbreak of hostilities in August 1914. As the only official document concerning Futurism in England, 'Vital English Art' must be considered the basis by which we judge England's only Futurist painter. This being the case, the majority of his work, albeit different from that of the Italians, is a legitimate form of Futurist art. To judge him in the light of the Italian manifestos is more difficult, and largely counter-productive, as many of the Italian Futurists could not have remained consistent and loyal to these in themselves. Likewise we assume that Futurism in itself was unchanging over the period 1909 to 1914, and this further weakens the validity of the investigation into the legitimacy of the title. Futurism evolved, adapted and changed from one time to the next, from one country to the next and from one artist to the next. There is no basic Futurist guideline as to what painting should or should not be, as observed by Severini who, in a letter to Soffici, lamented that manifestos 'came out without being known to the others'.[154] But Richard had never managed to break away from the basic desire to illustrate, albeit using a complex and modern language *derived* from Futurism, though Severini claimed that this was not necessarily a refutal of pure Futurist rhetoric, and despaired 'We are unfairly accused of severing all connection with tradition.'[155]

Unlike Severini, who remained in Paris for the duration of the war, Richard became involved and in doing so brought Futurism to the Western Front. Indeed the contents of a letter from Marinetti to Severini, dated 20 November 1914 could more accurately have been destined for the English artist when it said 'Try to live this war pictorially, studying it in all its marvellous forms.'[156] The Italian Futurists were frustrated by their country's indecision and resultant delay in entering the conflict, and so for a time he was perhaps the only Futurist actively involved in this modern war. In theory at least, they should all, though importantly not necessarily Richard, have welcomed it as a form of global hygiene and purge. Futurism in many respects found a new impetus in the war. There was a genuine fear that pre-war society had both accepted and adopted the movement, and in so doing, had confined it to a form of respectability which undermined its basic tenets. When war came, Richard proclaimed: 'This war will have a violent incentive to Futurism, for we believe that there is no beauty except in strife, no masterpiece without aggressiveness'.[157] These words still strongly echo the initial Futurist dictum that 'Art can be nothing but violence, cruelty and injustice'[158] and suggest that even if Britain had tired of the Futurist novelty, Richard had not, nor would he do so, at least publicly, for eighteen months to come. In this respect, then, the energy, vitality, dynamism and modernity of Futurism, previously only witnessed in peace-time society, were being brought to the Front with enthusiasm and optimism in order to depict the 'great bloodletting'.[159]

But to evolve is not necessarily to betray and so in taking to war his experiences of Futurist painting in England he aimed to abandon objective reality in search of an appropriate and convincing abstract and subjective expression to depict and convey the impact of this first truly modern war.[160] Futurism was both relevant and directly applicable to the war subjects that were to follow and therefore exempt from Somigli's generalization that argued: 'Modernism, and its champions...would find themselves somewhat isolated by the retreating tide'.[161] On the contrary, it would seem, Futurism was ready for the war when it broke out. Alternatively one could argue that Richard, having alienated himself from the rebel generation and the peacetime coteries of London by August 1914, might have seen war as a necessary, and very timely, change in direction. By going to war as the lone Futurist continuity could be guaranteed and credibility assured, regardless of what Lewis and his cohorts were doing.

Henry wrote of Futurism: 'It is a violent stimulant . . . deadly as whisky . . . but never an opiate, never narcotic with sleep . . . Let us not laugh too soon . . . It is violent, it is insolent.'[162] Considering these words were written in November 1914, it is obvious that at least one intellectual was propounding its suitability for surviving in the time of war. His son also observed the metamorphosis saying, 'In retrospect it certainly would seem that some of us were already preparing our technique to express the horror, the cruelty, and the violence which were to be our destiny.'[163] It was a belief that was shared, perhaps surprisingly, by many others. But while Henry was propounding the idea of 'De l'audace, encore de l'audace, toujours de l'audace'[164] his son was beginning to harbour some reservations about the future to which he had committed himself.

Writing his autobiography over twenty years later, Richard reminisced: 'It is a black thought for me to look back and see that I was associated with Italian Futurism, which ended in Fascism.' Fallen into the wrong hands, principally those of Mussolini, he bemoaned: 'What a fate for an intellectual idea!'[165]

6

The Successful Transition to War Modernism 1914–1915

I found, in brief, that all great nations learned their truth of word, and strength of thought, in war; that they were nourished in war, and wasted by peace; taught by war and deceived by peace; – in a word, that they were born in war, and expired in peace.[1]

And like that of our counterparts, our world seemed most beautiful just before it disappeared.[2]

Henry had been to Germany and then to the Front before the war was even two weeks old. There had not been a moment to spare, though his journal entry for 13 August 1914, reported that the same degree of enthusiasm had not been shared by his son. Rather, he observed that Richard was in great misery at the absence of success in art, and money, and that he exuded no apparent desire to go to become one of 'Kitchener's Million'. Henry paused briefly in London then was off again to Dunkirk, Nieuport, Fourness and all the other places where his son would serve some months later. On his return in October there was no further sign of Richard getting into uniform, in fact, quite the contrary, as he now seemed to be having doubts about the associations he had been keeping in the past, especially as they advocated the merits of modern conflict and the dynamism and heroism that would be the positive result of it all. Whereas he was still content to believe that the vocabulary of Futurism was the only medium for depicting such a modern and brutal conflict, he had apparently lost the enthusiasm for being at the centre of it all and for promoting, as his Italian colleagues did, the philosophy of 'war as hygiene'. Henry's journal records, revealingly, 'Rich much disturbed about war & the Futurist support of its horror. Declares he will abandon Futurism & call his new movement Mintalitist.'[3]

It was, it appears, the father who took the initiative in associating Richard with the war when on 27 October 1914, he 'wrote to Hector Munro about Rich and myself going out'.[4] By the 30th, the association with the Friends' Ambulance Unit had been established, and while he was waiting for the papers to be completed, Henry went back out to Ypres for a few days. The day after he got home he wrote to Nicholl's to get his son's uniform ordered,[5] by 10 November they were in London together getting Richard's papers, by the 12th he too was in uniform, and on the 13th father and son were crossing from Dover to Dunkirk together. There can be little doubt as to who was the driving force behind the young artist's decision to go to the Front.

The Artist's War

This is not the impression of the dawn of his war service that Richard gave, either then or in subsequent years. Immune to the propaganda campaigns and to the posters and brass bands, he said, he had simply felt the need to do the right thing, though he knew that the army would never accept him on account of a limp. On being told that, due to the urgent need for ambulance drivers, he could go directly to the Front, however, he recalled that this situation was 'excellent' and that he left at once for Dover. His autobiography talked of how 'I was pursued by the urge to do something, to be "in" the war; and although I succeeded in the end and was "in" it, I was never "of" it.'[6] He made no particular nationalistic claim saying that 'I regarded myself as having no patriotism' though 'I preferred the English'.[7] Professing his own strength of character and the independent nature of his decision to fight is again seen when he wrote 'Brass bands, union jacks, and even "Kitchener wants YOU" had no power to move me.'[8] Over everything else, he reported a sense of calm and rational thinking. In 1932 he recorded in an interview how he had been 'Eager to do my bit for Old England, Home and Beauty'.[9] He also wrote in his autobiography 'was there not something I could do?'[10] then mentioned how a chance conversation with his father led him to understand that there might be a possibility of serving in the Friends' Ambulance Unit. Cancelling all appointments at the Dore Gallery and training himself in motor mechanics and driving, he was ready for mobilization almost immediately. The dominant role of the father is scarcely mentioned and neither is the fact that three full months had passed before his departure (fig. 25).

What we do know from the records kept at Friends' House is that Richard served at the following: 13 November: stretcher-bearer at Dunkirk; 20 November: chauffeur at Woesten; 22 November at Kursal; 28 November: night orderly at Saint-Pierre; 30 January: England on leave. After this he was discharged for 'Business Reasons.'[11]

The aftermath of the Battles of Mons, the Marne and the Aisne, and the commencement of activities at Ypres, would have been the theatre into which father and son arrived. Richard recorded 'A few hours from London . . . just an hour or two away, and here we were working in a shed that was nicknamed "The Shambles".'[12] By all accounts it was a baptism of fire that exposed him immediately to the true horrors of war, and to the practicalities of heavy work at the front. Henry recorded that the day after they arrived he 'Found Rich had been dressing the wounded in the sheds with some success. But his driving of the motor ambulance was very poor.'[13] His father also recorded, before Christmas, that he received a letter from Richard telling him about how he knocked someone over in the unwieldy vehicle.[14] It is an ironic observation as he obviously prided himself on his ability to drive such a modern contraption and had his photographic portrait taken in front of it to send to Marinetti (fig. 26). He also painted a self-portrait of himself at the wheel of it, this being an image he liked to promote, in keeping with the dynamism, or vitality, of the modern artist at the Front. Ironically, he was not given a driving job until 20 November, which seems to have ended again by 28 November, a total service time of

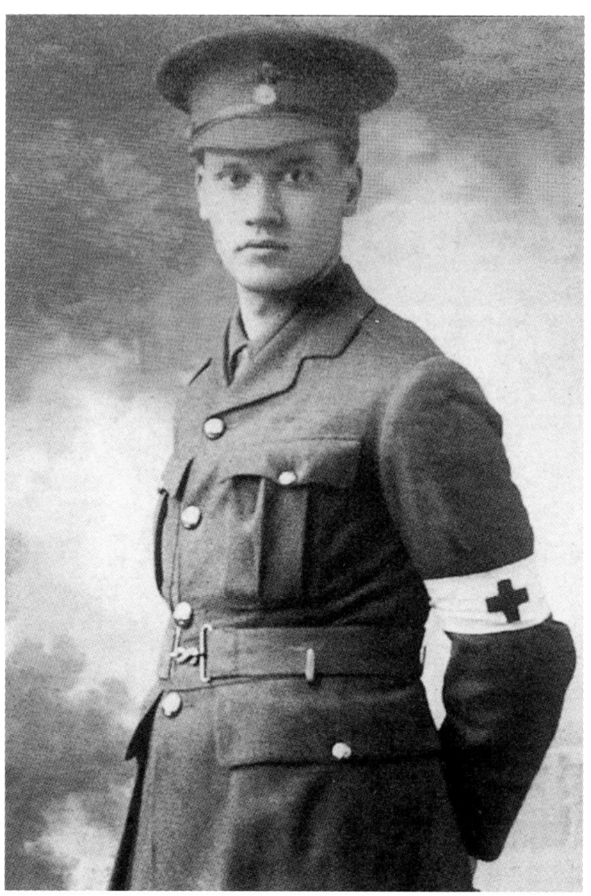

25. Nevinson in Uniform. Postcard, 1914. Artist's estate.

about one week. The nature of the heavy work inflamed rheumatic pains in his arms and led to his being made a male nurse at Malo-les-Bains.

Another of his war stories, recorded in *Paint and Prejudice*, also stems from the ambulance when he maintained that a shell had passed directly through the canvas rear of it as he had been driving. He implied that had the sides of the ambulance

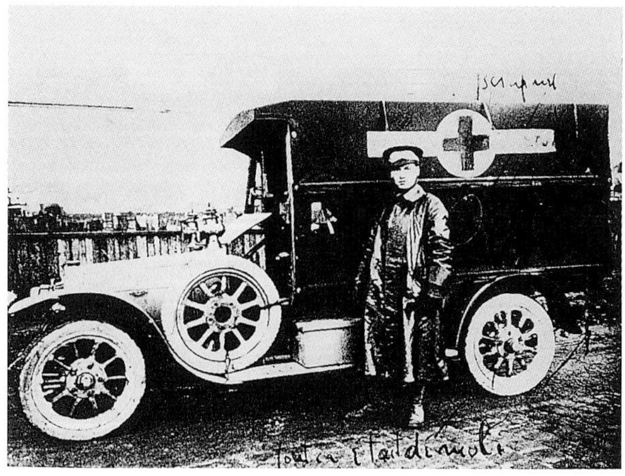

26. Nevinson in front of his ambulance. Palazzo Grassi, Venice.

been solid it would have exploded. The rumour is substantiated by a card addressed to his wife to be, Miss K. M. Knowlman, and dated 24 November 1914, which stated 'A damned shrapnel shells [*sic*] exploded under the back wheel of my "bus" & smashed it.'[15] The father's entry in his journal however talks of receiving 'a long letter from Rich describing a drive to Boulogne and a night at Woesten when a shell smashed his ambulance'.[16] The implication here is that it could have been destroyed while parked at night in Woesten.

Regardless of these ambiguities, what he observed in 'The Shambles' must have been a harrowing experience. His father, after staying with him a couple of days to get settled in, departed again on 15 November and recorded that he 'Left Rich apparently fairly happy though very apprehensive about going to the front.'[17] His autobiography described very clearly the conditions and atmosphere in which later compositions like *La Patrie* and *The Doctor* were rooted:

> By the time I had been at 'The Shambles' a week my former life seemed to be years away. When the month had passed I felt I had been born into a nightmare. I had seen sights so revolting that man seldom conceives them in his mind, and there was no shrinking even among the more sensitive of us. We could only help, and ignore shrieks, pus, gangrene and the disembowelled.[18]

The official history of the Friends' Ambulance unit tends to back up this nightmare scenario recording that at Dunkirk at the time of their arrival 'there was not less than 3,000 wounded men in the goods sheds at the station with only half a dozen men to attend them'.[19] This description goes on to remove any doubt as to the nature of the horror Richard faced on arrival:

> In the half-darkness of these bare sheds lay hundreds upon hundreds of wounded men stretched on the straw covered floor – Frenchmen, Belgians, here and there a few British and Germans. They had been there, many of them, for three full days and nights, practically untended, mostly even un-fed, the living, the dying, and the dead, side by side . . . It required a great effort of will to face the sight and stench of the countless gangrenous limbs that lay there helpless among the foul straw. None who were there can ever forget the horror and the hopelessness of that sight.[20]

Richard seemed to settle in fairly well however, and when his father returned towards the end of December he could observe that 'I joined Rich doing orderly in a ward of 10 or 12 wounded, some very terrible. He seems to be a great success as orderly, interpreter . . . but has been put off driving thro' rheumatism'.[21] He was now in charge of the nursing staff at the hospital and adapting well to the grim environment into which he had so suddenly been thrust. Even the prospect of missing Christmas at home didn't seem to bother the young artist and his father recorded 'Said goodbye to Rich who is quite content with his work there and is much liked by the wounded for his sympathies.'[22] Before his return he recalled several other stories, from which painted compositions would later emerge. These were exemplified by the occasion when he saw a dead child lying on the streets of

Dunkirk after a Zeppelin raid, and which led to the painting *A Taube*.[23] Other Nevinsonian tales came home from the front such as the cinema-like drama when he got the wheels of the ambulance stuck in the railway points as a train rumbled out of the night towards him, the ambulance and his injured men, only to be stopped a hair's breadth from disaster. Also noticeable, however, was his obvious reluctance to fight, and on one occasion when it looked as though there might be little choice he simply commented 'Could we not have claimed immunity because we were Red Cross men?'[24] Regardless of the nature of his war commitment he could comment on the positive elements of it and say 'A man is all the sadder for seeing war; but I grew better and painted.'[25]

London, the Press and the Creation of the Soldier/Artist

It is unclear when he actually left the Friends' Ambulance Unit: his service card records 12 January whilst his father's journal notes on 27 January, 'Heard Rich was coming over next Sunday.'[26] It is also unclear why he left. In *Paint and Prejudice* he recorded 'I crocked up and was sent home',[27] while the Ambulance Unit official records site 'business reasons' as the fundamental cause.[28] His father's journals make no mention of excessive illness at this particular stage. Whatever the reason, he now had something dynamic, emotive and original to work with and he was not slow to let the press know that the soldier/artist had arrived home after being at the Front.[29]

There had not been enough time to manipulate the press before his departure, but as soon as he came back from his first period at the Front he was quick to create a more acceptable public façade in issuing statements like: 'All artists should go to the front to strengthen their art by a worship of physical and moral courage and a fearless desire of adventure, risk and daring and free themselves from the canker of professors, archaeologists, cicerones, antiquaries and beauty worshippers.'[30] Surprisingly, after his harrowing experiences, he did not renounce his affiliation to Futurism; rather he assured the press and public that he had come home stronger and better than ever, invigorated by the experiences and in no way in two minds concerning his pre-war allegiances. In a lengthy piece entitled 'Painter of Smells at the Front: A Futurist's View of the War' in the *Daily Express* on 25 February 1915, he cut out any malignant philosophies that might damage his reputation when he said 'Unlike my Italian friends, I do not glory in war for its own sake, nor can I accept their doctrine that war is the only health-giver.' That done, he returned to the more familiar rhetoric and talked of the war as a 'violent incentive to Futurism' saying that 'there is no beauty except in strife, no masterpiece without aggressiveness'. Lastly, as the newly created soldier/artist he could now confidently declare 'The public cannot realise soon enough that the modern artist is not the puny and effeminate long-haired creature of the eighties.' He was presenting himself as the man, the modernist and the soldier, whilst not renouncing his status as an avant-garde painter. Likewise, a suggestion that he had returned home due to shell-shock was quickly refuted by the artist in an open letter in which he declared 'Beyond a severe attack of rheumatism, my health is better than before the war, and I am absolutely in no way suffering from any form of nerve trouble.'[31] The last thing he wanted was to be seen to be returning home a changed or damaged man, at the hands of everything that he had been praising, the impetuous youth who had been taught a man's lesson. It does, however, contradict his own version in the autobiography of why he left the Front in the first place. To maximize the military impact of his war service he also got a letter off to the *Manchester Guardian*[32] ruling out any ambiguity which may have existed concerning the role of the Red Cross on the Western Front, and confirming the dangers that faced its members. He drafted, though never sent, a letter to *The Times* too, in response to an article by Clutton-Brock entitled 'Sowing of Wild Oats in Art', which implied that young artists were still carrying on with their pre-war antics despite the seriousness of the situation unfolding in Europe. Had the response been sent it would certainly have had all the hallmarks of Nevinsonian defence as it declared:

> I have spent the last three months at the front in France & Belgium amongst wounds, Blood, Stench, Typhoid, agony and death & as a member of the Friday Club I resent your critic writing 'about the sowing of wild oats and managing to amuse myself with Art in spite of the war'. He ought to discover that I take Art as seriously as he take [*sic*] criticism flippantly.[33]

The *Daily Graphic* also received a letter in response to an article that said that he had 'paid a visit' to the front, in which the point was clarified that he had been out there full time and was by no means a visitor.[34] In short, he did not want his military service to be seen in any way as second class or transient. Rather he laboured the connection to the ambulance, not mentioning the period of time actually spent driving it, and this acted nicely as a bridge between the Futurist artist and the new image of the soldier/artist. Continuity was crucial and so the *Daily Express* article confirmed the allegiance to Futurism declaring 'Our Futurist technique is the only possible medium to express the crudeness, violence and brutality of the emotions seen and felt on the present battlefields of Europe.'[35] Richard, on his return and via the media, was crafting his own image, and using his *bona fide* credentials, perhaps generously, to establish himself, away from any pre-war groups, into a vital, though essentially positive role, unique to himself.

Almost immediately after arriving home he was exhibiting with the Friday Club[36] and according to the father's journal the Futurist bust of *The Chauffeur* reappeared, hinting that, as yet, there was no effort to publicly refute the artistic pre-war association. In fact the ideal compromise was reached when the *Daily Graphic* printed a photograph of him, in full uniform, explaining the Futurist bust to a wounded patient (fig. 27). Artist, soldier, Futurist, patriot and carer, were all neatly rolled into one image. To facilitate this process Nevinson distributed to journalists military photographs of himself for their use (fig. 28).[37] Now his original and poignant subject matter, harnessed to his avant-garde vocabulary and newly acquired military pedigree, was attracting attention, a substantial amount of which was positive. Peters Corbett addressed this issue in the following way: 'Moreover,

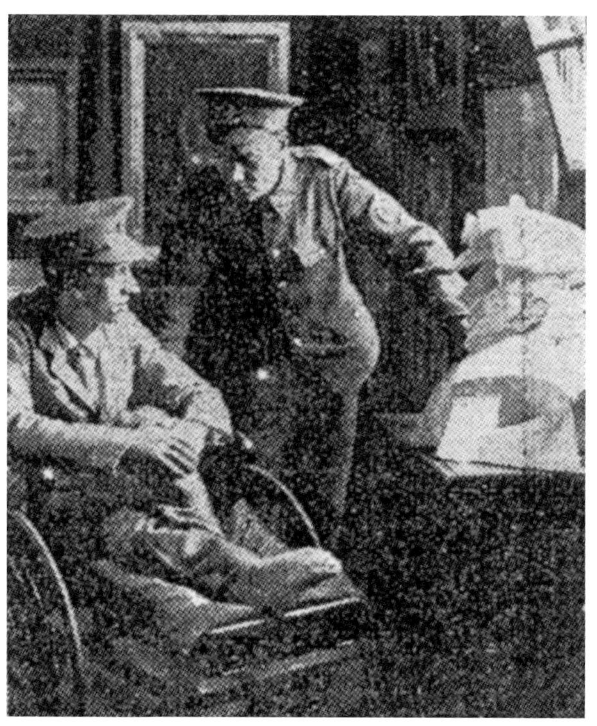

27. Explanations. *Daily Graphic*, 11 September 1915.

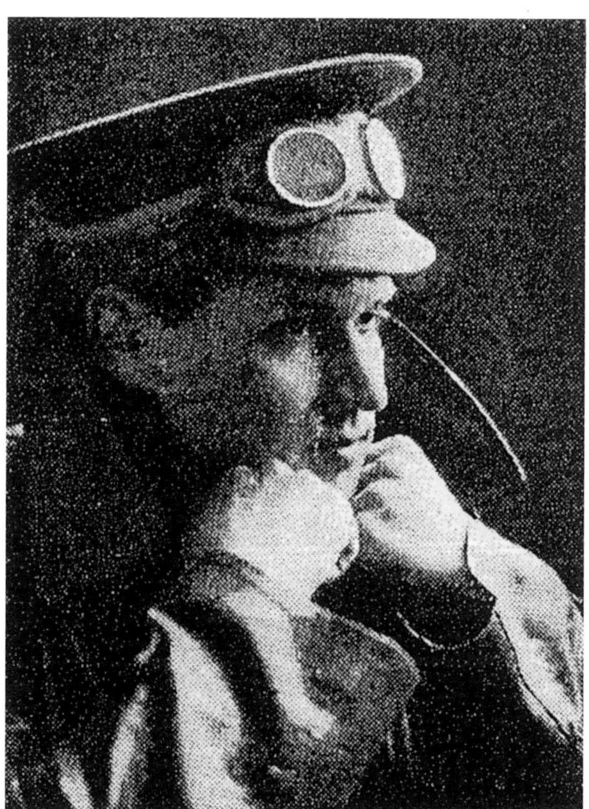

28. Photographic portrait by Malcolm Arbuthnot, reproduced in *Gazette of the Third London General Hospital*, vol. II, March 1917, p.164.

Nevinson's war service as an ambulance driver was a gift to the journalists, who could present him as a basically sound fellow, brought back to his senses by a dose of real life at the Front, and willing to talk about it.'[38] Richard himself had recorded this in *Paint and Prejudice*, though suggesting it was a coincidence, when he wrote 'The very fact that I was a private in the Army made a good story for the newspapers, and I had one of the boosts of my life.'[39]

The Outbreak of War and Art in London

But merely being a soldier and an artist was not enough to guarantee a successful homecoming, nor the celebrity status that was in store for Richard. London had changed and taken with it the attitudes that had easily been gauged, and outraged, prior to the outbreak of hostilities. What was especially unpredictable was what impact the outbreak of war would have on the more extreme artistic coteries in London with which painters like Richard had previously been associated.

Perhaps surprisingly, it was not universally seen as a negative phenomenon: not everyone saw lights 'going out all over Europe'.[40] For many the advent of war did not augur a period of darkness following in the wake of Victorian and Edwardian halcyon days. It was not the tragic end of something, rather the welcome beginning of a new era. The victims of civil, class and sex war mourned neither the passing of these eras nor partook in the fallacious nostalgia for a golden existence in pre-war England. The war, it was felt, was going to have a deep and lasting impact, which would either purge England of the 'spectres of national decay'[41] of previous years, or conversely, herald a new era which would make pre-1914 beliefs belong to an identifiable, and definitive, past. One way or another, throughout the various factions, there was room for optimism as to what the outcome might be, though predicting exactly where that line might fall within the arts was almost impossible. For example Samuel Hynes wrote 'What the war did was to make the condition of England a social disease for which war was the cure.'[42] By identifying the maladies in the 'condition of England' as, say, industrialization or feminism or modernism, he could conclude that war on Germany was seen as a war on these domestic conditions too. This was an echo of a contemporary review, which had stated: 'It was high time war should come with its purifying fire. A wave of diseased degeneracy had submerged Philosophy, Music, Literature, and Art to such a depth that, looking forward, I venture to prophesy that future centuries will gaze back with pity upon this period of mistaken morbidness. The futurists, the cubists, the whole school of decadent novelists.'[43]

Other writers saw the purge as an altogether more general sweeping away of social deviancies leading society to 'a masculine new age, with no feminist politics, more masculine literature, and a reversion to traditional art'.[44] Likewise, though diametrically opposed to the Futurist glorification of machinery, noise, destruction and 'war as hygiene', an old debate reappeared (originally put forward by Ruskin), in which the relationship between art and war was examined and extolled as beneficial. Ruskin had said 'There is no great art possible to a nation but that which is based on battle.' Citing Egypt, the great Gothic cathedrals of Europe, the Renaissance and other great periods in history he observed that 'all the pure and noble arts of peace are founded on war'.[45] Basing his argument on the grounds that society can only benefit from a war that is morally just, as opposed to one for material gains, the 'knock-on' effect clearly is that culture will benefit directly too. Though written almost fifty years earlier his words would have been seen by many to have rung true for the years leading up to and including the Great War. This argument was brought up to date and presented by the Slade Professor of Art at Oxford, Selwyn Image, in the autumn term of 1914. In a lecture entitled 'Art, Morals and War' he observed that 'War and Art are not always enemies, and Peace is not always Art's best friend.' The 'artist turned warrior' (precisely what Richard was destined to become though perhaps not in the way Image had intended) would be the new knight, defending not only his country and culture, but protecting it from the 'lowest and most inhuman conception of civilization'.[46] In short, through this crisis the nation could look forward to a purge in British civilization that would make this conflict worthwhile. Richard had to ensure that he, and his art, was not the focus of such a purge.[47] Collins Baker, keeper of the National Gallery, and critic for the *Saturday Review*, in one of the first articles to deal with the subject of art and war, dated 22 August 1914, predicted that 'Art will benefit if the war be great enough to engrave the world's mind deeply.' What is more, far from being a negative force, it might act as a purge to redefine 'that vague and chaotic groping',[48] which had characterized the pre-war years. If war strengthened society, made it less frivolous, and more serious and thoughtful in its pursuits, then the resultant art could only benefit from this phenomenon, so long as it was noble and just in spirit. The decadence of peace would be swept away and the great release of energy bound to follow a great conflict would manifest itself most beneficially in the arts. Clutton-Brock expanded on the theme of the great release of energy saying that 'It was inevitable, then, that the greatest war of all time should call out the poets.'[49] But benefits would not come only in the form of a positive rejuvenation of decency and culture, but in the extinction of 'undesirables' *en route*. A. R. Orage, for example, talking specifically about Ezra Pound said 'Whether he knows it or not, Vorticism is dead. It was, at best, only a big name for a little thing, that in the simmering of the pre-war period suddenly became a bubble, and is now burst. Compared with the war it is incomparably feeble.'[50] W. S. Sparrow saw war as a sobering phenomenon which might go some way to recovering from the pre-war frivolity 'after fools and their folly' whose theories and practices had been 'as destructive as they were ridiculous'.[51] The soldier was needed by society to replace the *dilettanti*, so closely associated with Lewis, Richard and the other rebels, who now had become the bohemian and debauched icons of the pre-war era. If this did not happen 'Future historians will say that the age went dancing to its doom.'[52]

On a more moderate stance, others believed, that war might act as a uniting force giving art a common *raison d'être* again, a common focal point if not, in fact, a common language. If addressed properly it could even, through its socially relevant subject matter, narrow the fissure between art and public, which had been growing rapidly up to, and including, August 1914. Perhaps this common cause could help to redress part of the pre-war crisis. It might also return art to having its social and narrative function and thus take it off the path to autonomy, 'art for art's sake' and abstraction, which had been making distinctive headway in Britain for half a decade now. This idea was shared by some of the younger artists of the rebel generation, who had seen the need for a cohesive event, though with different goals in mind, before the war started. Laurence Binyon projected: 'What is needed now is the fusion of one imaginative effort that shall make art again a single language expressing the whole modern man.'[53]

Or perhaps the war simply would not affect art and the two could remain separate entities. While the *Burlington Magazine* advocated 'business as usual', Roger Fry, Clive Bell and the Bloomsbury Group, with whom Richard had little sympathy, went further by proclaiming 'aesthetic disinterestedness', saying that their contribution would be the preservation of culture in the midst of the destruction which would inevitably follow. [54] Roger Fry later despaired 'It is all up with our ideas.'[55] Other avant-garde artists shunned the war too but for entirely different reasons. Jacob Epstein dismissively declared 'Really I am too important to waste my days thinking of matters military.'[56] For Lewis the war threatened an almost fatal interruption in his work, though he was confident that the roots ran deep enough to restart it after the conflict, and indeed that it was the artist's duty to recast English culture when hostilities had ceased. However, he wrote: 'Murder and destruction is man's fundamental occupation', then went on to state that 'the machine reflects man's basic violent nature' and observed that 'art must reflect the forms of modern life'.[57] If anything, surprisingly, it was the rebel artists who seemed the least enthusiastic as the war, to them, posed the greatest threat by changing what had been a fertile society in which change, at last, had not only been possible, but probable. The *Studio* had a much more passive role envisaged for art: 'In times such as these, when the air is filled with echoes from the battlefield, it is a welcome relief to turn for a moment to the things which remind one of the calm and the peace of the sanctuary.'[58] The galleries around London were also unsure of what the impact of war would be and certainly, Oliver Brown of the Leicester Galleries, where Richard would later triumph, recorded: 'The younger ones did not want to plan an exhibition that they might never live to see.'[59]

All told then, the concept of war, for many, and its related purge, as an aesthetic and social doctrine, for whatever goal, however disparate, seemed welcome. Art would find a new context, and gravitate to a new set of values, in which it would stand or fall in terms of a country, and a population, now at war. Hall described art then, in this period, as 'a kind of barometer of cultural health'.[60]

At the Outbreak: Nevinson and Futurism

Within the cacophony surrounding the opening months of the war Richard's voice was heard, his actions scrutinized, and his affiliation with his Italian counterparts closely observed, in what must have been a difficult philosophical stance to defend.

His association with Futurism was, by this stage, inescapable, though importantly, he at no stage had ever defended the Italian idea that war was a form of hygiene. Neither did he ever push for England's entrance into the war in the manner that the Italians were doing for their hesitant nation. He was not, however, on the surface, scared of the war. The arts, he believed, were ready and would certainly benefit from this catalyst. In 1919 he retrospectively mused that 'The war did not take the modern artist by surprise. I think it can be said that modern artists have been at war since 1912...They were in love with the glory of violence. Some say that artists have lagged behind the war, I should say not! They were miles ahead of it.' [61] The war, he propounded, was a social phenomenon to be embraced, to be learned from and overall to be observed, experienced, and comprehended. There were going to be negative elements to the conflict, but that was not the point on which he chose to dwell at this early stage. The Futurist artists would go to war, experience it and be part of it, thus earning credibility whilst distancing themselves from the 'old men' who would later be seen, bitterly, to be running the war. For the Futurists there would be one further break in the war art tradition, that of absenteeism. The Futurist artists, Richard included, would go to the Front, experience modernity in all its power and glory, and be a part of what they would eventually depict. Though Futurism did not stand alone in welcoming the war it did seem to be the ideology that would benefit most immediately from, or adapt most quickly to, a conflict tailor-made for it. The skill would lie in extracting elements of Futurist philosophy, beneficial to the arts and acceptable to the public, whilst abandoning the more reactionary clauses which would most certainly lead to its extinction. That sentiment, and even the language employed was not, however, exclusive to Futurism as the headline from the *Daily Graphic* illustrated when it observed: 'The virile teaching of war. Slack Youth Yesterday, a Man Today.'[62] The Futurist ethos of cleansing, virility, youth, and destruction, albeit to destroy the past, not rejuvenate it, was clearly being used as was the language employed by Richard in *Vital English Art*. The *Athenaeum*, within weeks of the outbreak of war, optimistically acknowledged that 'In an age of brutal strife, the art, if any, will be brutal also, the extremes of Futurism being alone suitable to express its spirit.'[63] The feeling was that in a brutal, and soulless conflict, only the most a-cultural, dehumanized and resilient medium would suffice. As uncomplimentary as this might be, Futurism was being given a modicum of worth, if in a roundabout way, before its artists went to the Front. *Colour* had the most exiting outlook for the impending months of conflict, as far as Futurism was concerned:

> Signor Marinetti has given some wonderful pictures of war in his poems. Probably now some of his followers will give us emotional aspects of the war in paint. It is a splendid opportunity. The explosive style of the Futurists is eminently suited to the character of modern warfare, and battle subjects are the very things that would appeal to their anarchic views of life. The Futurists should give us the true expression of War in Art.[64]

But neither Futurism nor Richard had unified or widespread support; nor did they have a *carte blanche* to success, or indeed survival, in the impending conflict. The hostility that awaited, if he pitched his art at the wrong level, can be gauged by published sentiments such as that by St John Ervine in the *North American Review* when he declared: ' The Vorticists and the Imagists and the Futurists and the rest of the rabble of literary and artistic lunatics provided slender entertainment for empty days; but our minds are empty no longer; and we have no time to waste on monkeys on sticks.'[65] There were other writers, to say nothing of the public, who were sure that the era would augur doom for the pre-war avant-garde: 'All those pretty little fancies, only to be explained by algebraic symbols, Cubism, Futurism, Vorticism, will receive their death blow.'[66] This altering perspective and revised toleration is a theme which Peters Corbett touched upon when he wrote: 'The hold which modernism had on its audience as an expression of their modernity proved extremely fragile and susceptible to challenge, and enthusiasm for its account of the contemporary crumbled away under the impact of the First World War.'[67] If the values of the public were to change, then so too was the role of the artist and his place within society in the pre-war years. The same writer sums up those closing months, prior to summer 1914: 'The imaginary artist – potent, caped or business-suited, secure in the status that opposition conferred – could strut upon the stage of the London art world and receive in return for his entertainment value the image, the complicit impression of the reception he desired. That moment was not to last long.'[68] The transition period would be the crucial time for both Futurism and Richard as an individual. Futurism in England was neither doomed from the outset nor guaranteed safe passage through the war years, but if it was to survive, indeed flourish, it would have to convince a hesitant and divided public. This is precisely what Richard would have been aware of in an environment where the 'post-Rossettis with long hair under the sombrero'[69] were to be replaced by the virile Englishman, uniformed and in the front line of modern war.

Nevinson and a New Approach to War Painting

Futurism in Italy, though importantly not in England, had a commitment to embrace this war and to live up to the words of the manifestos of the pre-war years. Marinetti had written: 'We wish to glorify war – the only health giver of the world – militarism, patriotism, the destructive arm of the Anarchist, the beautiful ideas that kill.'[70] Apollinaire, in France, believed that the war was the inevitable result of a series of experiments to which the twentieth century had committed itself, and enthusiastically joined up. Regardless of the philosophical or moral standpoint of the individuals concerned, the assassination at Sarajevo 'was the signal to roll up the amiable and idyllic screen, to set in motion the huge and destructive machinery which waited behind it. One by one, protesting, insistent and reluctant, the nations of Europe swirled into the vortex of war.'[71] Certainly, Marinetti advocated pro-intervention, though he was frustrated by the Giolotti government, in what he was coming to regard as this Futurist hour. M. W. Martin went further to suggest that the

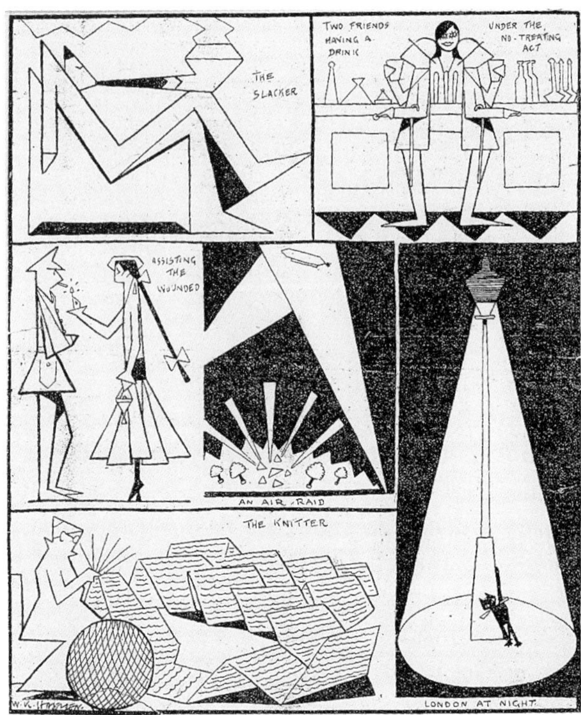

29. 'Our Futurist Artist on the War'. Cartoon, *Daily Mirror*, February 1915.

outbreak of war couldn't have happened at a more perfect time, saving Marinetti from the inevitable truth that the movement, which had been so widely known over the previous half decade, had now ceased to exist.[72] Yet condemnation, if condemnation was to come for Futurism in England, was far from immediate. The *Illustrated London News*, in the very week in which Britain committed herself to hostilities, still supported the concept that an artist was free to do as he pleased, claiming 'England is at any rate a free country, and all the advantages that free institutions can yield Mr. Marinetti and Mr. Nevinson need never lack.'[73] The English press, far from feeling threatened, could even parody what the Futurist role in the war would be (fig. 29).

The problem for Richard was how to depict the war, how to identify a suitable compromise in subject matter and technique, and how to isolate himself from the negativity surrounding extreme Futurist rhetoric, whilst retaining his avant-garde, and possibly, rebel, status. Beyond acceptability, Richard also had to wrestle with the concept of presenting this new, and very modern, though often visually mundane, war. In the same way that Victorian high diction was no longer sufficient or relevant as a means of literary communication to relate the trench experience, the same could almost certainly be said for painting.[74] The colourful uniforms had been replaced with khaki, the heroic charges and defences with long-range shelling, the sweeping military manoeuvres with trench warfare. The era of the machine gun, the U-Boat, the aeroplane and poison gas was going to guarantee that this war would not be picturesque in the way that the conflicts had been depicted in the past. A new language would almost certainly be required to depict this most modern of wars; the first total war. This was recognized at the time too:

> Old wars, so late even as the Russo-Turkish War of 1878, were still full of glitter and colour; the very rags of long campaigning held some picturesque traces of ceremonial parade; the plume, the hussar's floating sleeves, the flying sabretache kept the rhythm of war alive; the soldier made a gallant figure to the eye amid the grime and smoke the hot engagement, and the brush of Delaroche could dwell with loving fidelity on the dust stained uniform of Napoleon. The man was still paramount; he had not been lost behind a utilitarian disguise: it is this disguise that now confronts the battle painter with a task that will try his skill to the uttermost.[75]

In short, the picture had been vacated of the clear subject matter which had once occupied the space, the previously glamorous *style historique* now reduced to 'a game of moles'.[76] Even *The Times*, in an article entitled 'The Passing of the Battle Painter' declared that 'The trench is the enemy of military art.'[77] It might have become difficult to depict but that did not mean that it had become impossible to represent, and this is where Richard decided to focus his attention. No longer was it sufficient for the battle painter to paint only the pathos, patriotism and sentiment of manly conflict. Britain was, after all, believed to be a peace-loving nation, anti-militarist by nature, appalled by the activities of her European counterparts, and as such involved in a heroic struggle in the most un-heroic and un-glamorous of environments. According to a lecture given by Lawrence Haward, curator of the Manchester City Art Gallery, entitled 'The Effect of War upon Art',[78] the modern artist, like the soldier, had therefore to respond, but with caution. The response must be carefully weighted to embrace the anti-militarist ideal, the modernity of the conflict, whilst still attaining the status and legibility of high art. From now on the genre solution would have to be rejected as would the glorification of war advocated by the military, in favour of an expression ultimately modern in character, and therefore symbolic of the intact nature of a contemporary culture in the face of national crisis. For Haward the war was a 'purge' that was unnecessary, though it was an opportunity to advance, adapt and prepare, for a new renaissance in English painting, possibly based on the Post-Impressionist foundation of Cézanne. It was precisely here that Richard would find his niche.

In a letter to the *Observer*, dated 4 October 1914, even before his departure for Flanders, Richard was still seeing a chance for the war to result in a positive outcome for the arts, especially in London. He took the opportunity to have another attack, as he had often done before the war, on the art establishment that Futurism had set out to target, writing, 'Sir, – The love of art and architecture displayed by the English journalists and the nation in general during this war is most encouraging to British artists. In time of peace this same public has shown a contempt and neglect of art (especially architecture) as cynical as the monstrous vandalism of the Germans.'[79] On his return from Flanders some months later, however, he consciously aimed at the 'middle ground' of public tolerance, clarifying what it was he wished to depict before tackling the issue of how this depiction was to be approached: 'I have tried to express the emotion produced by the apparent ugliness and dullness of modern warfare. Our Futurist technique is the only possible medium to express the crudeness, violence and brutality of the emotions seen and felt on the present battlefields of Europe.'[80] Though he talked of 'our' Futurist technique, it is unclear with whom he was associating. Certainly the Italians would not have wished to take such a conciliatory stance had they been involved, and the affiliation was not with other English artists, none of whom would have permitted the association with the 'ism'. Now Richard, apparently acting alone, was taking Futurism in a different direction and, convinced of its ability to convey sensation, utilized it to depict the banality of war, not the beauty. But Lewis was quick to spot the change, and identify the reasons for it, writing in *Blast* No. 2:

> Marinetti's one and only (but very fervent and literal) disciple in this country, has seemingly not thought out, or carried to their logical conclusion, all his master's precepts. For I hear that, de retour du Front, this disciple's first action has been to write to the compact Milanese volcano that he no longer shares, that he REPUDIATES, all his (Marinetti's) utterances on the subject of war, to which he formerly subscribed. Marinetti's solitary English disciple has discovered that War is not Magnifique, or that Marinetti's Guerre is not La Guerre.[81]

If anything, he and his brand of Futurism was being forced into an anti-militarist (though not pacifist) role away from its earlier militarist origins. Marinetti with his militaristic opinions, was rapidly becoming *persona non gratis* in the light of the unfolding and very real war across the channel. Lewis had written that 'nobody but Marinetti, the Kaiser, and professional soldiers WANT war'.[82] He continued with the negative imagery elsewhere: 'There is one man in Europe who must be in the seventh heaven: that is Marinetti. From every direction come to him sounds and rumours of conflict. He must be torn in mind, as to which point of the compass to rush to and drink up the booming and banging, lap up the blood! He must be a radiant figure now.'[83] Richard would certainly have noticed this fall from grace and distanced himself from the principle points of objection. Futurism still had value and worth for depicting this modern conflict, but only when it had removed itself from the self-destructive ideas which would forever eclipse its positive elements. It was clear, however, that the art of this war, like the battles themselves, would be conducted and paid for by the young. It was his task to reconstruct, or readapt, Futurism in England accordingly, and this he did successfully throughout 1915. His memoirs recorded that the transition was far from smooth and not immediately appreciated or understood:

> Of course the Clive Bell group dismissed them as being 'merely melodramatic'. The *Times* was horrified, and said the pictures were not a bit like cricket, an interesting comment on England in 1915, when war was still considered a sport which received the support of the clerics because it brought out the finest forms of self sacrifice, Christain virtues, and all the other nonsense . . . To me the soldier was going to be dominated by the machine. Nobody thinks otherwise today,

> but because I was the first man to express this feeling on canvas I was treated as though I had committed a crime.[84]

Nevinson and the Modern *Guerrapittura*: 1914–1915

At the exhibition of the Friday Club in February 1915, Richard cautiously revealed to the public the first of his experiments on a war theme in the company of two pre-war compositions.[85] Perhaps the most experimental of these was *Searchlights* (or *First Searchlights at Charing Cross*) (fig. 30).[86] Interestingly it did not draw on his experiences at the front at all, being a depiction from Hungerford Bridge, of a London 'nightscape' during a threatened air raid. This suggests that the painting may have been executed before his departure for Flanders.[87] In appearance it boasted a geometric design of rectangles, triangles and arcs of light, intersecting throughout the composition. It was devoid of conventional narrative and was a depiction of a modern phenomenon utterly lacking in human presence or natural forms. The picture plane too was treated in very much the same way as his pre-war compositions where a fragmentation, and its collage-like effect, replaced the conventional use of space and perspective. The affiliations, both in subject matter and in the resultant composition, which exuded the stylized lines of force, made the association with Futurism both immediate and undeniable. The association was by no means detrimental to the overall success of the painting and its critical reception was, on the whole, favourable. The *Evening News* described it as a 'rational arrangement of cubes and rules and T squares, and most convincing'.[88] Even Richard's rival, Lewis, complimented the originality and success of the work declaring 'Mr Nevinson's *Searchlights*, the best picture there, is perhaps too, the best he has painted.'[89] Though the *Athenaeum* interestingly referred to it as a 'relic from his Futurist past'[90] the survival of Futurism, at least in the short-term was, by others, acknowledged and celebrated. The dogmatic adherence to extremist pre-war and early war rhetoric, however, would not last for much longer as even a cursory glance at a similar theme from 1916 testifies (fig. 31). For the moment though P. G. Konody in the *Observer* revelled in the fact that the war had not killed off the vitality of the pre-war avant-garde and of essential related components of modernism: 'Futurism and the other fashionable 'isms' of the last few years have been somewhat prematurely inserted in the casualty lists of the great war. Regular funeral services have been read over their alleged corpses. But here they are again in the exuberant vigour of their boisterous spirit.'[91] For Konody the war had changed only the direction and pace of the pre-war avant-garde. The vitality and dynamism were still there which, when coupled with the energy and daring of youth combined to make an interesting and welcome twist in the experiment of modernism. A second parting glance at his peacetime Futurism, or at least those Futurist paintings done after the outbreak of war, but before the artist's departure for Ypres, may be obtained through the descriptions of the now lost *Declaration of War*. It may usefully be seen as a bridge between peacetime and war-related Futurist subjects. The composition was described by Konody as being 'defiant gaiety and wholesale rejection of all for-

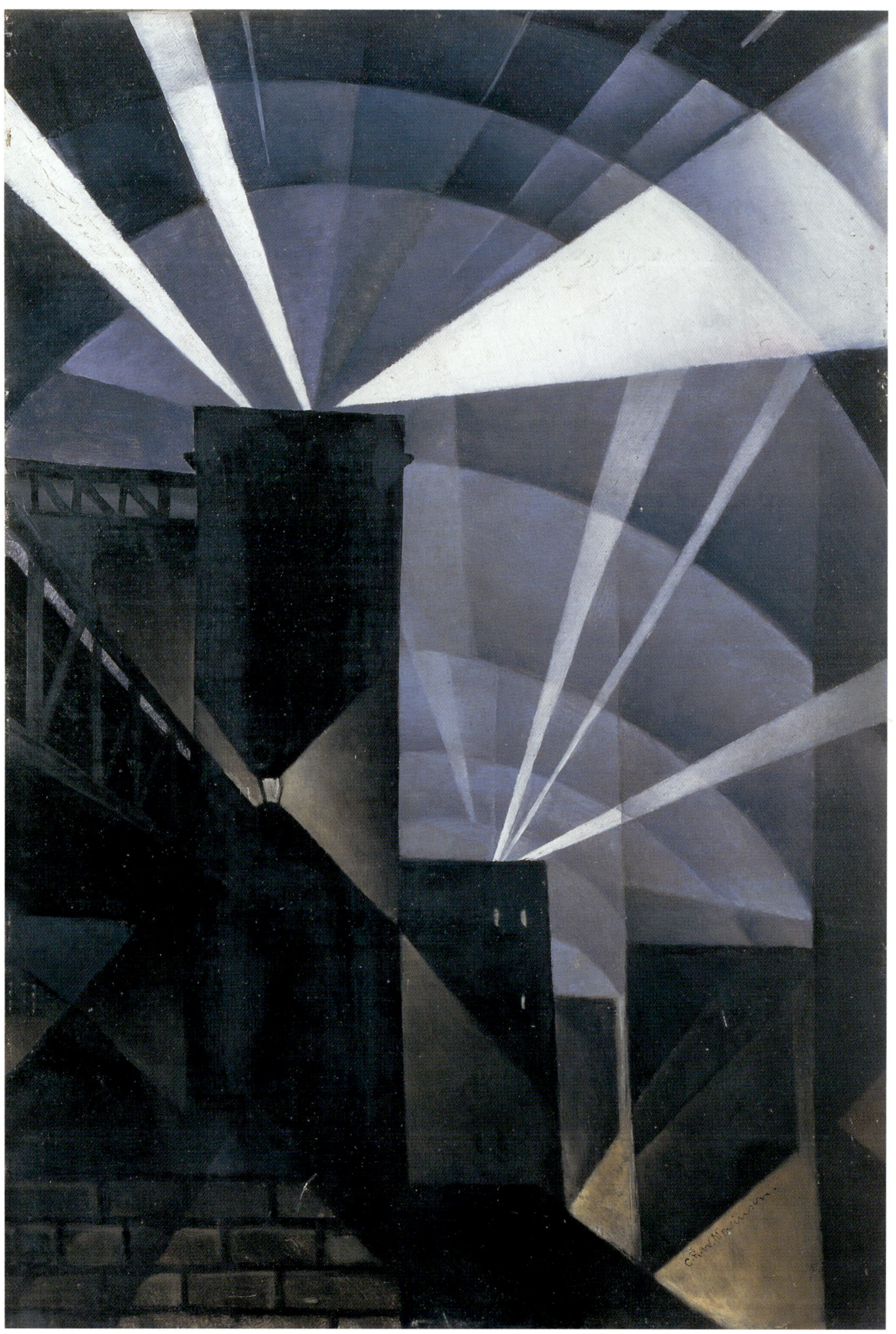

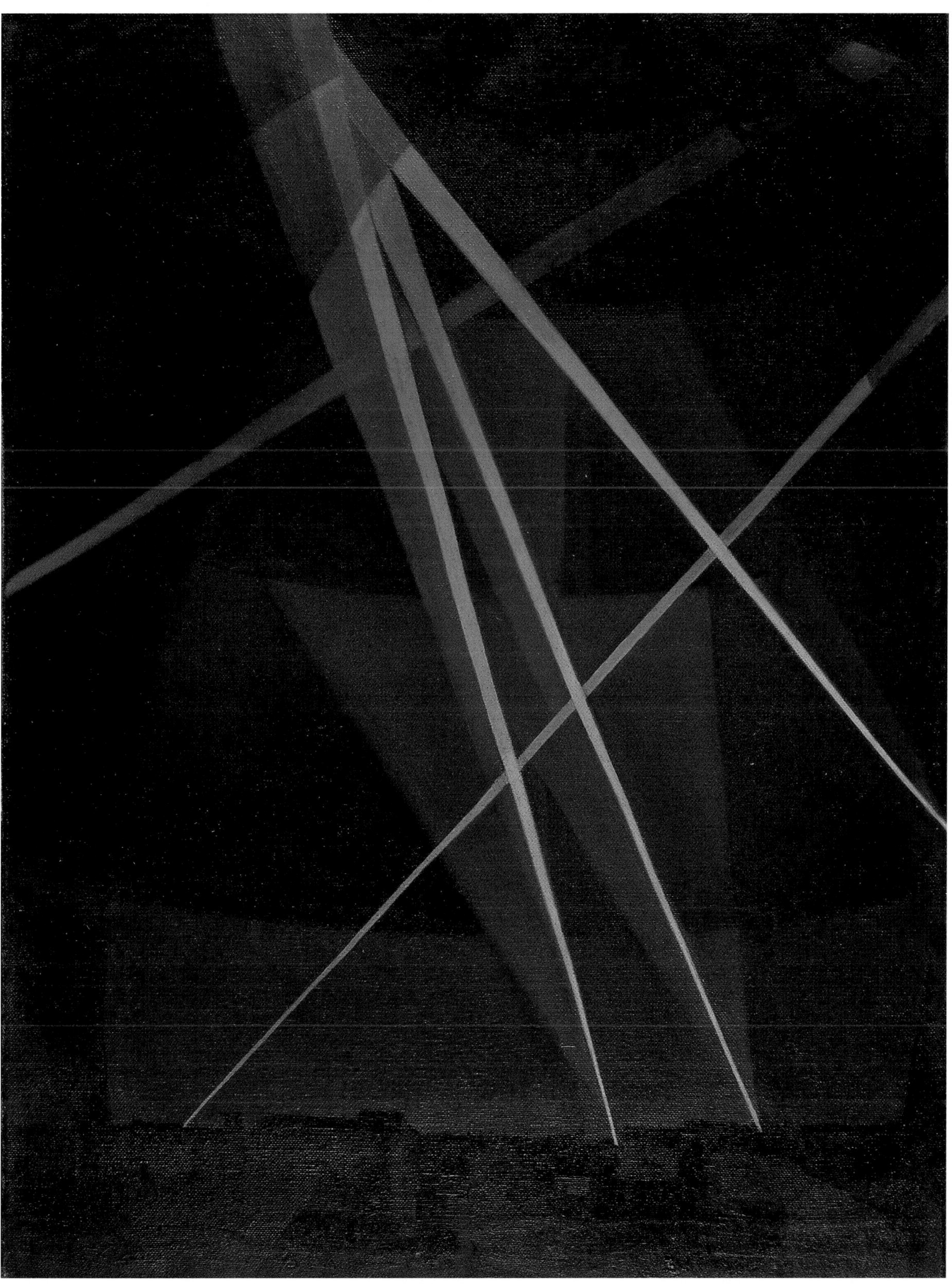

mal artistic conventions in what he later termed 'uncompromising Futurism'.[92] The critic made comparisons once again to the jigsaw images of Severini, while to W.L.H. the artist adhered to the 'geometrical convention of the Futurists'.[93] Reference was made once again to the fragmented picture plane, the mosaic, while the colours used to depict the rowdy crowd scene were those of the union flag encapsulating the dynamism and sensation of a jingoistic crowd in Trafalgar Square on the night war was declared against Germany:

> But no special preparation is needed to discover in this gay patchwork, in the general rhythm of waving flags and hats and insistently repeated wedge-shapes a suggestion of the enthusiasm, the excitement, the patriotic impulse which swayed the crowds in the streets of London on that memorable August night. No method of exact representation, not even a clear snapshot photograph, could ever have reproduced so happily the spirit of that scene.[94]

Another article talked of how the artist had 'returned to the geometrical convention of the Futurists, and very successfully conveyed an abstract dynamic and mental impression of the thing we call "mafficking"'.[95] For the reviewer of the *Evening News* it was 'an optical illusion – hats and flags and canes with features slightly mixed – half close, and then blink the eyes, and at once one sees what it means'.[96]

The links with Severini, and in particular his *Pan Pan at the Monico*, were again evident and the painting was very much in keeping with the artist's themes and techniques of the previous fifteen months and therefore consistent with the main thrust of Futurism in England before the war. Once again Futurism, in a diluted form, won critical appreciation and was seen as a perfectly acceptable and effective means of depicting something that mere visual accuracy would be incapable of doing. In short, Richard's early brand of war-Futurism seemed to be making the transition from peace to war with comparative ease. If this adaptation were to continue the war could act as a vindication for this element of modernism as opposed to being any form of threat to it. In terms of the predicted purge that the war was to have on art, opinion was divided as to whether Richard and his brand of modernist painting were rising above it or whether in fact they were the products of it. Regardless, and importantly, Futurism was neither being seen as an irrelevant form of pre-war degeneracy nor was it viewed, like many other branches of extremist modernism, as a symbol of threat. Early criticism, then, implied that the continuation of the pre-war experimentation was to be encouraged, that the war subject was to be addressed not ignored, but that the relevant balance would have to be found. Acceptance of Futurism simply for the self-indulgent sake of it was not likely to be tolerated, but as a vehicle of expression and relevant modernity it would, on the whole, be encouraged.

The articles generated by the exhibition of the Friday Club had scarcely disappeared when the next significant event for Richard, Futurism and the English avant-garde took place with the Second London Group exhibition at the Goupil Gallery in March. In all, ninety paintings were exhibited including four key works by him: *My Arrival at Dunkirk* (fig. 19), *Taube Pursued by Commander Samson* (fig.

Preceding pages:
30. *Searchlights (The First Searchlights at Charing Cross)*, 1914.
Oil on canvas, 60.9 x 40.6 cm.
Leeds Museums and Galleries.

31. *Searchlights*, 1916.
Oil on canvas, 76.4 x 56 cm.
Manchester City Art Gallery.

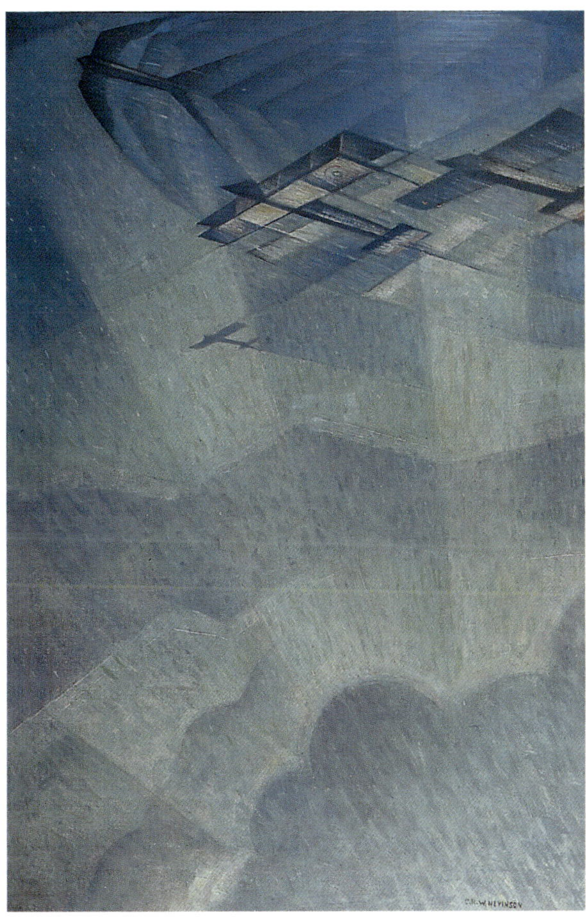

32. *Taube Pursued by Commander Samson*, 1915. Oil on canvas, 85.7 x 49.5 cm. Hendon Royal Air Force Museum, London.

32), *Ypres after the First Bombardment*,[97] and *Returning to the Trenches* (fig. 33), though the artist himself was unable to attend due to illness. The *New Witness* gauged public curiosity saying, 'One never saw so many folk assembled for a private view before, except at the annual academies. Futurism, Cubism etc are evidently still popular.'[98] Most reviews focussed on Richard's *Returning to the Trenches* and to Epstein's *The Rock Drill*, the latter of whom was still being described, confusingly, as a Futurist. The overall impact of the exhibition was to prove that modernism was as well and defiant as ever it had been before the war. Indeed, far from fighting for their survival, Hall feels the works of art on display here represented icons of the 'heroic' phase of British modernism.[99] The pre-war debate on purge seemed to have remained in the realms of theory and to many in the press this was a source of great disappointment. The *Star* for example, proclaimed that 'the Cubists and Futurists still live and do their worst' and even though they were known to have been to the front 'it does not seem to have done them any good'.[100] Naïvely the reviewer explained that Richard's *My Arrival in Dunkirk* was basically a painting that had been good but was then cut up into pieces and stuck back together again in the dark.

If anything, modern painting was as extreme as ever. The public had changed, not the artists, and Collins-Baker summed this up in the *Saturday Review* of the London Group exhibition when he wrote: 'So in August, to our horror, we were tipped right into things that really mattered. And now, when we have an opportunity to look again at those ingenious notions, our nerves still tingling with the impact of reality, we simply wonder what on earth was up with us that we should ever have been entertained by them.'[101] Though the whole group was classified as Vorticists, the members were also branded 'fakes', their work being every bit as dishonest as the sentimental anecdotes produced by the Royal Academicians. *My Arrival at Dunkirk* drew the first barrage of attack, being described as a 'deliberate perversion', a picture that 'bores us' at 'a moment [when] we have no use for elaborate ingenuity'.[102] For the *Tatler*, 'Nevinson and Wadsworth and Co. are weirder and wilder than ever, for war, it seems, hasn't toned down *all* the cranks.'[103] If anything, the lack of purge as predicted at the outbreak of war was adding to the hostility that the artists received, especially those who continued with the extreme modernism of the pre-war years. Richard's work, however, did not entirely fit into that category. Though the *Daily Express* had published a version of his *Returning to the Trenches* with the heading 'Will these pictures help the Germans?'[104] and though modernism was now being closely associated with Prussianism,[105] he, on the whole, avoided the critical backlash that his peers were subjected to. In short, extreme modernism and militarism were now being linked, one being seen as nearly as abhorrent as the other. For other reviewers it was the other way round. This was the state of society, why should art not reflect and interpret it? One way or another modernism was being rethought, its position and value within society and the arts reconsidered and its effectiveness as a language reassessed. So, while Lewis, Roberts, Wadsworth and Epstein drew most of the negative comments and the Camden Town contributions seemed dated, Richard's war pictures, in many, but not all, reviews were seen as epitomizing a modernism with a difference. One painting, *Returning to the Trenches*, rose above the rest and was treated as a successful artistic experiment.

Returning to the Trenches

It is worth exploring this composition carefully as perhaps it is at this specific moment in time, and with this particular painting, that the fragmentation occurred that was destined to lead to Richard's success in England, especially in the early war years, in the midst of the collapse of the more extreme forms of pre-war modernism. Critics such as P. G. Konody, who launched vehement attacks on the Vorticists, found sympathy for his paintings and in doing so proposed the earliest recorded explanation for why Futurism, or at least his interpretation of it, should still be acceptable. 'Mr. C.R.W. Nevinson, who has now definitely adopted the Futurist principles of dynamic art . . . is at present the most acceptable of all these revolutionaries, simply because he has resorted to compromise.'[106] It is interesting however, that a critic who had been familiar with the work of Richard for some time should only now be noting that he had taken to Futurism definitely and unreservedly, almost as if war had been the missing component. The relationship

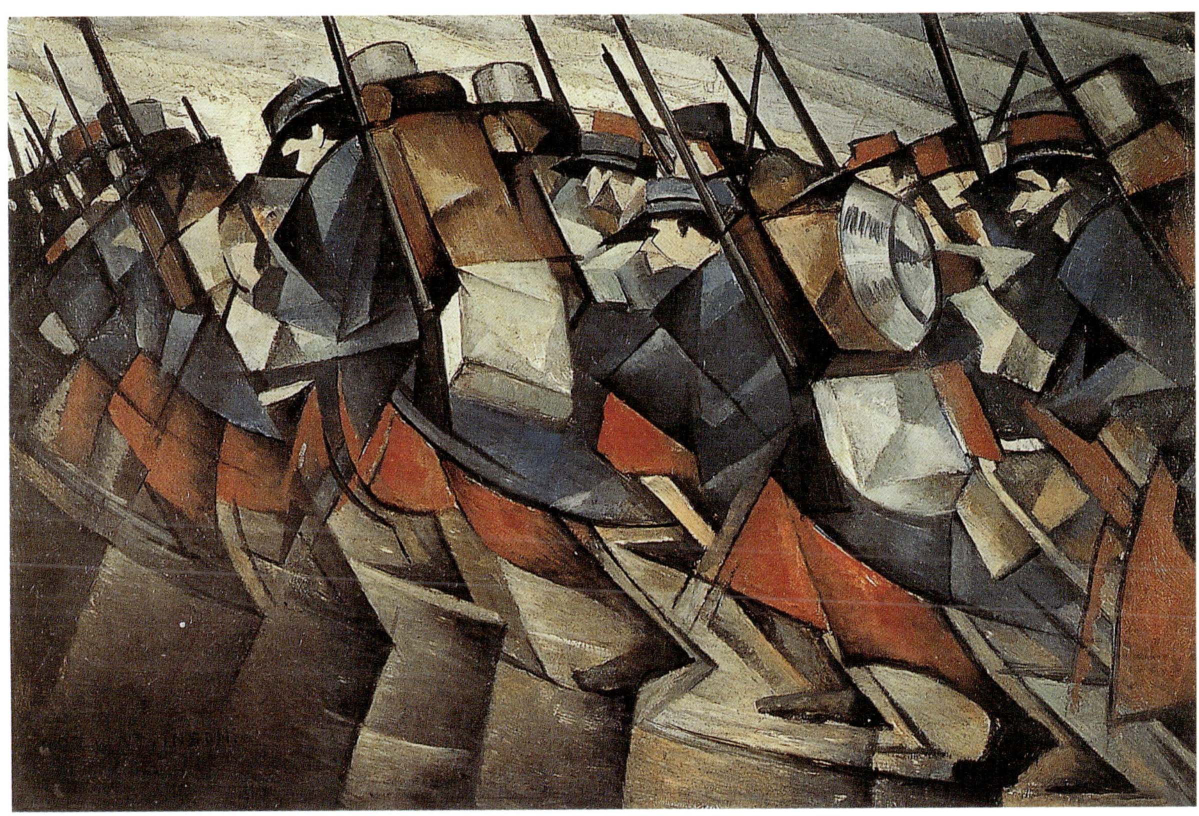

33. *Returning to the Trenches*, 1914. Oil on canvas, 50.8 x 76.2 cm, National Gallery of Canada, Ottowa.

between Futurism and modern war, so far as he and the critics were concerned, was working more effectively than any other brand of the pre-war avant-garde, as the *Manchester Guardian* grudgingly conceded.[107] Aesthetic radicalism, harnessed, had a place in the art world of the war years, the more extreme and uncompromising factions did not. Konody went on to explain the nature of this compromise:

> He has realised the uselessness of painting pictures that have no meaning for anybody but the artist himself, and therefore places his Futurist experiment on a lucid basis of realism. His *Returning to the Trenches* is really an uncommonly interesting picture, in which he has found an extremely expressive formula for the rhythmic marching of a body of French infantrymen fully armed and laden with all the paraphernalia for a prolonged stay in the trenches. While avoiding anything like literal representation of objects, he leaves the spectator in no manner of doubt concerning the meaning of every touch of the brush.[108]

For other critics his success lay in the fact that he was in the process of abandoning Futurism all together. Even the hardened anti-modernist writers such as Clutton-Brock, whilst mourning the survival of Cubism and Futurism, could observe 'Mr Nevinson, in his *Returning to the Trenches*, has himself begun to return from the barren wilderness of abstractions.'[109]

Returning to the Trenches was probably based on a photograph of marching men, in a state of preparedness and readiness, which were popular at the time. There are, in addition to the finished piece, several surviving sketches and one woodcut version. These act as a useful insight into how the picture was created and with what priorities in mind. The impulse to record momentum and direction are obvious and they appear harnessed to the formal rigid discipline associated with the Futurist technique of Russolo.[110] As in the photographs edges are blurred, abrupt angles pervade to represent arms, caps, feet and bayonets in motion. Futurist force lines are evident as the soldiers march on, and the compositional repetition suggests comparisons with a giant military machine, devoid of sentiment and human feeling. The repetition might also suggest the monotony and boredom of modern warfare as the artist had suggested in his previous interview. They may have been depicted using a Futurist vocabulary, but as Cork points out, they were not marching towards a 'Futurist victory'.[111] The soldiers are not recognizable individuals, no rank is evident, no expression visible, nor any other identifiable feature, other than that, by their uniforms, they are French. Rather they are shaded and moulded together into one active unit. Black argues that the subject treatment reduces the 'soldier to the dehumanised status of an easily expendable, roughly manufactured, mass produced component within a vast military organisation'.[112] There is a reference to abstraction in a Futurist sense, not least in the bottom half of the composition, but this is offset against the recognizable forms on the rest of the picture plane. Whether Richard was simply using an image of war or whether this was a personal recollection, the image was subjected to modified formal disciplines in its treatment. The depiction is not simply a reportage of French soldiers marching to the Front nor does it serve a narrative or propaganda function. One feels that the technique, the exploration of the medium, is as important as the subject itself, although still subservient to the meaning of the composition as opposed to being the focal point. Its strength lies not in the visual accuracy of the scene being depicted, but in the rendering of atmosphere and expression, and through the equality of technique with narrative function. The woodcut version, which appeared in *Blast* No. 2, is especially successful in its employment of the Futurist vocabulary to these ends. The fact that the subject is French might also have steered the artist clear of stronger patriotic sentiments in his viewing public and thus let their attention focus on the composition as opposed to any personal narrative implications. Clearly this painting then must stand as one of the distinct examples of Richard's moderation discussed earlier, being modern, relevant, comprehensible and not, in the light of recent press statements, extolling the values of war as his Futurist pedigree might have implied. Osbert Sitwell could have been describing this particular work when he said of Richard, 'Nor, on the other hand, did he reduce warfare to an abstract and rather unmeaning arrangement of planes and cones, tokens of men and guns, transmuted into one indistinguishable mass, beneath smoke that creaked through the air, as if cut out from yellow cardboard.'[113]

The artist was singled out from the rest of the group exhibiting at the Goupil Gallery and described thus: 'Mr Nevinson, the English disciple of this movement

[Futurism], is a very oasis of intellectual clearness among a babel of artistic gibberish.' Futurism and 'intellectual clearness' were being spoken of in the same sentence. The article went on to clarify why this might be and concluded that 'he does not carry Futurism to its logical, or illogical, climax, but effects a clever compromise between "dynamic art" . . . and realism'.[114]

Other Compositions: Novelty and Compromise

But Richard was not only depicting the routine of modern war in a modern way, he was also actively searching for novelty, originality and dynamism in his subject matter, which on its own account would enthrall and intrigue audiences. Aviation was perfect for this, and also lent itself to Futurist principles in terms of technique. *A Taube Pursued by Commander Samson* (fig. 31) represented some of the first ever attempts to capture in paint the entire concept of aviation and aerial conflict and would certainly have generated public interest.[115] On top of everything else, pioneers of flight, and emerging 'aces' would have been seen as glamorous, and Commander Samson himself was the perfect Marinettian character.[116] The resultant composition was hailed widely as a success bringing a further respectability to Futurism with an audience that might previously have harboured hostile feelings. The *Sunday Times* reported: 'If all Futurists gave us such beauty of colour and conveyed movement with such imaginative power as Mr. Nevinson shows us in these aeroplanes rushing through space, we should have no quarrel with them.'[117] The *Evening Standard* too found a new tolerance for the modern 'language' employed by the artist to depict the modern phenomenon of mechanized war, beyond even the potential of realism and visually precise depictions. It commented that his work was treated with 'a force a convincingness that no realistic snapshot could equal . . . It is the best flying picture that has yet been done.'[118] Charles Marriott also singled out this painting for specific praise, noting how Futurism is an excellent language for depicting 'a very convincing impression of a stern chase' capturing the essence of the scene in a way which 'no realistic snapshot could equal'.[119] Aviation certainly was a very suitable subject for any Futurist artist, especially in the context of combat and manly heroics, in defence of one's nation.[120]

By March 1915 it was generally accepted that art would be permitted to move away from the practice of imitation, rejecting literal representation in favour of an abstraction with which to communicate, though there were clearly acceptable and unacceptable levels in doing this. The Vorticists, on the whole, took it too far in some critics' eyes, as now their message or meaning was obscured, art being reduced to a system of patterns and designs which may, or may not, have a pleasing appearance. Richard, on the other hand, had established a balance between literal representation and the abstract language of modernism prevalent in the pre-war era. At the time there were those who would treat his work with scepticism, accusing him of playing to 'the mob', describing his work as being that of a journalist and classifying it as 'sentimental vulgarity'. There was no merit in basing art on the level of comprehension of the majority. To do this would be to relegate literature to the level of tabloid journalism.[121] Alternatively, it might also be seen to be returning the relationship between art, artist, public and critic to a safer period when it was not so strained. In so doing there existed both truth to nature and truth to materials, harnessing pre-war developments and techniques to produce a convincing and comprehensible language with which to comment on the modern subject of war. For the reviewer in the *Daily News and Leader*, however, the analogy was to that of drunkenness when he talked about the artist being 'under the influence' of Futurism, with the 'inability to co-ordinate one's vision'.[122] He did however at least review his work, something he refused to do with that of Wyndham Lewis.

Certainly Richard's own published writings show no 'backing down' from his original stance. He declared: 'I am firmly convinced that all artists should enlist and go to the front, no matter how little they owe England for her contempt of modern art, but to strengthen their art of physical and moral courage and a fearless desire of adventure, risk and daring.'[123] The voice of the Futurist was still sounding strong and unrestrained, showing no sign of wavering commitment to a movement which had been causing him private concern. By developing a confident appearance he might buy himself a modicum of artistic autonomy from this point on. This would then permit a partial return to a form of realism whilst deflecting attacks that a group association, especially with Futurism, was almost certain to invite. But for the moment the relevance of his work, the choice of subject matter, the hints at modernist references, the level of intelligibility and yet the originality of it made his early efforts an overnight success. Richard's notoriety, based on the war theme, was well and truly launched by the combination of the Friday Club and the London Group shows, though perhaps now he was beginning to see the advantages of disassociating himself from the Futurists all together, and going it alone.

There is nothing to suggest that Richard by mid-1915 was in the process of commencing the U-turn which would characterize his late war work so distinctly. Now was to be about his personal ideas, aimed at a British audience, dressed effectively, though deceivingly, in Futurist clothes. So too his proclamations were vociferous and outspoken very much in the manner of his pre-war days. A letter written from his studio on 18 April, and published in the *Manchester Guardian* on the 20th, entitled 'Dry Rot in Art', epitomized this point, and is worth reproducing here. There can be little doubt about what Richard believed, or perhaps more importantly, what he wanted to be seen to believe:

> I insist it is impossible to get any inspiration from the antique, or to let us dominate it, because evolution and change in vital art are essential, and has no eternal truths. The beauties and [?]eals of yesterday are the ugliness and sentimentality of today. Above all, it is impossible for an artist at the present time to have the same emotions, sensibilities, or modes of expression as an Egyptian, and early Italian, or a Michel Angelo, surrounded as he is by steel construction, speed, machinery, and high explosives, for art must represent, and always has represented, the spirit of its age.[124]

The tone obviously is still pro-modern, anti-establishment and to use his own word, vital. The affiliation was reasonably closely associated with Futurism, though the absence of the name and some of the better-known clichés associated with the movement are conspicuous by their absence. Perhaps the label now was becoming limiting and restrictive with the artist preferring an association only with the *Zeitgeist*.

7

Artistic Breakthrough 1915

He is a disciple of Marinetti and Marinetti's Futurist painter friends, but he is the only one to have the courage to proclaim it.[1]

The RAMC and the Third London General Hospital

Richard would have been acutely aware of the degree of attention, and acclaim, he was now attracting. The combination of patriotism and youth coupled with modernism and truth, were attributes in his art which were proving not only tolerable, but preferable to the incomprehensible abstractions of his more extreme peers, or the 'armchair dramas' which times like this traditionally produced. He would also have been aware that these military credentials would need to be refreshed and kept entirely up to date if he wished to remain at the vanguard of the wartime avant-garde. Accordingly, May 1915 saw the first avowed intentions of the artist to return to active service in the Friends' Ambulance Unit.[2] This was not a smooth procedure. In fact, Henry's journals show him struggling in vain to get him back in at all, recording, 'tried to arrange Rich's return to Quaker Unit', but wrote in an isolated sentence: 'Very unhappy and agitated'.[3] It is not quite certain who was unhappy and agitated, either Richard at the thought of returning to the Western Front, Henry himself or the ambulance unit, reluctant to take back someone who had overstayed their leave as badly as he had done. The following day, 28 May, Henry recorded 'Difficulties about Rich's return to the Quakers'[4] and by 31 May, the project seems to have been abandoned permanently with the new idea emerging to join the Royal Army Medical Corps (RAMC). Again, with no time being wasted, father accompanied son to Wandsworth on 1 June, watched him being sworn in as an orderly and extracted the assurance from the commanding officer that this form of military service would not involve being sent abroad. Richard was now in a favourable situation, engineered by his father. His autobiography recorded the whole affair much more nostalgically, 'Soon I heard that the 3rd London General Hospital had made an appeal to the Chelsea Arts Club (of which I was not a member) for men of intelligence. With an impulsiveness, that afterwards made me ponder, I threw up everything and joined the army.'[5] It is clear now that this was not almost immediately

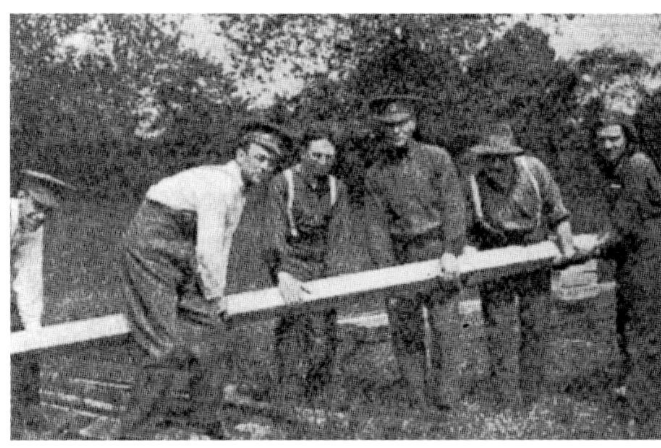

34. Nevinson (far right) in a work party. Reproduced in *Gazette of the Third London General Hospital*, vol. III, October 1917, p. 21.

after his return, rather after an absence of about six months and was neither spontaneous nor impulsive. In Paint and Prejudice he also depicted himself as the enthusiastic volunteer who had had to trick his way into the army by enlarging on his experiences in Flanders and keeping his rheumatism quiet. Regardless, the artist, with war service to his name already, was back in uniform. His military credentials were fresh and being kept as up to date as any other artist living in Britain, to say nothing of his patriotic stock rising in value too. An acceptable face was now being applied to the rebel from the pre-war era who had done so much to upset so many people. And all this at no actual risk to himself as his father had been given the vital promise that the private could not be detailed for overseas, and therefore dangerous, duties, at precisely the time that mobilization was under way for the impending Dardanelles campaign.[6] Of course, life at the Third London General Hospital in Wandsworth was far from perfect and had its stressful and unpleasant moments, but at least it was safe. Within a few days the concerned father started to record in his journals how unhappy his son was with the food,[7] then the next day, 'Very bad account of his life at Wandsworth hospital from Rich who seems unutterably miserable among the men, nurses and officers.'[8] Again, records show the mood swings and depressions, seen at the Slade and now in the army, which were to get progressively worse, and at an ever-increasing pace. Certainly he was not entering back into the spirit of the army, on which his reputation was being built, with anything less than absolute contempt. Far from leaving him to it however, his father was constantly inviting him to dinner and even went into the hospital from time to time to make sure his son was in reasonable spirits.[9] But the work in the army was hard and regimented in comparison to what he had known in the Red Cross, and before long he found himself undertaking a variety of grim tasks which included emptying bedpans, building roads, cooking, unloading hospital trains, helping in operating theatres and dealing with shell-shock victims (fig. 34). The lack of liberty he found appalling and the seemingly unlimited variety of tasks to which he could be set depressing. On a light-hearted note he recorded in his autobiography that a colleague had commented to him, on hearing his complaints, that the only thing the army could not do to you was 'put you in the family way'.[10] With little time to paint or sketch, and with the demand for blind adherence to orders, Richard saw a whole new element to the war, away from dynamism, excitement, noise and heroism. In fact, he had landed himself in the worst of both worlds where now as a private soldier he had to suffer the regimentation of the military, whilst experiencing none of the artistic benefits of being near to the Front. Only months earlier he had had exactly the opposite situation. Later he wrote that this had been 'the worst job I have ever tackled in my life'[11] and hypothesized that had he not been removed from it he would have ended up 'catching' the nervous and mental disorders of the men he was looking after.[12] The threat of being shipped out to Mesopotamia added to his concerns, as did the whole atmosphere created by his 'fellow' artists at the hospital. The latter, most probably, was the consequence of his pre-war days as a rebel artist, and particularly as a Futurist, the co-author of the inflammatory Vital English Art. Here he got 'my first real taste of the jealousy of artists and the nastiness of intellectuals'.[13] Perhaps jealousy is not the correct sentiment to attach to the Chelsea artists who had read of themselves, only months before, that they represented 'The old, grotesque idea of genius – drunken, filthy, ragged, outcast; drunkenness the synonym of Art, Chelsea the Montmartre of London.'[14] Revenge is presumably a more accurate sentiment. The hospital magazine jokingly referred to Richard now as their only Futurist, a joke that could be sustained in the absence of the threat of the extreme original doctrine, in the heart of an environment that would not have tolerated it. Futurism, or at least his version of it, was no longer a threat, though derision still came from the older artists within the community, for whom he was still an enigma. This is substantiated by an article written in 1928, which observed that 'life was not made more pleasing by his fellow artists'. The writer went on to observe that 'a certain state of war existed at Wandsworth which was too trying for Nevinson's constitution, sapped by his experiences in the field'.[15]

While Richard was in his first week at the hospital, the Vorticist show opened at the Dore Gallery, and again his father was there to see his son's work, even in the latter's absence. Faithful as ever he wrote: 'Rich's *Searchlights*, *Return to London* & *Wound* alone seemed sane.'[16] Likewise he was continuing to push his son's work while he was at the hospital and he even recorded travelling around London with 'Richard's very beautiful lampshade' to show it to people who may be interested in commissioning more work when there was a little more time.[17] Secure in the knowledge that everything had settled into place Henry turned his attention to Salonika and Gallipoli, not to return until October.

Marriage to Katherine Knowlman

Richard was somewhat dismissive of his father in Paint and Prejudice when he reported that he had not come to his wedding, on 1 November 1915 at Hampstead Town Hall (fig. 35). He also made an unfair insinuation when he remarked that, even months later, he didn't think that his father knew about the wedding.[18] Overall one gets the impression of a father who had neither the time nor the interest in his

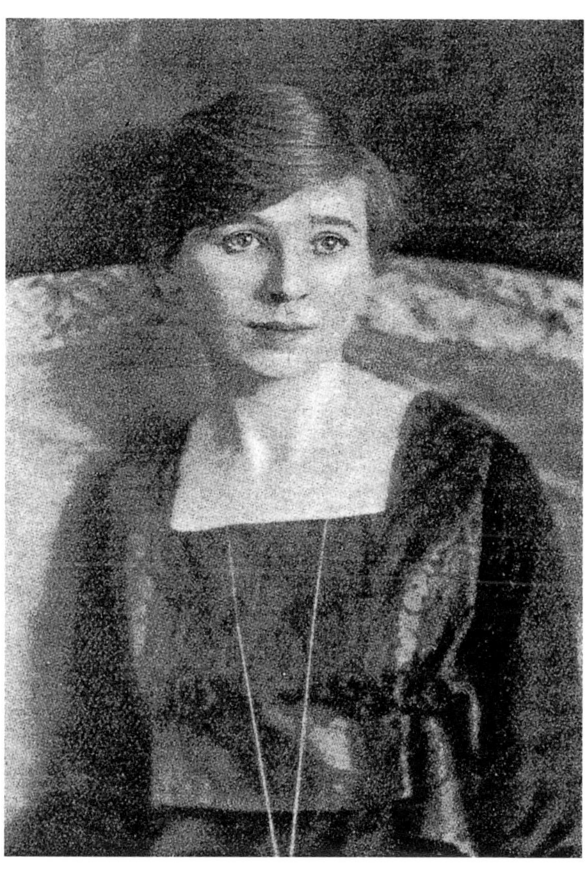

35. Kathleen Knowlman. Photograph, *Sketch*, 8 March 1918.

son to bother with even these large, life-changing, events. The reality of it is rather different. Immediately on returning from his first trip to Gallipoli, and before the wedding, he invited 'Rich and Miss Knowlman to dinner.'[19] He dined twice more with the couple before his return to the Dardanelles.[20] On one occasion his diary recorded that the true nature of the wedding of his son and Miss K. Knowlman didn't give him much choice with regard to attending. The entry reads 'Dined at home to say goodbye to Richard before his sudden marriage next week to the sweet draper's daughter of Islington.'[21] It is hardly surprising that there is a hint of sarcasm in the entry as he had patently been excluded from something which he would very much have liked to have been a part of. Richard's mother, too, confirmed this, writing 'My son informed me, suddenly, one evening that, though not engaged, he meant to get married before he was killed.'[22] She implied that the period between the announcement and the service was a mere six days.

For Richard himself marriage came at a time when he was, once again, involved with a model at the Slade, called Leila, who had become pregnant during the summer months of 1915, at around the time he was on leave from the RAMC. As Albert Rothenstein, Alvaro Guevara and he had all had been involved with her during this period it was not clear who the father was. But Leila disappeared from their lives shortly after the birth, which Richard himself arranged to take place at the Royal

Free Hospital, and so removed any potential embarrassment for the newly married couple.[23]

Henry opened the doors of his house for the couple to live in following their honeymoon in Ramsgate,[24] then wrote to his son from Messina telling him to come to the hospital in Palermo.[25] When he returned to England on 26 March 1916 he found 'Kathleen and Rich established in 3 rooms & whole house hung with his Futurisms.'[26] Richard, in the meantime, had been invalided out of the RAMC a couple of months before in January 1916 for health reasons. Whether this gravitated around psychosomatic rheumatic fever[27] or the 'heart weakness' that his mother suggested[28] is not clear. The hospital *Gazette* in its February 1916 issue, fondly reported his departure and confirmed the ill health: 'It was with very real regret that we recently bade farewell to Pte. C.R.W. Nevinson, who, after a severe illness, was invalided out of the service. We hope that Mr. Nevinson will find the time to send us some other examples of his remarkable art, and thus keep in touch with our community through the *Gazette*.' Richard himself recorded that his discharge came on the orders of a certain Dr Humphreys and that it was confirmed by Sir Alfred Gould.

Finding the Artistic Formula

However focussed and forward looking the artist may have appeared, it is worth observing that he had not completely 'gone over' to the depiction of war subjects, nor to the more moderate form of Futurism evident in his recent compositions. Though initial experimentation with modernist treatment of war subjects had yielded positive results, he was still in the process of finding out what, exhibited where, and with whom, met with critical acclaim. For example he was exhibiting watercolours with the Leeds Art Club[29] whilst simultaneously showing *Hampstead Heath on a Bank Holiday Monday* at an exhibition by the London Friday Club and also *La Circulaire, Paris* (lost) at the NEAC show towards the end of May. It may seem ironic, if not hypocritical, that he was exhibiting with the group that he had so openly and specifically attacked in the *Vital English Art* manifesto, less than a year previously, but it was still too soon to know whether or not he could succeed entirely without them.

He would have been aware too of the lukewarm reception that John Lavery and William Orpen had received for their more 'traditional' depictions at the War Academy in Burlington House. An alternative form of realism, beyond the purely visual traditions of the genre was openly recognized as being required, away from the theatrical and sentimental emphasis, which, clearly, was not telling the truth. The form of painting espoused by Lavery and Orpen served neither art nor the reality of war. In the light of this critical reaction to the 'establishment', and with his understanding of the attitudes towards extreme modernism, it became clearer why exactly his type of painting was rising to the top so quickly. His 'compromise' served neither the descriptive realism that was seen as an un-authentic aim in art and war, nor the meaningless and socially disengaged abstraction of the rebels.

The other extreme was also tested in the counter-offensive of the Vorticist exhibition of June 1915, with which he once again associated himself. In itself this was an act of defiance and a solid indication that extremist modernism was by no means dead. The exhibition at the Dore Gallery represented a heterogeneous group including Jessica Dismorr, Frederick Etchells, Henri Gaudier-Brzeska, William Roberts, Helen Saunders, Edward Wadsworth and Percy Wyndham Lewis. Other non-members of the group were invited and included David Bomberg, Richard Adeneny, Lawrence Atkinson, Duncan Grant, Jacob Kramer and Nevinson, the latter being identified in the catalogue as a 'Futurist'. The Vorticists had their own separate agenda however and Lewis identified their goals as different from the 'fuss and hysterics of the Futurists'.[30] Richard now was exhibiting with the group that, collectively, had so violently attacked him in June 1914. Either the ill feeling had been forgotten or the pre-war rebel artists had felt the need to group together as the best form of defence in these troubled and unpredictable times. Richard, despite all personal differences, might also have been seen as a useful addition to the group with which he had previously been associated as he, and he alone, had survived, then thrived on, the transition to war. He exhibited *War Crowd*, *The Wound* and *Caught: A Night Attack on Dunkirk*. None of these paintings has been traced. Apart from these three, a painting by Saunders and another by Wadsworth, the exhibition made no direct reference to the war. The irony here lies in the fact that far from producing furious and high-profile reviews, the exhibition generated very little press reaction at all. It seemed, at least from press responses, that extremist modernism, in the form of Vorticism, and its pre-war and non-war subjects, had run its course, exhausted the patience of the critics and exiled itself through its very ideology to the realms of the peripheral, if not the irrelevant. The *Westminster Gazette*[31] talked of 'artistic bankruptcy' and isolated only Richard's *War Crowd* for the mildest of praise, though the reviewer found it bewildering that he should make chaos out of unity. The *Daily Graphic* summed up succinctly, claiming 'nobody cares twopence about the lot of them'.[32] It was not only a rejection of the group and what it stood for, but also represented a distinct lack of patience which became tantamount to a personal attack, especially when it asked why more artists in the group had not followed Gaudier-Brzeska to war (and to death). For the critics, these radicals were still linked to *kultur*, threat, Prussianism, if indeed they were worthy of an accolade at all, and this was a reaction Richard would have noted with interest, and made a mental note to avoid in the future. In the 'War Number' of *Blast*, containing the woodcut version of *Returning to the Trenches*,[33] which was published in July 1915, Lewis reflected an appreciation of this when he parodied what others might be saying of him and the group. 'May the mortality amongst the Cubists, Carnivorists, Fauvists and Vorticists at the front be excessive. May those who survive have nothing but their feet left to paint with, and may those not at the front die of starvation.'[34] It is perhaps worthy of note that Lewis did not include the Futurists in this list. The war was changing art and the public reaction to it, whether Lewis accepted the fact or not. In the eyes of the public, their bohemian cloak and hat was now synonymous with the German *pickelhaube* helmet.[35]

Frank Rutter explained why Richard's brand of Futurism was thriving while Vorticism was in its death throes: 'The argument would seem to be that the representative element can never wholly be eliminated from painting: but, on the other hand, it ought always to be subordinated to the significance and harmony of design.'[36] This is the balance, or compromise, that Richard had found and which had acted as his passport into public acceptance and credibility. That is not to say that his acceptance was universal as the *Westminster Gazette* review of the Vorticist exhibition suggests. 'Mr Nevinson does make use of his mind, his confusion is never quite confounded. We can, if we will, pick up the threads; but we need a greater reward for our labour than Mr. Nevinson offers us.'[37] The *Athenaeum* was not slow to realize either that 'Mr. Nevinson . . . seems out of place in this particular gallery'.[38]

Charles Harrison, writing in 1981, acknowledged this crisis of degrees in modern painting when he wrote 'Had the dubious concept of the necessity of an abstract art perhaps been pushed too far? Could the Vorticists' claims for the representativeness of their art still be sustained? Did anyone much care in 1915?'[39]

The 'Tommies' Royal Academy'

A positive side-effect of Richard's time in the RAMC was his participation, alongside the twenty-five other artists serving there, in the hospital publication, *Gazette*, edited by family friend Ward Muir, and also in the *R.A.M.C. Exhibition, Third London General Hospital* in September 1915. This was organized by a certain Lieutenant Colonel Bruce Porter, who converted a recreational hut in the grounds of the hospital for an exhibition of the artists employed there and for which there would be no admission to the public, except on special application.[40] This 'Tommies' Royal Academy' set up an interesting new context in which art was to be viewed, out of the national spotlight, away from the critics and the press, and yet caught between the alpha and omega of the art world, the 'common man' and the artist himself. Perhaps, it was felt, the exhibition would be of benefit to recuperating patients and certainly the proceeds of any sales would benefit the hospital's benevolent fund. The *British Architect* patriotically and enthusiastically talked of the Empire's sons and questioned:

> What can artists, sculptors, musicians, and men of letters do to help their Motherland at such a time as this? Some of the younger men have put aside the palette, the chisel and the pen, to fight for her; not a few have laid down their lives for her. But the others – those who are too old or physically unfit – what of them?[41]

The same report quoted Bruce Porter as saying 'even the arts of peace can be brought in to alleviate pain and suffering. It is all a question of putting every man's genius, or services, to the best and proper use for the nation.' Over one hundred paintings and sculptures were eventually exhibited, the majority of which were watercolours, flower studies, landscapes and portraits, making Richard's contribution atypical. These were: *The Automobilist*, *Returning to the Trenches*, *Arrival at*

Dunkirk and *Ypres After the First Bombardment.* The exhibition itself was as diverse a collection of paintings as was exhibited together throughout the duration of the war with all styles and 'isms' represented, from the Royal Academy to Richard's own Futurist pieces, to say nothing of studies for artificial limbs. Away from the hardened art world this was a military and a medical affair, with the ex-rebel taking patients around, dressed in his own private's uniform (fig. 27).[42] Some critics were admitted, such as Marriott, Konody and the critic from the *Athenaeum*, but they all decided that this was neither the time nor the place to commence the usual barrage of abuse aroused in the normal London arena. Besides, Richard's pictures had all been exhibited before. That is not to say, however, that the audience was not a critical one, for whatever they lacked in art education, they made up for in matters military learned at the Western Front. Of all the audiences that would not tolerate the romanticized panoramas of heroism and patriotism associated previously with battle painting, or indeed the indecipherable compositions of the extreme modernists, this would surely be the most critical. To the common man, the soldier and the youth of Britain, Richard was now exhibiting his art in what would be an alternative test of worth, and one on which his future would very much depend. Observing these reactions and then talking of *Returning to the Trenches*, Konody could observe that it was 'the sanest, the most logical, the most convincing demonstration of Futurist principles that I have so far seen. No purely representative method could ever render so happily the swinging rhythm of the marching soldiers' movements'.[43] Marriot observed that 'the exhibition has, properly, nothing to do with war' and suggested that perhaps that was precisely the last thing a wounded soldier might want to see in his convalescence.[44] Also, for the critic from the *Athenaeum*, his paintings, though artistically sound, were inappropriate here as they were very definitely for the healthy, not the vulnerable.[45] The exhibition then was not dependent on commercial or critical success. It did, however, serve as an interim report on the state of his art, and the progress of English Futurism, one year into the conflict. Certainly there was nothing to suggest the demise of the 'ism', rather the implication that, if anything, it was gaining in respectability and credibility in addressing the pictorial war issues of the day, with an audience that would be critical in an alternative way of both subject matter and technique.

Where criticism might be levelled at Richard is in his frequent straying from the parameters of Futurist theories altogether for the more utilitarian depictions that were to appear in *The Gazette of the Third London Hospital* then later in the *Daily Sketch*. These, at first, were mere illustrations of the hospital 'from the water tank tower'.[46] Artistically they hardly compare to any of the main canvases examined so far. The next issue in November, however, contained a much more serious image entitled *Night Arrival of the Wounded* (fig. 36). Though used to illustrate a story, 'The Captive's Homecoming', specifically relating to an event on 7 October 1915, the image was seen to be an authentic interpretation of a concrete event. Here too the compromise between truth to materials and truth to nature was evident, epitomizing the balancing act between 'realism' and 'modernism', between purely artistic and being relevant to a specific public. If anything the pictures are more reminis-

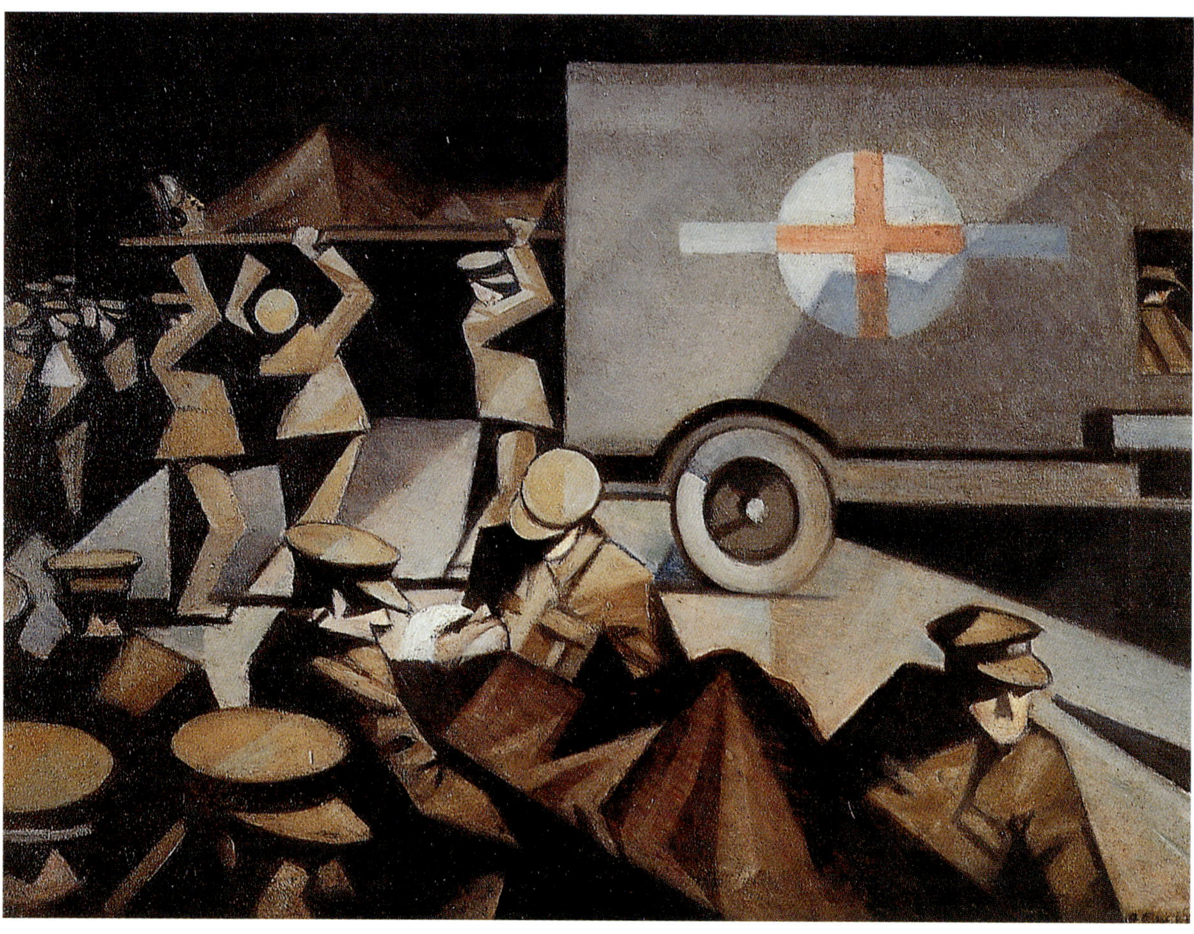

36. *Night Arrival of the Wounded*, 1915. Oil on canvas, 46.3 x 61.2 cm. Private Collection.

cent of his Parisian compositions such as *Bravo*, but they are, after all, illustrations for a magazine and should be treated as such.[47]

Refining Acceptable Parameters in Subject and Technique

November 1915 saw the opening of the third exhibition of the London Group at the Goupil Galleries, which, though distinctly limited in numbers and in extremist modernists (Lewis, Bomberg, Etchells and Epstein were all non-exhibitors), found Richard representing the 'far left' with four paintings: *A Bridge at Marseilles* (lost), *A Deserted Trench* (possibly *Flooded Trench on the Yser*), *Bursting Shell* (fig. 38) and *La Guerre de Trous* (fig. 37), and the only sculpture in the show, entitled *Une Americaine* (lost).[48] Perhaps the 'purge' expected of the war was now finally making its presence felt, and the press was not slow to observe this and speculate upon it, agreeing that the absence of the Vorticists was no loss. The London Group could now be taken seriously. Claude Phillips wrote succinctly 'The white heat of this great world crisis through which we are passing will sooner or later separate the pure ore from the dross, and under penalty of utter extinction compel a return to artistic sanity.'[49] For Konody, even Richard, 'our one and only Futurist, is becoming ever more rational and intelligible'.[50] The suggestion was that the return from the wilderness of abstraction was continuing and hopefully would soon have his modern painting more in line with that of the Cumberland Market Group also exhibiting at the show. The dogmatic and belligerent Vorticists were desperately conspicuous by their absence and this alone was seen as a positive homogenizing effect on English painting. Neo-Realism was heralded as the success story of the day, though Richard too took the spotlight, admired for both fighting spirit and intelligible work. P. G. Konody, once again, became his chief apologist writing at length about his aims and objectives and defending his work to a public that remained, even yet, in need of convincing:

> Mr. Nevinson's steadfastness of purpose must surely remove any doubt as to his sincerity. He is a firm believer in the theories of Futurism as expounded by Boccioni and his Italian followers: the displacement and interpretation of objects, the search for 'force lines' dynamism, and the cutting of the very atmosphere into geometric planes – a meeting point of Cubism and Futurism. But unlike the Italians, who are getting ever more abstract and incomprehensible, Mr. Nevinson applies himself to finding a compromise between the Futurist ideal and the normal vision.[51]

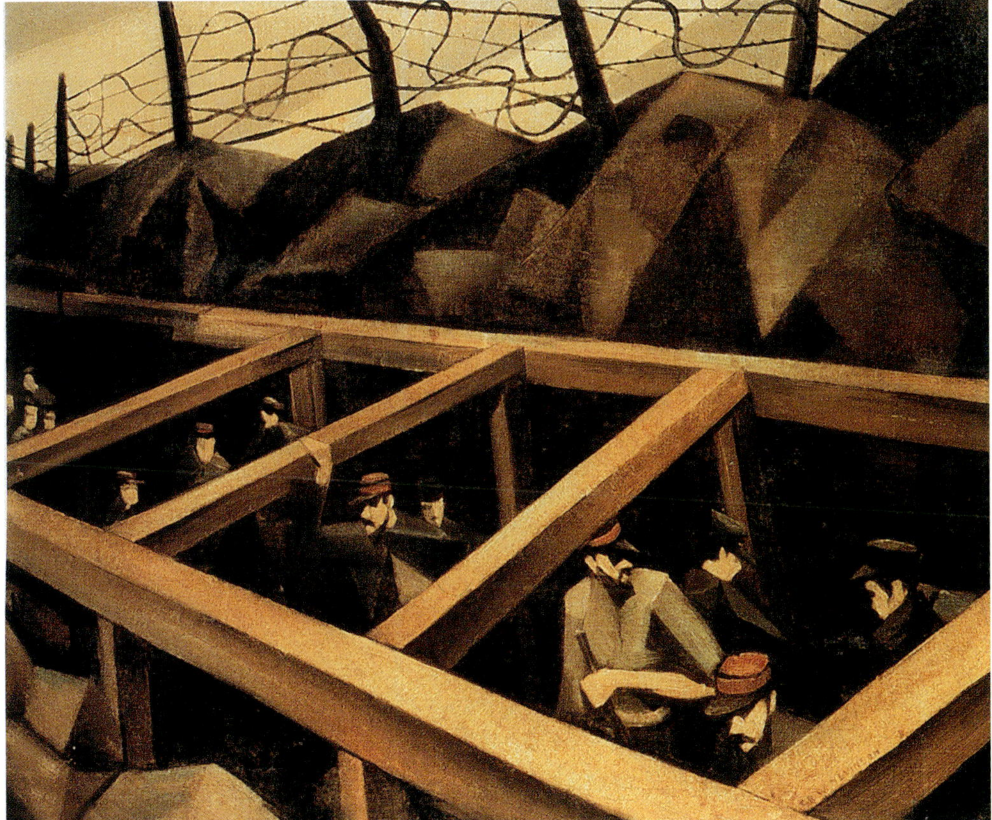

37. *La Guerre de Trous*, 1915. Oil on canvas, 51 x 61 cm. Private collection.

That said, the critic was not forthcoming with praise for the two non-war Futurist works, *Une Americaine* (a sculpture which was generally recognized as aiming to be humorous) and *The Bridge at Marseilles* (lost), preferring the other two paintings exhibited, which were, on the whole, more moderate and thus less thoroughbred Futurist. It was not the first time that non-war scenes were not being well received. Konody, in the same review, expressed the intolerance with which Futurism could be viewed when taken out of the war context when he wrote of *The Bridge at Marseilles* that the artist 'amuses himself, but not his audience'. Peacetime Futurism had no place, according to the critic, in this age of war and now represented only 'a tiresome repetition of the worn-out kaleidoscopic formula – bits of objects thrown together pell-mell with a sprinkling of letters'.[52] Interestingly it appeared that the survival of Futurism, even amongst Richard's more ardent supporters, now depended on the subject matter of war.

Other critics, such as Frank Rutter, tended, when acknowledging the success of paintings like *A Deserted Trench*, to shift the emphasis, and thus the reason for success, onto the emotional and expressive response of the viewer to the painting. Instead of celebrating the modernity of war in the vocabulary of modernism and capturing the dynamism and force of the destructive moment, the writer talked of the success of the composition stemming from the 'powerful, dramatic and emotional presentation of the thing seen and felt'.[53] Similar reviews were to follow which praised the sentiment, talked of emotional intensity, praised the intensification of reality, and mused as to how the formalizing influence of Futurism enhanced this ability beyond anything that an optical reality could offer. Line, form and colour, as a language in itself, was accepted as a viable and efficient means for relating back to the gallery what was happening on the Western Front, so long as it was adequately rooted in a pictorial realism that made the work accessible. Charles Marriot removed any ambiguity when, using *A Deserted Trench*, he explained what the theory was behind Richard's work:

> The object, we take it, of all such expedients is to intensify reality; and they always come off most successfully when the suggestion of optical illusion is frankly avoided. The eye is accepted as the channel to the mind, but not as a critic of reality in itself; and any person of ordinary intelligence soon learns his way about the new convention.[54]

The *Observer* too noted the shift in Futurist priorities as seen in this work when it recognized that the essence of the work lay in 'the substitution of plastic for expressive values'.[55] This did not lead to confusion or infuriation with modern techniques as may have been expected. On the contrary, the *Standard* claimed that it was 'as convincing a picture of the conditions of modern warfare as one could wish to see'. The acceptance of the technique used in depicting the scene was understood entirely when the same article explained: 'The object, we take it, of all such expedients is to intensify reality.'[56] Randall Davies summed up by writing that 'as a piece of pure translation it is perfectly marvellous'.[57] For others 'Mr. Nevinson's formula has vision behind it; he is an interesting artist, and his Futurism, or Cubism, needs no defence.'[58] This was the acceptable face of modernism, the moderation that would secure the artist relevance in a society with very much graver concerns. Eksteins, more recently, has attributed this success and acceptability not only to compromise on the part of the artist but also to the developing aesthetic sensibilities which had been maturing from the first Post-Impressionist exhibition at the Grafton Galleries. Basically, he argues, the two sensibilities moved to meet each other as opposed to one making a total compromise.[59] That is why newspapers could report 'If the modernists can show us things like this instead of cutting absurd capers and making picture puzzles there is perhaps, after all, a future for the most refactory of them.'[60] But the experiment was only acceptable up to a point, and Richard believed that he had reached a high-water mark, in terms of abstract compositions, with *Bursting Shell*, which had attracted mixed reviews. In so doing he had identified an important parameter beyond which it would be inadvisable to proceed.

Running at the same time as the London Group exhibition was the winter show of the NEAC and, regardless of the attack in *Vital English Art*, Richard exhibited at least one painting here, entitled *Campden Town* (lost). The exhibition, held at the galleries of the Royal Society of British Artists, was widely reviewed, the critic for the *Westminster Gazette* pinpointing the artistic dichotomy by saying that it was 'mildly surprising to find [Nevinson] in this dignified company'.[61] The *Daily Chronicle* talked of how even 'young blood runs coolly',[62] and how his contribution, in addition to the title, was very much in keeping with the Camden Town style of painting. Much more interestingly is how the *Observer* treads with care when noting that he was returning from his strong Futurist affiliations. 'To say that the change would be regrettable does not exactly imply an unconditional approval of Futurist principles, but the conviction that Mr. Nevinson alone among the artists of his group seemed able to exploit these principles in intelligent and intelligible fashion.'[63] His presence as a Futurist seemed welcome, perhaps even valued, even though the writer still believed that there were other, less credible, Futurists operating in England, even in late 1915. The *New Witness* also propelled him to a level of credibility denied to his colleagues when it said 'He is a disciple of Marinetti and Marinetti's Futurist painter friends, but he is the only one to have the courage to proclaim it. Most of Marinetti's other disciples in England, whilst helping themselves liberally to his ideas, have not only forsworn their master but publicly abused him.'[64] Grudgingly, there appeared to be a changing atmosphere, which, in acknowledging the success of some of his war paintings, also implied that some critics would not like to see his retreat from Futurism go too far. And so the second parameter was set, identifying a level of conservative realism behind which it was no longer deemed necessary to retreat. Richard still had his own doubts, as seen in a letter to Professor Sadler, remaining firm in his conviction that his modern painting must be upheld in this time of war. His fears were summed up in his own words when he talked of the 'art-dealers war' where 'he will push nothing but the "pretty-pretty" or "antique" & run no risks with the public that seems getting more sentimental & reactionary as the war goes on'.[65] Now, however, he had a clearer idea of what acceptable modern painting might be. Perhaps Douglas Fox-Pitt, owner of several of Richard's paintings, came closest to the artist's impending autonomy when he wrote in a letter to the *Pall Mall Gazette*: 'We want a picture to remind us that under no conceivable circumstances can war be described as glorious. I do not think that Mr. Nevinson would describe himself as a 'Futurist.' He would probably be content to call himself a painter.'[66] It would be naïve, however, to believe that Richard just happened to chance upon the right formula, introspectively pursuing his individual goals as a painter. An individual, as Fox-Pitt suggested, yes, but also fully aware of the demands of the society in which he was living also, and determined to cater for its apparent need.

In these early stages of the war, Peters Corbett believes, 'Nevinson captured the ground available to modernism', by introducing a 'new traditionalism' to replace what had been seen as 'an oppressive orthodoxy'.[67] The environment of 'freedom' in which his work thrived, merely represented the eye of the storm. His moderation had helped push the extreme coteries even further to the 'left' in the eyes of the critics, and in turn, to eventual, if only temporary, obscurity. He had side-stepped, perhaps even catalysed, this artistic cull. The critics would have favoured his war modernism as their understanding was still sympathetic, broadly, to the era of the 1910 and 1912 Post-Impressionist exhibitions, as opposed to the developments of the previous eighteen months. It would be naïve, however, to believe that this would be anything more than a temporary arrangement. Nevertheless, when war broke out Richard had taken that Futurist vocabulary to the Front, only to have his fears confirmed by what he witnessed in the opening weeks. Distancing himself publicly from the suicidal clauses of Futurist dictum concerning war, he continued to operate, though cautiously, in the mode of Futurist technique, with which his apprenticeship had so usefully been served, and in doing so produced some of the most powerful images from the conflict. This output was agreeable to the artistic and critical community of which he was now a part, and to the public to whom his work became almost universally acceptable. The nature of his affiliation to Futurism had, however, changed from that of pre-August, 1914. Firstly, he abandoned the high-profile publicity occasions which had accompanied his pre-war work, letting the painting, and complimentary reviews, do the talking. Secondly, he adopted a selection procedure which meant that he could use Futurist techniques where necessary, and move away from them entirely in other circumstances. In this respect he could be accused of displaying a lack of consistency, or even a lack of loyalty to one doctrine, in a radically changed environment where obedient adherence would have been counter-productive. Conversely it could be argued that the implementation of a selection procedure, through trial and error, in a rapidly changing environment over the course of the opening seventeen months of the conflict was the natural evolutionary process to undertake. The reason for the change may also be due to his experiences at the front or it may simply have been the product of common sense in realizing that there was no sympathy, and therefore no future, in pretending that the Great War was not happening and that the public psyche was not going to be deeply affected by it. To embrace the subject of war, and yet to display appropriately an extreme shift neither to the left, nor to the right, was essential to critical acceptance. This reaction swung public sympathy away from the pre-war extremes of modernism and academicism, and Richard, through his exhibitions and experimentation, would have realized this. To equate modernism with Prussianism, and academicism with deceit, clearly suggests that a middle course was advisable. His path was that of moderate modernism, though it could be suggested that an equally successful route could have been that of moderate academicism. Peters Corbett acknowledged the former, saying 'The equation of a successful traditionalist art with the positive qualities of the nation was the obverse of the conceptual coin which equated modernism with the violence and destructiveness of war.'[68] Lastly, Futurism as the English public perceived the Italian notion of it, with its pro-war rhetoric was not a good movement with which to be too closely associated. His rejection of the extreme Italian rhetoric removed a foreign threat from perceptions of his work, returning it to an English form of modernist depiction, and this would have been welcome at a time when subservience to any foreign idea would have been extremely unwelcome. In his introduction of a personal, and moderate, modernism he side-stepped the awaited purge which had led to the decline of his more radical artistic peers. His compromise was all the more tolerable in the light of the still existing confusion surrounding what exactly Futurism was. Though the label was widely used, not least in association with his name, it was done so ambiguously, creating enough space for lateral movement on the part of the artist to adjust more readily to the needs of the war and the artistic climate of the time. More importantly, he recognized his own set of goals and artistic objectives, rather than merely imitating those of his Futurist counterparts, and in doing so created his own artistic identity, perhaps for the first time in his career. The fact that he had labelled himself a Futurist before the war would obviously have implications even after the conflict had begun, but it did not, in his eyes, condemn him to an inescapable commitment to a philosophy now partially redundant. The debt to Futurism remained clear though by now it was by no means a blind commitment. In an environment of countless dichotomies of expectation and reality, propaganda and experience, pastoral settings and murderous technology, Richard approached the subject of modern art and modern war. In his findings, with compromise, the two were far from mutually exclusive. Perhaps then, Harrison was accurate when he described his work as a 'moderate brand of post-Cubist modernism'.[69] He was certainly not accurate when he wrote: 'He was not, after all, an original painter, but he was a good reporter.'[70]

Finally, Futurism itself was changing in the face of conflict. To compare Richard's war painting with that of pre-war philosophy is hardly a valid comparison especially in the light of the fact that Marinettian Futurism itself saw the need for change. Perhaps his defence is best rested with the words of a letter from Marinetti to Severini three months after the outbreak of war (but before Italy's involvement):

> What we need is not only direct collaboration in the splendour of this conflagration but also the plastic expression of this futurist hour. I mean a more ample expression so strong and synthetic that it will hit the imagination and the eye of all or almost all intelligent readers. I don't see this as a prostitution of plastic dynamism but believe that the Great War, intensely lived by Futurist painters, can produce true convulsions in their imaginations, pushing them to a brutal simplification of radiantly clear lines...Paintings or sketches will probably become less abstract, perhaps a bit too realistic, perhaps in a way a more advanced form of Post-Impressionism.[71]

Marinetti himself, though almost certainly not speaking for the Futurist movement in general, perfectly, though perhaps coincidentally, described the Futurist metamorphosis that occurred in Richard's painting and if anything suggested that it may have been evolutionary as opposed to a form of betrayal. In the light of the ensuing *rappel à l'ordre*,[72] on a European-wide basis, the moderate shift to the right is neither surprising nor dubious. Watney, in *English Post-Impressionism*, confirms this belief and observes quite logically that 'No art can exist without an audience, be it real or imaginary.'[73] The fact that Richard's brand of Futurism survived, and indeed went from strength to strength, is testimony in itself to this fact.

8

Credibility and Crisis 1916

I became the talk of London[1]

Building on the successes of 1915, discharged from the army for legitimate health reasons, and with time to concentrate on his work, Richard could identify and cater for the critical tastes of the era. He lost no time and at the Allied Artists Association, in March 1916, he exhibited three works, each with an explanatory title to assist comprehension.[2] These were *Violence: An Abstraction* (lost) *La Mitrailleuse: An Illustration* (fig. 39) and *Night: Light: Crowd: An Interpretation* (lost). *La Mitrailleuse* was the first to draw attention and Rutter commented: 'It is one of the best war pictures I have seen this year, sufficiently "futurist" to be piquant and distinguished, yet not so relentlessly futurist . . . as to be bewilderingly disintegrated'.[3] Marriot said of the same painting that 'It shows Mr Nevinson can beat most Academic painters on their own ground'[4] whilst Lewis-Hind enthusiastically believed that it was 'the best and most ruthless illustration of the menace of the deadly machine-war that has been produced'.[5] All the paintings propounded the theme of war in an exhibition that promoted the artist as patriot and martyr, through special displays of Henri Gaudier-Brzeska and Henri Doucet, recently killed on the Western Front, and through a 'Roll of Honour' in the catalogue, which listed which artists were serving where and with whom. The implication was that this was not a time to abandon the war theme, but that on the contrary, it was precisely the time to make the most of any military credentials available. Likewise, a 'modern' approach to painting was to be encouraged, so long as it was tempered with moderation.

Later, in March, Richard exhibited six works at the Friday Club, in the Alpine Galleries, all on war-related subjects.[6] Once again, critics began to comment on the success of his moderation in technique, the suitability of his subjects and, perhaps more than anything else, his military credentials, which gave him the authority, and right, to paint the war as he had perceived it. Now, it was commented, 'his gropings in the past have led him to a compromise between clear illustration and Futurist abstraction, which is absolutely intelligible without being . . . literal representation'.[7] Moreover, he was an individual, a lone voice of truth, reason and daring, both as a soldier and an artist. Having taken what was necessary from pre-war eccentricities and excesses he had now, with the catalyst of war, found his niche. In short, according to Konody, Richard, the modernist artist, had 'arrived'.[8] Observantly, *Truth* attempted to get to the bottom of this success and concluded: 'In doing so Mr Nevinson has stooped to sufficient realism to make himself intelligible to the layman.'[9] It was a claim that would be reiterated over and over again, even by the artist himself. The article also tended to use the word 'cinematography' to describe his work, rather than its more aggressive forebear, 'Futurist'. By creating a new definition, an alternative path was suggested to lead away from the troublesome polemic movement and its pre-war associations.

In May he exhibited a further three war subjects at the NEAC, hinting that the pre-war antagonisms had now been forgotten and that he, even as a non-member, was winning respect from factions previously hostile to his art.[10] Certainly, the self-destructive pre-war antagonisms within artistic circles were being put on the back burner and now Richard was even being discussed in articles with grand titles such as 'The Reward of the Patriot'. Here his military credentials eclipsed almost all other considerations and made his works, in the eyes of Salis, both 'somehow different' and 'the real thing'.[11]

But a new, and much more daunting, crisis was emerging simultaneously and this first appeared in Henry's journals on 3 May 1916, taking the form of a rather understated and ambiguous comment, which read: 'Anxious too about Rich and the new Bill'.[12] This new legislation, which followed in the wake of conscription at the hands of the Military Service Bill, was the Compulsion Bill. This called for the re-examination of every discharged soldier with the strong possibility that they would be compelled to rejoin the ranks and return to military service at the Front. In short, a soldier discharged once was not necessarily out for the duration of the war unless he failed a second examination. Richard had been discharged from the RAMC due to a possible attack of psychosomatic rheumatic fever at the end of 1915, and he had even been hospitalized in the Wandsworth ward where he had been working up to that point. Returning his attentions to the art world, and now outside the armed forces, yet with military credentials and honour intact, he had assumed that his role in the war was now over. With the assistance of his father, his friends, critics and public figures, and with the strong collection of paintings on which he had been working, the future now seemed secure and the risk of a return minimized. The new Bill, if passed, could put an end to all that and could find the artist taken away from London and put in the 'firing line'. Perhaps too this time, his father would not be able to secure him work behind allied lines, or, better still, at home. On 5 May, with a sense of relief, the journal entry was 'Rich is clear as a discharged soldier'.[13] Less than a week later the doubt returned as there was a 'Threatened inclusion of discharged soldiers in army again [which] makes Richard's position again uncertain.'[14] The crisis would re-emerge later in the year.

The NEAC exhibition, tellingly, overlapped with the fourth London Group exhibition at the Goupil Gallery in June, where Richard exhibited three more paintings and a collection of illustrations from the *Gazette* of the Third London General

Hospital.[15] As 'honourable secretary'[16] and member of the hanging committee, he was now moving closer to the centre of this reputedly extremist group, assisted by the complete absence of Lewis, Bomberg, Wadsworth and Roberts. Much of the work exhibited there, such as *La Patrie* (fig. 41), whilst being socially engaged, was definitively moving away from the unintelligibility of pre-war abstractions. Or at least, where modernist vocabulary was used, it was not as an end in itself, but as an expressive component, crucial to the nature of the composition. Rutter later commented: 'It was true that Nevinson's paintings left something to be desired in their quality of paint, but they had enough virtue to carry their message home.'[17] He had also combined the interests and priorities beneficially in addressing 'the claims of war and art'.[18] The press now referred to this much more frequently as Cubism, rather than Futurism, and it was not an error that the artist did anything to redress. Certain factions encouraged him to drop the gimmicks and be who he wanted to be, writing 'Come out of it, Nevinson, and let us see you as you are!' They went on to say 'Leave the tomfoolery to idle or ungifted youths, who use it either to convince people they are clever, or to avoid the hard work that is necessary for all sound art'.[19] Richard would not have been unaware of the number of critics who now believed that the association with Futurism had had its day and was instead now holding him back.[20] In addition to this came a 'leak' to the press that he was to be sent to the Front as an official war artist, an idea that appalled writers who asked 'But why send a Futurist?'[21] Throughout early June the press was full of the story, which once again, placed him in the same articles as the words 'banned', 'censorship', 'genius', and, not for the last time, depicted him as the truth teller, stifled at the hands of officialdom.[22] (Later Lady Cunard came forward as the originator of the idea.) Though a false alarm, it was noted by the artist how the association with Futurism, or extreme avant-garde theories, might have stood in the way of a genuine offer.

Exhibition of Paintings and Drawings of War by C.R.W. Nevinson (Late Private R.A.M.C.)

The Leicester Galleries show in September 1916 was undoubtedly the exhibition that made Richard's name as the painter of modern war, or indeed the modern painter of war. *Paint and Prejudice* attributed the concept of a one-man show entirely to Charles Lewis-Hind, who, during Richard's illness following his discharge from the RAMC, had taken several of his works to Messrs Brown and Phillips of the Leicester Galleries, and confirmed a booking. This is substantiated by Lewis-Hind himself when he wrote that, having seen *La Mitrailleuse* in the artist's studio, he 'was conquered, [and] went in hot haste to the Leicester Galleries, and told the proprietors that they must, and quickly, hold a Nevinson exhibition'.[23] This was made possible by the cancellation of the planned Alfred Munnings exhibition. Fired by the opportunity Richard recorded that he 'painted and painted and painted'[24] and that with the help of previous patrons he borrowed back paintings that he had previously sold.

A valuable relationship formed by his father during the Boer War and strengthened during the Gallipoli campaign when he was based with him on the island of Imbros, was with the commander of the fated expedition, Sir Ian Hamilton. Within a fortnight of his return Henry was at the Hamilton home asking Sir Ian if he might consider writing the foreword for the catalogue of his son's forthcoming one man show at the Leicester Galleries.[25] Three days after the suggestion the journal records Lady Hamilton coming round to 'take away one of Rich's pictures'.[26] Using his influential friends, Henry was, once again, taking his son's military credentials to an unprecedented height, especially for a private, and placing him within a social sphere which would encourage the patronage of the 'establishment', and attract the spotlight effectively, and beneficially, to the best of his ability. The way was not yet clear, however, and having attended both the NEAC[27] and the London Group at the Goupil Galleries,[28] both of which had had Richard's paintings on display, Henry continued to push for the maximum opportunity for his son. On 30 June (the eve of the Battle of the Somme), he was dining at Sir Ian and Lady Hamilton's, where *Barges on the Thames* (lost) was hanging, discussing the involvement with the Leicester Gallery show again. The next evening he was giving dinner to 'The Whites and the Leicester Gallery man', and by the end of August he had had the official acknowledgement that Sir Ian Hamilton would write the introduction. Though he had hardly jumped at the opportunity Sir Ian came the following evening to see the pictures and was apparently 'very charming & friendly & admiring'.[29] It was the father directing operations, however, and this continued when, on 1 September, he wrote 'Helped Rich with his preface to the programme of his show.'[30] Henry also took charge of the distribution of invitations and even before the opening oversaw every step of the hanging procedure and made sure that those who might be useful to his son saw it too.[31] On 9 September Henry went again to watch the preparations at the Leicester Galleries with his old friend and head of the Department of Propaganda, C.F.G. Masterman. This prominent Liberal, and government figure, would play a central role in Richard's future in the light of the conscription crisis of 1917–18, which was, at this stage, beginning to unfold.

On the same day, having received Sir Ian's first draft, it was the father who wrote to thank him, not the son. Once again the autobiography made no mention of Henry nor of the groundwork that had gone into this distinction. Rather it says 'General Sir Ian Hamilton honoured me with the following preface'.[32] Sir Ian's preface gave it, in effect, a soldier's blessing albeit in a form of 'high diction' which hardly seemed relevant to the works on display, or, for that matter, to the priorities of the artist himself. Hamilton wrote of the quality of truth and of the symbolic relevance of the artist's compositions 'crossing the bloodiest pages of history' resulting in the fact that 'we come away feeling that the cup of war is filled not only with blood and tears, but also with the elixir of life'.[33] The importance of the introduction came perhaps from the author's identity, as opposed to what he had actually said.[34] The general's introduction, however, had at least placed his painting in an acceptable context of war, just as the artist himself would do for his painting in the context of art in 'Note by the Artist'. This preface to the catalogue clarified and justified his eclecticism and moderation, further claiming 'But it will be seen from the later examples of my painting that (though working within a geometrical convention) I free myself from all pedantic and academic theories of "Post" or "Neo", as well as from the deadening influence of the idolatry to "Primitives" and "Old Masters" which has lately caused so many enfeebled and emasculated revivals.'[35]

Through the platform of the catalogue he had dissociated himself from the artistic movements and coteries of the day, whilst leaving his reputation as a modernist very much intact. His military credentials were used with maximum effect by his neither praising nor glorifying the war, whilst avoiding becoming one of the growing, and largely unacceptable, band of conscientious objectors. Having the support of one of the British Army's most senior generals, albeit not at the peak of his popularity, did nothing to hurt his standing with his newly targeted audience either. Ironically, or perhaps tactfully, his key images at the show were not of British soldiers but rather the French *poilus* (or squaddies). This, it could be argued, kept him clear of the censor, of overtly sentimental and patriotic emotions and expectations on the part of the public and critic, whilst boosting the legend of the artist's own internationalism. In later interviews he would quite often state that he had been 'attached' to the French army during the opening stages of the conflict. Appearing at the show, with a limp and a walking stick, increased the insinuation that he was 'just home' from the Front. In fact he had been home for eighteen months and had been at the Front for ten weeks in total. He had never lied, but the ambiguity of his statements and implications was open to misinterpretation. In short, he was now perceived as the intelligent and vital young artist who hated modern war, but who could depict it well, and indeed, who could fight it well. It was because of their admiration for the soldier/artist in general, his mother recorded, that visitors flocked to the house, like Robert Nicols, Siegfried Sassoon and Osbert and Sacheverell Sitwell.

Announcements concerning the opening of the Leicester Galleries show were abundant throughout the national press, promoting Richard as a hero and patriot, but also, tantalizingly, hinting that the preface for the exhibition was going to be written by 'A very Distinguished Soldier.'[36] When *Paintings and Drawings of War by C.R.W. Nevinson (Late Private R.A.M.C.)* opened on 26 September 1916, Richard was already on the crest of a wave critically and was rapidly becoming one of the most respected and admired 'modern' artists in wartime London. Oliver Brown, the gallery owner, reiterated this over fifty years later when he wrote: 'It was not until 1916 that we found a young English artist who provided a sensational vision of modern warfare.'[37] Sitwell agreed, saying that for the first time the public was 'given the whole business of modern warfare'.[38] Elsewhere it was enthusiastically reported that 'Never have the conditions of modern warfare been interpreted with such vital force and convincing realism.'[39] Even traditionally conservative newspapers called him 'the first British artist to give really profound and pictorial expression to the emotions aroused by the war' saying that the inherent significant form and pattern appealed to the artistic sensibility while the quality of truth appealed to the soldier.

It was, in their summation, 'le beau dans l'horrible'.[40] A glance through the catalogue of the exhibition at the list of lenders gives us an indication of how successful the artist had actually been up to this point.[41] The *Daily Mirror* echoed this when it reported, before his Leicester Galleries show, 'he is distinctly "catching on". He has sold more pictures this year than ever before, three of them having been actually acquired for public galleries.'[42]

It is interesting that an ambiguity is created even in the title of the exhibition itself, and this, it could be argued, was an intentional military/publicity stunt in the light of the rising reputations of artist martyrs such as Rupert Brooke and Henri Gaudier-Brzeska. The insinuation certainly appears to be that the artist was dead, presumably killed while in the service of his country with the ambulance corps.[43] Alive, but in ill health, Richard prepared, or borrowed, thirty-five paintings, eighteen drawings and etchings, and one sculpture for the show (see appendix). He then promoted it using two photographs taken by Malcolm Arbuthnot (see jacket and fig. 28)[44] of himself in military uniform, goggles and cap complete.

Richard believed that, such were the demands of the subject matter being depicted, no one style or set of theories was sufficient to grasp effectively the range and potency of the scenes. He had learned from his experiences in 1915. Now a degree of eclecticism would be required, based on a diluted set of modernist principles, unique to the individual artist, and inevitably, in the eyes of some, seen as a form of artistic wandering. For Richard, his training in the ideologies of Cubism and Futurism (when he had expounded the concepts of virility, masculinity and the end of the era of the *dilittanti*) could scarcely have been more relevant for the task in hand. He retrospectively concluded: 'I was the first artist to paint war pictures without pageantry, without glory and without the over-coloured heroic that had made up the tradition of all war paintings up to this time.'[45] This he said he had done subconsciously, as he had seen no glory in the trenches, and had been surprised that this had brought the older generation and the clergy against him.

The exhibition represented everything he had done, on a military theme, up to that point, and to some extent was a microcosm of the works of art that had led up to his 'coming of age'. It represented no denial of styles or theories with which he had experimented previously, rather it encapsulated the path taken to this zenith of artistic credibility. The *Glasgow Herald* was quick to pick up on this point, though tempered it by saying that the seriousness of the new subject matter had almost certainly saved him from the inevitable excesses and eccentricities associated with the aforementioned movements.[46] The *Daily Chronicle* too traced the valuable pedigree and combined them with his valuable military credentials: 'He is an artist, a fighting artist, who has rampaged like a "Tank", through all the modern movements; he has bustled through Impressionism, Post impressionism, Cubism, Vorticism; and out of Cubism he has brought to birth a curious geometrical formula, sharp and glittering as a sword, which is admirably suited to his vision of this scientific, mechanical war.'[47]

For Lewis-Hind the war had given Richard's subject a gravitas which had previously been lacking in the years when he was learning his trade and was merely a 'technician'. Lewis-Hind added 'but the war has not made him, it has hastened his development, thrust his talent into a kind of intensive culture'.[48] Now he could depict not only the modern appearance of war but also the dehumanized sense of modern war, in a mechanized environment where, to quote Clutton-Brock, 'He has emptied man of his content.'[49] Importantly, however, on all but a few occasions, he managed to steer a course whereby his work was not associated with the dehumanized, mechanical militarism of Prussian *kultur*, which had dogged the radical extremes of the avant-garde from the outbreak of war.[50] This, Cournos believed, was due to the fact that the artist had come back from the extremities of pre-war rhetoric and had laid the ashes of Futurism to rest, not, as was otherwise suggested, because the medium had found itself in a new, suitable, context.[51] Lewis-Hind didn't agree and wrote: 'Then came the war, and this vivid revolutionary, eager and intelligent, had the luck of his life, got his subject, in horrible completeness, straight and deep, as you will see if you visit the Leicester Galleries.'[52]

Through a wide range of different subjects and through the different techniques used in their depiction, Richard was attempting to approach a variety of different aspects of the war, and to appeal to an equally disparate audience. Though not glorifying war, he was at least in awe of its industrial force, and the impact that that was having on the individual who fought in its midst. Through scenes of destruction, the impersonality of the conflict was being attempted, in a way that subverted the human role to that of the machine. Modern war, for Richard, was not only marvellous in all its new forms, but was dehumanizing, mundane, routine, and above all merciless. But war was also a human activity, a human tragedy, and that could not go unrecorded. It did not, and in such paintings the artist shifted both the emphasis in subject matter and technique towards a means of expression more suitable for the task in hand. But in so doing, he was also appealing to the popular beliefs that portrayed the dead civilian or allied soldier as victim of the fabricated and fictionalized atrocities of the Central Powers. This swung his subjects advantageously towards the pro-patriotic and anti-German sentiment of the day, which guaranteed the legitimacy of Britain's efforts in the conflict. It would also return his work to the mainstream of public sentiment and would compensate the public for the less intelligible mechanical imagery elsewhere in the gallery.[53] The techniques he employed, though often diverse, attempted to address these disparate elements, but not to alienate his public through use of an unintelligible medium. Likewise he had no desire to hark back to the now redundant methodology associated with the conventional depiction of war in art. Instead, in approaching a variety of themes he would have to use a variety of technical considerations, and these employed in such a way as to find the balance between an 'art for art's sake', with which the public had almost exhausted its sympathy, and a strong comprehensible narrative content, which did not owe its existence to the redundant vocabulary of tradition. H. W. Massingham reiterated this in the *Nation* when he wrote:

> For the first time in recent years, the pioneer seems to be seeking a manner which will not be merely the amusement of a coterie, but might by its directness, its force, and its simplicity, appeal even to the unsophisticated perception. I can

> imagine that even Tolstoy might have welcomed this rude, strong style, a reaction against the art of leisure and riches.[54]

On top of everything else, Richard was being cast, or was casting himself, in the role of uncompromising truth teller, appealing to the masses, and unafraid of what the repercussions might be. Not only was he in the perfect environment for a modern painter of his pedigree, but he had also served in Belgium and France, the latter of which he claimed to have been the home of his artistic education.[55] He could do this with confidence as he had been there in peace and in war and he was seen as no armchair journalist, illustrator, or creator of the myth of glory in conflict. In order to do this with maximum effect he distanced himself in the introduction, in a rather bombastic and therefore vaguely Futurist manner, from all groups, 'isms' and theories, to create some leeway in terms of how his pictures would be judged. For one reviewer, this, combined with his attitude, now 'masculine and sane',[56] was the key to this success, while others started a retrospective assessment that proved all along that they had known he was 'the only one of the English Futurists who had a future'.[57] The uncompromising truth teller was poised to expose to the public, in a perfectly intelligible vocabulary, the reality of war, as he himself had known it, using the most up to date technique acceptable to popular taste, and, as usual, in contempt of tradition and pedigree previously associated with the genre.[58] As expected, however, unified approval was not forthcoming. *The British Architect* wrote of his 'mechanical puppets', then pondered 'Are we not better served by pictures which illuminate for us the fine spirit of endurance and the nobility of action.'[59] To Ezra Pound there was no mystery in his success, and almost as little credibility, when he observed that the masses had come to see the war, not the art. He concluded that 'It is manifestly an exhibition for the wide public, and not for the connoisseur in new movements. There are troops on the march, rather than new discoveries in form and form composition.'[60]

Through the soldiers visiting the exhibition, and approving of it, the public was assured of the validity of the truth of the depictions. How else would a civilian know whether it was 'the real thing' or not? It was this aspect of Richard's work that H. M. Tomlinson chose to highlight with his review in the *Star*, which told of the young officer who, on seeing the exhibition declared, 'Well, I'm strafed.'[61] Richard's depictions were actually used elsewhere by the military themselves, completely out of the context of painting, in articles such as that by 'An Officer' in the *Daily Mail*, which described the build up before going 'over the top'. In this he said that the soldier, both as an individual, and as a collective group, was 'as full of angles as he is in a Nevinson war picture'.[62] A telling accolade indeed and an indication that his painting was both known and accepted by those well outside the usual pre-war art public. This was one vital key to their widespread success, and one in which other war artists had not shared, as Muirhead Bone found out when his Somme series was described as 'the laughing stock of the army'.[63] Instead, the press could confidently create headlines for Richard, their new champion, the 'Warrior and Artist'.[64]

38.(facing page) *Bursting Shell*, 1915. Oil on canvas, 76.2 x 55.9 cm. Tate Gallery, London.

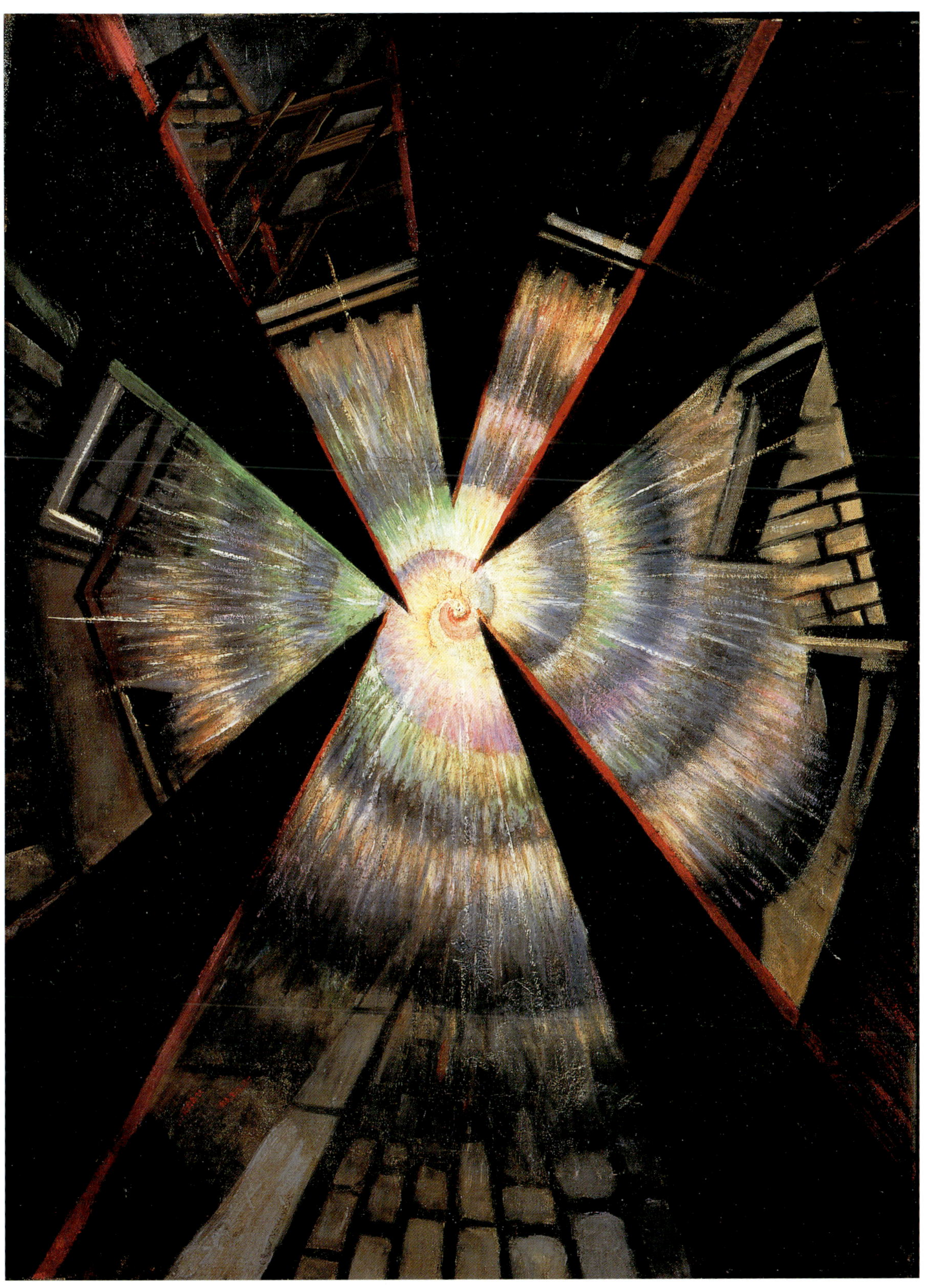

Bursting Shell

For a Futurist, or ex-Futurist, the force and sensation of *Bursting Shell* (fig. 38) would be an irresistible theme. In the 1916 exhibition at the Leicester Galleries, Richard included four such scenes. He had tackled the subject in 1915, but it was at this exhibition that the painting came in for most critical comment. The view point was an aerial one, depicting the outward force of the explosion, reduced in composition to five dark triangles and a colourful whirling epicentre. There are realistic references to bricks, rafters and other identifiable objects in the flash of the destructive moment, though the surface is shattered like broken glass. The viewer is undoubtedly thrust to the centre of the canvas, to the heart of the vortex created by the explosion, where the urban motifs, such as bricks and walls, remind us of the wholesale destruction of towns such as Ypres, and remind us also that this was by no means removed, or restricted, to a faraway countryside. It depicts no human form, recoiling or suffering from the blast, but shows an industrial, modern and urban war, far removed from the traditional concept of the battlefield. The function of the picture is not to provide the viewer with an exact replica of the destruction wrought by shells; it is to convey the sensation of the force at the heart of this new means of mass destruction. In other words it embodied a great many of the Futurist claims in art. Konody had been very aware of this and called it 'Futurism, pure and simple . . . an extraordinary sense of irresistible, destructive force is conveyed by that revolving rainbow-coloured spiral from which radiate black, orange bordered shafts'.[65] Reviews originally ranged in enthusiasm and competence, and cynicism pervaded many reports. Reproducing Richard's *La Guerre des Trous*[66] and *Bursting Shell*, the *Daily Graphic* simply reported 'The War as Viewed by the Impressionists'[67] while the *Evening News* reported that he (as part of the London Group) was 'at it again'.[68] Frank Rutter had felt that *Bursting Shell*, though an example of Futurist phraseology, was not altogether successful, being eclipsed by the rather more conventional *La Guerre des Trous*.[69] Charles Lewis-Hind, however, far from being shocked at what was being exhibited found it all rather *passé*, lacking originality and experimentation, and using Cubism and Futurism as time-tested formulas for being radical. His overall review was tainted with pessimism and one feels that the description of *Bursting Shell* was far from sufficient when it was described as 'a Neopolitan ice tormented by radium'.[70] Konody more specifically attributed the painting to the influence of Balla, in producing a compromise between abstraction and representation, illustration, and the depiction of a destructive force.[71] In short, this was both a novel and innovative depiction of a relevant subject, comprehensible to most, yet not regressive in terms of art theory. It was perhaps the most abstract, and Futuristic, of all Richard's wartime depictions. It had duly earned a very mixed response and he would have been aware that this must surely represent a high-water mark for the degree of abstraction that was going to be acceptable to public and critics alike.

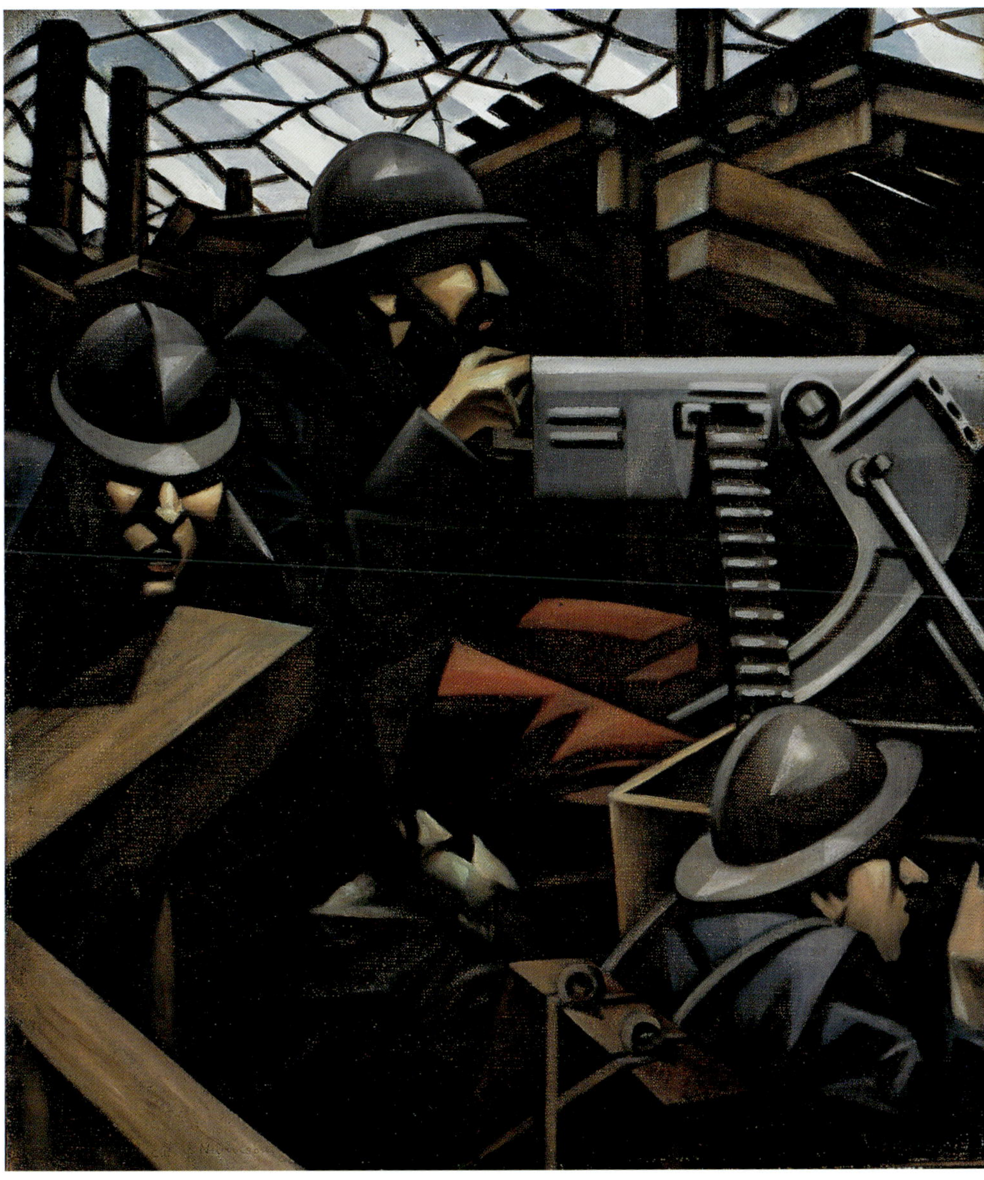

39. *La Mitrailleuse*, 1915. Oil on canvas, 61 x 50.6 cm. Tate Gallery, London.

La Mitrailleuse

La Mitrailleuse (fig. 39), allegedly painted with *Flooded Trench on the Yser* (fig. 40) on his honeymoon in late 1915, and previously exhibited at the Allied Artists exhibition in March, became the focus of critical attention and admiration, and has, as a consequence, been reproduced innumerable times since. Stepping back from the extremities of Futurism, as seen in *Bursting Shell*, Richard employed a more moderate geometric vocabulary, firmly rooted in an identifiable narrative, to depict what might be interpreted as the triumph of machine over man. War was stripped of its

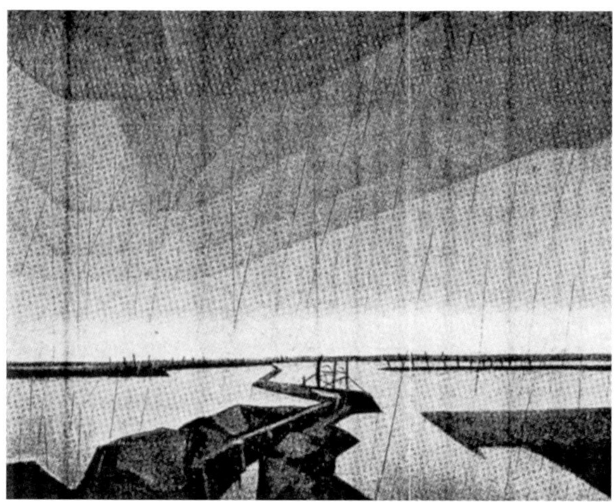

40. *Flooded Trench on the Yser*, 1915. Oil on canvas, 50.8 x 61 cm. Private collection.

glory and heroism in a scene that equated the modernity of modern weaponry in a symbiosis with the impersonal nature of the men directed towards the ultimate goal of mass destruction. His French gunners, in metallic colours and geometric form, are barely differentiated from the weapon they depend upon for their survival, both being angular, steely-grey and devoid of sentiment. There is a reminder of their deadly pursuit in the form of a fallen comrade lying slumped at the foot of the gun-pit, to whom they seem oblivious. Lewis-Hind had been quick to appreciate this, writing in the *Daily Chronicle*: 'He has seen, and has been deeply moved by the sight of this grim pit in the French lines covered with barbed wire through which the reluctant daylight peers; he has seen the crew of the mitrailleuse crouched in their pit (one dead), angular, implacable, machine-brains of destruction, the men like the gun, the gun like the men.'[72]

For Lewis-Hind, the machine had created man in its own image, stripping the individual of that sentiment and consciousness which in other environments would have prevented the men from their deadly pursuit. Now the two are inextricably linked, alike, remorseless and bound together in their pursuit of destruction. In another article he elaborated on his description:

> You peer into a pit in the zone of fire; barbed wire stretches across the surface of this machinomorphic pit; above is the grey, clear sky of France. In the pit are four French soldiers. One lies dead. The three living men are conscious of one thing only – the control of their death-scattering mitrailleuse. There it lurks, rigid and venomous, ready to spit out immense destruction. And the gunners? Are they men? No! They have become machines. They are as rigid and as implacable as their terrible gun. The machine has retaliated by making man in its own image . . . The crew and the gun are one, equipped for one end, only one – destruction. Horrible![73]

Another careful balance, in addition to technique, was attained by the artist insofar as the subject could be interpreted as a protest against the war, or could merely be a clinical observation, or perhaps an interpretation, of what the artist had seen at the Front. If it was to be seen as an anti-war statement it was at least balanced precariously or ambiguously enough not to be relegated to the ranks of pacifist politics and rhetoric, and in turn unacceptability. Likewise, whatever sentiments the painting carried, it was still a depiction of the honourable, though ghastly, pursuit of allied soldiers against the misapplied technical innovation of Prussian militarism that was the fundamental cause of the war.

Neither aiming at a photo-realism, nor at an abstraction in its entirety, the composition sought to convey, through modern means, a message which was clear to all but the least perceptive viewer. There can be little doubt that the painting represents a form of extreme realism, though not the conventional, or entirely visual realism, that we may otherwise associate with this genre. If anything, it invited the viewer to reconsider the expressive potentialities of painting and the means, in subject matter and technique, by which these could be achieved. If the overall aesthetic impact of the composition was unpleasing, it was because the subject of modern was also unpleasing. It may not be pretty but it is appropriate and infinitely more relevant than the theatrical pieces of the Royal Academy tradition of battle painting. Philosophically, if not visually, modernism, as utilized by Richard, was being equated with metaphorical 'realism', not in the conventional photographic sense, but in the deeper implications of the war, to present an accurate synopsis of events on mainland Europe. Besides, the geometric form of modernism was to some extent literal realism as well in that this was a mechanical, industrialized conflict, a seemingly obvious invitation for the use of modern geometric, but not incomprehensible, forms. In this respect, his balance and restraint in applying modernist principles to his subjects was clearly being received as a form of representation preferable to any other alternatives, both conservative and radical. Konody previously had claimed that it 'was the most interesting picture so far shown in London'[74] whilst Sickert went so far as to call it 'the most concentrated and authoritative utterance on war in the history of painting'.[75] Moreover, it was depicted by an artist in uniform who therefore had a sound pedigree, and was in turn, worth listening to. John Salis, himself a serving war artist, reiterated this point when he wrote: 'Why, when these men are risking everything for us, should the plums of their profession be handed to our unfits and conscientious objectors, who have had the leisure to haunt the boudoirs and such places through which these appointments filter.'[76] Richard had found the balance, in image, subject matter, technique and sentiment to appeal broadly at this midway stage in the war.

La Patrie

Retreating further from Futurist doctrine, and moving more definitively towards a more identifiably realist set of principles, was *La Patrie* (fig. 41). The title itself, Doherty argues, could be drawn from 'La Marseillaise' when it proclaims 'allons enfants de la patrie', then later prides the citizen in 'amour sacré de la patrie'.[77] Richard clearly was employing ironic and cynical overtones as he had done in *La*

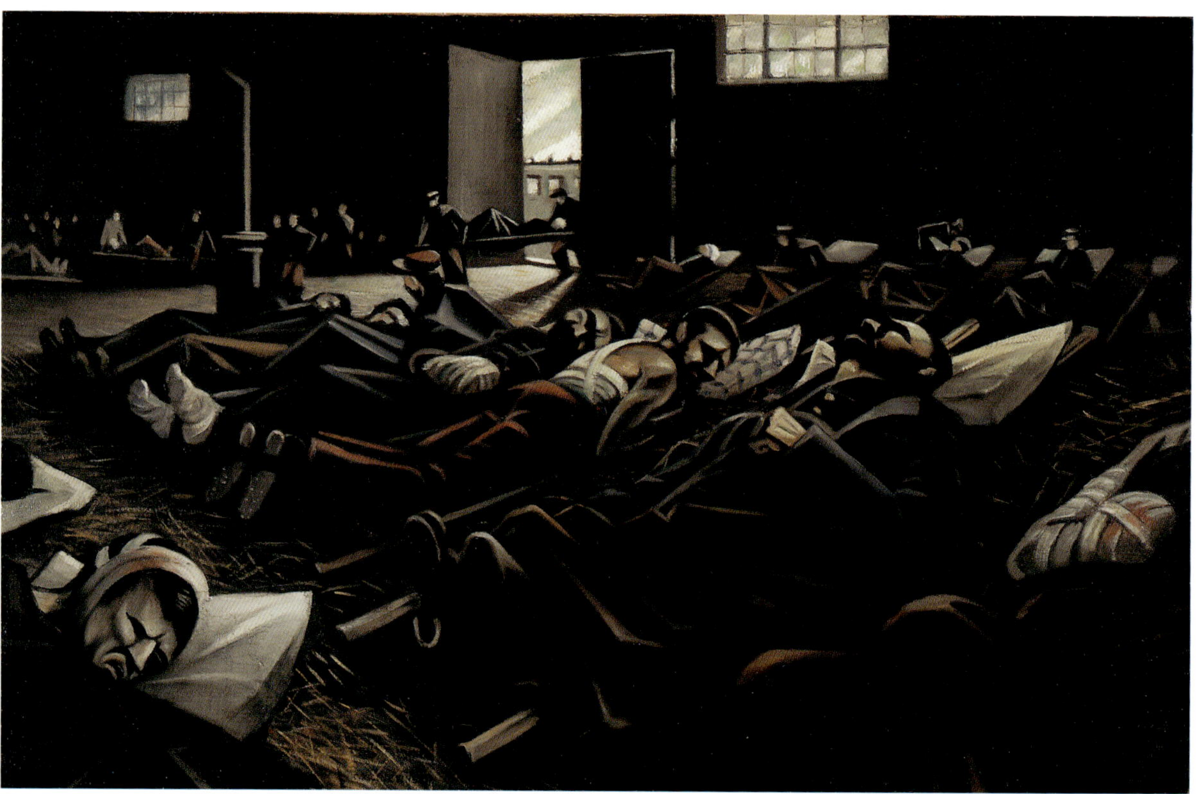

41. *La Patrie*, 1916.
Oil on canvas, 60.8 x 92.5 cm.
Birmingham Museums and Art Gallery.

Guerre de Trous and would later do in *Paths of Glory*. Henry entered in his journals, supportive of his son as always, that at the London Group show at the Goupil Galleries '*La Patrie* attracted much attention, being also the best.'[78] Rutter had agreed saying that the artist had 'chosen the method of the epic poet rather than that of the sensational journalist' to depict, as never before 'the pitiable horror of war'.[79] Lewis-Hind went further, to say that it had 'an almost unbearable intensity',[80] then several months later declared the permanence in value of the depiction saying '*La Patrie* will stand, to the astonishment and shame of our descendants, as an example of what civilized man did to civilized man in the first quarter of the Twentieth Century.'[81] Richard's technique was deemed acceptable, even desirable, by conservative critics such as Claude Phillips, who wrote: 'Here, at any rate, Mr Nevinson vindicates his right to the use of his now mitigated cubist technique: for has he not through its cold, calculated violence, its cruel, metallic angularity, expressed something of the awful unconsciousness of Fate controlling yet ignoring the tragic destinies of man.'[82] This painting epitomized another subset within his artistic repertoire, by subjugating the technical and theoretical considerations in his production, to the importance of the narrative content, and above all to the intelligibility of the overall composition to the viewer. The impact of his experiences in Flanders whilst with the Red Cross, had to be conveyed to those who as yet had not been to, or seen, the war. He could not afford, with such powerful and important subject matter, to risk a medium which might not be understood or which might elicit negative sentiments in the viewer. In short, it, when viewed with the other works on display, demonstrated what Harries referred to as his 'adventurous peripatetic approach'.[83] Nevertheless, when it was reproduced in *Bystander*, it was under the caption 'Futurism Finds the War'.[84]

The bleakness of *La Patrie* is captured in the artist's use of dark colours and of sharply angular forms. These represent coldness and death more than promoting any sensation that the soldier's duty is now done and that the worst has passed. If anything it has only just begun. He also did nothing to disguise or camouflage the wounds of the men, rather he made them the focus of the composition. Their expressions further tell of the suffering they are experiencing. There is little attempt here to depict the 'happy hero', the patriot and the youth who willingly gives all for King and Country. On the contrary, the dressing station is depicted more as a mortuary than as a warm and comforting place of solace. In short, the conventions for depicting the war wounded and the British hero, post conflict, were ignored. Nor need there be any ambiguity as to who these subjects were:

> These soldiers had been wounded during the retreat onto the frontiers at Furnes just before the Battle of Ypres. They had been roughly bandaged and packed into the cattle trucks which were to carry them to hospital. Here they lay, men with every form of horrible wound, swelling and festering, watching their comrades die. For three weeks they lay there until only a tortured half of them were alive; and then, a staff officer happening to pass that way, there were protests because the train should have been used for other and more important things, and the men were dumped out of the way in a shed outside Dunkirk.[85]

Richard, now back to full health, was taking the opportunity to exorcise the ghastly memories of his early war experience.[86] Bitterly he had recorded in his autobiography that the dead, all of whom he had tried to assist, had been from Germany too. But now this was ignored, or reinterpreted, epitomized by Lewis-Hind who wrote: 'La Patrie! War! Which the German military party, in beautiful clothes, was once accustomed to regard and to preach as a normal method of national expansion.'[87]

It was clear that Richard had found the balance between relevant modernist simplification, charged with a high degree of both subject and technical relevance, whilst retaining a degree of expression, patriotism, realism, even sentimentality, and all the other key ingredients essential to the success of a work of art for the audience at which he was aiming. Other critics saw it differently – instead of them coming round to his way of thinking, they believed that he was being 'reeled in'. The *Morning Post* expressed this explicitly when it declared that he 'had felt the moral influence of the trenches. It has given him greater respect for nature and is curing him of eccentricity'.[88] In depictions such as these, therefore, Richard was taking an old formula and subject matter, was adapting it to be modern and relevant to a modern war, and was becoming popular as a result. This might also explain how and why he believed that 'the public . . . showed more intelligence than the intelligentsia' and why 'I was also well treated by the general Press'.[89] Perhaps the more *élite* coteries and writers would not have enjoyed the populist feel of the exhibition and Pound certainly believed this, concluding an article on the show by writing 'a fig for aesthetics and theories'.[90] But this is exactly what Richard was reacting against, claiming now that stylistic consistency was a luxury, unique to the aesthetes who had not as yet embraced the fact that there was something much more significant to concentrate on than the theories and ideologies of pre-war years. The *Graphic* accordingly concluded that it was definitely an exhibition for the 'average man'[91] and the *Manchester Guardian* saw the target audience as 'the ordinary man'. In the same article it was stated that he was now *the* British painter of modern war by 'general consent'.[92] This may, however, have proved an unstable platform on which to build an artistic career in anything other than the short term, especially when the unity and passion of a nation in crisis had passed.

Both *La Mitrailleuse* and *La Patrie* were recommended for purchase for the nation, the former by Sickert, and the latter by Lewis-Hind. This, to some extent, implied that they were seen as not only worthy of merit as works of art, but also as accurate and poignant records of war. It was for a variety of reasons then that these paintings made their impact on wartime Britain.

In the end, the exhibition was extended by a week due to popular demand. It was attended, as usual, by a society set including Winston Churchill, Ramsay MacDonald, Joseph Conrad, John Galsworthy, Arthur Balfour, Mrs Asquith and Bernard Shaw, and caused the greatest of interest in the press.[93] The autobiography makes little other reference to it and goes on to talk about the developing and beneficial friendship with the Sitwells, which was made through this event via friend and critic P. G. Konody.[94]

But such was it's outstanding popular success, a full study of Richard's war pieces was conducted in a book by P. G. Konody, published by Grant Richards, entitled *Modern War Paintings by C.R.W. Nevinson*. When it was published in January 1917, it placed the artist firmly in the tradition of the great battle painter, as Konody traced a linear progression from the ancient Greeks, through Uccello, Leonardo, Michelangelo and Goya to this artist of the Great War. The fighting artist, the intellectual able to relate to the soldier and the civilian, the truth teller, the product of the modern age and the rebel generation – all were qualities that thrust the artist into this hallowed company.

Konody concluded: 'He returned with many illusions shattered. He had witnessed too much suffering and misery to believe any longer in war as the "hygienics of the world".'[95] Richard himself had been eager to dispel that rumour from early 1915, but had been reluctant to dispose completely of Futurist technique as he believed it was still a perfectly valid means of depiction for the subject in hand. If anything, his compromised, or diluted, Futurism had done more to win over the public to its merits, than had all the violent and bombastic proclamations of the pre-war era. His depictions of searlights, then his aviation pieces, announced this compromise clearly and unmistakably. But flexibility too had counted for a lot in the utilization of different modes of painting for different subjects and therefore more immediate relevance to the subject matter. Basically, he had sought public success, and had attained it by speaking a language they understood to convey a message with which they had sympathy. Neither did he force an opinion on them, simply offering the 'truth', as he perceived it, in an objective way, and leaving the interpretation up to the individual. It is interesting to note that Konody, like Richard, saw this as being a finishing point for the study of war, concluding his essay 'He has done with the interpretation of the war and may be confidently expected soon to start in search of new artistic adventure.'[96] Richard reiterated the point in the *Daily Mirror* saying 'I have painted everything I saw in France and there will be no more.'[97]

Confident that his reputation had now been built to the point that he could diversify from the war subject he exhibited four non-war subjects, in a pre-war fashion, at the fifth London Group show, in November, to scanty and unenthusiastic reviews.[98] In order to appear 'open' and not typically enigmatic, he, in the company of Gilman, Ginner, John Nash and Bevan, made it clear through the press that they would be 'at home' every Saturday from 3.00 to 6.00 p.m. In the Grey Room of the Goupil Gallery, in the company of their paintings, the artists made themselves available to assist and to discuss the works of art with those who were interested or confused.[99] However, it was becoming obvious that Richard's success had been built as much on his subject matter as it had been on his method of depiction, and so, despite his intention to abandon the genre of battle painting altogether, he had been served a timely reminder that that was not necessarily the most pragmatic or profitable way forward.

For Richard therefore, the Leicester Gallery exhibition had marked a major turning point in his career, not only as it had been a remarkable success, but in that it had reminded him of the value of war as a subject. He had identified the middle ground, between the extremes of the élitist academicism of both left and right, and there, putting a new emphasis on the value of relevant subject matter, had expressed his patriotic condemnation of the war. Aesthetic puritanism was rejected, by artist and public alike, and substituted with the knowledge of a soldier and a moderate, intelligent, and patriotic rebel from the pre-war era. As a consequence Richard's return to a form of 'realism' was by no means interpreted as a 'retreat' by anyone other than the avant-garde coteries who, as yet, were not involved with the war and who were making little artistic headway anyway. But he had also cast the nets very wide in both subject matter and technique, and so most, if not all, of his visitors, could find something they liked in the exhibition, though few would have appreciated it in its entirety. On this high note he began to feel that this experiment had almost come to an end and that he had little or no intention of returning to the Front, in whatever capacity. The reality, of course, was quite different. Writing to William Rothenstein, Richard suggested that the nature of his success was more to do with the public's fascination with the war, than with their appreciation of his painting, and he suggested a break with this theme on those grounds. He concluded: 'In fact, I intend to paint no more war pictures for some time. I hope to change my method of painting...I wish always to work within the limits of some self-imposed convention and a different one in relation to each new subject'.[100] Accordingly

Clutton-Brock mused, prophetically, 'Will Mr Nevinson have the power to paint for us, some day, the daylight after the nightmare?'[101]

The Military Crisis of 1916

By 17 October, Henry was feeling the strain of possible enlistment for his son and recorded 'I grew most wretched again at possibility of discharged soldiers being called up, & Rich being forced into either munitions or active service.'[102] The fears of both father and son escalated throughout October and into November. On 9 November Henry wrote of how he had 'Much trouble about Richard's anxiety as to recall into the army'[103] and by 15 November, the situation had deteriorated to 'Extreme misery at night owing to Richard's terror of being called up again.'[104] Neither the private viewing at the London Group,[105] nor even Richard's contribution to the NEAC show,[106] could eclipse the panic that was setting in at the Nevinson household.

On 2 December, when his father returned from visiting Lavery's studio, he found that his son had made plans to escape to Spain, one of the few nations remaining neutral in the war. The idea was discussed at length by father and son over the following days and by 5 December, Richard was at the passport office making sure that everything was in order. In fact everything was not in order and by 11 December, Henry recorded 'Rich & Kath were refused passports for Spain because of my political opinions.'[107] He later described the incident as follows:

> The Official asked him: 'Are you related to that man, Henry Nevinson?'
> 'He is my father' Richard replied.
> 'He is a man of very violent opinions, isn't he?' asked the official.
> 'Oh dear, no!' said Richard, who had known me from his childhood; 'he's the mildest of men.'
> 'When I say violent opinions,' the official replied, 'I mean he doesn't see eye to eye with the man in the street. Now does he?'
> It was an official definition of violence unsurpassed in precision, and I understood then the grounds of my evil repute.[108]

The following day an official note came forbidding their move to Spain and, despite Henry's efforts at the permit office, the situation was clearly not going to change. His efforts there with a man named Walker resulted in the statement that 'discharged men sh. not go to any neutral country but Switzerland lest they should be interned as belligerents'.[109] This only intensified the efforts of the father and 14 December was spent going from office to office and official to official in an attempt to aid his son's case. Firstly he established that he, not his son, was regarded as a conscientious objector by the government and was thus to be treated with the utmost suspicion. Secondly, at the permit office he found out from a Lieutenant Wynne that all discharged men were forbidden from going to Spain or any other neutral country. Thirdly, and more hopefully, at the Foreign Office he found an officer who told him that his son's relocation could be effected by altering the destination to the

South of France, simply by presenting an address and a doctor's certificate. That plan went wrong too when he was accepted but 'the French would not pass her'.[110] It is one of the very few times that Henry referred to Kathleen in a cold or derogatory way.

It was time for a different approach, with Henry once again at the helm. Exemption was looking less and less likely, and doing so with any degree of self-respect, out of the question. Henry's diary entry for 19 December, however, suggested the start of a new plan. It talked of how the essay by Konody, which was appearing in the form of a book entitled *Modern War* on his son's art, was 'quite excellent'.[111] The following day he 'Went to the Galleries and got Rich's book wh. I left at the War Office for Adj. Gen. MacReady with a note.'[112] Accordingly he could record more optimistically, 'Horizon looking rather clearer about Richard.'[113] To make sure there could be no way that the art of his son escaped the attention of the powers at the War Office General Haig also received a copy the very next day. On 27 December, father and son went together to Sir George Newman to see what the future might be for an artist in uniform. In the meantime Richard was suffering from 'nervous apprehensions'[114] and was consulting a nerve specialist. In a final communication, dated 'Decembre 18 1916', Severini wrote from Paris to relay the news of his child's death to his friend in London. Importantly, he added, echoing Richard's own sentiments 'J'espère que vous n'êtes pas rappelle dans l'armée.'[115]

9

The Official Commission 1917–1918

He is a desperate fellow and without fear…only anxious to crawl into the front line and draw things full of violence and terror.[1]

January and February 1917 were quiet months with Richard exhibiting beside Epstein at the Leicester Galleries and winning the general sympathy of his society friends, including Lady Hamilton, over his treatment concerning Spain. However, in the light of what his father was trying to do in order to keep him out of the ranks one wonders at the wisdom of his holding a large party on 11 January 1917 at which many 'distinct French and Germans [were] present'.[2] But March was to bring the worst news that he could have expected: the Discharge Bill was definitely to be voted upon in parliament, and worse still, 'rheumatic fever does not count for exemption'.[3] Immediately he went to a specialist to get a second opinion on his condition, both mental and physical, the result being that 'A Dr. Rackham told him: his nerve all gone: almost insane: says he will never go back to the army alive.'[4] The problem was clearly getting more pressing and the following was a 'wretched and sleepless night of terror for Richard'.[5] The full impact of the calamity came on 29 March, when Henry recorded: 'The Bill recalling discharged soldiers was passed second reading – & so fate moves nearer.'[6] By 5 April 1917, the Military Service (Review of Exceptions) Act was fully operative. Consequently, and rather tactfully, Richard made a gift of *Swooping Down on a Hostile Plane* (fig. 42) to the National War Museum (later the Imperial War Museum), just before writing to C.F.G. Masterman[7] to advance his own suggestion.[8] On 1 April he had had an interview with Masterman and later in the week he made his way back to Wandsworth hospital 'and saw Bruce Porter who told him he was utterly unfit for active service and would let it be known if need be'.[9] Father and son were now using contacts and friends in order to secure a form of eleventh hour exemption. Accordingly his father wrote to Lieutenant General Sir David Henderson, with whom he had served in South Africa at the siege of Ladysmith, to see if his son could be accepted into the Camouflage Corps.[10] Richard too wrote at length to Edward Marsh asking what was 'the best means of getting attached to the camoflage [*sic*] section . . . that paints and disguises guns etc for invinsibility [*sic*] from aeroplanes'. This letter emphasized his desire not to be sent back and to 'be put in the ranks of some infantry regiment'. His

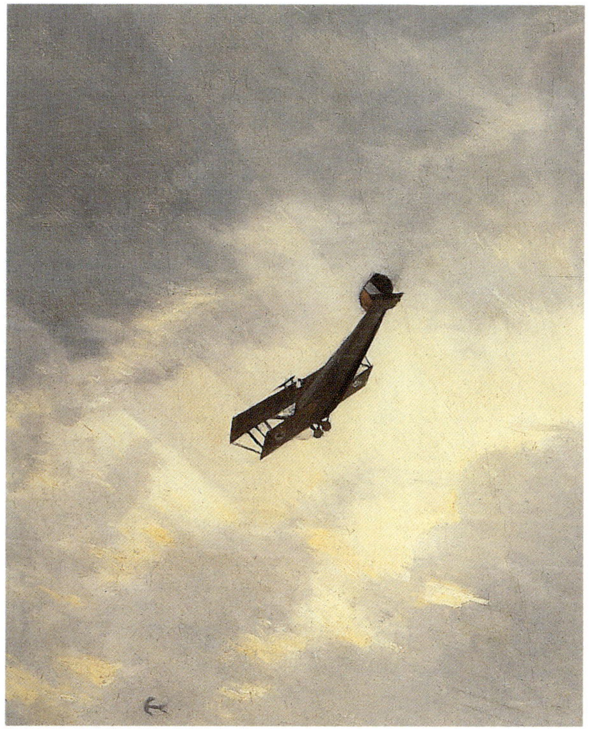

42. *Swooping Down on a Hostile Plane*, 1917. Pastel, 48.3 x 32.4 cm. Private Collection.

health, he claimed, would not take it and besides, he argued, his 'knowledge . . . of colours, tones etc would be of more use to the country' than in a situation where he would simply be another soldier.[11] Just over two weeks later he was writing to Marsh again to express his concern at how his plan might have been misinterpreted as he had just received a letter from the War Office which advised him that he was to be sent out to France as a 'private-sapper in the camouflage'. This did not appeal to him at all as it was as a private, once again, that he would be employed, and this involved associating with men who had no loftier 'ideals than "grub" and "booze"'. Besides, he knew that he was not sufficiently fit for a return to the ranks and the hardships that that entailed, or to 'the loneliness which breaks my spirit'.[12] Perhaps, he suggested, if there was something in London, and especially with a rank, the situation might be more palatable. Otherwise, he might turn his attention to a commission in the Artists Rifles, via their cadet school.[13]

Only five days after parliament passed the Military Service (Review of Exceptions) Act on 5 April, work in the cartography department of the Machine Gun Corps in Grantham came up, though Richard seemed far from relieved to be offered it. His father commented 'Rich heard of possible work at Grantham, but was much distressed at the thought of the army and its sergeants.'[14] The next day his father wrote: 'I induced him to go to Grantham for appearance'[15] and so he did, coming back resigned to his fate. *Paint and Prejudice* suggests that it was an eager artist who went to Grantham to try out for the Machine Gun Corps, and that it was with frustration that he was rejected on health grounds one more time. Nonetheless, it was at precisely this stage that fate dealt a kinder hand. Within twenty-four hours of his arrival home he found out that his *Taube* had been bought by the War Museum 'and Mond thought he sh. go out as an artist'.[16] The idea of becoming a war artist, whether the result of his father's efforts or not, had finally become associated with his name. He wasted no time in going to the War Office and then on 'to see Klein in Hyde Park with promising result'.[17]

The Friday Club show, and the London Group exhibition which followed within two weeks, though very poorly attended, seemed not as important as they had done previously, but were used to re-enforce Richard's case. Masterman, for example, went along to have a closer look at the young artist's work and confirmed what he already had suspected: that his friend's son really was a painter of worth. It would be Masterman who would be the chief link between Richard and the army. As a fellow journalist with Henry on the *Daily Chronicle* and the *Nation*, and both members of the National Liberal Club, strings could almost certainly be pulled. Richard further backed this up with a letter to Alfred Mond, MP and chairman of the National War Museum, which asked him to 'put in a good word for me at the proper quarter'.[18] A week earlier he had written to Marsh again asking him to 'put in a word for me if an opportunity occurs'. The same letter also lets us see that the idea of becoming a war artist, though 'strictly confidential', had been mentioned and that he believed he had a 'vague & sporting chance of getting it'.[19] Two days later Marsh received another letter asking him, through General Lowther, to write a letter to assist his application to the Special School of Works. Otherwise he would find himself in front of the recruitment board, and he was not convinced at all that they would give him a proper examination.[20] By 1 May, Henry was writing again to Masterman, telling him of the success of the Leicester Galleries show and saying that his son was 'very anxious to go to France as one of the authorised War Artists'. He reiterated that it was on Muirhead Bone's recommendation that he had known where to direct the letter.[21] As a result Masterman wrote to Richard 'I have received a letter from my friend your father', and proceeded to tell the young artist that he would be happy to see him.[22] Contrary to the claims made in *Paint and Prejudice* that a number of generals were supporting his application, it appears, through communications like this, that Muirhead Bone and his own father were the two who championed his cause most assiduously. The misconception was enhanced a decade later by Richard when he reported that Masterman had said 'I have never seen a man with so many generals' recommendations.'[23] A further letter to General Charteris from Masterman advanced his case, and stated that through illness he would be unfit for any other form of service. This saw Richard getting selected to 'go out' as an artist before Lavery, and the confirmation, which father and son had hoped for, that, if called up for active service, there would be those who would fight his case against it. Masterman, in the same internal document, supported his friend's son's claim saying 'there is no doubt he has genius' and reported that his successes, which had extended now to the USA and Russia, could be beneficial for all concerned.[24] Richard's case was supported further by Masterman, when the latter described him as a 'desperate fellow and without fear' being 'only anxious to crawl into the front line and draw things full of violence and terror'.[25]

This is an image that we now can appreciate is far from reality, but of which the artist would certainly have approved. Indeed it is testimony to the combined efforts of father and son that this image should have prevailed despite the true desperation that was rife at home. Clearly Masterman was keen, and though the timing of Henry's and Richard's efforts could hardly have been more perfect, it was clear that Wellington House was perfectly aware of the nature and potential of his painting as a propaganda tool. Richard was now, through the Department of Information, safe from the terrors of the trenches, and secure in the knowledge too that this could be just what his painting had been waiting for.

Paint and Prejudice presents a different picture, the entire episode being remembered as follows: 'I thought I would apply for a commission before the rush came. My outlook was that the war was a loathsome job from which there was no escape; but if I must go back, I was this time going as an officer. After all I was a public school man.'[26] It glosses over the whole affair simply by saying 'Imagine the nervous state I was thrown into when I was suddenly rung up by the War Office.'[27] From here the description tells the story of how a surprised, nervous and somewhat uncomprehending young man was swept through the corridors of power to a destiny as a war artist over which he had no control. The section reproduced below hardly does justice to the events of summer 1917:

> 'But I understand that you want an artist's commission,' he said.
> 'All right,' I agreed in my innocence. 'I should be happy to join the Artists Rifles.'
> He referred again to the letter, then glanced at me.
> 'But Douglas Ainslie says you ought to be made an Official War Painter,'
> I had just enough presence of mind to give him the right answer.
> 'Of course,' I said. 'If it could be arranged it would be ideal.'[28]

That aside, he was no doubt one of the more dynamic and youthful painters of the day and had also had a highly successful Leicester Galleries show. When this was combined with the strong references provided by his father, Masterman and Mond, the outcome, to some extent, must have been obvious. One could however speculate that he was taken on as a favour to his father since, unlike Bone, he was not commissioned and received neither salary nor uniform.[29] On 29 June he received his contract from Wellington House, which he amended slightly, before writing back to Masterman.[30] The latter then returned an optimistic letter saying 'I am delighted that you are going out now, and I hope very much that you will have a thoroughly interesting time, and come back with some war drawings equal – if not excelling – in merit the wonderful series which you showed at your last exhibition here.'[31] Severini, once again, wrote to express his satisfaction that his friend had become the 'peintre d'armée' and hoped that the inevitable return to France would afford the opportunity of a visit to Paris and to a collaboration on a scheme he was working on there.[32]

Flying practices with Sir Sefton Brancker[33] were organized almost immediately at Hendon with the intention of working on some aerial pieces at the front. Allegedly,

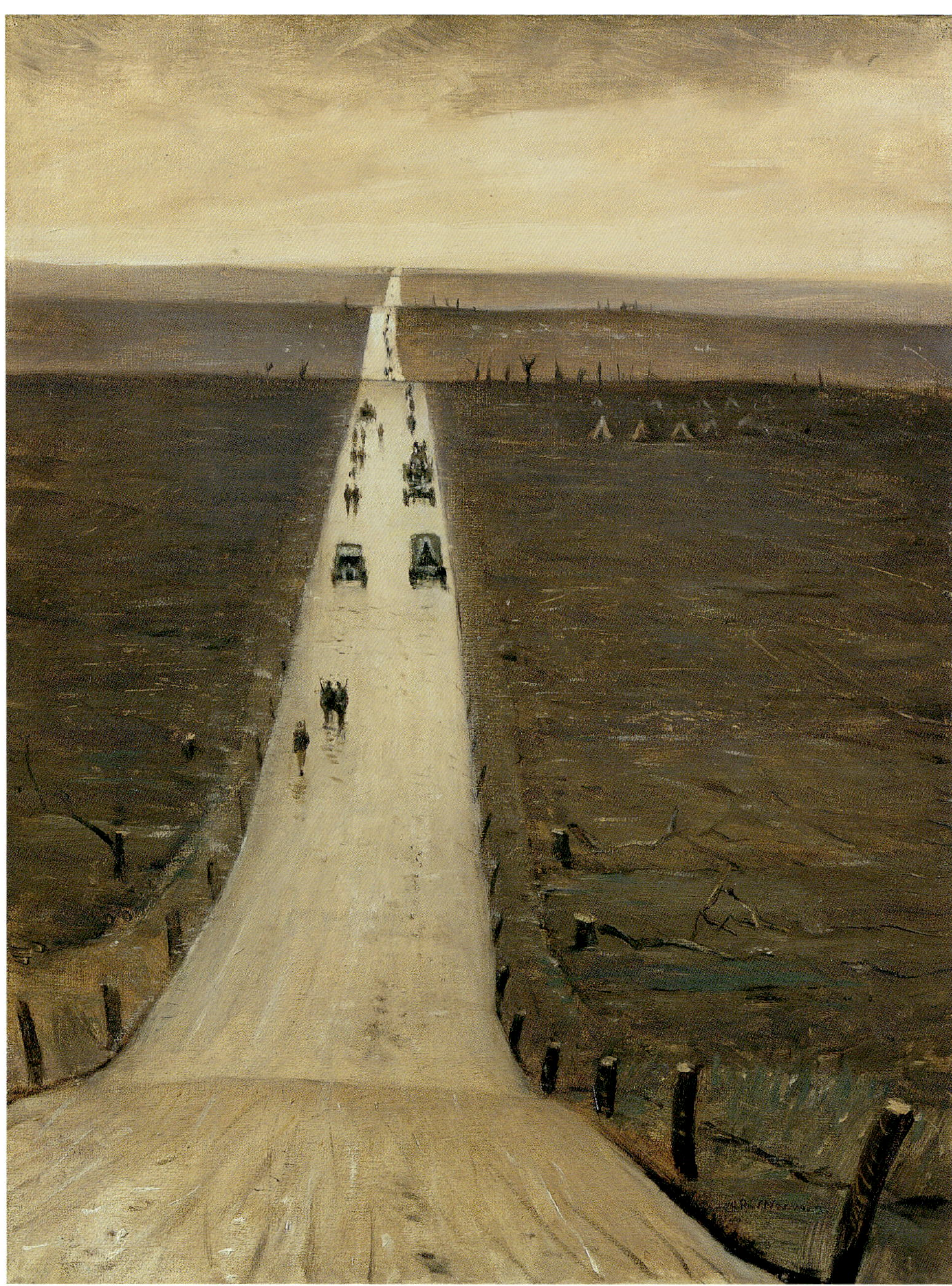

43. *Road from Arras to Bapaume,* 1917. Oil on canvas, 60.9 x 45.7 cm. Imperial War Museum, London.

the young artist was also given permission to take to the London skies in a hot-air balloon, a feat that would be repeated at the front in the months to come.[34] In the meantime he would start some compositions on the making and flying of aircraft throughout Britain for the *Aims and Ideals of War* series.[35] By the end of June it was only a matter of days until the telegram arrived ordering his departure to France and on 1 July it came. The day before he had written to Masterman outlining his aims saying: 'I hope I shall be able to make a fine record & that my pictures will give the civilian public some insight as to the marvellous endurance of our soldiers & the real meaning of hardships they are called upon to face.'[36]

The Return to France

Far from being terrified, his father noted, following a lunch with his son and Kathleen, 'He is asking to go by aeroplane wh. shows a fine recovery of nerve.'[37] After a short delay he departed at 12.25 on 5 July for the Château d'Harcourt, replacing George Bernard Shaw there, and returned home a month and a day later. While the major preparations were underway for the third Battle of Ypres, or Passchendaele, and in the immediate aftermath of the Battle of the Messines Ridge, Richard was billeted in this sixteenth-century château, eighteen miles south of Caen, and a long way from the front line. He later transferred to join the Fourth Division of the Third Army at Scarpe, near Arras.[38] At the château he saw the *Times* war, officers and gentlemen in white gloves, which he believed to be as fake as the chaâteau itself.[39] In his personally driven car, and his father's war correspondent's uniform,[40] he visited areas of the Somme, Etaples, Montreux, Calais, Abbeville and even Paris. It is hardly surprising that he felt under pressure to produce something dramatic having had all this service lavished upon him. In a letter to Masterman, dated 24 July 1917, he wrote: 'I am very worried that my pictures will not justify the wonderful opportunity that you have given me not to mention the petrol I have used up.' The same letter, however, goes on to justify his time in France by saying that he had been 'all about the line North & South in trenches, balloons, aeroplanes, batteries dug-outs & most of the roads behind the lines'.[41] The resultant canvases from this period were: *Road From Arras to Bapaume* (fig. 43), *Survivors at Arras*, *Very Lights at Monchy* (lost), *Roads of France* (fig. 44), *Destroyed Canal at Ytres* (lost), *Hindenburg Line* (lost) and *Inside Brigade Headquarters* (fig. 45). His father wrote that his son had been 'rather overwhelmed with the confusion'[42] and that, on the whole, everything seemed so much more grand and complicated than it had been on his first visit. This is understandable in the build-up to the Passchendaele campaign, which began on 31 July 1917.

One of Richard's favourite stories from his autobiography relates the time when he went up in a balloon, with Richmond Temple, to monitor the constantly changing positions of the German guns, best done in the dark due to the flashes. The balloon was attacked by a German aeroplane, almost requiring an immediate parachute decent, but in the end, the attack passed off without serious incident.[43] Another attack found him crash-landing in a tree, presumably after a parachute descent, where he hung 'like a fly in a spiders web until dark [when] I was able to cut myself free'.[44] This, it could be argued, marked a return to some of the ideologies of the Futurists and their pre-war beliefs, though, understandably, he never felt at home in the air, especially when being fired upon, even by friendly 'Archies'.[45] He believed that the resultant aerial pieces, or 'airscapes', were amongst the best of his career and certainly press reviews for 1917–18 tend to support this. [46]

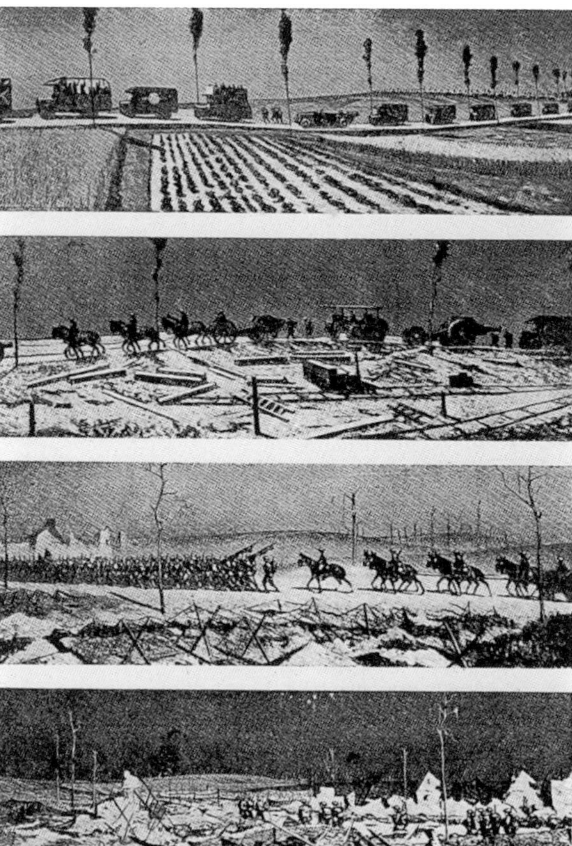

44. *Roads of France*, 1917.
Oil on canvas, each painting 63.5 x 170.2 cm.
From top: *Mechanical Transport Leaving the Base; Heavy Artillery and the Dumps; Field Artillery and the Infantry; Infantry in Extended Order, Within the Lines.*
National Gallery of Canada, Ottowa.

A letter to Masterman from the Front, suggests that the artist came close to the firing line and certainly must have convinced his employers of the genuine nature of his pursuits. 'I nearly got done in a few days ago at an Observation Post with some "Lovat Scouts". We were spotted and got shelled, had to stick glued against a bank for an hour, wondering when Fritz would leave off.'[47] This, as he went on to say, had occurred on all but one occasion when he had gone down the line. A similar story, or perhaps the same one enhanced, appeared a year after the war finished and was described thus: 'For an hour and a half the entire fearfulness of the German army and the most expensive ammunition were turned on us...After that I could paint just exactly what it feels like to lie in a shell-hole.' The description went on to talk about the death of the man next to him and of his efforts to get the body back to British lines under heavy machine-gun fire.[48]

Later, taking the car one more time, he was driven up to Ypres, where it was believed some major engagement was about to occur. Sketching, for what would later be painted up into *Shell Holes* (fig. 46) and *Harvest of Battle* (fig. 47) was done in and around Passchendaele and this earned him the reprimand, from a Major Lee, of Intelligence F, that would get him sent home. He arrived in London in the first week of August, having made no attempt to actually depict one of the bloodiest battles of the Great War, only peripheral elements, and was replaced at the Front by Eric Kennington. His account was that he was sent home for rank insubordination.

London and the Reaction to Nevinson's War Images

At home there seemed to follow a serious downturn in his mental condition and before long his father was writing, 'Richard still nervous and miserable'[49] though not specifying about what. The next month observed a slight shortening of patience on the part of Henry when he wrote 'Richard again distressed with anxiety about some scare which was nothing.'[50] Nor was his art living up to expectation. When the Mastermans came to see the fruits of his labours, they seemed to feel that 'they missed imagination and originality'.[51] Edward Hudson, who was preparing *British Artists at the Front*, focussing on Richard, was also dissatisfied with the work he was seeing. He went on to say 'I do not wish to be rude to Nevinson, but there is an approach to the pavement artist touch in it.'[52] Department of Information documents from October 1917 tell a similar story of disappointment with officially commissioned works such as *Survivors at Arras*. Derrick, after viewing the works, and in a letter to Masterman, speculated that they were tame 'with the intention of gaining official approval' which is understandable, but 'to the point of dullness'. In the same letter he summed up by hoping that Richard's 'own un-restraining savage self, can appear in subsequent work, without giving offence in official quarters . . . and that his restrained, decorous, official self, is valued rather less highly'.[53] Some of the

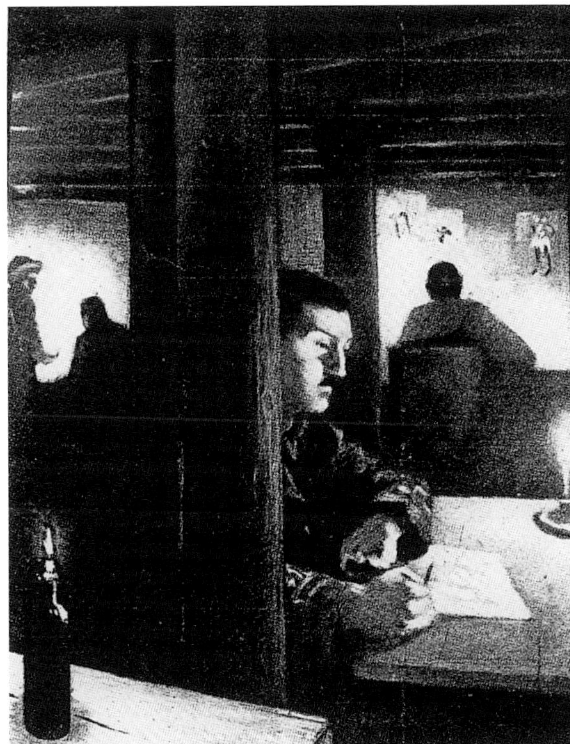

45. *Inside Brigade Headquarters*, 1917. Oil on canvas. Whereabouts unknown. Reproduced in *Illustrated London News*, 2 March 1918.

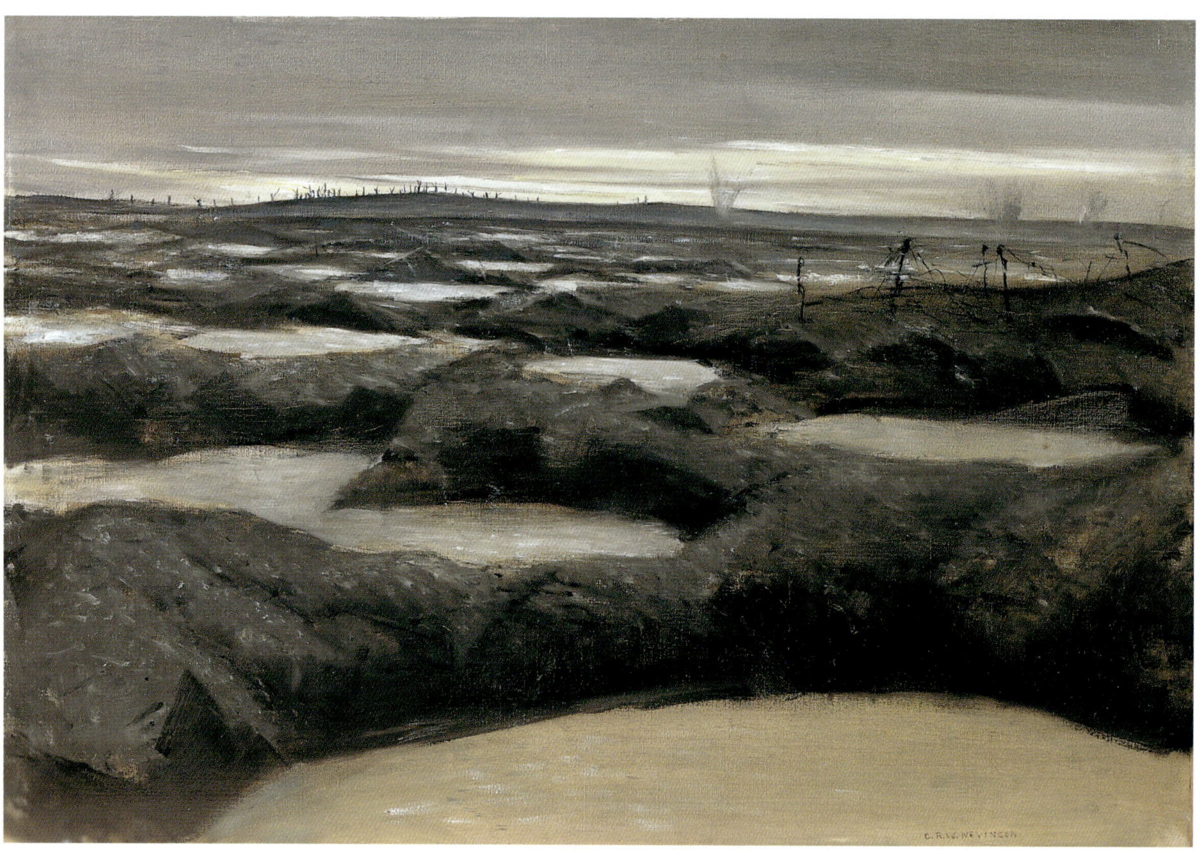

46. *Shell Holes* (also known as *After a Push*), 1917. Oil on canvas, 57.1 x 80 cm. Imperial War Museum, London.

blame may rest with Masterman, however, as the goals he desired were obviously unclear. He wrote that 'they [Nevinson and Kennington] both ask me continually to tell them what I want'[54] Malvern recounted also: 'When Nevinson asked Masterman if there were any subjects he should avoid Masterman replied, with a wave of his hand "No, no, paint anything you please"'.[55]

On 22 December 1917, news came through, once again, that Richard was going to have to register like any other discharged soldier. Henry, despairingly, could only record that 'The torture of life is hardly bearable'.[56] It was a miserable Christmas by all accounts and Boxing Day was little better with the shadow of enlistment hanging over the house. His father entered in his journal 'Sad and distraught.'[57] The year closed with Henry continuing to introduce his son to useful personages and in preparing for the NEAC show which would be opening on 4 January 1918.[58] Writers and personalities were invited to the house to see his works and the occasional trip was made to the Foreign Office, to find out if there had been any further developments regarding his son's military status. On 21 January 1918 momentary relief came after one such trip when the father met John Buchan who had 'said Richard need have no fear at all of going back into the army. If Head's letter didn't work, Buchan's department would take him for the whole war. An unspeakable relief.'[59] And so it was back to 'business as usual', apart from a rogue Zeppelin which damaged Richard's lithographer's studio and three of his stones, one of which was *The Road From Arras to Bapaume*.

Towards the end of 1917 and in the opening months of 1918 Richard exhibited widely through the London Group, the NEAC, the Senefelder Club, the Allied Artists, and at a host of other fund-raising events in Hampstead and Chelsea. He had continued his dalliance with non-war subjects, and had continued to experiment with degrees of abstraction in his work to find the most commonly acceptable medium. On the whole, however, reviews were poor and now his diluted depictions were ridiculed as simply displaying a lack of artistic direction. Frank Rutter, previously a staunch supporter, started to make comments that he had '*tout Paris* in his portfolio'[60] whilst Ezra Pound mockingly noted that he had a 'habit to choose a "different style" on what seems an average of once a fortnight'. In the same review he had gone on to highlight the credibility crisis by suggesting that the artist 'leave off trying to suit everyone all at once'.[61] It appeared that following the absolute success of the first Leicester Galleries show in 1916 the artist had found out, perhaps to his surprise, that his moderate modernism was not acceptable as a means in itself for the depiction of all things, rather a tool by which the war subject, exclusively, might be presented.[62] Success was deemed only possible through the inextricable linking of the two and through their development hand in hand.[63] But also he felt it vital to retain the role of the outspoken, uncompromising truth teller, and so in press releases he retained the polemic tone though it almost seemed unnecessary considering at whom it was aimed, and inappropriate considering the conservative nature of the paintings being presented. Or perhaps this was the very point, that now, more

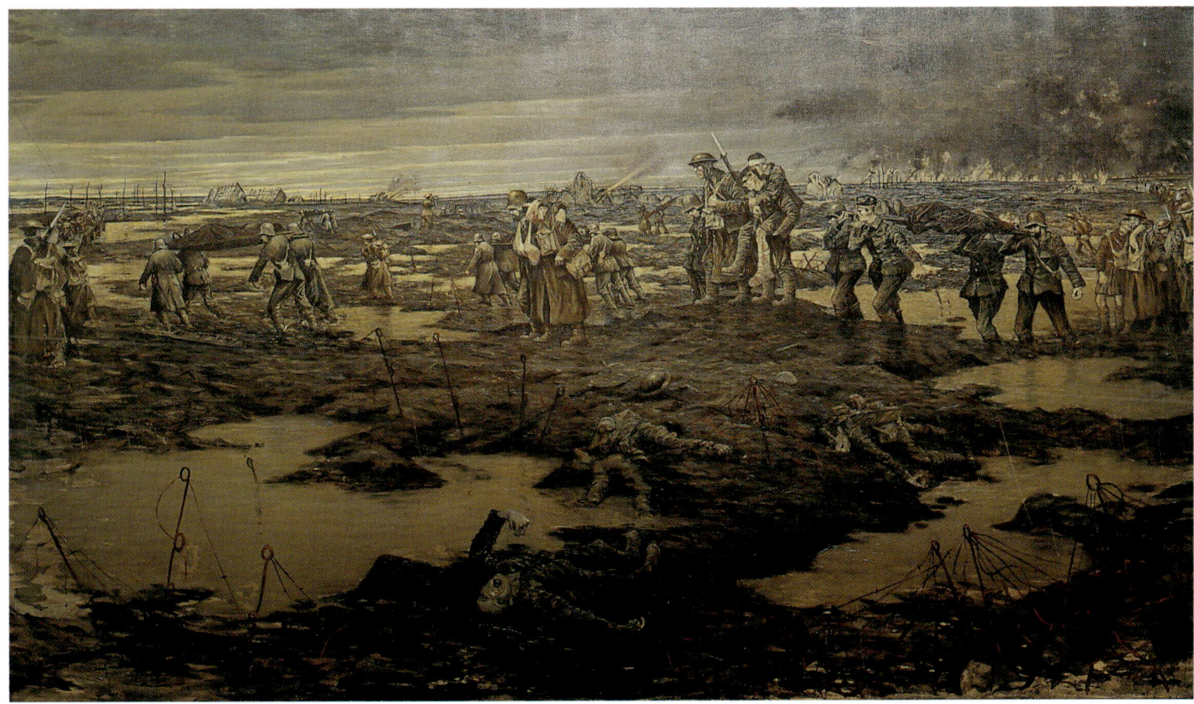

47. *Harvest of Battle*, 1919. Oil on canvas, 182.8 x 317.5 cm. Imperial War Museum, London.

than ever, the artist had to specifically declare himself the rebel, and create scandals of his own, or risk being seen exclusively as the 'official' painter at the Front.

'Alas! In time the Brass-Hats got at Nevinson.' [64]

In an attempt to win his way back into the favour of the Department of Information, Richard wrote to Masterman again in the new year suggesting ways of making the imminent exhibition of official war art at the Leicester Galleries a guaranteed success. The letter survives, dated 4 January 1918, and in it the old Futurist spirit, as propounded by Gabriele D'Annunzio,[65] requested 'If I could fly over London on the opening morning of my show chucking out handbills on the heads of "men in the street" this would start great publicity in the press.'[66] Offering to pay for the leaflets, and counting on help from General Brancker once again, he felt that this would be a means of getting the publicity that he believed the propaganda machine wanted, and from which he, and the War Office, could so directly benefit. It might also counteract the fact that his work was perceived as being somewhat 'dull'. The idea was declined by Masterman on 7 January 1918. Undeterred, the artist wrote back again, saying that if it was not seen as too vulgar, he might proceed anyway. Later, in yet another letter to Masterman, he admitted that considering the state of his nerves it would probably be for the best if the plan were abandoned.[67] Henry was doing his bit too, writing again on 5 February to ask if Jan Smuts, another acquaintance of his from the days in South Africa, would open his son's Leicester Galleries show, entitled *Exhibition of Pictures of War by C.R.W. Nevinson*, followed by a letter requesting the same thing from Lord Derby only three days later.[68] Richard tried Winston Churchill at the Ministry of Munitions but was turned down. Lord Derby requested that if he was to open the show he would only do it without publicity, which rather defeated the point of the invitation. Perhaps Derby had anticipated the trouble that even Henry had not seen coming until he was asked to read over the preface to the catalogue for the show which his son had written. This he described as 'a terribly provocative document'[69] and pondered on how it would backfire.

The opening and speech was conducted by Lord Beaverbrook[70] in the Hogarth Room of the Leicester Galleries, on 1 March 1918 and seemed to focus greatly on Henry, though it did at least say 'that Rich was an instance of inherited genius in a different art'.[71] The military, high society and the critics appeared to be sanctioning Richard and his work more so now than ever before. This coincided nicely with the decision on the part of the Department of Information to publish a book of his images with introductory essays by Dodgson and Montague, entitled *British Artists at the Front*. Also, in the days leading up to the show father and son were both sent the Mons Star by the Friends' Ambulance Unit and so the military credentials were once again revitalized at precisely the right moment.[72] Behind the scenes however, Major Lee, who had sent Richard home from the Front, was yet again incensed: 'I am going to see Nevinson's effort and shall find him out too and tell him what I think of his rotten little booklet. Bad from start to finish.'[73] Richard's dealings with Lee were by no means over. In fact, the Ministry of Information was openly involved in the show, and the fact that it was opened by Lord Beaverbrook, as Minister of Information, did nothing to hide the fact that it was to be a propaganda affair. This, from the very outset, set it aside from the private 1916 exhibition.

In his memoirs Richard reproduced the entire catalogue preface as it appeared. It is a lengthy document clarifying who he was, what he stood for, and perhaps more importantly, what he was, and what he did not stand for. Firstly, the exhibition was of works conducted over the previous seven months, and was therefore a synopsis of his officially commissioned work. It was also made clear that 'This exhibition differs entirely from my last in which I dealt largely with the horrors of War as a motive.'[74] The focus was now the human activity and the prodigious organization of 'our' army, recorded from countless trips to the Front, in aeroplanes, balloons, and over enemy lines. This he combined with the ability to work from memory, a skill acquired in Paris in student days, and a desire not to over-intellectualize painting as the Bloomsbury Group would do. He went on to distance this exhibition from the last by stating that in the interim he had experimented with various new styles. Clarifying the point he said 'I do not believe the same technique can be used to express a quiet static moonlight, the dynamic force of a bomber, and the restless rhythm of mechanical transport.'[75] Going on to explain that the individuality and personality of the artist should triumph over an intellectual mannerism, he expressed the desire to exhibit to the largest possible public. This eclecticism then catered for 'truth to subject', as opposed to any one set of theories or blinkered principles, and this was wholly in keeping with the priorities of 1916. He also claimed that he had no hidden agenda which could be linked to politics, theory, aesthetics or anything else, only a devotion to truth and honesty in fulfilling his role as a war artist. But by 1918, and in the knowledge of how the Vorticists, the Bloomsbury Group and even the Royal Academicians had not thrived during the war, this may be seen as a case of preaching to the converted in an environment that had already rejected the excesses of the movements and 'schools' Richard had highlighted. The catalogue displayed an increasing confidence and intolerance of those who disagreed with him and set a certain distance between the 1916 show and this one, in an awareness that two further years had passed and that the expectations of the public would be different. Extracts from it, however, may remind us forcefully of the pre-war artist and the proclamations made before August 1914:

> I have no illusions about the public for, owing chiefly to our Press, our loathsome tradition-loving Public Schools and our antiquity-stinking Universities, the average Englishman is not merely suspicious of the new in all intellectual and artistic experiment, but he is mentally trained to be so un-sportsman-like as to try to kill every new endeavour in embryo, especially if it shows signs of developing a future health and strength.[76]

In a condescending and increasingly inflammatory way the artist was in the process of alienating the public who were the very means of his success. Whether he intended this, or not, he was treating the art public as an uneducated mob, whom he would not criticize, and for whose tastes he would not cater, but for whom he was happy to use his art in the process of education. Once again the pre-war rhetoric is evident throughout the catalogue: 'I also feel convinced that it is the duty of every sincere artist to have the courage of this bellicose ideal, giving his finest, singing his song from the roof-tops, even using a mega-phone if necessary to overcome protesting howls.'[77]

Richard would also have been aware that his 1916 success was based very largely around the unprivileged, and therefore common, man, both as subject and as consumer. His depictions had not been of the official, privileged, or officers', war. It is therefore interesting to note that despite, allegedly, aiming his work at the common man and away from the intellectual *élites*, his second Leicester Galleries exhibition was attended by anything but the man on the street. The guests who attended the exhibition, were hand picked by him from *Who's Who*, and from this list of notables came further private sales.[78] A glance at the *Westminster Gazette* proves this point by listing some of the visitors: the Princess Royal, Princess Beatrice of Connaught, the Duchess of Marlborough, Herbert Asquith, Arthur Balfour, Lord Ribblesdale, the Marquis and Marchioness of Sligo, the Countess of Scarborough, Lady Tredegar, Baroness d'Erlanger, the Countess of Lytton, Lady Cunard, Countess Drogheda, Lord Desborough, General Sir Ian Hamilton, Sir John Lavery and so on.[79] As such, by 1918 the artist appeared to be bridging many of the traditional fissures in the art world and ostensibly winning recognition from critics, the public and the establishment alike. At a time when his pre-war peers were finding the atmosphere in wartime Britain detrimental to survival, let alone progress, Richard had fabricated a route to make him the most celebrated and talked about artist of the day. But this time he did not project himself as the soldier/artist, rebel and patriot. Rather, he felt sufficiently secure to let the image of the artist come to the fore again, and so *Sketch* could report seeing him in a black velours hat and a red crêpe scarf round his neck'[80] while the *Star* spotted him in a 'black student hat and orange muffler'.[81] He was no longer solely the artist in khaki (fig. 48).[82]

It seems strange then, that if anything, he retreated yet further from the modernism he had employed in the 1916 show, to become, as the *Illustrated London News* called him, 'a Realist'.[83] A glance at paintings such as *Inside Brigade Headquarters* (fig. 45), or *Reliefs at Dawn* (fig. 49) confirm that suspicion, though must be offset against clear examples of eclecticism which afforded depictions as diverse and as extreme as *The Bomber* (fig. 50). Once again, as with the 1916 show, Richard was clearly utilizing the subjective treatment of form to illustrate his autonomy from theories or doctrines that might prove restrictive or irrelevant to what was being depicted. Frank Maclean acknowledged this claiming that the 'Great Catastrophe' had made artists reconsider pre-war beliefs and made them question whether or not some 'constructive' and 'reconciling doctrine for the future of art might not be evolved'. Richard, and perhaps Richard alone, in his opinion, had done this, and in so doing had created a microcosm of harmony in the arts, of universal popularity among critics, artists and public alike, and was thus reaping the

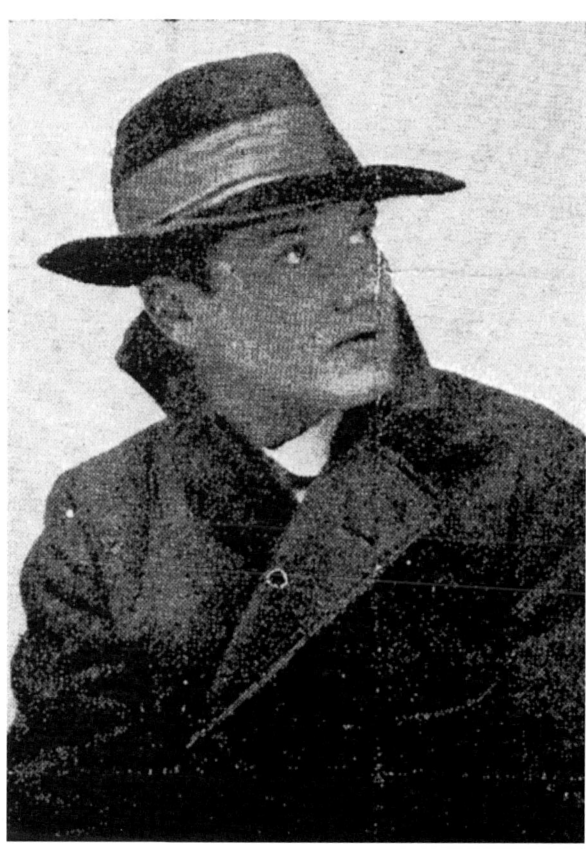

48. The Official War Artist. Reproduced in *The Sketch*, 27 March 1918.

reward for observing, maybe even creating, the 'New Freedom in Art'.[84] For others, then and since, it simply displayed the end of his 'moral anger'[85] and marked the dawn of works which were 'stridently obvious'.[86]

Overall, however, his retreat in style and subject matter in painting was not as a direct result of his official commission as has previously been suggested. Rather it had manifested itself in the six months prior to the commission and so the two facts, though closely related, are not interdependent. It should also be noted that although his style may have become undeniably more conservative, this did not prevent him continuing to exhibit with the old rebel coteries such as the AAA and the London Group. In other words it would be dangerous to comment too firmly on the magnitude and permanence of the shift to the 'right', even though, from a glance at his 1917 production, it would be tempting to do so.[87] The government's choice of a modernist, indeed a Futurist, as an official war artist, would have at one time seemed unthinkable, even outrageous.[88] Perhaps they had employed an ex-Futurist, as they had finally woken up to the strength and potential of a harnessed, modern, virile art – or perhaps not. The fact that the momentum of his radical past took a while to die down, and that his previous image was not easily or quickly shed, does not imply that the government, or the establishment in general, had come round to a more avant-garde way of thinking or had come to appreciate the

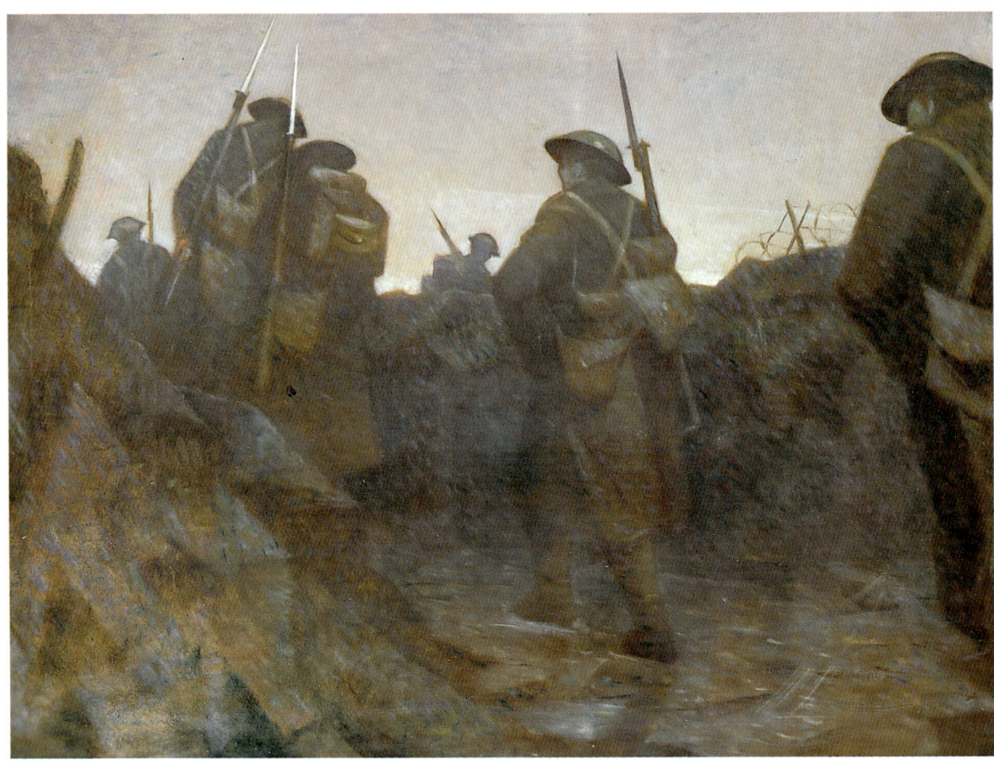

49. *Reliefs at Dawn*, 1917. Oil on canvas, 71.1 x 80 cm. Imperial War Museum, London.

usefulness or appropriateness of this means of depiction. Therefore, it is difficult to share the opinion of the *War Budget* which excitedly declared: 'Yet this ultra-modern experiment has come off with flying colours.'[89] Other reviews also did not shed the association with the past, or appreciate the dawning of a new set of artistic priorities on the part of the artist. In an article entitled 'Futurism Today', the *Globe* had the following to say: 'Mr Nevinson's contemporary work should be studied by all those people who laughed at Futurism in its infancy, without attempting to understand its underlying ideas, and who have since imagined that it has passed into the limbo of ephemeral absurdities.'[90] For them it was a mature form of modern representation, rather than a betrayal or an abandonment of pre-war ideologies. The *Saturday Review* could not have agreed less and wrote: 'Not to beat about the bush, the Trustees of the Imperial War Museum have put their money on the wrong horse.'

The hostility did not stop with art criticism alone and the artist himself was checked as being 'self-righteous', and patronizingly dismissed as displaying all the 'rawness of youth'.[91] Richard of course responded in kind and as a result the editor got a lengthy letter, which complained of 'hack-journalists', defended his good character, which he believed had been attacked, and dismissed the writers' artistic sensibility as that of 'some Italian woman'.[92] As if to buttress the artist's defence, many of the paintings exhibited were bought by official institutions: four going to the Canadian War Memorial Fund and a further eight going to the Imperial War Museum.

Conveniently, running in parallel to the exhibition once again, was the publication of a further book dedicated to Richard's war paintings entitled *British Artists at the Front*, with an introduction by Campbell Dodgson. As this was a Wellingtom House publication it serves as a useful insight into the 'official' perception of Richard's painting as opposed merely to the critic's or indeed the artist's own. They too promoted the originality of his work, the eclecticism of it and the moderation in statements such as 'He has not forsworn the practice of Cubism and Futurism, but he has adapted these methods successfully to the treatment of subjects which interest the average man.'[93] Again, the benefit of the war as subject matter had facilitated the artist's return from what had been a ruinous course into abstraction and irrelevance, and which, epitomized by the 1916 exhibition, had saved his career. It also, in its overtones, suggested that the artist had changed his focus from depicting the negativity and destructiveness of war to the positive aspects apparent even at this late stage in the conflict. Instead of a chaos of destruction, these had become records of organization and construction. Noticeable also was the lack of human presence, so prevalent in his earlier pieces. Where humans were depicted it was in the context of routine or organizational work, not in the front line or in a life and death grapple. But this shift had also brought him to paint what some believed to be the 'side show', not the actual fighting or the suffering so prevalent in the first exhibition. For many, including the officials at Wellington House, this was not necessarily a step in the right direction, and led to the previously recorded comments on

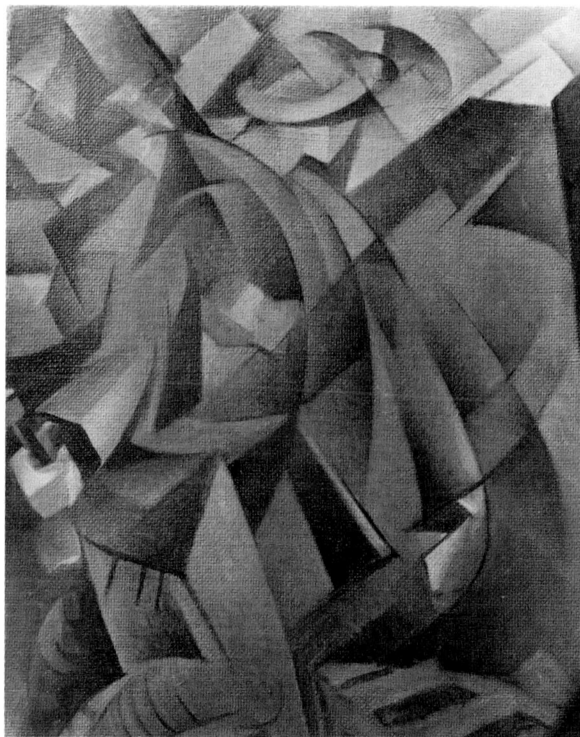

50. *The Bomber*, 1918.
Oil on canvas, 50.8 x 40.6 cm.
Whereabouts unknown.

dullness. For others, most notably in the military, there were no such complaints. A letter to the *Saturday Review* from a lieutenant in the Royal Warwickshire Regiment, read: 'Show them to any fellow who has inhabited a dug-out. Pass them round any mess in France or Flanders. Ask the man next to you in hospital in town what he thinks of them . . . I think you will find he has a pretty whole-hearted admiration for the Art of the man who has realised it so wonderfully.'[94]

The retreat from the avant-garde pre-war and early-war sympathies was now well underway, towards an intelligible form of illustrative depiction which, whilst appealing to many, disappointed others and marked the end of his experimentation with anything other than representational painting. John Salis observed, and explained this, when he warned

> There may be some who will not find these pictures quite as exciting as were the first red-hot impressions which Mr Nevinson brought back from France, but in those early days war was not as yet a business...there was shift and makeshift which gave it a character entirely different from the war of to-day whose sad motto is 'Business as Usual.' And it is this latter aspect which Nevinson has set out to show and with complete success.[95]

In technique *The Times* couldn't find the exact pigeon-hole for him, between Van Gogh in his treatment of landscapes, and the Royal Academy, for which they said his paintings would be considered 'superior'.[96] But despite the dramatic proclamations in the preface to the 1918 show the exhibition was by all accounts tame in comparison to the 1916 one. It was, however, more successful and profitable than its predecessor, and Richard's paintings, photographs and caricatures had never been in the public eye more (fig. 51). Henry recorded that the 'tubes [were] red with his picture of spiky bayonets' (fig. 52),[97] which was, of course, his self-designed poster advertising the show.

Some Key Works and Comparisons

Only one glimpse of Richard's radical past is afforded in *The Bomber* (fig. 50); the dynamic, human, active past on which his reputation up until to this point had been built. Indeed, it is as Futurist a composition as perhaps one would have expected from the 1914–15 era, with the figure reduced to 'lines of force', geometric simplification, and placed on the obligatory fractured picture plane. It is a mechanical reduction, focussing not on the human but on the dynamism of the movement, like one individual isolated from *Returning to the Trenches*. Perhaps it was a token gesture on the part of the artist to demonstrate that no significant U-turn had taken place, no abandonment of principles, whatever the overall appearance.[98] But this was not typical. The disparity between compositions of 1916 and those of 1918 is best seen through other direct comparisons on similar themes. *Swooping Down on a Hostile Plane* (fig. 42), though tackling the imminently modern concept of military aviation, epitomized the retreat of the artist in terms of technique if not subject matter, from the early depictions of similar subjects such as *Pursuing a Taube*

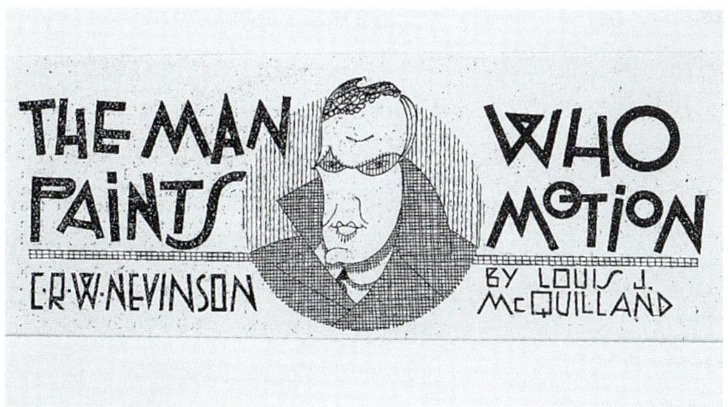

51. 'The Man Who Paints Motion'. Caricature, Lloyds Magazine. Tate Gallery Archive.

(Taube Pursued by Commander Samson) (fig. 31) of 1915. The latter canvas depicted the concepts of speed, force, motion and direction in a composition that was described as cinematographic. Richard had attempted to introduce a kinetic element to convey the modernity of the subject, utilizing the angular forms and 'lines of force' so typical of his pre-war early-war modernism.[99] He had not attempted to create a representative copy of anything he had seen but rather to reconstruct the sensations one might have felt in the heat of the chase and in a struggle to the death

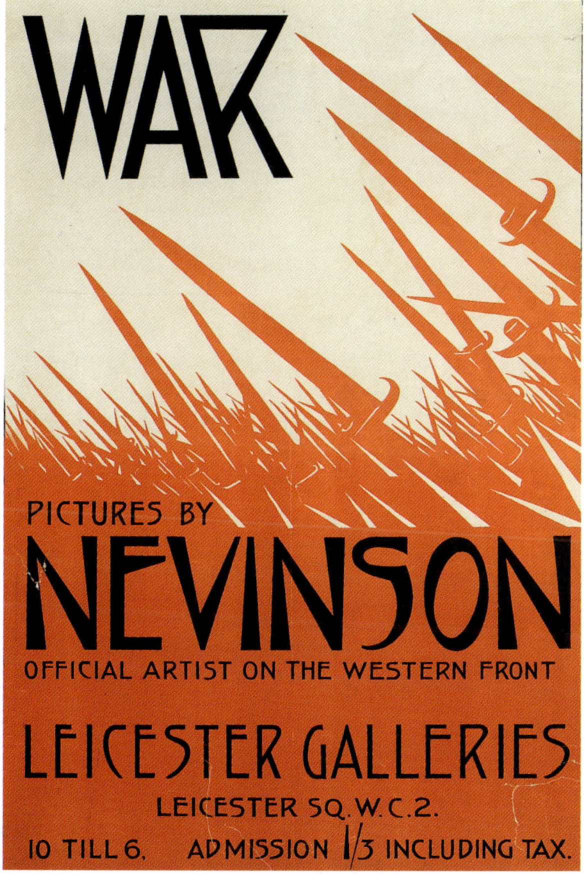

52. *War: Pictures by Nevinson Official Artist on the Western Front*, 1918. Lithograph, 75 x 49.3 cm. Imperial War Museum, London.

in the most modern of man's war machines. Konody wrote: 'It is inconceivable that anything like it could have been expressed by any other means' and went on to say 'It is not too much to say, that never before has flight been expressed in paint so convincingly, so clearly.'[100] And so the painting was seen as dynamic, innovative, topical and more than anything, original. *Swooping Down on a Hostile Plane* was wholly different as it was an almost photographic representation of an aeroplane beginning its descent on a virtually unseen enemy. Though aesthetically pleasing, and almost certainly an accurate representation of what the scene must have looked like, the canvas essentially conveyed little more than a well taken photograph of the same. Dodgson, nevertheless, believed that 'Any people who look at these drawings a century hence may feel that they are wiser than we, and yet that we had the best of it – we and not they had the visions of the prime.'[101]

But Richard's job as an Official War Artist as he saw it, was to record what was happening in France, not to comment upon it or to expose it to some illegible artistic interpretation. As a consequence, much of the 1918 show was made up of conventional depictions of the Western Front, encapsulated best perhaps, by the series *The Roads of France* (fig. 44). Here, in a frieze-like composition, one follows the procession of soldiers and equipment from behind the lines, at the railhead, right up into the firing line, in a deteriorating countryside. The theme of the 'never-ending procession' was one that he had attempted on several occasions before in successful compositions such as *Returning to the Trenches* and *The Road to Ypres* and so, here, the artistic gulf between 1915 and 1917 is most evident in terms of treatment and in artistic goals. The latter hardly compares favourably to the former.

Now he was more concerned with the 'before' and 'after' scenes of battle rather than with the heart of the conflict, as had been seen in earlier canvases such as *Bursting Shell* or *La Mitrailleuse.* Rather, he now was attempting to capture the preparations of the army prior to the Passchendaele campaign, and where possible to record the aftermath of such activity. *Shell Holes* (fig. 46) is a record of such an aftermath. Here is the landscape of modern war, un-picturesque, sodden and the result of the collision of two titanic forces. Nature alone is used to depict the enormity of the conflict, not individuals or images of wounded and dead. The apocalyptic vision, by implication, is more powerful than a more typical illustration of the time, and, using a different means, still aims at the emotions aroused by previous compositions such as *La Patrie.*

But the extent of the change in his work is perhaps only fully comprehended when one turns to canvases such as *War Profiteers* (fig. 53) and *He Gained a Fortune but he Gave a Son* (fig. 54).[102] Here, Richard forayed into commenting on aspects of morality surrounding the conflict on the 'home front',[103] abandoning completely the radical technical approaches of the pre- and early war years, in order that the subject of the painting should be unmistakable. The artist now had an opinion and a comment to make, as opposed to merely an aesthetic theory or an advanced method of recorded interpretation to propound. The war, he acknowledged, was not only fought at the Front, neither was it for everybody, the tragedy that it had been for the majority. In *War Profiteers* he depicted two women, neither threatened by the war

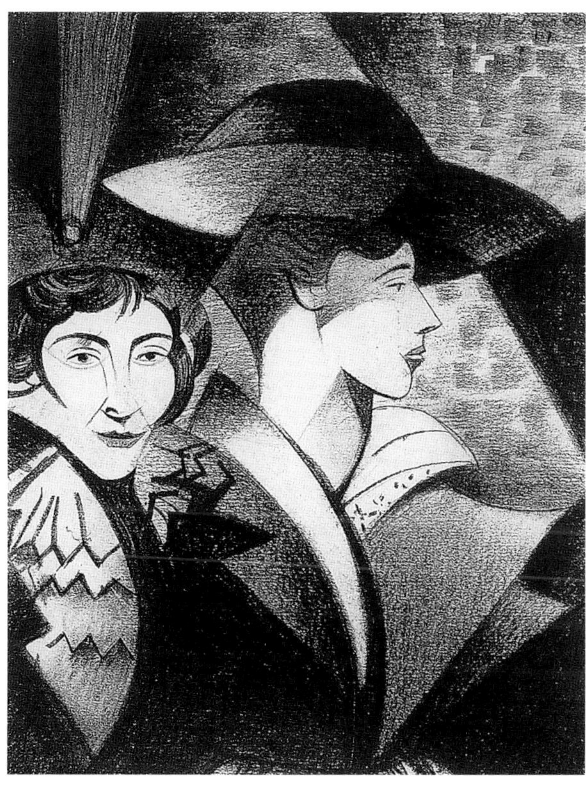

53. *War Profiteers*, 1917.
Oil on canvas, 91.4 x 71.1 cm.
Russell-Cotes Art Gallery,
Bournemouth.

nor in any way the worse off for it. On the contrary they had clearly benefited from it and were now living well off its proceeds. They are well dressed, well fed and immersed in the London night-life that could only have been afforded by the few. The artist put the ladies in a context of moving light, which Doherty sees as a direct metaphorical reference to searchlights and to the war around them to which they appear oblivious. He also noted that the colours used, albeit subtly, are those of the British flag, and so patriotism and profiteering advance hand-in-hand.[104] Whether they are wives or daughters of industrialists making money from the insatiable demand for munitions, or whether they are prostitutes, making money much more directly from the war, is unclear. The message was not lost on the critics who reported that they were 'clearly course and repulsive young women'[105] though deflected a lot of the controversy by suggesting that they were French.[106] Likewise, in *He Gained a Fortune but he Gave a Son* Richard commented on the relative price that had been paid in the war, even by those who came out better off financially. Though obviously comfortable now, the subject of the painting knows that it was through the very trade that made him rich that he had paid the price of a son. He is also left to speculate as to how many other sons it took to fall on the battlefields of Flanders and Picardy to make him as wealthy as he is today. There is a memento on the mantelpiece of his son, in military uniform, surrounded by all the trappings of wealth, creating the paradox within the composition. Richard clearly, in this painting, subordinated all form of artistic experimentation and innovativeness to the

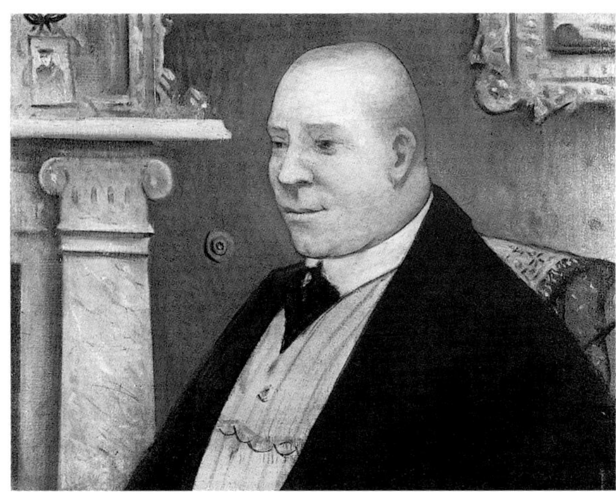

54. *He Gained a Fortune but he Gave a Son*, 1918. Oil on canvas, 40.6 x 50.8 cm. University of Hull.

function of conveying a moral message. There can be little in the artistic merits of this sentimental work to appeal to the purist, the historian or the critic, the latter of which was apt to calling it 'A crude, childish portrayal.'[107]

In a letter from Richard to Masterman, dated 10 March 1918, Richard could write enthusiastically of the record-breaking attendance at the galleries, only to be superseded the following week when the crowds were apparently so dense that it was difficult to see the pictures at all. This had shocked him and he wrote 'I am the more surprised at this popularity, as the general quality of the work is so much higher aesthetically than the last, and has very little appeal to the sensational which is so dear to the literary-minded Englishman.'[108] Gallery owner Oliver Brown also recorded that the show, at least, was as successful as the first.[109] Conveniently a further publication entitled *The Great War Fourth Year by C.R.W. Nevinson*, which had an introduction by J. E. Crawford-Flitch, was published in September of the same year, and so the debate was kept alive surrounding his paintings, long after the show had closed its doors. Designed by Grant Richards as a sequel to Konody's *Modern War*, it was independent from the influence of Wellington House, though read very much in the same vein as the earlier publication. Richard, as an ex-Futurist, had 'dethroned Venus only to enthrone Mars',[110] but not to glorify in the subject or to protest about it, simply to observe it without comment. In short, Crawford-Flitch advocated that his painting was the 'truth' from the trenches at last, and that was where its merit lay. He also finished his introductory essay by saying that there was a lot more for him to do on the subject of war, even after the conflict had ended.

The Censorship Question: *A Group of Soldiers* and *Paths of Glory*

But something had happened to Richard's mental state, and his nervous condition from later 1917. Any doubt about that was removed when his father started to observe the depression and despair in his son 'who [was now] much affected by the raids'.[111] Zeppelin raids had started again on 1 October in the area of London where they were living, and the Nevinsons, like many other Londoners, had taken to the tube for safety. With this ever-present nervous stress, combined with his already obdurate nature, his temper was short and he was more intolerant than ever. This manifested itself clearly when Major Lee, an old Uppingham peer, censored *Old Contemptibles*, later called *A Group of Soldiers* (fig. 55), on the grounds that the work was too ugly, despite the fact that Richard had simply set out to depict 'the British working man in khaki'.[112] His work had to undergo compulsory censorship since it was carried out in an official capacity,[113] and now as a result, Lee had dismissed the work saying that it depicted 'the type of man...not worthy of the British Army'.[114] There appeared to be a physiological code for the depiction of British troops as opposed to Germans, the latter of whom would be depicted as brutes or at best, merely uncultured and uneducated. Richard's depiction of the British army therefore was seen as an unacceptable self-portrait of what, in essence, was the nation's sons, brothers and fathers. Henry noted his son's response and wrote 'Richard in great trouble and rage.'[115] The nature of the artist's consequent rage can be felt in an undated letter, which, though written to Lee, was actually given to Masterman by Richard, and is reproduced in full here:

> Dear Major Lee,
>
> I am writing to you to ask if you would be good enough to let me have an idea of your ideal type of manly beauty as I have just heard that you have censored one of my best pictures as 'too ugly.' When I took on this job I of course understood that my work would be submitted to a military censor but I had no idea that it would also be submitted to an aesthetic censorship. So if you would just let me know what you consider a pretty man, I will in future paint all my soldiers up to your ideal, only I must know what it is . . . On the other hand I will not paint 'Castrated Lancelots' though I know this is how Tommies are usually represented in illustrated papers etc . . . high-souled eunuchs looking mild-eyed, unable to melt butter on their tongues and mentally and physically incapable of killing a German. I refuse to insult the British army with such sentimental bilge.[116]

Almost two weeks later, feelings still ran high over the whole censorship issue and a week after that his father was still concerned for his son's mental welfare. Further letters were written to Masterman claiming that there must be some form of appeals system as even the Royal Academy had that, and that Lee, working on those criteria, would have censored paintings by Forain, Rubens and Goya. Masterman nullified the censorship order and wrote telling Richard of his decision on 26 November 1917 and then the following day to Lee. This could not have pleased the latter who had a personal dislike for the artist, claiming that 'he deserves all he gets' and observed that the painting, which he called *A Group of Brutes*, was like a collection of ventriloquist's dummies.[117] More seriously he did genuinely believe that these paintings would help the Germans were they to fall into their hands.[118] The matter ended with a letter from Masterman to Richard, which said 'I entirely agree with you that Lee should only censor things from a military point of view and that there is of course nothing of any military significance in the picture to which

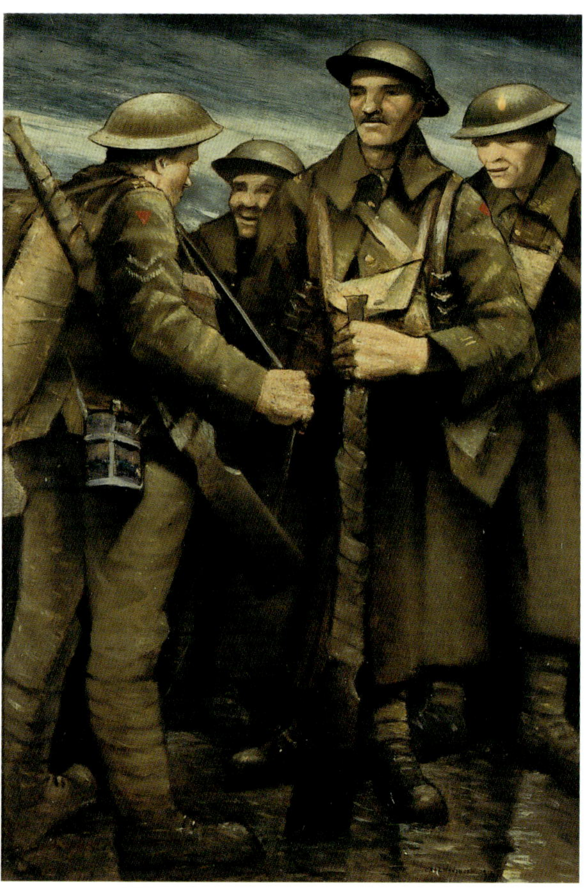

55. *A Group of Soldiers*, 1917.
Oil on canvas, 91.4 x 60.9 cm.
Imperial War Museum, London.

exception could be taken.'[119] He also wrote to Lee for future reference, saying 'If we judge of its ugliness or beauty as censors we are "in the soup" at once!!'[120] In fact, when the painting was exhibited the critics rather agreed with Lee and the work attracted comments suggesting it was a depiction of 'a crew of dummy hooligans...semi-idiotic puppets . . . a gang of loutish cretins'.[121] It had been a useful lesson for Richard, however, as the ambiguities in his 'official' status were now being questioned. In France he was subject to the will of the military, but at home he was a civilian – the boundaries were often blurred between the two.

There was another 'fly in the amber'[122] and that was *Paths of Glory* (fig. 56), which led him to fall foul of the military officials operating under the Defence of the Realm Act (DORA), in March 1918. The painting had been causing problems from November the previous year when, entitled *Dead Men*, it had caught the attention of Lee who admitted that it wasn't beneficial to the enemy but that it did raise 'a point of policy'.[123] By 3 December, Richard knew of the problem. The following day his father was entering into his journal that his son's future was 'very obscure' and the day after the two went together to see Buchan about the controversy. Richard said of this that he was delighted to have no official rank as in his own defence he could talk to the 'brass hats' on a man-to-man basis, something which would never have been possible had he been of a junior rank. But the result was the same. Images of the dead were to be rigidly suppressed – no exceptions, unless of course they were the enemy. Richard argued, saying that 'My picture happened to be a work of art',[124] depicting no actual person to be identified by a grieving relative, and having as a subject something that the British public had hardened to. But this was still the era when journalists such as W. Beach Thomas could write of the dead Tommy: 'Even as he lies in the field he looks more quietly faithful, more simply steadfast than others.'[125] In this context Richard's depiction of putrefying corpses seemed hardly appropriate. He also pointed out that, at this stage in the war, 'civilians, at any rate, know that war causes casualties, even if soldiers do not'.[126] Even the name *Paths of Glory* contained more than a hint of cynicism, taken as it was from the popular 'Elegy Written in a Country Churchyard' by Thomas Gray (1716–71). The original verse reads

The boast of heraldry, the pomp of power,
And all that beauty, all that wealth e'er gave,
Awaits alike the inevitable hour,
The paths of glory lead but to the grave.

The subdued polemic is reiterated in the knowledge that Richard had originally thought of calling it *Shall their Sacrifice be in Vain?* Later, he explained the censorship situation to American journalists: 'A Don't had been issued to the censors on pictures of dead bodies. Cause – some poor mother had recognised the mangled

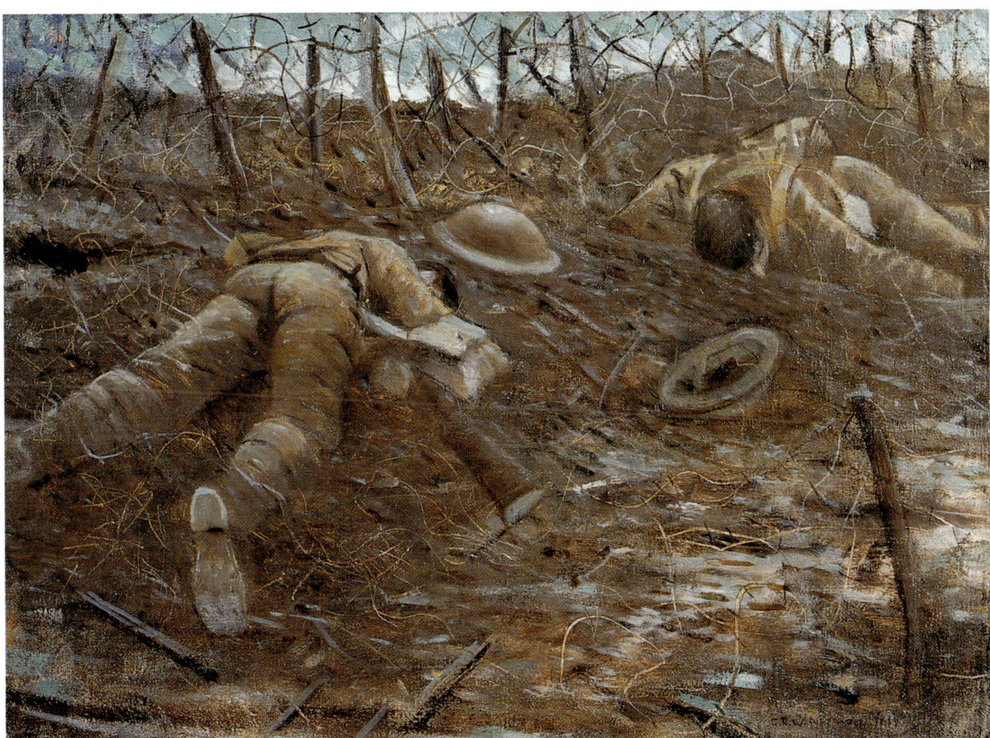

56. *Paths of Glory*, 1917. Oil on canvas, 45.7 x 60.9 cm. Imperial War Museum, London.

body of her own son in an official photograph. A painting which I made of corpses, of course, had no portraits in it, but nevertheless the rule applied.'[127]

In similar vein he wrote to Masterman, 'My only instructions from you were to paint exactly what I wanted, as you knew my work would be valueless as an artist and propagandist otherwise.'[128] The censorship battle went on for months and Masterman stopped answering his letters and refused to see him. On the whole, however, Richard's handling of the entire issue, with the assistance of his father, was to keep his name to the forefront of the press, not as the anti-establishment rebel, but, once again, as the victim of the establishment in pursuit of the truth. His action, therefore, in exhibiting *Paths of Glory*, albeit with the word 'Censored' scrawled across it in blue chalk on brown paper and stuck to the canvas, was leading him into a dangerous position concerning his hard-fought-for status of official artist (fig. 57). A letter from Alfred Yockney to the artist, dated 20 December 1917, had made the ban final and there should have been no further ambiguity.[129] His father's journal recorded on 15 March 1918, 'Rich was in trouble as I expected about the exhibition of the censored picture'.[130] Whether naïvety, or carefully crafted media manipulation it cornered the press reviews and this could not have endeared him to the military authorities. Could it have been an attempt on the part of the artist to instigate a debate on the relationship between art, war and the authorities? Might it have been a direct way of placing the whole question of censorship up for examination? Or was it simply a very risky publicity stunt carried out in the hope that he would not upset his patrons too much, while benefiting from the publicity which was bound to flow his way as a result?[131] A letter to Masterman suggests that during the controversy the gallery had submitted the frame and the pasted paper to another censor who had subsequently passed it[132] and so the artist could plead ignorance of the law as it was inconsistent and virtually unintelligible. The censor had been cast in the role of villain while leaving him once again in the role of innocent and much misunderstood artist striving for the truth. The media in the weeks leading up to the exhibition asked: 'Things we want to know . . . what is hidden by the patch?',[133] while mysteriously and hastily, the Imperial War Museum bought the painting, presumably in order to control its exhibition and reproduction. *Paint and Prejudice* innocently suggests that he hung the painting, as he was sure the censors would change their minds at the last minute. Malvern is not sympathetic however, saying 'The painting, because of its notoriety, acquired a significance it did not warrant and since it was, and still is, perceived as a martyr to censorship it had attributed to it an authenticity derived from circumstances.'[134] One way or another it was removed before the end of the show and replaced with *A Tank* (fig. 58).

A tactful departure to St Ives for a few days seemed advisable, based on the advice of Dr Head, as a cure for 'nerves and acute insomnia',[135] though Henry continued to go to his son's exhibition in his absence. Just before departure Richard tried to appease the establishment with a letter to Masterman explaining that he had been summoned to the War Office to be interviewed by a Captain Foster. The letter read 'It appears there is some regulation which forbids the mention of censorship; as

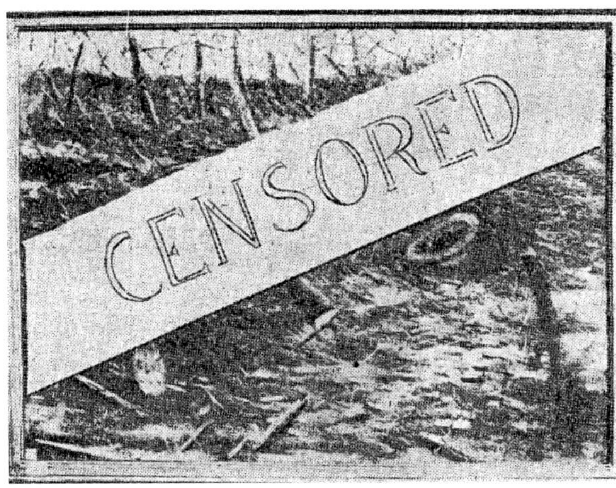

57. *Paths of Glory 'Censored'*, 1918. Oil on canvas and glued paper, 45.7 x 60.9 cm. *Daily Mail*, 2 March 1918.

usual I did not know about it, and I hope I made it clear to Captain Foster that I have better things to do than offending the censor.'[136]

When Richard and Kathleen returned from their break on 3 April, Henry was dismayed to note that 'he is almost insane with anxiety as I feared'.[137] And not without cause. Henry could only lament in his journal 'If one is defiant, one must expect disturbance and face it.'[138] Not only had Richard upset the authorities over the censorship issue, and thus called into question his position as an official artist serving in relative safety and only periodically, but he had done it at exactly the time that the Germans were launching their 'spring offensive' at Saint-Quentin. The horrors for the British army at Passchendaele had left enormous gaps in the ranks and now, more than ever, every eligible British man was required in the field. The Military Service Act (no. 2) of 1918 was within days of being passed, further invalidating all previous exemption clauses and extending the eligible age to fifty-one. In short, it was a national emergency. The following day Henry entertained his son and Kathleen at Maxims, 'to distract R's haunted mind'[139] and three days later Henry contacted Masterman who 'assured me that Richard is absolutely safe'.[140]

Once again it was one of Henry's friends, this time Konody, who came to the rescue. Now, as head of the Canadian War Memorials Committee, he transferred Richard out of the unpleasantness by offering him another commission specific to the Canadian government. After an initial aviation piece he would be set to work painting workshops and the like, all of which would be purchased at a fair rate. On hearing the news Henry rushed to the Friday Club to tell his son the good news, though missed him there.

The rest of the month settled back into a degree of normality. Richard exhibited at the Friday Club on 12 April. The following day he sold a blank canvas at an auction at Christie's as part of the wartime fundraising efforts of the Red Cross, for the princely sum of £120.[141] During this month too he was negotiating with his father's friend Robert Ross, who was an advisor to the British War Memorials Committee, a commission for the planned permanent exhibition to the war dead in the Hall of Remembrance.[142]

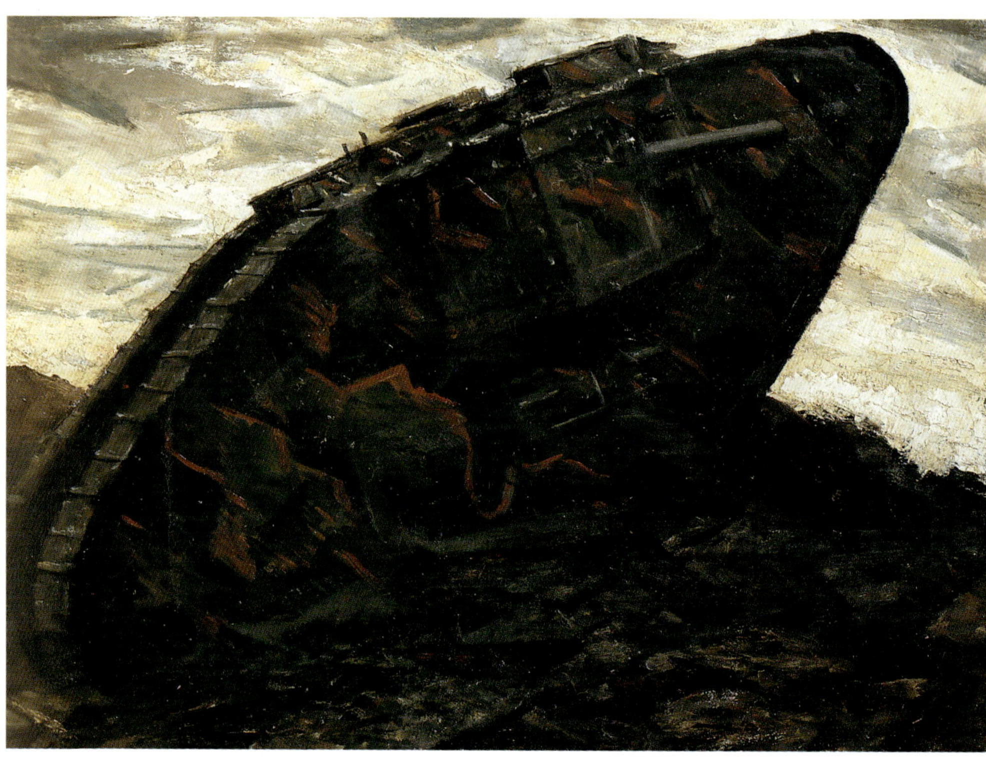

58. *A Tank*, 1917. Oil on canvas, 44.2 x 59.3 cm. Imperial War Museum, London.

Throughout April Richard had been writing to Ross trying to suggest his own direction. He said 'I wish someday I might have permission to paint a huge works up north. I paint that type of thing with far greater enthusiasm than these eternal aeroplanes. Oh! I'd love to paint a camouflaged liner at the docks.'[143] Later in the month he suggested a return to an old, successful theme, that of the field casualty stations. He said 'I feel most competent to do this side of the war as I became familiar with it in the ranks, and it is the side that interests and moves me the most.'[144]

Both Richard and Kathleen were now entering the realms of celebrity status with the press, a position that Richard did everything to encourage. Even retrospectively, critics were now beginning to acknowledge that in the pre-war years he had stood like 'a young oak amidst a tangle of creepers' and that he had forged ahead while 'his contemporaries were preaching anarchy and painting piffle'.[145] The public persona, and the charisma of the artist, were now beginning to eclipse his actual paintings, which were undeniably relinquishing their claim to any bona fide stance within the avant-garde of English painting.

On 1 May, Henry attended the NEAC exhibition to see a painting of the sky and broken trees by his son, which had been attracting a lot of criticism. For once Henry wasn't supportive of the effort, claiming 'I agree, there is not enough stuff or guts in it.'[146] Regardless, Richard was happier and there were even instances again of he and his wife throwing large house parties with drinking and dancing until the early hours of the morning.[147]

A chance diary entry on 29 June shows that the rift between Lewis and Richard had not healed, when Henry tried to speak to him and found him 'sullen and hostile on account of Richard.' A matter of weeks later Richard started receiving anonymous telegrams saying 'Stop your slanderous activities or I will stop you!' and this, Henry believed, was also the work of Lewis.

On his return from France on 28 August Henry reported to the War Office to confirm his re-entry into Britain and to check up on his son's position with Major Foster. It seems ironic that the old man was still in uniform and had been to the various theatres of war many times now, while his son, who had built his reputation on war and on his depictions of it, remained out of uniform and moreover 'in distress again about his visit to France'.[148] Richard went to France again for a week, returning home on 24 September, but this was both disappointing and unproductive as the subject Konody had set him (an air battle involving Canadian ace W. A. Bishop) proved too difficult to recreate. His attempts resulted in the composition *War in the Air* (fig. 59). In fact, in France he suffered a further breakdown of sorts that necessitated an immediate return home. This continued artistic retreat, or degeneration, had been observed by Arnold Bennett who, in an internal memorandum, had noted 'There is not by any means the same striking creative force. My opinion is that this artist is running short of inspiration for war subjects at the front. I suggest that he should either have a rest or be put on to a different sort of subject in England. If he continues on present lines the result is likely to be unsatisfactory.'[149] In a return document Ross talked of 'monotony', 'sameness' and 'repetition'.[150] In short, Richard was losing ground, though it was never underestimated how well he was known to the public and how he was capable of selling out an exhibition.[151] Luckily this crisis was averted by the end of the war on 11 November 1918.

For Richard the news of the Armistice led to the predictable relief of a man who had been living in fear for years and who now had had all threat removed. This manifested itself at the favourite pre-war haunt, the Café Royal, when 'I climbed the pillars of the old café'.[152] His claim that the Armistice led to the total cessation of his painting of war scenes is untrue as, armed with a letter of introduction from Yockney, he was once again in France during the last week of November and the first few weeks of December,[153] working towards a composition called *The Harvest of Battle*, which had been commissioned by the British government for £300.[154] On hearing of the cessation of hostilities Henry returned to mainland Europe, not even returning for Christmas, and wrote on New Year's Eve in Cologne: 'So another year ends: a year which at last brought peace and woman suffrage: and to me personally Richard's safety.'

A Dangerous Artistic Legacy

Notoriety had come at a price to his status within the avant-garde, and the war years, as represented by both Leicester Galleries exhibitions, had thrust him into the spotlight giving him the prominence he had desired as an artist. It is not coincidental, therefore, to see early projections suggesting that this change in direction

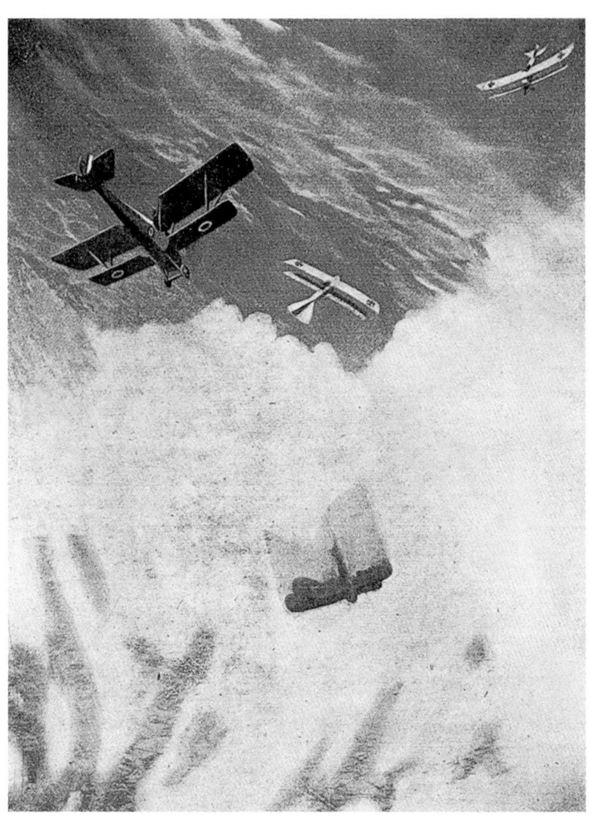

59. *War in the Air*, 1918.
Oil on canvas, 304.8 x 243.8 cm.
National Gallery of Canada, Ottowa.

was permanent, indeed irreparable. Arnold Bennett had observed this, writing, 'As Nevinson is admittedly the chief war-painter a special observation about him may be made. I saw his new show on Friday last. It contains some fine things, but as a whole it can scarcely be compared to his previous show a year or so ago. There is not by any means the same striking creative force.'[155] Indeed the recession from the image of the rebel painter continued and by November 1918, the *Saturday Review* suggested that he was 'predestined for the Academy at an early date' and went so far as to suggest that this path would lead to 'the Presidential Chair itself'.[156] Konody himself, with more than a little cynicism, commented 'Who knows? Mr Nevinson may yet become a pre-Raphaelite.'[157]

With the end of the war imminent, and with so much of his success having been based on the war image, Richard was going to have to identify with something other than the war subject following the Armistice. He had not identified a 'hallmark' technique throughout the war years, indeed he had been notable for exactly the opposite. Peters Corbett observed that 'a collapse into uncertainty' was inevitable.[158]

Though his popularity was immense during the 1915–18 period, he was now running the risk of falling between two stools when the conflict ended. Already ostracized by the purists, and now employing a vocabulary sustained substantially by the dynamism of the subject matter, peace could, and would, bring an evacuation of the picture and create a subject vacuum. In the place of the dominant subject would return the primacy of technique and of theory, but by this stage Richard had renounced that for the intelligible medium of the second Leicester Galleries show. Though riding on the crest of a wave by the Armistice on 11 November 1918, a crisis of identity in artistic terms was imminent. As the public lost their taste for the war theme, so would they lose their enthusiasm for Richard's art. Rutter was not slow to anticipate this and wrote 'There is a danger that Mr Nevinson may have survived the war only for his art to be killed by his popularity.'[159]

10

The Transition to Peace and the New World 1918–1919

For Nevinson there is no armistice. He is always at war.[1]

Richard recorded in *Paint and Prejudice* that the end of the war had categorically brought the end of his war painting with it. He wrote: 'I may have varnished one of them and framed another, but after the Armistice I did not do a stroke of painting which dealt with the war.'[2] This coincided nicely with the invitation by Charles Sims to put his name forward for the Royal Academy.[3] As optimistic as this may have seemed, he also recorded that it was in this period once again that he encountered the hostility of the 'intellectuals'. Attacks came from all sides; Claude Phillips, for one, was remembered as a hypocrite and Rutter, though not named, was singled out for an article entitled 'Exit Nevinson'. Even joining the Chelsea Arts Club on the suggestion of Alvaro Guevara did not help; he revoked his membership after only one night following a series of insults by Derwent Wood. On top of everything else, 'officialdom' had ousted him as they felt that he would not subscribe to the national sentiment that, however cruel and costly the war had been, it had, on the whole, been worthwhile.

But if post-war life was perhaps difficult, it was certainly not idle or unproductive, and by January 1919 he was exhibiting at the *Canadian War Memorial Exhibition* at Burlington House.[4] The introduction in the catalogue said that the artists had been selected in 'the most catholic spirit, to represent every school and group, from the most academic and traditional to the most revolutionary and advanced'.[5] The attitude to Richard's work, however, contrary to that of the exhibition on the whole, was only fairly positive. Even former allies wrote that the artist had peaked in 1915 and had been declining ever since, congratulating 'the Canadian authorities on having acquired some of Mr Nevinson's good early works' but going on to 'advise them to lose the later ones in the Atlantic'.[6] But if criticism was to be levelled at him, it was not going to be taken lying down. In a return letter to the *Sunday Times*, he stated:

> However, when your critic announced, with thinly disguised pleasure, my deterioration, he ought to prove his case – to be able to distinguish between my early

> and later work. This he has failed to do; therefore I feel I am entitled to some explanation, not to mention my 'ignorant and contemporary public' whom I presume your critic is employed to enlighten.[7]

Phillips too observed that Richard could 'no longer be counted among cubists, hardly indeed among the ultra-moderns'.[8] Without a war, and without the 'rebel' kudos, it appeared the artist was quickly being side-lined from the forefront of the arts as post-war Britain perceived them.[9] That said, the *Daily News and Leader* did title its article on the exhibition 'Canada in the War: Futurist Painters' Impressions of the Battlefield'[10] while the *Daily Express* ran an article under the heading of 'Rebels in the Fortress'.[11] Despite these claims, however, it was generally agreed that he had 'largely disembarrassed himself of Cubist theories'.[12] In fact, he removed all doubt when, in an article entitled 'Are Futurists Mad?', he openly declared: 'I have now given up Futurism and am devoting my time to legitimate art.'[13] This too had its apologists and his close friend, Chadwick Moore, wrote to the *Sunday Times* claiming that leaving Futurism and Cubism behind was actually a progressive step, and one which most artists in Paris, including Picasso, were now doing in what was a continental *rappel à l'ordre*.[14]

Inevitable too was the return of the newly liberated pre-war modernists who now poached the spotlight in Room V, which was nicknamed 'the modernist gallery',[15] and in which Richard was not exhibited. It was this room, and these artists, who stole the show, and it is little wonder that he recorded the misery he experienced at becoming so peripheral so soon after the cessation of hostilities. The Canadian authorities had, however, made it very clear that 'cubist work would be inadmissible for the purpose' and Bomberg had had one of his works rejected as a 'futurist abortion'.[16] It was, therefore, reasonably difficult to ascertain exactly where the line should be drawn between representation and abstraction, and between literal images and interpretations. For the first time concerning the war, as far as the critics were concerned, it seems that Richard had miscalculated where this line fell. The *Manchester Guardian* didn't mention him until the last sentence of their review, and then only to say 'Mr Nevinson, in his large picture of an air fight, works in the ordinary convention.'[17] This went hand in hand with the first press pronouncements that he had had his name put forward for the Academy.[18] Indeed, satirical comments were aimed his way at this irony and the press were not slow to pick up on it. One report, on the eve of his departure for the United States, stated 'I see that a farewell dinner is to be given to Mr Nevinson before his departure to New York. I wonder whether he is going to be feasted by his erstwhile colleagues of the advance guard in art, or by his future fellow-members of the Royal Academy.'[19]

Nevertheless, Richard was busy recreating himself in a post-war world that, for him, and for many of his peers, would not only be impoverished, but would require a redefinition of the value and nature of their painting in order to traverse the transition period successfully. Unlike Nash, however, he did not wish to hide away or to retreat into convalescence, but turned once again to the city. Reporters observed him and his fashionable wife at the Café Royal,[20] singing 'a coon song' at the Poet's

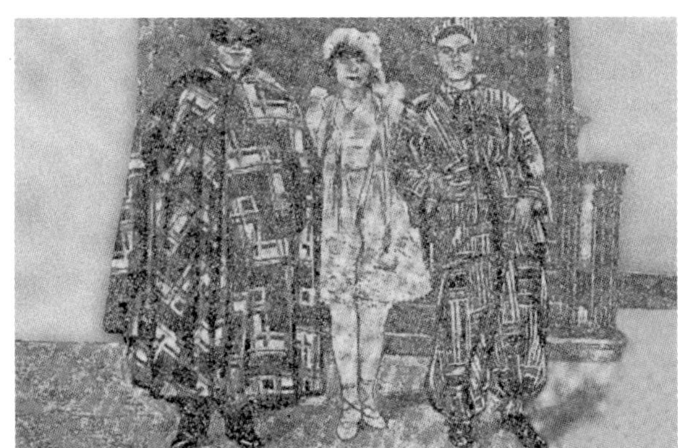

60. Chelsea Arts 'Dazzle' Ball at the Albert Hall. Nevinson is on the right. Photograph from *The Daily Graphic*, 14 March 1919.

Club,[21] and dancing and sketching at London's clubs.[22] They also attended the Chelsea Arts Club Ball at the Royal Albert Hall, entitled the Dazzle Ball, and photographs appeared of them in 'Futurist' dress in many society magazines and papers (fig. 60).[23]

By early March reports were being made publicly that Richard's work, alongside those of other 'official' war painters, would be making its way to the Worcester Art Museum, in Massachusetts and that a lecture tour would ensue.[24] Before leaving, however, much was to be done in London in keeping his high profile to the fore and his artistic identity intact. On 10 March he published a lengthy article in the *Daily Express*, typically entitled 'Bolshevism in Art: Catering For the Intellectual Snob'. In this he attacked once more the élitist coteries who did not destroy in order to rebuild, but who worked for a minority intelligentsia, who prided themselves in the comprehension of the obscure as a form of 'one-upmanship'. These groups he claimed were a 'parasitic growth', and should not be the voice of all labelled 'rebels' in the capital. Inevitably 'the liberty-loving artist prefers to leave the paths that end in the dreary and oppressive cul-de-sac of the so-called art rebel'.[25] The previous day he had also been reported on in the *Weekly Dispatch* and had given his views on war and art and on the path forward. In it he talked about 'an enormous longing for order', however ironic that may have seemed coming from an artist who had preached, then painted, chaos in the not so distant past. He put the point beyond ambiguity stating 'My joy in chaos is gone' and claimed that to stick to the polemics of 1913 was now very dated. Making exception only for *Harvest of Battle*, he said that all war work was finished with and that the new focus would be on modern industrialism and on human activity, the latter of which he defined as his epitome of beauty.[26] Thus the distance was finally created, the official abandonment of pre-war and wartime associations complete, and the reasons stated. Sitwell argued that this was not through fear or conservatism, but simply an indication of Richard's permanent quest for change and relevance in the depiction of modern life and in adherence to the artist's dictum of 'art rules the artist'.[27] Consequently, it was now time to replace that void with a new and original identity. [28] It was to this period that works such as *Old Southwark Bridge* (fig. 61), *Hampstead Heath* (fig. 62) and

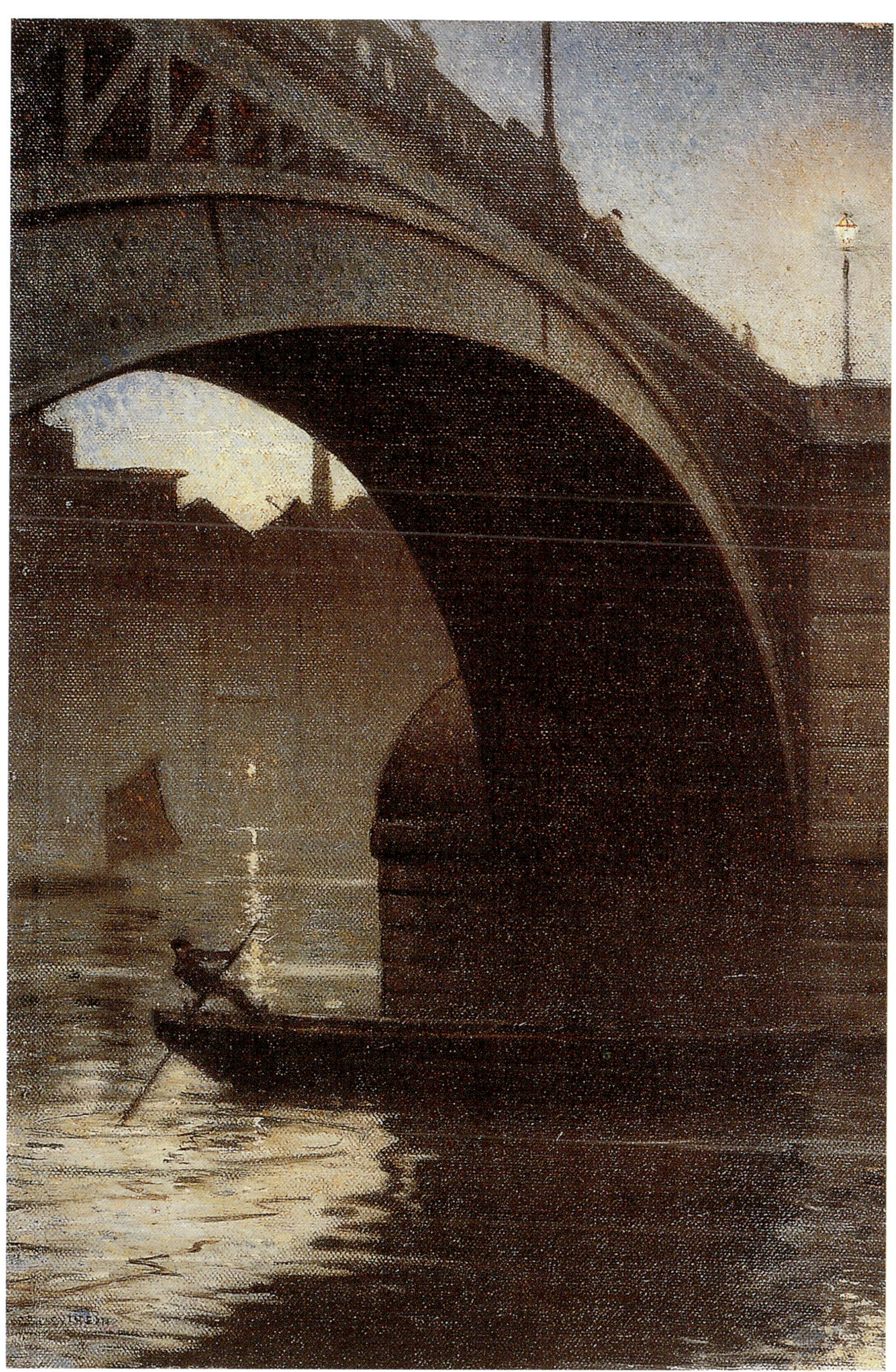

61. *Old Southwark Bridge*, 1919. Oil on canvas, 76 x 51 cm. Private collection.

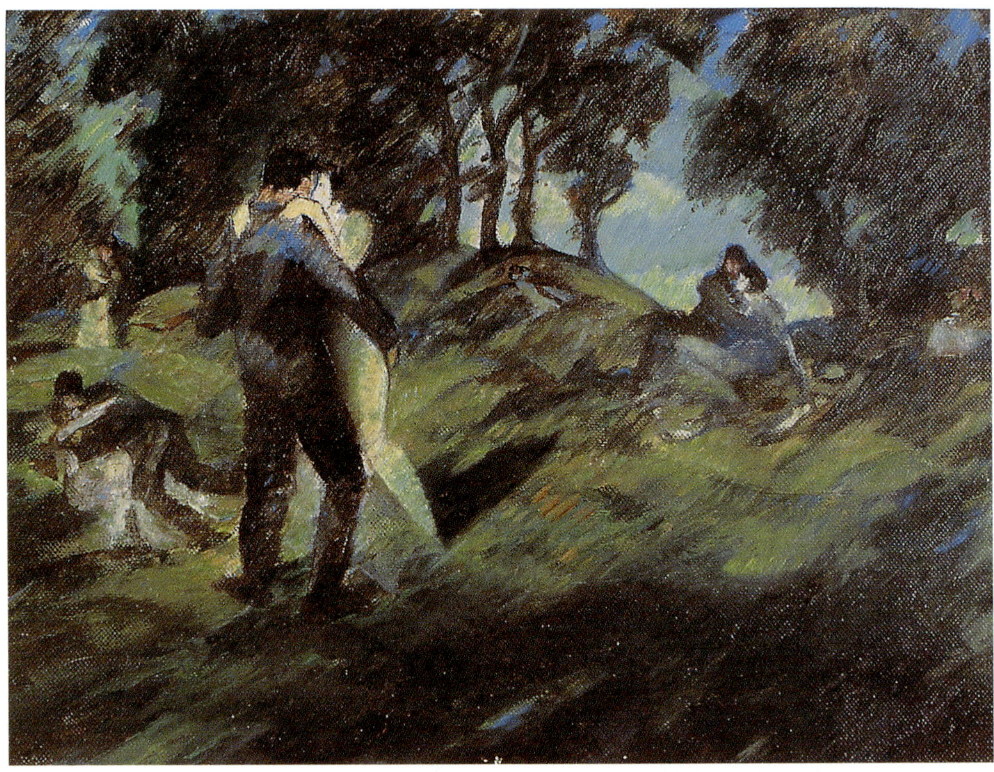

62. *Hampstead Heath*, 1919. Oil on canvas, 44 x 60 cm. Private collection.

Clapham Common (fig. 63)[29] belonged, in a first glimpse of how the post-war approach to painting, both in subject matter and technique, would materialize.

Preparing *Harvest of Battle*

Henry had been abroad for almost three months by the time of his return in the first week of February. Following his visit to the Leicester Galleries on 7 February 1919, to see *Port* and *Oxford in the Rain* [30] he turned his attention to the large-scale

63. *Clapham Common*. Reproduced in *Colour*, November 1919.

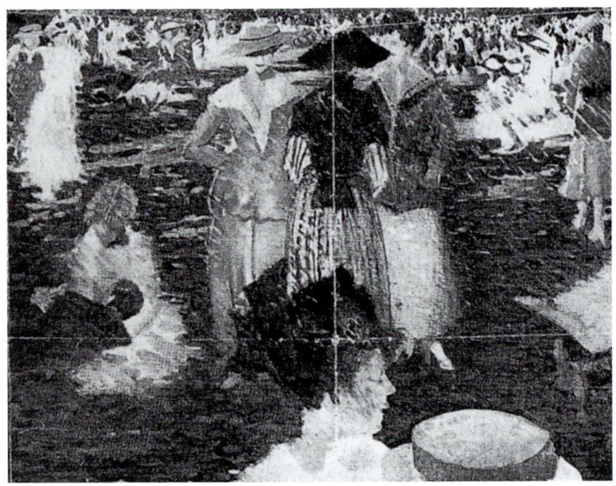

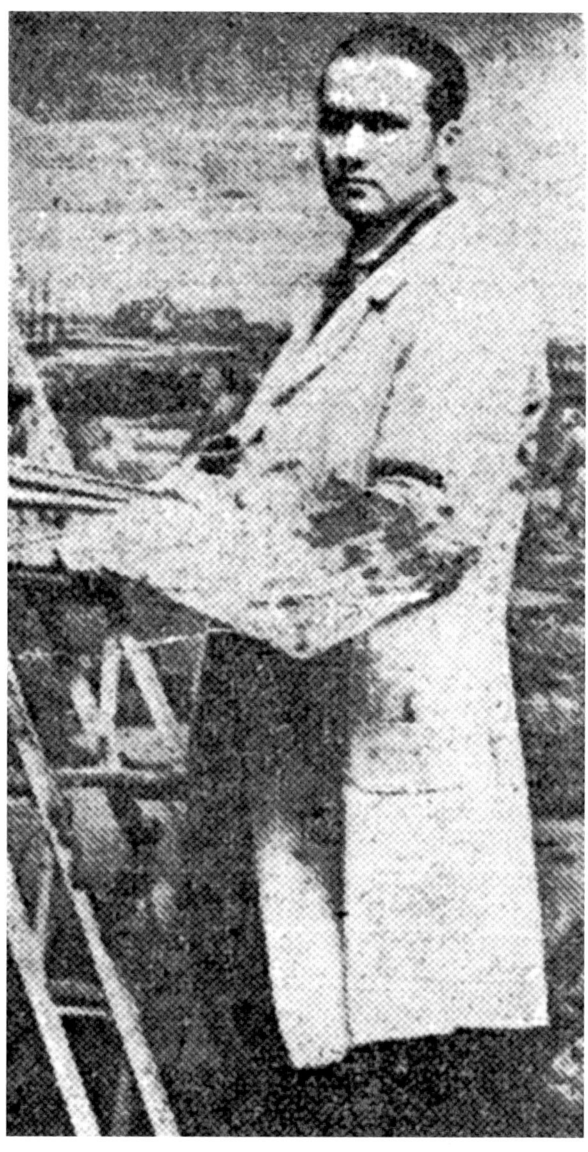

64. War Painting Withdrawn. Photograph, *Leeds Mercury*, 1 April 1919.

work, *Harvest of Battle* (fig. 47), which Richard was now completing and planning to exhibit privately in his own studio. Henry attended the private show with Tomlinson, the critic from the *Star*, and recorded a big crowd and an overall favourable reception. As Richard's intention had been to exhibit it at the May 'Peace Show' at the Royal Academy the preview might serve as a valuable guide to the painting's acceptability. There was however, an ulterior motive. Alfred Yockney had actually forbidden Richard from exhibiting at the May Royal Academy show, as it would have diluted the impact of his 'The Nations War Pictures and Other Records' exhibition in the autumn.[31] Likewise, the *Daily Express* was denied its request to photograph the artist at work on his large canvas for the same reason, the resultant publication showing only the artist and a very cropped version of the painting (fig.

64).[32] Richard's response, especially in the light of the fact that the same restrictions had not been placed on John Singer Sargent's *Gassed*, was to send invitations to a private viewing of the work, complete with bus and tube routes to his studio.[33] The press obviously attended, and the stories concerning censorship, once again, ran rampant over the newspapers of the day. The *Daily Express*, for example, printed the story under the title 'Mystery of a War Picture. Academy Closed to Grim Flanders Scene',[34] while others conjectured that 'it is considered to be not only his finest painting, but the most wonderful of all war pictures'.[35] Of course it had not been the academy which had closed its doors to the painting, nor had there been any issue with its 'grim' contents, but nevertheless, that is the way the press reported the story, and so, once again, as with the 1918 censorship issue, he had manipulated his way into the spotlight. Immediately and characteristically he wrote to Masterman disclaiming anything to do with the press coup, saying he had only given them 'the basic facts'.[36] Typically, he also suggested that he should look on the bright side as it had already boosted publicity for when the painting would finally be unveiled. His studio show had once again promoted him to the role of the truth telling, uncompromising, modern, military and often misunderstood, artist, once again a victim of the establishment. In the end his painting did not appear in the Royal Academy Peace Show of May 1919, and Sargent's did. But Richard had made sure that even his absence created attention.[37]

The New World and a New Era

Two days later a dinner was held in his honour at the Café Royal, organized by Grant Richards, at which about sixty people were present, including Sickert.[38] *Paint and Prejudice* recorded the presence of about one hundred people. Henry's diary entry reads 'Then Richard spoke and read a long defensive offensive as to his position in art against narrow cliques & little sets who try to scorn and reject him as successful. Many of the wounds & illustrations were daring and violent: but the general effect fine and powerful.'[39] Richard recalled it very differently in his autobiography saying that he spoke dreadfully and that 'I still go hot when I remember it.'[40] The press reported more fully on his 'fiery and warlike response' saying that it was worthy of Marinetti himself, in which he proclaimed absolute freedom from all groups and ideologies, against which he was happy to declare war if they would not respect his autonomy. He once again renounced his extremist associations, then went on to say 'An artist cannot be too aggressive. As I have often said, an artist should be a bellicose Jesus Christ: a man convinced of his mission and unashamed, with a song to sing impossible to repress, and determined to be heard.'[41] Other papers published a summary of his speech or extracts, which reported his attack on 'little Revolutionary groups in art which call themselves free, yet tyrannise their members into one formulated expression and turn themselves into narrow little academic societies'.[42] Complete with photographs, the artist's departure to America, typically, did not go unnoticed (fig. 65).

On 3 May his father said goodbye to him at Waterloo station.[43] Richard left with

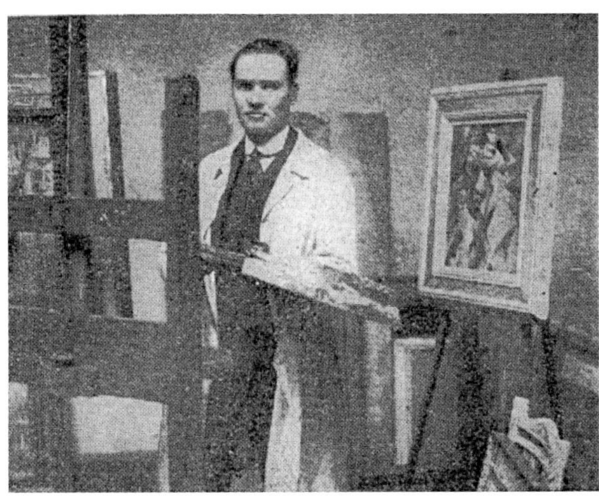

65. Cubist for the States. Photograph, *Daily Sketch*, 29 March 1919.

66. (below, left) A Cubist 'Cubed' – By the Camera. Photograph by Bertram Park, *The Sketch*, 21 May 1919.

67. (below, right) Mr C.R.W. Nevinson. Photograph by Bertram Park, *Bystander*, 21 May 1919.

a heavy heart, not least because his wife was in the advanced stages of pregnancy and now in a nursing home. Following his trans-Atlantic passage on board the *Mauretania*, he arrived in New York, armed with a new series of dramatic photographic portraits by Bertram Park (figs 66 and 67). He was also quick to get the press working for him and soon his post-war position was being made very clear. In an interview in the *New York Times Magazine* he declared: 'Having lived among scrap heaps, having seen miles of destruction day after day, month after month, year

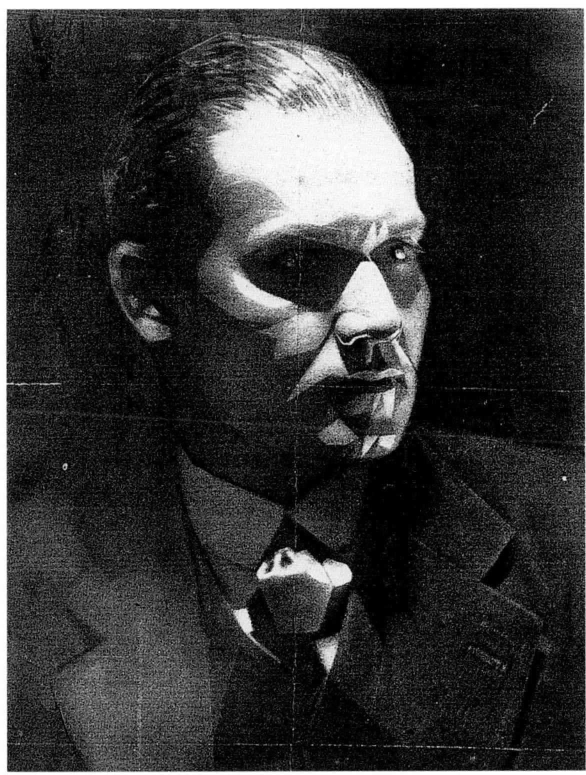

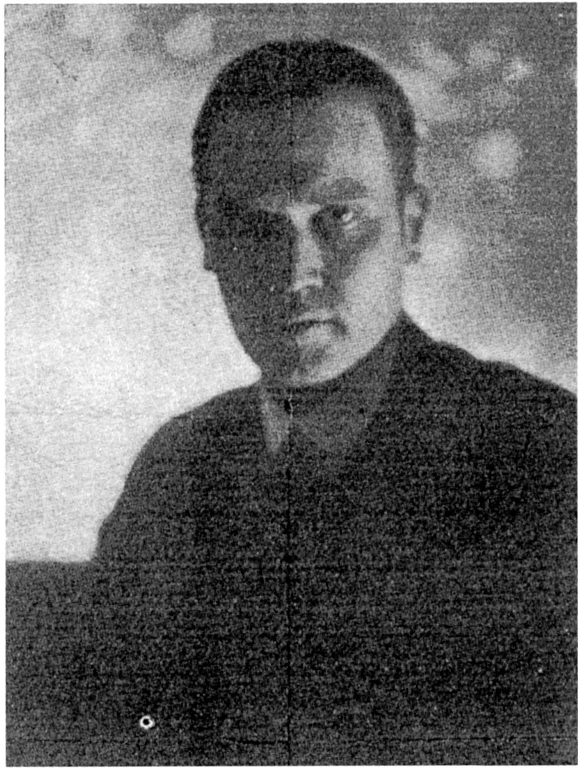

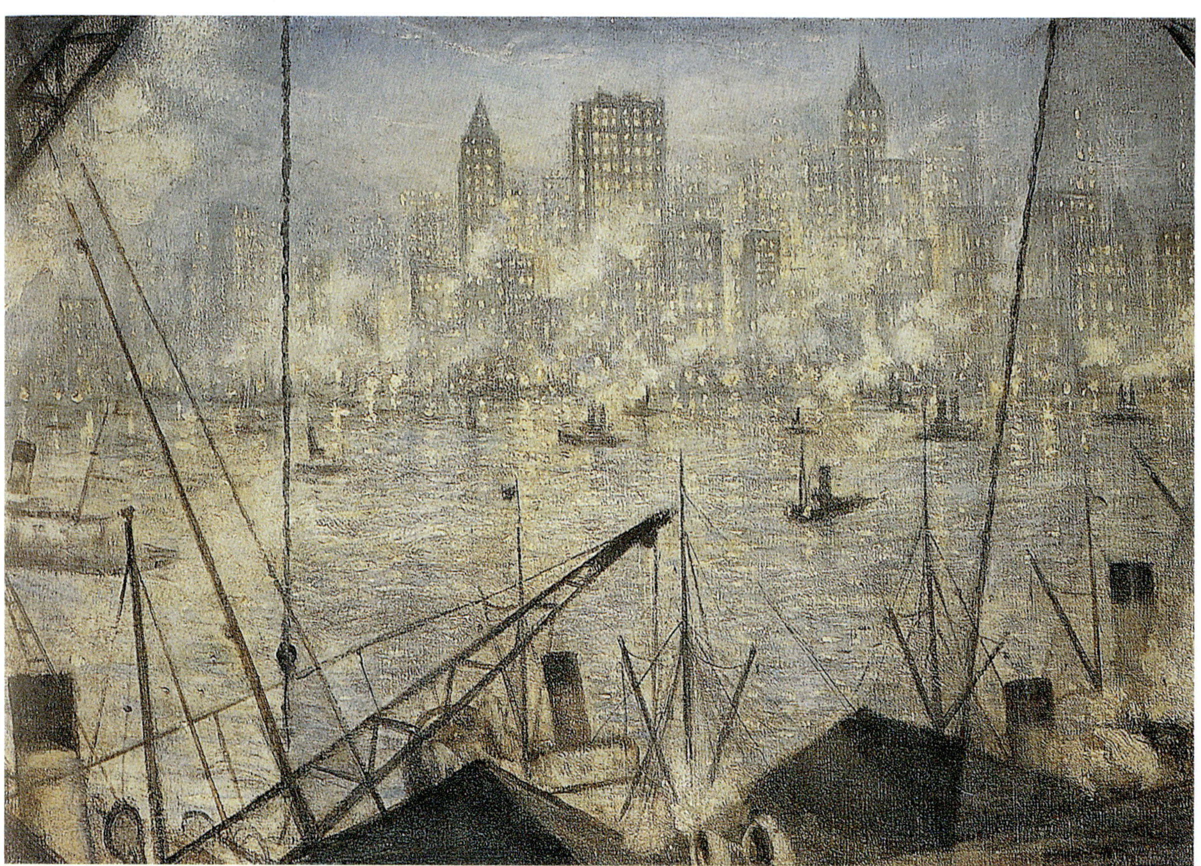

68. *New York by Night*, 1919–20. Oil on canvas, 50.8 x 76.2 cm. Private collection.

after year, they are longing for a complete change. We artists are sick of destruction in art. We want construction.' He reaffirmed this hatred of the negative consequences of modernity saying 'the effect of the war has been to create among artists an extraordinary longing to get static again. Having been dynamic since 1912 they are now utterly tired of chaos.' [44] Whereas the implication augured the end of the artist's extreme modernist vocabulary, and the war subject, it did not, however, in his view, mean the end of the experimentation with modernity on the whole. Trying to find this new balance was to be the challenge, and Konody, retrospectively, applauded: 'Mr Nevinson stands indeed in splendid isolation . . . he has been through the mill, he has passed through a period of flirtation with every movement of recent days. He has learned from them all: he has become enslaved to none.'[45] Rutter, interestingly, put a totally different interpretation on the move to the American subject. He felt that the reason Richard would be attracted to, then inspired by it, was because he was only capable of painting that which he hated. Just as the war had brought out the best in him, so too, might America and Americans, with their love of money and their lack of respect for tradition.[46]

Certainly his initial attempts to depict the metropolis, in canvases such as *New York by Night* (fig. 68), suggest a debt of gratitude to the subject matter, as opposed to the technique, in any claim to modernity. We sense no apparent apathy to the great city either, as Rutter had suspected. Manhattan from the Hudson River would have been one of the first sights he would have had of the city, although, according to *Paint and Prejudice* he arrived on board the Cunarder in the morning. Certainly he must have been 'overjoyed by that glimpse of beauty'[47] though, this time he felt little impulse to depict it by the radical means utilized in *The Arrival*. Instead, very much in the way he had depicted *The Railway Bridge, Charenton*, the artist returned to a single-point perspective, in a homogenized picture plane, designed to depict clearly and legibly the modern subject.

Richard was quick to talk of ambitious schemes to bring the Canadian and British Memorial exhibitions to New York, which he envisaged would require the use of Madison Square Garden to house, such would be the enormity of the show.[48] But if it seemed that in subject matter and technique he was returning to pre-war themes and methods, so too it appeared that through naïvety or intentional polemicism he was returning to the spotlight as a personality in a very Marinettian way. He gave high-profile presentations at the Society of Independent Artists at the Waldorf Astoria, at which over two hundred artists were present, and generated countless other press releases and interviews to remain very much in the public eye. However, his tone was often far from subtle as seen in his speech at the Kevorkian Gallery, New York City, in late May, 1919. In this he declared: 'Americans are splendid painters, but no artists . . . They have no soul, no feeling, no emotion . . . They are so artistic that they represent nothing but themselves.'[49] Later he would comment that the American idea of art was a 'well appointed bathroom' with their Raphael being a plumber.[50] Even later in life he would assert 'The average American citizen is essentially a slow-minded, inefficient, and credulous person, with a juvenile love of mechanical toys.'[51] One may sense hints of Marinetti and his pre-war assault on the English artists reappearing. Later, a journalist for an English paper could report, 'Anyway, if he could hear the things they say about him now he would not be so keen to come back in the autumn as he was when he left America the day after that speech was made.'[52] It is little wonder that Charles Lewis-Hind wrote in the introduction to the catalogue for Richard's second one-man show in America, 'It is something, at the age of thirty one, to be among the most discussed, most successful, most promising, most admired, and most hated of British artists.'[53]

Without a doubt his time in New York was busy. From the National Arts Club, he sent notes to key figures in New York society to meet and discuss art with him. An undated letter to Dr Rabin, from this address, suggested meeting to walk around the city at night, to talk, sketch and experience the modern wonder which was New York.[54] Even if Americans were subject to his negative comments, their city was spared, for Richard could proclaim 'Today New York is, for the artist, the most fascinating city in the world. She is like a young woman, splendid in her unconscious strength and beauty, cold and hard perhaps, but only as youth always is. She doesn't soothe the nerves; she stimulates action.'[55] New York, he believed, was the rightful heir to Venice as the world's most beautiful, dynamic and technically bewildering

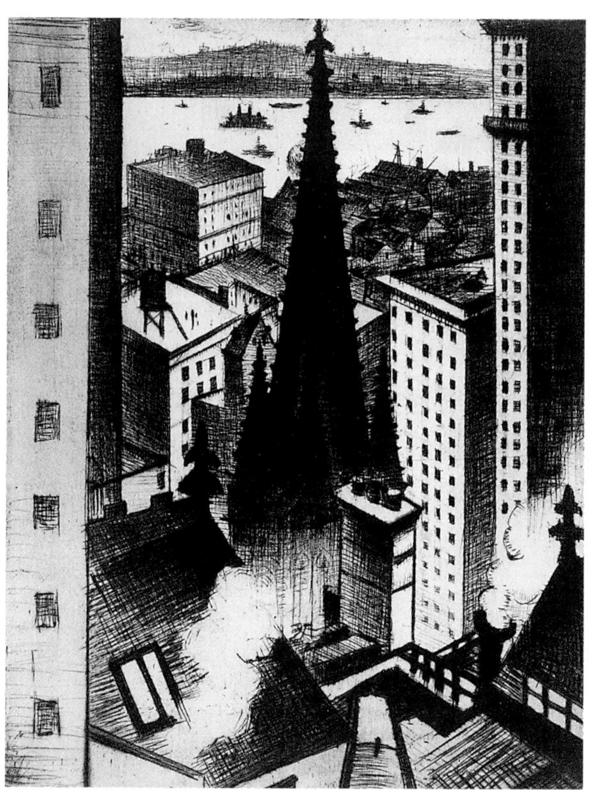

69. *The Temples of New York*, 1919. Drypoint, 19.7 x 15.2 cm. Victoria and Albert Museum, London.

city. The skyscraper would later also be described as 'the most vivid art works of the day',[56] being the epitome of utility, efficiency, man's achievement and the spirit of the age. And yet, paradoxically, he loathed the products of this environment, such as suburban development, commercialization, traffic, social mobility, female emancipation and the despoiling of the countryside.[57] Perhaps it was with a degree of cynicism, as propounded by Rutter, that he approached works such as *The Temples of New York* (fig. 69), which had as its focal point the spire of Trinity Church. The spire is dwarfed by the newly emerging skyscrapers, though the church remains central to the business community, being situated at the head of Wall Street. The composition could be interpreted to represent a comment on the material and financial values of the modern America, which had benefited so considerably from the Great War.

Regardless, he sketched the modern city rapidly, if superficially, and possibly photographed it, in order to work the images up into full compositions on his return to London.[58] Here was a modernity that was, on the face of it, positive, unlike the negative modernity of war, and one which was infinitely more human, rather than merely mechanical. It was upon icons such as the skyscraper and the Brooklyn Bridge then that Richard would focus,[59] proclaiming himself, typically, to be both the first and the best artist to do so. He chose to overlook other contemporary artists such as Samuel Halpert, Charles Sheeler and Joseph Stella who had tackled the same subject matter, often in a technically more adventurous, original and dynamic way.[60] So too Alvin Langdon Coburn, Paul Strand, John Marin and Max Weber were carefully ignored in Richard's sweeping self-acclamation.[61]

Eugene Gallatin, painter and modern art collector, also became a friend and confidant, and wrote the introduction to the catalogue for the exhibition at Frederick Keppel & Co.[62] Entitled *Etchings and Lithographs by C.R.W. Nevinson*, the catalogue promoted Richard as one of Britain's 'most vigorous and original painters', whilst stating that no American, not even John Marin, could have painted the way he had done on the Western Front.[63] The style of the work, seen throughout the forty-one works exhibited (see appendix) was described as 'a compromise between Futurism and illustration', but once again included the key words 'dynamic', 'synthesis' and 'abstraction'. More than anything it was 'free from all music-hall and journalistic heroics'.[64] The modernity, it was clear, would be in the selection of his subjects as opposed to any radical technique of depicting them. Indeed, the show did demonstrate a profound diversity of images, from the first year of the conflict through to the last, utilizing both 'freelance' and 'official' styles. Strong pieces such as *Returning to the Trenches* and *A Flooded Trench on the Yser* were offset against literary pieces such as *That Cursed Wood*,[65] and non-war themes such as *Wet Evening, Oxford Street*.[66] The autonomy as an artist that he had fought so hard for was certainly on display at the show that introduced him to the United States of America.

Richard was not long home before he became aware that an American journalist called James Montgomery Flagg was attacking him in the *New York Times*. Once again Richard claimed that this was the product of a misquotation and a misunderstanding and appealed to his new-found friend, Gallatin, for help. Ironically he went on to say that 'I am not the type of man to gratuitously insult Americans, especially after the amazing kindness I received in New York.'[67] There were problems too with the Worcester Art Museum, as mentioned in *Paint and Prejudice*, and these were destined to provoke a predictable backlash by the artist.[68] It appears that a contract was signed, though not by Richard, which gave the Worcester Art Museum his paintings for exhibition until August 1920. They were therefore not available for exhibition or sale prior to that, even though a show had been organized for the Bourgeois Gallery, New York, that spring. Richard wrote to Gallatin saying

> Who ever signed this contract (if it exists) had no right to sign away my property – as definitively stated by H.M. Government when sent to N.Y. – & I refuse to be bound by a contract I never was party to. If the Worcester Art Galleries still have the audacity to stick to my work I shall have to come to America earlier than I intended, find the show & cut out my property from their frames as all my pictures and prints were my personal property & for sale.[69]

The letter went on to say that he had government support on this affair and that they, too, readily agreed that he had been 'robbed'. On a more positive note he told Gallatin of plans to mount a show in Paris at the hands of the dealer of Picasso and Derain, who recently had chosen his work over that of Fry and Lewis. He also observed the temperature rising amongst jealous artists and critics and wrote 'they are just beginning to find their jaundiced spittle, I expect to be drenched soon'.[70]

Both in Europe and in the USA Richard seems to have antagonized artists and press alike by the closing days of 1919 and the opening ones of 1920. Likewise, he reiterated how he believed war was behind him when, in the build-up to his trip to Prague, he sensed possible conflict between 'Czech-Slovakia and Hungary...in which case I certainly shall not go'.[71]

If Richard was leaving behind the subjects on which his success had been based in the past, it was with difficulty that he was embracing the subjects that would carry his career into the future. In technique and creed however, there was no major radical U-turn from late war to peace paintings. Even as late as 1920 familiar, though adapted, ideas were self-evident. A letter to Lewis-Hind, who was writing the introduction for the 1920 Bourgeois Gallery show in New York, gave a few pointers as to what should be said. It started with the familiar call to be disassociated from 'any possible clique, school, ist, ism, post, neo, pro, anit, academic, un-academic, conventional or unconventional'. It was a familiar plea for individuality and subjectivity to triumph over everything else, and a renunciation of any attempt to create an art that was wholly original. It went on to say that a painting should have 'guts', unlike the 'pretty-pretty water-colourists & Royal Academicians'.[72] The final, published, introduction, entitled 'My Art Creed', also went on to resurface old arguments in new clothes with statements such as 'I maintain it is impossible to use the same means to express the flesh of a woman and the ferro-concrete of a sky-scraper.' Art was once again, referred to as 'virile'.[73] He had returned to an urban theme, employing a roughly defined technique last seen almost a decade before in his Slade days, and had virtually erased from his palette the legacy of pre-war and wartime modernism. At the end of his visit Brodsky advised him 'You've made good here, and they seem to like you. Beat it and get away with it, and don't come back. I know these New Yorkers.'[74]

The Life and Death of Anthony Christopher Wynne Nevinson

The birth of Richard and Kathleen's child attracted media attention, and the *Daily Sketch*, in his absence reported the arrival of 'The Cubist Baby' on 21 May 1919. Henry too recorded the event in his journals, though the entry for 3 June read that 'Rich and Kath's child must die.' He observed a sorrow, which he attributed more to the hopelessness now of 'the desire to carry on a name'.[75] The following day he wrote 'Richard's and Kathleen's child lay dying & died. I was strangely unhappy at the thought.'[76] Then by 6 June, he could record unreservedly that he was 'Overwhelmed by the death of that poor child, now lying still in the studio.' He also observed how he was essentially taking his son's role in this drama saying 'looked in on Kathleen, sitting in the garden of the nursing home. She cried a great deal when I was "kind". Spoke much of the child, its intelligence and strength of will. All very sad.'[77] The following day 'We buried Richard's and Kathleen's little son in a white coffin. Happily the service was short. The poor little thing was dropped into a hole on the top of my father in the old Hampstead Churchyard. His name which we never knew was Anthony Christopher Wynne.'[78] Margaret recorded that the child had lived for fifteen days, which had been 'just enough time to get fond of him'.[79] Not twenty-four hours later Richard returned home from New York. In a letter to Gallatin, he recorded coldly, 'Things were rather upset on my arrival as my son died just before I got back.'[80] The sole reference to the family tragedy in *Paint and Prejudice* was dealt with as follows 'On my arrival in London I was met by my mother, who told me my son was dead.' He added 'I am glad I have not been responsible for bringing any human life into this world.'[81]

London, Cézanne and the *rappel à l'ordre*

From this point to the end of the year Henry's journals charted the slow decline of his son to what could be classified as a nervous breakdown. Though it is not recorded in detail anywhere, not even in *Paint and Prejudice*, it may be assumed that the death of the artist's child, in the wake of all the anxiety caused by the war, and following trouble with artists and critics alike, to say nothing of financial worries, lead to a state of heightened nervous tension. When additional complications were added, it started to become an unbearable burden, which his father could do nothing to alleviate. More personal problems became evident on 18 June, when Richard found out that Lewis had taken the flat above the one that they had just moved to on the Euston Road. Kathleen even talked of 'the madman's violence'[82] though this amounted to nothing. Kathleen was still ill and so time was spent between the new flat and the country where they were guests of Grant Richards. Henry called almost every day before going to Ireland to report on the deteriorating political crisis there. When he returned he observed that his son seemed to be over-reacting to a quarrel he had had with American dealers, and that now the only topic on which he wished to talk was painting, but this in a negative way. Indeed the quarrel spilled over to Mrs Lewis-Hind and in the end Henry had to broker peace talks between the two as they had been the best of friends up until this point.

Shortly after this, Richard, once again, was busy in defining himself and his attitudes to art in the national press. The ideas had not changed radically from anything said before, only this time he summarized his beliefs: 'When a movement becomes a movement it ceases to be a movement; which means that organisation kills the idea.'[83] Once again, coteries, imitators, and intellectuals came in for his wrath, and echoed his dinner speech from before his departure to New York. He had also rethought his own position within the linear development of art history and had decided to regroup around the priorities of Cézanne as the basis for his own reconstruction. This was clarified in the *World*: 'The immediate need of the art of today is a Cézanne, a reactionary, to lead art back to the academic traditions of the Old Masters, and save contemporary art from abstractions, as Cézanne saved Impressionism from "effects".'[84] It seems that, while still denying the value of Bloomsbury aesthetics, he was now propounding a reconstruction in art that would root it firmly with tradition, interjecting only the Post-Impressionism of Cézanne.

In all it was a technical theory very similar to that of 1912, though he no longer looked to Paris for inspiration in subject matter but to London and New York.

Nevinson's 'Peace Show' at the Leicester Galleries

The Leicester Galleries proposed that his next exhibition would be mounted in parallel with a Matisse show, which, ironically, would be the source of much pride for Richard in years to come.[85] At the time however it was no source of pleasure and his father recorded how a family meal was ruined over this gripe.[86] September became October and preparations got under way for the show, which was to open on the 25th. Once again Henry was involved from the very beginning and in every stage up to the opening night, and after. Again, he thought that his son's preface to the catalogue for the show was too extreme, saying 'Rich showed me his preface & I made a few changes, but it is still belicose [*sic*] and too defensive.'[87] Once again, however, the artist was using the power of print to promote himself and to cause, wherever possible, a talking point to ensure his high profile. Again, he was fighting for his artistic autonomy and predictably his introduction read 'I wish to be thoroughly dissociated from every "new" or "advanced" movement; every form of "ist," "ism," "post," "neo," "academic," or "unacademic".' This was nothing new and one critic retorted 'Good! This saves me a heap of trouble. One need only describe these curious but forceful works as sheer Nevinson.'[88] Similarly he was sticking with his ideology concerning eclecticism in art by saying 'I refuse to use the same technical method to express such contradictory forms as a rock or a woman.'[89] The result of this was a 'confused and confusing exhibition' which contained, according to one contemporary essayist, some 'really dreadful pictures'.[90] Conversely, this was picked up on positively by the press at the time, which reported 'The versatility of the man is amazing. He can paint in half-a-dozen styles – according to subject – and you feel that, as often as not, he does it with his tongue in his cheek.'[91] A clear break with his pre-war past was once again being made and if anything, a continuity of late-war ideologies was being attempted, as had been seen in other interim exhibitions.[92] In subject too, all associations from the past, especially with Futurism and war, were almost totally replaced by works such as *When Father Mows the Lawn* (fig. 70), *The Sandy Path* (lost) and *The Inexperienced Witch* (fig. 71). There were pictures of New York and the dynamism and modernity of that great metropolis, such as *The Shimmy Shake* (fig. 72) and *Music Hall Patriotism* (fig. 73), but these were counteracted with nudes, portraits, landscapes, seascapes, comic pieces, jazz subjects, and many more (see appendix). Each required a different vocabulary in depiction and Peters Corbett observed this saying that he 'divides the world up into units of experience, to each of which he assigns its appropriate art historical dialect'.[93] This is precisely what Richard was trying to do, and had been clearly established in the 'introduction' when he had specified:

> Many painters today try to find some particular style of mannerism, and when found they never vary it, hoping always to hall-mark their canvases and deceive their public (the Intellectual especially) into the idea that they have individuality.

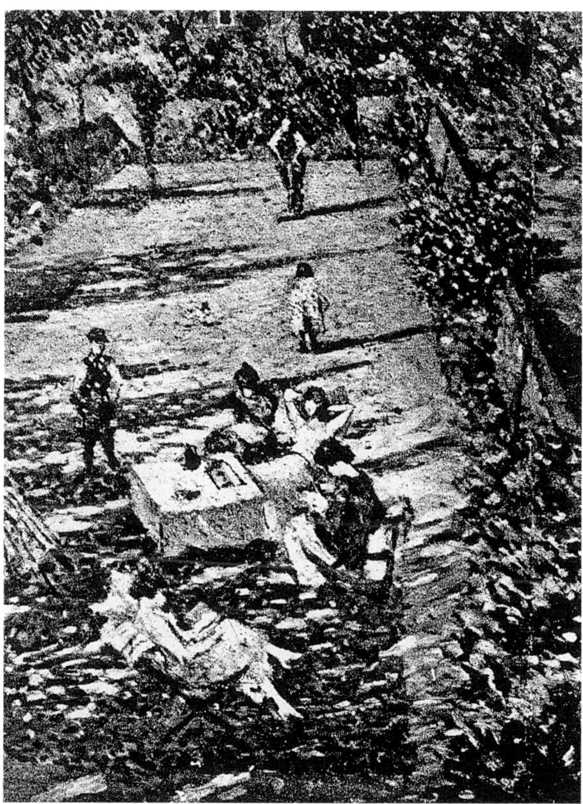

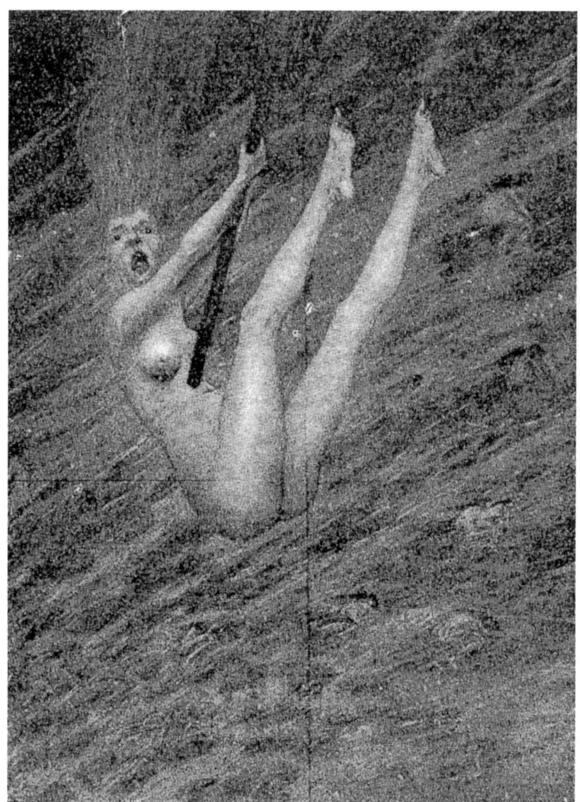

70. *When Father Mows the Lawn*, 1919. Oil on canvas. Whereabouts unknown, reproduced in *The Sketch*, 5 November 1919.

71. *The Inexperienced Witch*, 1919. Oil on canvas. Whereabouts unknown, reproduced in *The Tatler*, 5 November 1919.

> The truth is that the personality of a painter – if he has any personality, of course – enables him to withstand the test of any technical method.[94]

He was also overheard saying that he wished to return comedy and farce to art, just as they were permitted in literature and drama.[95] The *Daily News* reported gleefully that 'the lost sheep had returned to the fold' whilst observing that for others there would be 'wailing and gnashing of teeth as over one who has deliberately chosen to return to the realms of darkness'. The article finished by pondering how many more stages he would have to go through before finally finding himself.[96] *The Times* headline simply read 'Mr Nevinson's Return to Nature.'[97] Whether this was as a result of the return of peace and his resultant liberation from the war theme, or whether the searching attitude was inspired by the trip to New York, was subject of much speculation at the time. Konody, whilst not wholly approving of the eclecticism, tended to lean towards the latter, saying, 'The sky-scrapers and cabarets of New York are a happier hunting ground for him than Olympus or Parnassus.'[98] Michael Sadler, by implication, assigned him to being a 'popular', or possibly frivolous, artist now by saying he 'must be a great trial to those serious young painters who would have English secessionism move relentlessly from one abstraction to another'.[99] Charles Marriott could only comment 'But in spite of his disclaimer, I'm afraid that Mr Nevinson will always be a stuntist.'[100]

There could be little doubt that the show was an unmitigated success in terms of

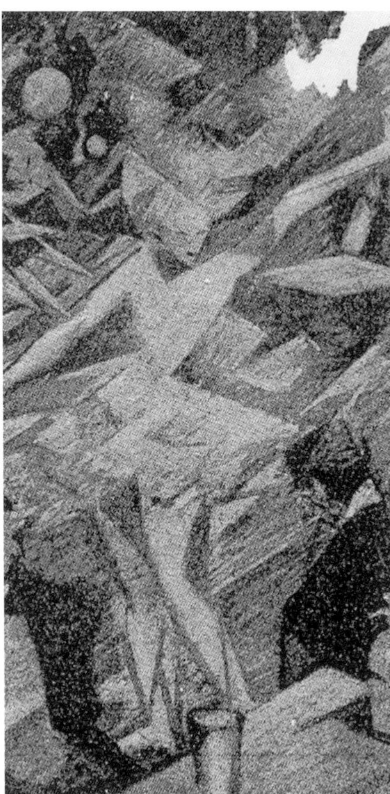

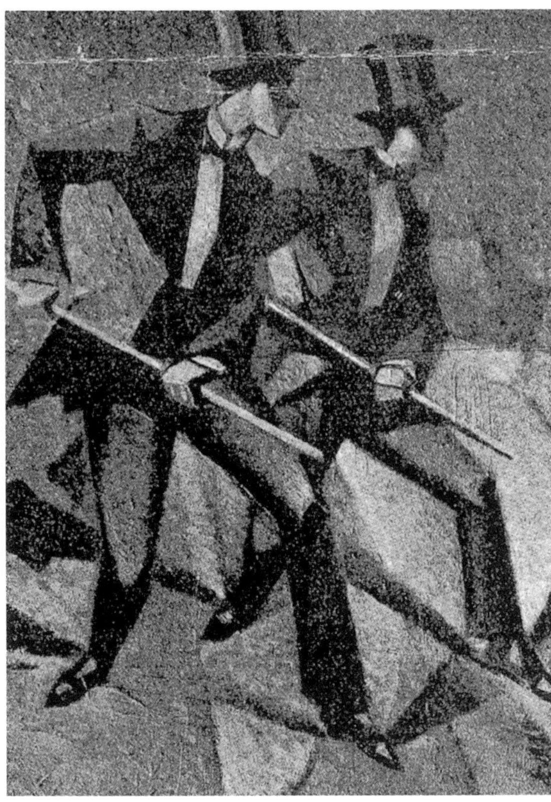

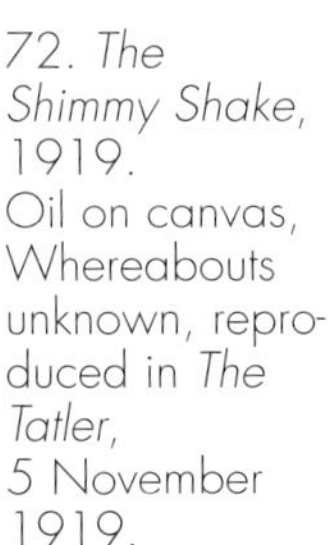

72. *The Shimmy Shake*, 1919. Oil on canvas, Whereabouts unknown, reproduced in *The Tatler*, 5 November 1919.

73. *Music Hall Patriotism*, 1919. Oil on canvas. Whereabouts unknown, reproduced in *The Tatler*, 5 November 1919.

attendance and profits and that the artist had seemingly bridged the gulf from war to peace successfully, and with the greatest of ease. Versatility, variety and adaptability seemed to be adjectives applied to his work in place of alternatives, which could have talked of inconsistency or artistic meandering in pursuit of public acclaim. Peters Corbett summed up that decision saying, 'Nevinson's defence of an eclectic art, choosing its idiom from all those available to suit its subject matter, is an argument for the abandonment of modernism in favour of the comforts of convention.'[101] Richard himself would have made no attempt to deny this.

Henry admired the exhibition in its entirety and the following day showed how he was still prepared to fight his son's battles, physically if necessary, when he recorded 'put off going to see Wyndham Lewis against whom I meant to brawl if he insulted Richard in his speech'.[102] His son, too, was apparently very pleased with the Leicester Galleries show and on this upbeat note Henry departed, once more, for business overseas, while his son and Kathleen left for Paris the following day to stay with Severini. The *Pall Mall Gazette*, after reporting the departure to France, commented that the Leicester Galleries show 'must be the most popular one-man show ever known'.[103] But when his father returned to the gallery once with Masterman, the latter complained that he 'wants a fixed and definite style. Says Rich paints in anyone's styles and says "Look here, I can do it better".'[104]

Richard and Kathleen were back in London in just over two weeks though, having been disillusioned with the post-war French capital.[105] Richard himself

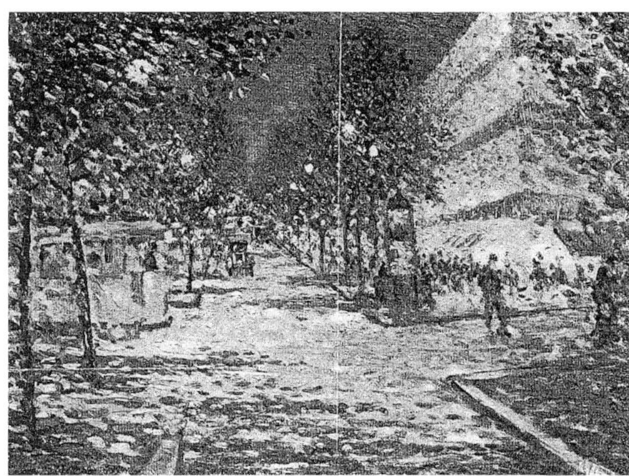

74. *Parisian Night*, 1919. Oil on canvas. Whereabouts unknown.

recorded in his autobiography that the stay had had its merits and that at least he had reacquainted himself with Kisling, Zadkin, Modigliani and Asselin, even if Picasso had proved a little aloof. The only identifiable painting from this visit, *Parisian Night*, clearly illustrates the retreat to his pre-war stance (fig. 74).

The Nation's War Paintings and Other Records

By the middle of November Henry had noticed a change for the worse in his son, provoked by the *Nation's War Paintings and Drawings* exhibition at the Royal Academy.[106] This show had been requested by Yockney as early as January 1919 and was designed to promote the idea of the Memorial Gallery scheme, which had been envisaged by the British War Memorials Committee.[107] Though not a Royal Academy exhibition the collection of the Imperial War Museum would be exhibited in the rooms of Burlington House and would represent artists of 'every sort of school' who had depicted the 'Titanic struggle'.[108] It was even reported that 'Millais and Leighton [would be] turning in their graves'[109] at the thought of pride of place going to Roberts and Lewis in such a hallowed sanctuary of art. In essence, it was to represent a *tabula rasa* at Burlington House, devoid of the usual prejudices and principles associated with painting and taste, and was to give equal opportunities to artists, despite their creed and priorities. Masterman himself publicly outlined the goal of the exhibition and described its origins.[110] The hanging committee, chosen to select one thousand of the three thousand paintings in the collection, included amongst others, Yockney, Bone, Dodd and Tonks, and this was clearly going to present problems for Richard from the very outset. When the exhibition opened in December 1919 that was to prove to be the case, though 'over a dozen' of his works were selected (see appendix).[111] Certainly none of his paintings made the Central Gallery, and everything was, in his opinion, divided and scattered throughout the many rooms of the show. This is clarified in a letter from Richard to the officials at the Imperial War Museum, which read 'every single picture but one of mine has been placed in an obscure corner, and every trick, well known to every artist who has hung an exhibition, has been used to dissipate my strength, and handicap me in every way.'[112]

Regardless of the selection committee's natural affinity towards the NEAC and the ex-Slade students, no favours, it appears, were extended to him. If anything, despite his age, his established name, and his return to the illustrative nature of depiction, as represented by *Harvest of Battle*, he was grouped with the older artists, and certainly removed from the dynamism of youth, which this show seemed to tolerate. If anything he was moving in the wrong direction as the review from the *Yorkshire Evening Post* implied:

> In those far-off days, before the war, we used to smile at the strange methods of the young London school of artists, and murmur that they would grow out of it some day. The war paintings now on view at the Royal Academy...show us that the young men were right. At any rate theirs is the only way of painting the war, and their stark angularities make the smooth work of the older men seem meaningless, sentimental things suitable for grocers' almanacs.[113]

Having been so instrumental in creating the belief that a form of moderate modernism was the ideal form of war realism, Richard had now retreated from his own stance, while others enjoyed his success on those terms. He was also surrounded by other artists who had served on the various Fronts of the Great War and so his position of soldier/artist was no longer unique and the role of truth teller was common to all.

Insofar as *Harvest of Battle* (fig. 47) in no way embraced modernist simplification as a form of expressive truth, it at least did utilize realism as a vehicle for telling the public of the grim reality of war. Richard himself described it as follows:

> A typical scene after an offensive at dawn. Walking wounded, prisoners & stretcher cases are making their way to the rear through the water-logged country of Flanders. By now the infantry have advanced behind the creeping barrage on the right, only leaving the dead, mud & wire; but their former positions are now occupied by the Artillery. The enemy is sending up S.O.S. signals & once more these shattered men will be subjected to counter-battery fire. In spite of the early hour our aeroplanes are already up spotting hostile positions.[114]

The *Daily Mail* described it thus:

> It is a large, steel coloured painting. Dawn: somewhere that looks like earth's most God-forsaken region, the sodden flats north-east of Ypres. Guns are blazing away in the half-light; the first of the "walking wounded" and prisoners of the morning's attack are trailing back amid the shell-holes and brimming craters. Terrible! The man who painted that has seen; the man who has seen that knows the bitterness of things.[115]

Ezra Pound, declaring it a 'bad painting', at least credited it as being 'a representation of reality and an excellent record of war'.[116] Chamot has agreed saying that the power of the subject matter detracted from its aesthetic worth claiming that it was 'too full of blood-curdling detail to be artistically impressive'.[117] Ferguson's interpretation noted the transition from *La Mitrailleuse* to *Harvest of Battle* and concluded pessimistically saying 'His soldiers became toy soldiers, rather than dehumanised human beings.'[118] For Bond the painting was a failure in its totality, suggesting 'There is a sense of his feeling he ought to fill a large canvas and having neither the imagination nor the ability to do so.'[119]

Long-standing ally P. G. Konody concluded that the painting had failed, whilst Rutter, Clutton-Brock, and Sadler all failed completely to mention the canvas in their reviews. Marriot and Wilensky mentioned it in passing and observed that, essentially, it was competent. In an Australian review, Richard was dismissively described merely as 'an illustrator and house decorator'.[120] In some ways Richard was being relegated to the role of journalist as opposed to that of artist, albeit a journalist with an anti-militarist conscience. This being the case, he found himself still to the fore in any discussion concerning war and the depiction of it, but very much in the periphery of discussions on the future of art.

Other writers began to question the value of his war art, asking 'Was it a good bargain or not to supply Mr C.R.W. Nevinson and Mr Eric Kennington with motor-cars in which they could proceed over the war zone and paint pictures?'[121] Of course Richard responded with a letter to the offending newspaper saying that the value of his work as a tool of the propaganda machine easily justified the cost of the petrol he had used up in the car and on his flights.[122]

But the show at the Royal Academy was perhaps the final straw in breaking his will. Henry recorded that having telephoned his son he had found him in 'a state of anger and despair'[123] saying that he had never been so insulted and that all his pictures had been badly hung. But his father seemed to feel the attacks too, implying that his son was either extremely convincing in his paranoia, or that they really were happening, for all to see. On 11 December, for example, Henry recorded that he had had a 'Sleepless night owing to the attacks on Richard',[124] though the next day, on visiting the show itself, with his son and daughter-in-law, and on having a good look around, believed that his son had been over reacting. Apart from the fact that a couple of newspapers didn't review his works, and that a few of the smaller images had been dispersed, and placed 'above the line', he felt, on the whole, that it had been a 'superb show'. He welcomed the change from the 'old sword waving, cavalry dashing pictures of Glory!'[125] Henry returned the following day to have another look and was delighted to report that there were queues to see *Harvest of Battle*. No other picture, he felt, was as dynamic or as impressive, except for Sargent's *Gassed*.

In the popular press too, Richard was still spoken of highly, but this was with the 'common man' who would soon forget his paintings. In the mainstream of artistic discourse he was now sidelined and in desperate need of a new identity if he was not to be eclipsed entirely by the younger or more extreme artists around him. It seemed, retrospectively, that the war, by giving a substantial subject to pre-war modernist beliefs, had vindicated the ideologies and styles employed, just at the time that he had firmly and definitively moved away from them. But the fact that this show was hung at all, and in Burlington House, led P. G. Konody to argue that 'The seal of approval has thus been fixed upon what the reactionaries still choose to regard as Anarchism or Bolshevism in art, but what in reality is healthy progress on legitimate evolutionary lines.'[126] Needless to say this opinion was far from universal and once again the debates, so typical of the pre-war years, emerged, though this time with the Royal Academy and its members as 'outsiders'.[127] It was harsh irony that Richard should now be associated with his former enemy, as were the extreme pre-war modernist coteries and the remnants of those who 'sat the war out'. Instead of this being a new Renaissance, the start of a great, new, vital and fresh movement, some critics could only observe that 'this country is . . . once again going to make itself the laughing stock of Europe'.[128] It was still clear that Richard, especially in the wake of the third Leicester Galleries show, was now out of the running in the extreme avant-garde coteries of the day. This, he believed, was the result of a direct conspiracy against him and a belief, whether true, partially true, or absolutely fictional, which he would carry with him for the rest of his life. More recent interpretations are less sympathetic and Ferguson summed up declaring that after the war the artist had been no more than 'a pontificating poseur' who 'for a few months had shown genius'.[129]

The End of the Decade: Breakdown and Thoughts of Suicide

London was not accommodating and Richard recorded 'Still the intelligentsia were showing me every form of hostility and contempt, and when I returned to London I found social life impossible. Everywhere I went I was wounded or driven to fury through some cheap insult from some superior Bloomsbury or an aesthetic bohemian.'[130] An attack by Muirhead Bone deepened his depression when he referred to the later paintings of the artist as mere 'pot-boilers'. Once again Henry had to negotiate peace terms between the two, and in the end, on 10 December, 'Muirhead Bone came to see Richard and apologise . . . He said he knew there was a violent set against Richard among a clique of artists'.[131] Henry Tonks was also at this time allegedly getting up a petition to have *La Mitrailleuse* removed from the Tate Gallery and asking journalists not to review Richard's work. This, incidentally, had the opposite effect and Richard recorded cynically 'I have always wanted to thank that old woman Tonks for how his malice ended.'[132] But Richard's nervous decline accelerated now and at lunch on 14 December, his father was perturbed and wrote: 'But the sorrows of Richard appal me & and his outbreaks of wrath against Tonks . . . and others only make things worse.'[133] The attacks he felt were bad enough, but his son's method of dealing with them was even worse. Time did not alleviate the problem and on Christmas Day, at the family home, Richard seemed to reach the nadir of his mental health. The diary entry for that day reads

> Richard came to dinner . . . in terrible state of rage and depression against critics and artists. He is 'obsessed' hardly sane, utterly wretched, incapable of reason or work. He does everything that the enemy wishes him to do. Has written again to Tonks, no doubt with abuse. One of his pictures was rejected by the New English. He must have known it would be, yet he rages, I am in despair of a way out.'[134]

Three days later, when the father called at his son's flat, he found him in bed 'having a sort of cure for his distracted brain'.[135] Henry, amid concern, guessed one more time that the mastermind behind this plot against his son was Wyndham Lewis.[136] Richard now, abhorring his role as a peacetime artist, declared: 'Everything ought to be done to prevent a man's becoming an artist', going on to extol the virtues of martyrdom, as had been witnessed in the case of Rupert Brooke and Henri Gaudier-Brzeska. Though perhaps the comment was only meant flippantly, when he said that the artist was 'better dead than alive',[137] it remained germane, as now, over a year after the Great War ended, Richard, again contemplated suicide.

CODA

But Richard did not commit suicide. Instead he came out fighting, as angrily and as vociferously as one would have expected from the ex-rebel, Futurist and soldier. His enemies were confronted both privately and publicly as he stepped up his attacks on the 'Sladey-Tatey' clique, on the 'dictatorship' of Sir Kenneth 'Napoleon' Clark, on 'Henrietta' Tonks and the ubiquitous 'Bonehead Muir'. Then, in addition, he rejected London in its entirety to become the travelling artist who lived and worked in an eye-catching converted Ford truck with the ever-present, and ever-patient, Kathleen. In tandem, modernism and modernity, alongside any desire to be at the forefront of the avant-garde, was rejected as he turned to landscapes and flower drawings. Nevinson himself seemed to cut the ties to his own successful past, convinced of his persecution by other artists and critics and tortured by his post-war lack of artistic alignment to either the left or the right.

But he never allowed himself to move, or be moved, out of the spotlight altogether, maintaining his frequent visits to the Café Royal and hosting house parties that were famous throughout London. He continued to associate with the literary and society set, which included H. G. Wells and T. S. Eliot, the latter of whom even named him specifically in an early draft of *The Waste Land*:

He the young man carbuncular will stare
Boldly about in London's only café
And he will tell her with a casual air
Grandly, I have been with Nevinson today.

When inspiration seemed on the wane for painting he reinvented himself as the artist turned writer, and became the author of the apocalyptic novel *Exodus AD*, co-written with Princess Paul Troubetzkoy. In his more popular pronouncements he never abandoned the controversial comment or the argumentative headline, both of which were to become his trademark. As the artist was replaced by the celebrity / social commentator, society articles appeared with titles like 'The Worst Women in the World – and alas! They're British', 'There Are Far Too Many Ugly Women',

'Wild Parties in Three Countries' and 'Visions of an Artist: C.R.W. Nevinson re-Plans the Empire'.

Ultimately, and perhaps paradoxically, the ex-rebel finally turned to embrace the establishment he had once fought so ardently and publicly against, becoming a member of the New English Art Club, an Associate of the Royal Academy (ARA) and a Chevalier d'Honneur in France. He would have argued that it was the establishment that turned to embrace him, but would also have admitted, perhaps grudgingly, that sometime after the war he was finally content to let the past remain in the past. Ironically, having been accepted into the conservative elements of the London art world he appeared as at home there as ever he had been with the 'rebels' of the pre-war and early war periods. By the time of his death he was a frequent exhibitor at Burlington House.

But to focus on, or indeed include, the later period in the main body of this text would be to dilute the significance of the artist's contribution to British visual culture in the decade surrounding the Great War. However entertaining and eye-catching the rest of his life may have been, its inclusion would only act as a distraction to what was, after all, his short, but vital, period of extreme influence.

Through his perceptive and analytical images, C.R.W. Nevinson emerged as the significantly respected recorder and interpreter of that turbulent decade in European history. He had begun, in the eyes of the public at least, as a high profile icon of the pre-war avant-garde in the cultural and international vortex of London. Later he had evolved to become the epitome of intellectual youth from the generation who marched away to fight the Great War. Though his images were valued highly during this period, his position of prominence was only lost following the Armistice, in a convalescent Britain that no longer valued the eccentricities, priorities and subjects on which he had built his success. This phenomenon was far from unique to him. The potency and significance of his work from this short period, however, is undeniable. It was recognized as such at the time and today it represents a vital legacy left by a young man who had succeeded, where others had failed, in producing memorable and original images of lasting power, spawned from his turbulent affair with 'this Cult of Violence'.

APPENDIX

I. *Exhibition of Paintings and Drawings of War by C.R.W. Nevinson (Late Private RAMC)*
September–October 1916, Leicester Galleries, London

1. *Twilight*
2. *Explosion*
3. *Bravo*
4. *In the Observation Ward*
5. *Declaration of War*
6. *Motor Lorries*
7. *La Patrie*
8. *Sprucers*
9. *A Taube*
10. *Road to Ypres*
11. *Bursting Shells*
12. *Southampton*
13. *A Flooded Trench on the Yser*
14. *Patrols*
15. *Pursuing a Taube*
16. *Troops Resting*
17. *A Column on the March*
18. *Ypres After the First Bombardment*
19. *Belgium, 1914*
20. *The Converted Factory*
21. *The Doctor*
22. *Portrait of a Motor Ambulance Driver*
23. *La Guerre de Trous*
24. *Bursting Shell*

DRAWINGS AND ETCHINGS

25. *On the Road to Ypres*
26. *The Sprucers*
27. *A Flooded Trench on the Yser*
28. *Belgian Peasant Woman*
29. *Troops Resting*
30. *Huts*
31. *Before the Storm*
32. *Ypres Before the First Bombardment*
33. *1914*
34. *Boesinghe Farm*
35. *Returning to the Trenches*
36. *Southampton*
37. *La Mitrailleuse*
38. *Troops Resting*
39. *Night Arrival of the Wounded 3rd LGH*
40. *Receiving Ward 3rd LGH*
41. *When Harry Tate Came Down*
42. *Column on the March*

PAINTINGS

43. *Searchlights*
44. *A Wood*
45. *Behind the Lines*
46. *A Dawn, 1914*
47. *The First Searchlights at Charing Cross*
48. *Before the Storm*
49. *Returning to the Trenches*
50. *La Mitrailleuse*
51. *Back in London*
52. *A Star Shell*
53. *A Strafing*

SCULPTURE

54. *The Mechanic*

II. *Exhibition of Pictures of War by C.R.W. Nevinson*
March 1918, Leicester Galleries, London

1. *Bursting Shell*
2. *Reclaimed Country*
3. *Inside Brigade Headquarters*
4. *Looking Down on a Leave Boat From the Quay*
5. *Bomber*
6. *Over the Lines*
7. *Crossing the Channel*
8. *Spiral Descent*
9. *Ramming Home a Heavy Shell*
10. *Archies*

11. *Destroyed Canal at Ytres*
12. *Self-Portrait*
13. *A Group of Soldiers*
14. *After a Push*
15. *Banking*
16. *The Road from Arras to Bapaume*
17. *Swooping Down on a Hostile Plane*
18. *Reliefs at Dawn*
19. *Gun in Elevation*
20. *Survivors at Arras*
21. *Mule Team*
22. *Nerves of an Army*
23. *A Tank*
24. *A Front Line Near St Quentin*
25. *'He Gained a Fortune, But He Gave a Son'*
26. *War Profiteers*
27. *Verey Lights*
28. *M.T.*
29. *Paths of Glory* (Censored)
30. *Study for War Profiteers*
31. *Reliefs at Dawn*
32. *A German Observation Post, Mount Saint-Quentin*
33. *After a German Retreat Looted Coffin at Roclincourt*
34. *A Group of Soldiers*
35. *View of Arras*
36. *A Tank*
37. *Hauling Down an Observation Balloon at Night*
38. *Vimy Ridge from Mount Saint-Eloi*
39. *M.T.*
40. *Hans and Fritz*
41. *View of Peronne*
42. *After a German Retreat Labour Battalion Making a Road Through a Captured Village*
43. *After a Push*
44. *After a German Retreat Bottles*
45. *Mule Team*
46. *Road From Arras to Bapaume*
47. *Tincourt*
48. *Ramming Home a Heavy Shell*
49. *Over the Lines*
50. *Peronne*
51. *Reclaimed Country*
52. *Survivors at Arras*
53. *Butte de Warlencourt*
54. *Bomber*
55. *That Cursed Wood*
56. *Roads of France*
    a. *Mechanical Transport Leaving the Base*
    b. *Heavy Artillery and the Dumps*
    c. *Field Artillery and Infantry*
    d. *Infantry in Extended Order, Within the Lines*

III. *Etchings and Lithographs by C.R.W. Nevinson* May 1919, Frederick Keppel and Co., New York

ETCHINGS

1. *The Cursed Wood*
2. *Survivors at Arras*
3. *Inside Brigade Headquarters*
4. *A Group of Soldiers*
5. *Bombardment of Ypres*
6. *Boesinghe Farm*
7. *Reclaimed Country*
8. *An Estuary*
9. *Flooded Trench on the Yser*
10. *Dressing Station*
11. *A Tank*
12. *Returning to the Trenches*
13. *Mule team*
14. *Twilight*
15. *Dawn, 1914*
16. *Southampton*
17. *Troops Resting*
18. *The Nerves of an Army*
19. *On the Road to Ypres*
20. *Greenwich*
21. *Le Port*
22. *Wet Evening, Oxford Street*
23. *After a German Retreat – Looted Coffin Rollincourt*
24. *Labour Battalion Making a Road*
25. *Over the Lines*
26. *Reliefs at Dawn*
27. *After a German Retreat – Bottles*
28. *Bomber*
29. *Southampton*
30. *The Wave*
31. *Hauling Down an Observation Balloon*
32. *Hans and Fritz*
33. *Dawn at Southwark*
34. *Road From Arras to Bapaume*
35. *After a Push*
36. Set of *Making an Aeroplane* (6 images)

WOODCUTS

37. *Motor Transport*
38. *Ramming Home a Heavy Shell*
39. *From an Office Window*
40. *Wind*
41. *Southwark*

IV. *An Exhibition of New Works by C.R.W. Nevinson* October – November 1919, Leicester Galleries, London

1. *American Patriotism*
2. *A Canadian Dawn*
3. *The Elder Tree, Suburbia*
4. *February*
5. *Bacchus*
6. *Venetian Twilight*
7. *When Father Mows the Lawn Suburbia*
8. *Clapham Common*
9. *Pan*
10. *Le Bassin, Bruges*
11. *Parisian Night*
12. *Hampstead Heath*
13. *Summer-night*
14. *The Sandy Path*

15. *The Towing Path*
16. *Issy-les-Moulineux*
17. *The Garden of Eden*
18. *A Cornish Sea*
19. *Sur les Fortifications de Paris*
20. *The Mill-Pond*
21. *Portrait of a Very Young Man*
22. *Looking Down into Wall Street*
23. *The Temples of New York*
24. *Boulogne*
25. *Brittany; a 'Pardon'*
26. *Among the London Searchlights, 1918*
27. *Snow on the Downs*
28. *Rottingdean*
29. *A Thames Regatta*
30. *The Seine at Rouen*
31. *Bruges*
32. *Night Shift, Merthyr* (lithograph)
33. *Below the Bridge* (drawing)
34. *From an Office Window* (mezzotint)
35. *La Porte de Montmartre* (drawing)
36. *Limehouse* (mezzotint)
37. *Broadway Girls* (woodcut)
38. *London Bridges* (watercolour)
39. *Portrait of an Actress* (pastel)
40. *The Lilies of the Café* (pastel)
41. *The Pit-door* (pastel)
42. *An Inexperienced Witch* (pastel)
43. *The Roof Garden* (pastel)
44. *Broadway Girls* (pastel)
45. *La Ceinture* (drawing)
46. *The Shimmy-Shake* (pastel)
47. *Wind* (mezzotint)
48. *The Temples of New York* (dry-point)
49. *The Roof Garden* (mezzotint)
50. *The Workers* (lithograph)
51. *Looking Down into Wall Street* (lithograph)

V. *The Nations War Paintings and Other Records* December 1919 – January 1920, Imperial War Museum, Burlington House, London

1. *A Group of Soldiers*
2. *The Road From Arras to Bapaume*
3. *Howitzer Gun in Elevation*
4. *Swooping Down on a Hostile Plane*
5. *A Taube*
6. *After a Push*
7. *The Harvest of Battle*
8. *The Doctor*
9. *Reliefs at Dawn*
10. *Making Aircraft* (6 images including: *Swooping on a Taube*, *In the Air*, *Assembling Parts*, *Acetylene Welder*, *Banking at 4,000 feet*, and *Making an Engine*)
11. *Over the Lines*

ABBREVIATIONS

AAA Allied Artists Association
ARA Associate of the Royal Academy
DORA Defence of the Realm Act
NEAC New English Art Club
RA Royal Academy
RAC Rebel Art Centre
RAMC Royal Army Medical Corps

BIBLIOGRAPHICAL ABBREVIATIONS

Cornell
Wyndham Lewis Collection, Division of Rare and Manuscript Collections, Karl A. Koch Library, Cornell University

Harvard
Houghton Library, Harvard University, BMS. Eng. 1148-1081-27

HRHRC Texas
Carrington Collection, Harry Ransom Humanities Research Center, University of Texas at Austin

HWN Journals
H. W. Nevinson Journals, MSS Eng. Misc. e. 610–628, Bodleian Library, Oxford University

IWM
Imperial War Museum Archive, C.R.W. Nevinson, First World War Correspondence, 1917–18 [226A/6]

MART
Museo di Arti Moderna e Contemporanea di Trento e Rovereto

NYPL
Berg Collection, New York Public Library

Smithsonian-Gallatin
Gallatin Papers, reels 507, 508 and 1293, New-York Historical Society, Manuscript Division. Copies at Archives of American Art, Smithsonian Institution, Washington, D.C.

Smithsonian-Radin
Herman T. Radin Letters, N17 frames 531–533, Archives of American Art, Smithsonian Insititution, Washington, D.C.

TGA
Nevinson, C.R.W., Collection of Press Cutting Albums, 14 vols, 1910–47, Tate Gallery Archive, 7311.1-14

NOTES

INTRODUCTION

1. 'How the War Vindicated "Modern" Methods in Art' (journal and reviewer unknown, 1919. TGA (7311.Vol.1).
2. Obituary: C.R.W. Nevinson', *New York Times* (8 October 1946).
3. 'Stricken artist dies in his native Hampstead', *Hampstead News* (10 October 1946).
4. J. Rothenstein, *Modern English Painters*, vol. 2 (London, Eyre & Spottiswoode, 1956), p. 120.
5. J. Beechey, 'C.R.W. Nevinson: A Controversial Modernist', *Lancet* (15 January 2001), p. 241.
6. O. McNally, 'Images from the front lines', *Hartford Courant* (24 February 2000), p. 32.
7. B. Sewell, 'Pictures that Pack a Punch', *Evening Standard* (19 November 1999), p. 34.

CHAPTER ONE

1. *T.P.'s Weekly* (7 August 1915).
2. Margaret Nevinson recalled that even the servants did not stay long due to the unusual nature of the family and the life styles they led. M. Nevinson, *Life's Fitful Fever* (London, A. & C. Black, 1926), p. 133. A full study of the Nevinson family, but with emphasis on C.R.W.'s father, has been conducted by Professor Angela V. John at the University of Greenwich. Her forthcoming book is entitled *Rebel Correspondent: H. W. Nevinson, War, Journalism and Justice*.
3. C.R.W. Nevinson, *Paint and Prejudice* (London, Metheun, 1937), p. 2.
4. This address is actually closer to Gospel Oak than to Parliament Hill. In *Life's Fitful Fever* Margaret says that she, personally, bought this house through an inheritance, moving from the previous address which she said they had had built specially to their own specification.
5. C.R.W. Nevinson, *Paint and Prejudice* (London, Metheun, 1937), p. 2.
6. *Ibid.*, p. 2. In fact, his father had not been a professor at Jena. Rather, following his formal education at Shrewsbury and Christ Church, Oxford, he had conducted research into German literature at Jena and had given some tutorials, whilst preparing a text on Goethe.
7. *Ibid*, p. 2.
8. There can be little doubt that Nevinson was competent in French. He acted as an interpreter at the Front in 1914, wrote to Severini and Marinetti and received his replies in French and gave speeches in that tongue. There is no archival substantiation for his claim that he could speak German.
9. C.R.W. Nevinson to Carrington, 14 January 1913. Carrington Collection. HRHRC Texas.
10. C.R.W. Nevinson, *Paint and Prejudice*, p. 9. According to Professor Angela V. John, at the University of Greenwich, Margaret had been there after the Franco-Prussian War and the Commune, probably in 1874, to attend school for one year.
11. George Nevinson was an amateur artist. Some of his works can be seen at the Society of Antiquaries at Burlington House, London.
12. Though this was later in life, not at the stage his son was remembering in his autobiography.
13. C.R.W. Nevinson, *Paint and Prejudice*, p. 18.
14. *Ibid.*, p. 11.
15. C.R.W. Nevinson to Carrington, July 1912. HRHRC Texas.
16. C.R.W. Nevinson, *Paint and Prejudice*, p. 5.
17. *Ibid.*, p. 4.
18. *Ibid.*
19. *Ibid.*, p. 5.
20. C.R.W. Nevinson to Carrington, 17 January 1913. HRHRC Texas.
21. The separation seems mutual and they never sought divorce proceedings.
22. C.R.W. Nevinson, *Paint and Prejudice* (London, Metheun, 1937), p. 18.
23. F. Rutter, *Art in my Time* (London, Rich & Cowan, 1933), p. 166.
24. M. Nevinson, *Life's Fitful Fever*, p. 117.
25. HWN Journals, e. 612/3, 5 May 1904.
26. *Ibid.*, e. 610/4. 5 November 1897. This entry reads

'Wrote to Stafford removing Richard.' After this he went to Peterborough to stay with his Uncle Lloyd.

27. *Ibid.*, e. 611/1, 7 April 1901.
28. *Ibid.*, e. 611/3, 13 September 1901.
29. *Ibid.*, e. 611/3, 14 September 1901. It is worthy of note that this was two full years in advance of his taking a place there and so the move was not as random, or as last minute, as the artist suggested. Indeed his mother suggested that his name had been on the books of all three schools from birth.
30. Later known as the Red Brotherhood according to his mother's recollections in *Life's Fitful Fever*.
31. C.R.W. Nevinson, *Paint and Prejudice*, p. 7. Professor Angela V. John has commented on the inaccuracy of the statement that he became a socialist later in life. Instead, she has suggested, he experimented with socialism and anarchism in the 1880s and 1890s, became a Liberal, then in post-World War I Britain became a fairly moderate supporter of the Labour Party. She also points out that Henry was never a 'party man'. Personal communication.
32. In *T.P.'s and Cassell's Weekly* (19 July 1926), Richard recalled that it was here he had won his first art prize and that it had been presented to him by Michael Sadler. His mother, in *Life's Fitful Fever*, went further and named the compositions as: *Arrival of the Viking Ships in England*, *Joan of Arc's Vision of St. Michael*, *The Knight's Vision Before the Battle* and *St Simeon Stylites*.
33. John Fulleylove was a family friend and the author of *Pictures of Classical Greek Landscape and Architecture* (London, J.M. Dent, 1897) for which Henry wrote the foreword.
34. C.R.W. Nevinson, *Paint and Prejudice*, p. 7
35. *Ibid.*, p. 10.
36. *Ibid.*, p. 7.
37. The Uppingham archive contains no records pertaining to Richard and his health. Further evidence for ill health in this period can be found in: Margaret Nevinson, *Life's Fitful Fever* (London, A. & C. Black, 1926), p. 156 and also Henry's journals: e. 613/3, 28 March 1906, and e. 613/3, 26 April 1906.
38. HWN Journals, e. 611/5, 21 March 1903. Though this report described Selwyn as 'not an impressive or splendid character'. Of the school itself he went on to say 'The workshops are all rather dreary and useless. One felt the immense waste of time in all the school and its course – the dreariness & isolation of it all.'
39. *Ibid.*, e. 612/1, 18 September 1903.
40. *Ibid.* Henry also had mixed feelings about his public school education at Shrewsbury where, as a scholarship student, he had come in for the harsh exposure to the class system that his son was about to experience at Uppingham.
41. *Ibid.*, e. 612/1, 19 September 1903.
42. *Ibid.*, e. 612/1, 26 September 1903.
43. *Ibid.*, e. 612/1, 22 September 1903.
44. *Ibid.*, e. 612/1, 4 October 1903.
45. *Ibid.*, e. 621/1, 5 October 1903.
46. Where HWN heard that his son was too proud to ask questions in class
47. HWN Journals, e. 612/1, 10 October 1903.
48. *Ibid.*, e. 612/1, 11 October 1903.
49. *Ibid.*, e. 612/2, 18 December 1903.
50. *Ibid.*, e. 612/3, 18 February 1904.
51. *Ibid.*, e. 612/4, 10 May 1905.
52. *Ibid.*, e. 613/1, 6 October 1906.
53. This operation is recorded in M. Nevinson, *Life's Fitful Fever*.
54. HWN Journals, e.613/1, 6 October 1906.
55. *Ibid.*, e. 614/1, 23 February 1907.
56. *Ibid.*, e. 614/2, 15 November 1907. On this occasion he 'wrote a letter of warning to Rich on women'.
57. H.W. Nevinson, *More Changes and More Chances* (London, Nisbet, 1925), p. 173.
58. H.W. Nevinson, *Changes and Chances* (London, Nisbet, 1923), pp. 309–10.
59. *T.P.'s and Cassell's Weekly* (19 June 1926).
60. HWN Journals, e. 614/1, 23 February 1907.
61. *Ibid.*, e.614/2, 9 September 1907, 'went to 32 with R's pictures'.
62. C.R.W. Nevinson, *Paint and Prejudice*, p. 14.
63. A. Eyre, *St. John's Wood: It's haunts, it's houses and its celebrities* (London, Chapman and Hall, 1913).
64. *Ibid.*, p. 267.
65. C.R.W. Nevinson to Carrington, 14 August 1912. HRHRC Texas.
66. C.R.W. Nevinson, *Paint and Prejudice*, p. 14.
67. *Ibid.*, p. 17.
68. *Ibid.*, p. 16.
69. Walter Richard Sickert RA, PRBA, NEAC, ARE (1860–1942).
70. C.R.W. Nevinson, *Paint and Prejudice*, p. 18.
71. Philippa Preston later married the film producer Maurice Elvey.
72. HWN Journals, e. 615/2, 20 December 1908.
73. C.R.W. Nevinson, *Paint and Prejudice*, p. 11.
74. *Ibid*, p. 19.
75. *Ibid.*, p. 19.
76. HWN Journals, e. 615/1, 8 October 1908.
77. *Ibid.*, e. 615/2, 19 December 1908. Though Henry did report that his son had done a charcoal, Russian in appearance, of a workman with a flag, and stated that he had quite liked it.
78. S. Chaplin, 'The Slade School of Art' (unpublished, Slade School of Art Archive), p. 131. He wrote that Richard was convinced on seeing the college magazine, *The Studio*, in 1907, and in particular the images of Augustus John contained within.
79. In an article in *T.P.'s and Cassell's Weekly* (19 June 1926), Richard implied for the first time that he had left the college through dissatisfaction with the direction and pace of his learning there.
80. C.R.W. Nevinson, *Paint and Prejudice*, p. 20.
81. *Ibid.*, p. 30.

CHAPTER TWO

1. K. Pople, *Stanley Spencer* (London, Collins, 1991), p. 16.
2. C.R.W. Nevinson, *Paint and Prejudice* (London, Metheun, 1937), p. 23.
3. P. Nash, *Outline: An Autobiography and Other Writings*

(London, Faber & Faber, 1949), p. 90. On the previous page Nash explained simply that 'Tonks was the Slade and the Slade was Tonks.'

4. For a complete, though unpublished, understanding of the history of the Slade, see: S.Chaplin, *Slade School of Art* (Slade School of Art Archive), p. 123. References to Richard are, however, based on *Paint and Prejudice.* M. Holroyd, *Augustus John* (London, 1974) however dismisses this triumphal period in the Slade history as 'mythology'.
5. C.R.W. Nevinson, *Paint and Prejudice*, p. 23.
6. P. Nash, *Outline*, p. 90.
7. Frederick Brown (1851–1941). One of the 'London Impressionists' to exhibit with Sickert and Steer. Slade Professor from 1892 to 1917.
8. Henry Tonks (1862–1937). In 1892 Professor Brown offered him the post of assistant at the Slade which he held until Brown's retirement in 1917. At this point he became Slade professor and held the post until 1930. See J. Hone, *Life of Henry Tonks* (London, Heinemann, 1939).
9. C.R.W. Nevinson, *Paint and Prejudice*, p. 24.
10. S. MacDonald, *The History and Philosophy of Art Education* (University of London Press, 1970), p. 276.
11. His enrollment in the second term was confirmed by Gertler who recalled the late arrival of a very confident young artist, keen to become the 'leader'. J. Woodeson, *Mark Gertler* (London, Sidgwick & Jackson, 1972).
12. The Heatherly School of Fine Art at 75 Newman Street. Based on the French atelier system and open to students without a formal entry qualification. Richard also studied sculpture in his spare time under Harvard Thomas. See: C.R.W. Nevinson, *Paint and Prejudice*, p. 28.
13. N. Carrington (ed.), *Mark Gertler – Selected Letters* (London, Rupert Hart-Davis, 1965), p. 34.
14. Edward Alexander Wadsworth ARA, NEAC, LG (1889–1949).
15. Mark Gertler LG, NEAC (1891–1939).
16. Adrian Paul Allinson, ROI, RBA, LG, PS (1890–1959).
17. Rudolph Ihlee, NEAC (1883–1968).
18. Maxwell Gordon Lightfoot (1889–1911).
19. Possibly William Lionel Clause, NEAC (1887–1946).
20. John S. Currie (1884–1914).
21. Sir Stanley Spencer, RA, NEAC, ARCA, CBE (1891–1959).
22. C.R.W. Nevinson, *Paint and Prejudice*, p. 29. The reference is to Augustus John.
23. *Ibid.* The reference is to Henry Tonks.
24. K. Pople, *Stanley Spencer*, p. 517.
25. P. Nash, *Outline*, p. 90. Ironically he gets Richard's name wrong in his book, calling him Charles.
26. K. Pople, *Stanley Spencer*, p. 15. Years later, in 1939, Richard and Stanley Spencer met again at the Carlines'. He later wrote to him 'Stan, I would like you to know how glad I am that we have met again. My gratitude to you is boundless. As you know, I consider you the only man with that indefinable touch of genius. I felt it for Picasso years ago.' C.R.W. Nevinson to Stanley Spencer, 15 June 1939. Nevinson, C.R.W. Correspondence,TGA, London, 733.1.1107.
27. C.R.W. Nevinson, *Paint and Prejudice*, p. 41.
28. *Ibid.*, p. 23.
29. *Ibid.*, p. 24. This might be a throwaway comment but it can be interpreted to back up the positively masculine stance that Richard always took in the presentation of his image. At the Slade, and certainly through Futurism, he wanted to be seen as the virile, dynamic, man's man.
30. A. Allinson, 'Memoirs' (unpublished). Cited in J. Woodeson, *Mark Gertler.*
31. Dora Carrington (1893–1932).
32. Christopher Martin has also observed that Paul Nash knew him as 'the Minataur' whilst Henry Williamson, in *The Phoenix Generation*, conflated the nick-name 'Chips' with 'Nevinson' to create the character 'Channerson'. C. Martin, 'C.R.W. Nevinson: The Artist and His Name', *Nevinson News* (Issue 5, 2000), p. 4.
33. C.R.W. Nevinson, *Paint and Prejudice*, p. 26.
34. R. Cork, *Art Beyond the Gallery* (New Haven and London, Yale University Press, 1985), p. 216.
35. A. Allinson, *Memoirs*, cited in J. Woodson. *Mark Gertler.*
36. C.R.W. Nevinson, *Paint and Prejudice*, p. 27.
37. Francis Vane Phipson Rutter (1876–1937) studied at Cambridge alongside C.F.G. Masterman. In 1903 he became the regular art critic for the *Sunday Times.* He also founded and edited *Art News*, was editor of the *Art Gazette*, and the editor of *Art & Letters.* In 1905 he established the French Impressionist Fund and in 1908 he established the Allied Artists Association. In 1913 he was responsible for organizing the *Post-Impressionist and Futurist Exhibition* at the Dore Galleries. Between 1912 and 1917 he was curator of the Leeds City Art Gallery, and there met Michael Sadler and Herbert Read. The pamphlet he wrote for the 1910 exhibition at the Grafton Galleries, entitled 'Revolution in Art', epitomizes his pre-war desire for experimentation and for the influence of France. He was open to the ideas of Futurism, in preference to total abstraction. He was central to Richard's rise to prominence in this era.
38. The photograph hides the tension between the three 'friends'. It was at this picnic that Gertler's hatred for Richard peaked, and his feelings for Carrington were reciprocated for the first time.
39. G. Cannan, *Mendel* (London, Lloyds, 1920).
40. The Hon. Dorothy Brett (1883–1977), daughter of Lord Esher.
41. Michael Reynolds, 'The Slade: The Story of an Art School 1871–1971' (unpublished), p. 181. Ironically, Nash too seems to have fallen for Carrington's affections and it was Richard who was given the job of forwarding a letter from Nash to her. He wrote to her 'I do not wish to get cut out but I heroically enclose my rival's letter, by the way, who is this Paul Nash? I do not seem to remember him though in a way his name seems familiar to me.' Nevinson to Carrington, 2 April 1912. Carrington Collection, HRHRC Texas.
42. Cannan reported of Mitchell (Nevinson): 'But Mitchell was often depressed and moody. He had letters every day, and every evening he wrote at great length.' G. Cannan, *Mendel*, p. 97.
43. Nevinson to Carrington, 8 April 1912. HRHRC Texas.

44. G. Cannan, *Mendel*, p. 124.
45. Nevinson to Carrington, 12 June 1912. HRHRC Texas.
46. *Ibid.*, 28 March 1912.
47. *Ibid.*
48. *Ibid.*, 2 April 1912.
49. *Ibid.*, 28 March 1912.
50. *Ibid.*, 8 April 1912.
51. *Ibid.*, April 1912. From 2 Toronto Terrace, Lewes.
52. *Ibid.*, Undated note from the Café Royal. Probably early 1912.
53. *Ibid.*, May 1912.
54. *Ibid.*, 28 March 1912.
55. *Ibid.*
56. G. Cannan, *Mendel*, p. 56.
57. Nevinson to Carrington, 10 June 1912. HRHRC Texas.
58. G. Cannan, *Mendel*, p. 56.
59. C.R.W. Nevinson, *Paint and Prejudice*, p. 25.
60. G. Cannan, *Mendel*, p. 79.
61. Mark Gertler to William Rothenstein, undated. Cited in N. Carrington (ed.), *Mark Gertler – Selected Letters*, p. 33.
62. G. Cannan, *Mendel*, p. 58. In return Mendel described Mitchell as 'a fine young Englishman, pink and oozing robustious health, ease, refinement and comfort'.
63. *Ibid.*, p. 57. Though Mitchell (Nevinson) did also exclaim 'Gawd! What can you do when your own father takes the shine out of you at every turn.' Later Cannan suggested that Mendel (Gertler) helped to bring Mitchell (Nevinson) and his father closer together.
64. H.W. Nevinson to Professor Sadler, 9 May 1911. Cornell.
65. C.R.W. Nevinson, *Paint and Prejudice*, p. 26.
66. HWN Journals, e. 617/2, 21 July 1912.
67. C.R.W. Nevinson, *Paint and Prejudice*, p. 30.
68. H.W. Nevinson, *More Changes, More Chances* (London, Nisbett, 1925),p. 288.
69. HWN Journals, e. 615/4, 2 and 8 December 1909.
70. *Ibid.*, e. 615/3, 13 September 1909.
71. *Ibid.*, e. 615/3, 8 July 1909.
72. *Ibid.*, e. 616/2, 6 November 1910. He commented 'The ribald scorn of the fatted rich who knew nothing of art even stirred Hind's rage.'
73. Charles Lewis-Hind (1862–1927) wrote for the *Art Journal* and the *Daily Chronicle*. He had been one of the more outspoken supporters of the Post-Impressionist exhibition at the Grafton Galleries in 1910. He wrote extensively too on more conventional subjects such as Velázquez, Rembrandt and Turner. A wide range of periodicals benefited from his writing such as: *T.P.'s Weekly* and the *English Review*. He was a close friend of the Nevinson family.
74. HWN Journals, e. 616/1, 10 April 1910.
75. *Ibid.*, e. 616/2, 4 January 1911.
76. *Ibid.*, e. 616/3, February 28 1911 & e. 616/4. August 11 1911.
77. *Ibid.*, e. 616/3, 30 March 1911 and e. 616/4, 13 August. Clearly his son's progress was discussed as, on 13 August, Rothenstein seems to have been suggesting some form of employment for Nevinson in Bradford.
78. *Ibid.*, e. 615/4, 1 December 1911.
79. *Ibid.*, e. 617/2, 12 July 1912.
80. *Ibid.*
81. *Ibid.*, e. 617/1, 15 February 1912.
82. M. Nevinson, *Life's Fitful Fever* (London, A. & C. Black, 1926), p. 217.
83. HWN Journals, e. 616/4, 6 November 1911.
84. *Ibid.*, e. 615/2, 2 February, 3 March and e. 615/3, 9 July 1909.
85. *Ibid.*, e. 616/4, 27 August 1911.
86. *Ibid.*, e. 616/4, 29 August 1911.
87. *Ibid.*, e. 616/4, 17 October 1911.
88. *Ibid.*, e. 616/4, 26 August 1911, 'Dined alone at 'Gustaves' reading R's final essay on Mona Lisa.'
89. *Ibid.*, e.616/4, 6 August 1911.This led directly to a composition which has not survived.
90. G. Cannan, *Mendel*, p. 59.
91. *Ibid.*
92. C.R.W. Nevinson, *Paint and Prejudice*, p. 30.
93. The Last Will and Testament of C.R.W. Nevinson states: 'I request my wife to destroy all sketches, drawings and paintings left by me which in her opinion are unworthy of me and if she should be in doubt I desire her to consult any judge of art, but not an artist.'
94. Recorded as being in the private collection of a Mrs Lloyd Jones (perhaps Richard's aunt).
95. My point is that though the immediate association is with that of late nineteenth-century French painting, there are significant roots in the English tradition. To include the former then is not necessarily to exclude the latter.
96. HWN Journals, e. 616/2, 26 November 1910. 'Went with Rich and Gortler [*sic*] to the Post-Impressionists.'
97. P. Nash, *Outline*, p. 93.
98. Only nine of the 228 paintings exhibited were by Manet.
99. M. Hall argues that this has been exaggerated and that 'England had in effect, already gone over to 'Post-Impressionism' well before Fry's show.' Her argument is that the ideology of the Post-Impressionists was not so very different from that of the NEAC and so did not break with tradition, simply modified it. She goes on to say that in an adaptation of the Ruskinian concept of art conveying noble ideas, now it was conveying noble emotions. The emphasis is all that has changed. M. Hall, *Modernism, Militarism and Masculinity* (State University of New York at Binghampton, 1994).
100. J. S. Sargent, *Art News* II (16 January 1911), p. 1.
101. W. C. Wees, *Vorticism and The English Avant-Garde* (Manchester, Manchester University Press, 1972), p. 23.
102. Cited in J. Ferguson, *The Arts in Britain in World War One* (London, Steiner & Bell Ltd, 1980), p. 10.
103. F. Rutter, 'Revolution in Art' (London, Art News Press, 1910), p. 1.
104. 'Round the Galleries', *Sunday Times* (month and reviewer unknown). TGA.
105. A group founded by Vanessa Bell in 1905, which Richard described as 'a remarkable little clique and which was eventually ruined by the amateurish dilettantism of Roger Fry'. Cited in C.R.W. Nevinson, *Paint and Prejudice*, p. 29. Richard is known to have exhibited with the group from as early as 1910.

106. 'Round the Galleries', *Sunday Times* (month and reviewer unknown). TGA.
107. Nevinson to Carrington, 2 April 1912. HRHRC Texas.
108. This painting and *A View of Bradford*, were both bought by American collector John Quinn.
109. 'Round the Galleries', *Sunday Times* (month and reviewer unknown). TGA.
110. C.R.W. Nevinson, *Paint and Prejudice*, p. 40.
111. 'Round the Galleries' *Sunday Times* (month and reviewer unknown). TGA.
112. W.R. Sickert, 'Idealism', *Art News* (12 May 1910).
113. C. Harrison, *English Art and Modernism 1900–1939* (London, Allen Lane,1981), p. 37.
114. Nevinson to Carrington, undated letter. HRHRC Texas. This was exhibited as *Boat Race Day, 1911* at the Friday Club in April 1918, where Konody again compared it to Boudin.
115. HWN Journals, e. 617/2, 29 March 1912.
116. Nevinson to Carrington, 28 March 1912. HRHRC Texas.
117. *Ibid.*, 2 April 1912.
118. *Ibid.*, undated letter.
119. *Ibid.*
120. *Ibid.*, 2 April 1912.
121. *Ibid.*, 28 March 1912.
122. *Ibid.*, 8 April 1912.
123. The setting is the Regents Canal, Camden, behind Gilbey's gin factory. This is also where he would set the later composition *Camden Lock, London* (1913).
124. R. Cork, *Vorticism and Abstract Art in the First Machine Age* (London, Fraser, 1976), p. 59.
125. R. Cork in J. Turner (ed.), *The Dictionary of Art*, vol. 23, pp. 15–16 (London, Macmillan, 1996).
126. Nevinson to Carrington, undated. HRHRC Texas.
127. Later in life Richard used to claim that he had been a member of the Camden Town Group. This is not true.
128. 'Round the Galleries', *Sunday Times* (date and reviewer unknown). TGA..
129. HWN Journals, e. 617/1, 12 February 1912.
130. *Ibid.*, e. 617/1, 15 February 1912.
131. *Ibid.*, e. 617/1, 25 February 1912. 'M' is Richard's mother, Margaret.
132. Nevinson to Carrington, 23 May 1912. HRHRC Texas.
133. *Ibid.*, June 1912.
134. *Ibid.*
135. *Ibid.*, 23 May 1912.
136. *Ibid.*, June 1912.
137. *Ibid.*, May 1912.
138. *Ibid.*, 28 March 1912.
139. *Ibid.*, undated note from the Café Royal.
140. *Ibid.*, 23 May 1912.
141. *Ibid.*, undated letter.
142. *Ibid.*, 8 April 1912.
143. *Ibid.*, May 1912.
144. *Ibid.*, June 1912.
145. *Ibid.*, 21 June 1912.
146. Gertler to Carrington, 19 June 1912. Cited in N. Carrington (ed.), *Mark Gertler – Selected Letters*, p. 36.
147. *Ibid.*, p. 37.
148. *Ibid.*, pp. 38–9.
149. J. Woodeson, *Mark Gertler*, p. 87.
150. *Ibid.*, p. 98.
151. G. Cannan, *Mendel*, p. 105.
152. *Ibid.*
153. *Ibid.*
154. *Ibid.*, undated.
155. The passage from 'The Ballad of Reading Gaol' actually reads: 'Yet each man kills the thing he loves,/...The coward does it with a kiss,/ The brave man with a sword!'
156. B. Wadsworth *Edward Wadsworth* (London, Michael Russell, 1989), p. 39. Wadsworth on his return from the Canary Islands stayed in Paris for a short time and, like Richard, did some work around Moulineux and on the fortifications.
157. N. Carrington (ed.), *Mark Gertler – Selected Letters*, p. 41.
158. Nevinson to Carrington, undated, probably July 1912. HRHRC Texas.
159. *Ibid.*, June 1912.
160. *Ibid.*, undated.

CHAPTER THREE

1. Nevinson to Carrington, 13 October 1912. HRHRC Texas.
2. C.R.W. Nevinson, *Paint and Prejudice*, p. 34.
3. *Ibid.*, p. 35.
4. *Ibid.*, p. 37.
5. *Ibid.*, p. 42.
6. *Ibid.*, p. 43. Kandinsky had been exhibiting at the AAA from as early as 1909. His works were well known in England and his book, *Concerning the Spiritual in Art* (1912) was widely read among English intellectuals.
7. *Ibid.*
8. *Ibid.*
9. *Ibid.*, p. 54. He recorded that he studied lithography under Ernest Jackson at the London County Council schools in Southampton Row.
10. M. Bradbury and J. McFarlane (eds), *Modernism* (London, Penguin Books, 1976), p. 172.
11. HWN Journals, e. 617/ 2, 22 July 1912.
12. Nevinson to Carrington, July 24 1912. From Hôtel de la place de L'Odéon, Paris. HRHRC Texas.
13. *Ibid.*
14. *Ibid.*, July (Sat) 1912, from Rouen.
15. *Ibid.*
16. *Ibid.*
17. *Ibid.*, August 1912, possibly from Le Havre.
18. *Ibid.*
19. *Ibid.*
20. *Ibid.* Professor Tonks, in *Mendel*, is Edgar Froitzheim, and the novel explains how he had taken a collection of £50 in order that the girl should go away. Calthrop gave £20.
21. HWN Journals, e. 617/2, 16 August 1912.
22. Nevinson to Carrington, August 1912, probably from Le Havre. HRHRC Texas.
23. *Ibid.*, 14 August 1912.
24. *Ibid.*
25. *Ibid.*, August 1912.
26. *Ibid.*
27. *Ibid.*, 14 August 1912.

28. *Ibid.*, undated, probably August 1912.
29. *Ibid.*
30. HWN Journals, e.617/2, 2 September 1912.
31. Nevinson to Carrington, 28 August 1912. HRHRC Texas.
32. *Ibid.*, undated, 1912.
33. *Ibid.*, 14 August 1912.
34. *Ibid.*, undated, from Bradford.
35. *Ibid.*, 4 September 1912.
36. *Ibid.*, September 1912.
37. *Ibid.*, 28 August 1912.
38. *Ibid.*, August 22 1912.
39. *Ibid.*, August 28 1912.
40. *Ibid.*, 8 September 1912.
41. *Ibid.*, 17 September 1912.
42. *Ibid.*, September 1912.
43. *Ibid.*, September 1912.
44. *Ibid.*, 17 September 1912. His father at this stage was in Enniskillen and was shortly to return to the Balkans to the report on the war there. It is here that he would meet Marinetti.
45. *Ibid.*, 12 October 1912.
46. *Ibid.*, 13 October 1912.
47. *Ibid.*, October 1912.
48. M. Nevinson, *Life's Fitful Fever* (London, A. & C. Black, 1926).
49. C.R.W. Nevinson, *Paint and Prejudice*, p. 13. One has to be very careful in adhering closely to the labels Richard attributes to himself. When he says he was a modernist, the reference will simply be to 'modern ideas'. It almost certainly does not make reference to the more complicated debate concerning Modernity and Modernism. See D. Peters Corbett, *The Modernity of English Art: 1914–1930* (Manchester, Manchester University Press, 1997), pp. 1–24.
50. The family was not Catholic: Henry was agnostic and Margaret was High Anglican, her father and brother were both clergymen.
51. Nevinson to Carrington, 26 December 1912. HRHRC Texas.

CHAPTER FOUR

1. Ford M. Hueffer, 'Those were the days', in G. Hughes (ed.), *Imagist Anthology* (London, Chatto and Windus, 1930), p. x.
2. V. Woolf, *Mr. Bennett and Mr. Brown*. Cited in H. Read, *Contemporary British Art*, p. 20. Woolf wrote 'On, or around December 1910, human character changed.'
3. Sir C. Petrie, *The Edwardians* (London, 1965), p. 231.
4. G. Dangerfield, *Strange Death of Liberal England* (London, 1935), pp. 107–8.
5. *Ibid.*, p. 67.
6. Sir O. Sitwell, *Great Morning*, p. 235. Cited in W.C. Wees, *Vorticism and the English Avant-Garde* (Manchester, Manchester University Press, 1972).
7. E. Pound, 'Affirmations VI', *New Age* (1915), p. 411.
8. M. Sinclair, *Tree of Heaven* (London), p. 240.
9. *Ibid.*, p. 163.
10. W.C.Wees, *Vorticism and the English Avant-Garde* (Manchester, Manchester University Press, 1972), p. 12.
11. C.R.W. Nevinson, 'War and Art', *Daily Graphic* (11 March 1915), p. 17.
12. T.E. Hulme openly criticized the Bloomsbury Group, notably in a series of articles from early 1914 in *New Age*: See January and February 1914.
13. F.T. Marinetti, 'The Founding and Manifesto of Futurism' (1909).
14. Cultural anarchism was promoted by Georges Sorel (1847–1922), a French social philosopher. Sorel consistently affirmed the moral importance of self-expression and self-realization through the free and creative exercise of the will. Change could only come in the wake of revolution and confrontation. This founded a basic tenet for Futurism.
15. The philosophies of Nietzsche were widely read at this time. Both Mussolini and Marinetti are known to have adapted a simplified version of some of these ideologies to serve their own ends, as did the Nazis in the 1930s. The best known of the publications include *Untimely Meditations* (1873–6), *The Joyous Science* (1882), *Thus Spake Zarathustra* (1883–92), *Beyond Good and Evil* (1886) and also *Ecce Homo* (his autobiography which was witheld from publication by his sister until 1908). Recurrent themes include the repudiation of Christian ethics, detestation of liberalism and democratic ideologies, the creation of the *Ubermensch* (superman), the death of God and the 'will to power'.
16. Gabriele D'Annunzio, (1863–1938). Writer, poet, politician, and believer in the second Renaissance. He urged strongly for Italy to join the Great War, then served as soldier, sailor and finally airman. In 1919 he seized and held Fiume as dictator, for over a year, despite the international will as set forth at Versailles. D'Annunzio was a contemporary and rival of Marinetti's. He also was an admirer of England and the English.
17. Henri Bergson (1859–1941). French philosopher, professor at the Collège de France, and Nobel Prize winner for literature (1927). He propounded the idea of the *élan vital* or 'creative impulse', implying that impulse and intuition are at the heart of evolution, not analysis. Key works include *Time and Freewill* (1889), *Matter and Memory* (1896) and *Creative Evolution* (1907). His chief apologist in England was T. E. Hulme who lectured on the reinvention of the artist as 'discoverer' as opposed to 'creator'.
18. 'Technical Manifesto of Futurist Painting' (March 1910). Signed by Boccioni, Carra, Russolo, Balla and Severini.
19. A. Bozzola and C. Tisdall, *Futurism* (London, Thames & Hudson, 1977), p. 8.
20. This format was later echoed in *Blast* when the subdivisions became 'Blasted' and 'Blessed'.
21. A. D'Harcourt, *Futurism and the International Avant-Garde* (Philadelphia Museum of Art, 1980).
22. *Ibid.*
23. 'Declaration of Futurism', *The Tramp; A Journal of Healthy Outdoor Life for the Adventurous Gentleman* (1 August 1910), p. 488.
24. The lecture was delivered in French as Marinetti could not speak English.
25. Cited in R. Banham, *Theory and Design in the First*

Machine Age (London, 1960), pp. 123–4.
26. R.W. Flint (ed.), *F.T. Marinetti: Selected Writings* (London, 1972), p. 59–60.
27. W.C.Wees, *Vorticism and the English Avant-Garde* (Toronto, 1972), p. 96.
28. The *Vote*, (31 December 1910). TGA. This was the journal of the Woman's Freedom League, a suffrage organization of which Margaret was a part.
29. F.T. Marinetti, 'War, the world's only hygiene' (1915).
30. M. Nevinson, *Life's Fitful Fever* (London, 1925), pp. 241–2.
31. From a lecture delivered at the Estorick Collection, London, by J. A. Black, entitled 'The "Caffeine of Europe" Hits England: F.T. Marinetti (1876–1944) and the Futurists in England, *c.* 1910–14.'
32. *Evening News* (4 March 1912).
33. J.A. Black, Estorick lecture. See note 31.
34. Boccioni to V. Baer, 15 March 1912. Cited in L. Somigli, 'Towards a Theory of the Avant-Garde Manifesto' (PhD diss. State University of New York at Stony Brook, 1996), p. 200.
35. He considered Marinetti's argument concerning the evils of British colonialism hypocritical considering that is what the Italians had tried, and failed, to do. Cited in W. Wees, *Vorticism and the English Avant-Garde*, pp. 94 and 96.
36. Cited in C. Ferall, 'Melodramas of Modernity', *University of Toronto Quarterly*, vol. 63, no. 2 (winter 1993/1994).
37. Marinetti could not get the cabins he wanted, the sailing was delayed by a coal strike and neither Russolo nor Boccioni wanted to go anyway. Thanks to J. A. Black for this research at the Beinecke Library, Yale University.
38. *Daily Chronicle* (20 March 1912).
39. W.C. Wees, *Vorticism and the English Avant-Garde* (Toronto, 1972), pp. 94–6.
40. Translations and extra notes were added concerning individual paintings by the gallery director, R. Meyer-See, and the previous attack against Cubism was withdrawn.
41. F. Rutter, *Pall Mall Gazette*, (1 March 1912).
42. C. Lewis-Hind, *Daily Chronicle* (4 March 1912).
43. *The Times* (19 March 1912).
44. Marinetti to Pratella, 12 April 1913. Cited in R. Carrieri, *Futurism* (Milano, 1963), p. 62.
45. Boccioni's *The City Rises* to Busoni, and Carra's *Leaving the Theatre* to Max Rothschild.
46. R. Carrieri, *Futurism*, p. 62.
47. P. Hamilton, 'The Role of Futurism, Dada and Surrealism in the Construction of British Modernism 1910–1940' (PhD diss. University of Oxford, 1987).
48. *Ibid.*, p. 58.
49. HWN Journals, e. 617/1, 4 March 1912.
50. C.R.W. Nevinson, *Paint and Prejudice*, p. 57.
51. H.W. Nevinson, *More Changes, More Chances* (London, 1925), pp. 378–9. Marinetti had also served as a reporter in the Tripoli Campaign of 1911.
52. M. Hall, 'Modernism, Militarism and Masculinity' (PhD diss., University of New York at Binghampton, 1994).
53. Paul George Konody (1872–1933) was born in Budapest, educated in Vienna and settled in London in 1889. He wrote for both the *Observer* and the *Daily Mail* and was personal art advisor to Lord Rothermere. He defended the artist's right to experiment, though, like Rutter, was often uncomfortable with the more extreme results. He defended the arrival of Post-Impressionism in Britain in 1910 and in time became the chief apologist for C.R.W. Nevinson.
54. C.R.W. Nevinson, *Paint and Prejudice*, p. 56.
55. The Rebel Arts Centre was officially registered as 'The Cubist Art Centre Ltd', at 38 Great Ormond Street, and was funded by Kate Latchmere (1887–1976)
56. C.R.W. Nevinson, *Paint and Prejudice*, p. 56.
57. *Ibid.*, p. 57.
58. *Ibid.*, pp. 77–8.
59. C. Bell, 'The English Group,' *Catalogue of the Second Post Impressionist Exhibition* (London, Grafton Galleries, 1912).
60. C. Harrison, *English Art and Modernism 1900–1939* (London, Allen Lane, 1981), p. 65.
61. HWN Journals, e.617/3, 4 January 1913.
62. F. Spalding, *British Art Since 1900* (London, Thames & Hudson, 1986), pp. 37–9.
63. Nevinson to Carrington, Wednesday, 8 January 1913. HRHRC Texas.
64. *Ibid.*, 14 January 1913.
65. HWN Journals, e.617/3, 22 January 1913.
66. Nevinson to Carrington, 14 January 1913.
67. *Ibid.*, 13 May 1913.
68. HWN Journals, e. 617/4, 22 May 1913.
69. *Ibid.*, e. 617/4, 15 March 1913.
70. Nevinson to Lewis, 2 March 1913. Cornell.
71. *Ibid.*
72. Nevinson to Carrington, 16 January 1913. HRHRC Texas.
73. *Ibid.*, Friday 17 January 1913.
74. *Ibid.*, 19 January 1913.
75. *Ibid.*
76. *Ibid.*, 20 January 1913.
77. *Ibid.*, 17 February 1913.
78. *Ibid.*, 17 February 1913 (second letter of that date).
79. *Ibid.*, 26 March 1913.
80. HWN Journals, e. 617/3, 28 January 1913.
81. *Ibid.*
82. A very early result of experimentation with Futurism was seen in January 1913 when Richard exhibited *Rising City* (now lost) with the Friday Club. The reference is very clearly to a Futurist work by Boccioni called *The City Rises* from 1910, the slight ambiguity in the name occurring only through the gallery translation for the catalogue. It does not survive and so we cannot know whether it was Futurist in composition as well as in name.
83. F. Rutter, *Art in my Time*, p. 165.
84. HWN Journals, e. 617/4, 21 April 1913.
85. C.R.W. Nevinson, *Paint and Prejudice*, p. 37. C. Doherty has suggested another possibility for the meeting saying that it took place at the 1912 Futurist Exhibition at the Sackville Galleries Show after which Nevinson 'managed to wangle an invitation to accompany him to Paris'. C. E. Doherty, 'Nash, Nevinson and Roberts at War: a

Catalogue Raisonne of First World War paintings, drawings, and prints by Paul Nash, C.R.W. Nevinson and William Roberts' (PhD diss., University of Wisconsin at Madison, 1988). Also Margaret Nevinson implies in *Life's Fitful Fever* that it was in Paris that they met.

86. J. Rothenstein, *Modern British Painters. Volume 2* (London, Eyre & Spottiswoode, 1956), pp. 96–7.
87. A. C. Hanson, *Severini Futurista: 1912–1917* (London, 1995), pp. 21 and 147.
88. *Ibid.*, p. 37.
89. As reported by J. Black in his lecture at the Estorick Collection. See note 31.
90. G. Severini, *The Futurist Painter Severini Exhibits his Latest Works* (London, Marlborough Gallery, 1913), p. 4.
91. Nevinson to Percy Wyndham Lewis, dated 5 November. Cornell. The reference in particular was made concerning a Futurist commission for a certain Lady Muriel Paget.
92. A.C. Hanson, *Severini Futurista* (London, 1995), pp. 158–9.
93. Nevinson to Lewis, 14 November 1913. Cornell. Richard hoped to bring Wadsworth to the meeting too, implying the latter's enthusiasm for the movement, as well as his own, but whether or not he came is unknown.
94. F. Rutter, 'Foreword' to the exhibition catalogue for *Post-Impressionist and Futurist Exhibition*, 1913.
95. W. Lipke, 'Futurism and the Development of Vorticism' *Studio International* (April 1967), p. 173.
96. Cited in C. Harrison, *English Art and Modernism 1900–1939* (London, Allen Lane, 1981), p. 88.
97. F. Rutter, *Art in my Time* (London, Rich & Cowan, 1933), p. 150.
98. Cited in R. Cork, *Vorticism and Abstract Art in the First Machine Age* (London, Fraser, 1976), p. 243. It is possible that this painting might also have been known as *Gare Saint-Lazare* as Rutter claims that the latter was the first English Futurist painting in *Art in my Time* (London, Rich & Cowan, 1933), p. 150.
99. R. Ingleby, 'Utterly Tired of Chaos' *C.R.W. Nevinson: The Twentieth Century* (London, Merrell Holberton, 1999), p. 15.
100. The work has since been lost. There is a reproduction however, from the *Daily Graphic* (25 October 1913).
101. R. Cork, *Vorticism and Abstract Art in the First Machine Age* (London, Fraser, 1976), p. 108. Here Cork describes the work as an 'academic travesty of Cubist principles.'
102. F. Spalding, *British Art Since 1900*, p. 49.
103. G. Severini, *The Futurist Painter Severini Exhibits his Latest Works* (London, Marlborough Gallery, 1913), p. 8.
104. J. Canaday, *Mainstreams in Modern Art* (New York, Rinehart and Winston, 1959), pp. 428–42.
105. T. M. Scheid, 'Experimentations in Temporal and Spiritual Techniques' (PhD diss., Ohio University, 1985).
106. Richard liked to 'play up' this friendship. Even in 1940 he wrote 'Picasso considers me the best of living artists'. Nevinson to Sir Kenneth Clark, dated 31 March 1941. TGA [8812.1.2.4659].
107. Sir R. Penrose and J. Golding (eds), 'Picasso and the Typography of Cubism' in *Picasso* (London, Paul Elek, 1973), pp. 53–5.
108. G. Severini, *The Futurist Painter Exhibits his Latest Works* (London, Marlborough Galleries, 1913), p. 9.
109. *Ibid.*
110. Nevinson to G. Severini, dated 28 April states 'Je fait un tableaux 4 metres x 3 metres!' Sev. 4.4. MART.
111. G. Apollinaire, 'Les Peintres Futuristes Italiens', *L'Intransigeant* (7 February 1912).
112. G. Severini (trans. F. Franchina), *The Life of a Painter* (Princeton University Press, 1995), p. 143.
113. *Daily Sketch* (18 October 1913), p. 5.
114. Sir C. Phillips, 'Post-Impressionists', *Daily Telegraph* (date unknown). TGA.
115. The press grappled with all the 'modern' terms and often used them inaccurately. Futurism, Cubism and Post-Impressionism were almost interchangeable in many cases.
116. 'British Artists and Post-impressionists', Publication, date and author unknown. TGA.
117. C. Bell, 'The New Post – Impressionist Show', *Nation* (25 October 1913).
118. *Ibid.*
119. *Ibid.*
120. Publication, author and date unknown. TGA.
121. 'Picture Puzzles at the Dore. Post-Impressionism and other Fatuities', Publication, author and date unknown. TGA.
122. 'The Confetti School of Painting', Publication, author and date unknown. TGA.
123. HWN Journals, e. 618/1, 16 October 1913.
124. G. Severini (trans. F. Franchina), *The Life of a Painter* (Princeton University Press, 1995), p. 88.
125. *Ibid.*, p. 119.
126. *Ibid.*, p. 134.
127. Nevinson to G. Severini, dated 28 April. MART.
128. H.W. Nevinson, *Newark Evening News* (17 January 1914).
129. W.C. Wees, *Vorticism and the English Avant-Garde* (Toronto, 1972), p. 99.
130. W.K. Rose (ed.), *The Letters of Wyndham Lewis* (Norfolk, Virginia, 1963), p. 53–4.
131. Nevinson to Lewis, 19 November 1913. Cornell.
132. Marinetti to Severini, 30 November 1913. MART.
133. F. Wadsworth to Lewis, undated. Cornell.
134. HWN Journals, e. 618/1, 19 November 1913.
135. Wyndham Lewis, 'Man of the Week: Marinetti', *New Weekly* (30 May 1914), p. 329.
136. Nevinson to Lewis, 19 November 1913. Cornell.
137. C.R.W. Nevinson, 'These People Taught Me How To Live', *Daily Express* (26 May 1931). Richard isolated four people as major influences in his intellectual development: Freud, Van Gogh, Marinetti and Lewis.
138. Nevinson to Lewis, 5 November 1913. Cornell.
139. *Ibid.*, 13 November 1913.
140. *Ibid.*, 4 December 1913.
141. *Ibid.*, undated letter. Lady Cunard had threatened to remove her business to the Omega Workshops if the RAC artists could not, or would not, do it.
142. Richard formally accepted the invitation to exhibit there on 28 October 1913 in a letter that expressed his desire to exhibit 'one or two things'. Nevinson to Lewis, undated. Cornell.

143. The terms Cubist and Futurist were often interchangeable, even by the artists themselves. It is our retrospective definition of the terms that make them so distinct. Richard postponed a one-man show in order to participate in the Brighton show as recorded in an unaddressed letter, signed by himself, and currently in the Cornell collection.
144. W. Baron, *The Camden Town Group* (London, Scolar Press, 1979), p. 64.
145. We should note that there was not yet universal acceptance of Futurism as in a letter dated 5 November 1913 from Richard to Lewis, he concludes by saying 'Fishburn has refused to have any more negotiations with Edinburgh as they refuse to show any work by "English Futurists".' Cornell. What is important is that Richard is talking about 'English Futurists' as a group, or movement.
146. Nevinson to Lewis, 4 December. Cornell. In doing so Richard was turning his back on the commission for the Countess of Drogheda.
147. Nevinson to Severini, 11 December 1913. 'When Marinetti was in London I saw a lot of him and I organized a dinner in his honour on behalf of the young painters of the avant-garde, it was a great success and I think that Marinetti was very happy to see that in England there was such a strong movement and that such a great sympathy for Futurism had started and that a group of English artists has come together in the cause of an advanced art and it will make us feel in the intelletual and international world like you Futurists'. MART.
148. Nevinson to Severini, 11 December 1913. Cornell.
149. Nevinson to Marsh, 25 December 1913. From rue Brea, Paris. Marsh folder.7 A.L.S. New York City Public Library.
150. 'Ommagio a Severini', *Critica d'Arte* (May–June 1970), p. 25.

CHAPTER FIVE

1. C. Lewis-Hind, 'An Appreciation', *The Old World and the New. Exhibition of Paintings, Lithographs and Woodcuts by C.R.W. Nevinson of London, England* (Bourgeois Galleries, New York, November – December 1920).
2. HWN Journals, e. 618/1, 2 January 1914.
3. *Ibid.*, e. 618/2, 16 February 1914.
4. Professor Angela V. John has emphasized that Futurism was only one movement with which Henry was associated at this time. The son's affiliation was much more focussed.
5. 'Some of the Manifestoes of "Futurism"; Amazing, Absurd, Amusing – As You Like', *Evening News* (17 January 1914). TGA.
6. R. Cork, *Art Beyond the Galleries* (New Haven and London, Yale University Press, 1985), p. 200.
7. Nevinson to Lewis, 24 March 1914. Cornell.
8. *Ibid.*, 24 May 1914. Cornell.
9. *Ibid.*, 2 March 1914. Cornell. Marinetti had agreed to lecture as a 'fund raiser' for the Blast Group.
10. 'Art & Artists: The London Group', *Observer* (1914). TGA.
11. There are two surviving cuttings of this painting, both in the TGA. Neither records the name of the newspaper or the date of publication.
12. 'Futurist Painting: Technical Manifesto 1910'.
13. 'The Cubist's Error: Exhibition of the London Group' (publication, author and date unknown). TGA.
14. 'The London Group', *Westminster* (1914). TGA.
15. G. Severini, *The Futurist Painter Severini Exhibits his Latest Works* (London, Marlborough Galleries, 1913), p. 8.
16. 'Art and Artists: The London Group', *Observer* (1914). TGA.
17. *Ibid.*
18. *Ibid.*
19. Where there are many overlaps in Richard's work and that of Severini, some exist with other Futurists, for instance with Carra's *What I Was Told by the Tramcar.*
20. W. Sickert, 'Post-Impressionism and Cubism', (11 March 1914). TGA.
21. W. Sickert, *'The Futurist "Devil-Among-The Tailors"'* (publication, author and date unknown). TGA.
22. C.R.W. Nevinson, letter to the editor, 'Post-Impressionism and Cubism', *Pall Mall Gazette* (13 March 1914). TGA.
23. G.R.S.T., 'Reflections', *The Limit* (9 March 1914).
24. 'Solemn Insanity of Futurists', *Daily Herald* (12 June 1914). Lewison reported that Richard introduced Wadsworth to Marinetti and so this could be the source of confusion. J. Lewison, *A Genius of Industrial England: Edward Wadsworth 1889–1949* (Arkwright Arts Trust, Bradford Art Galleries and Museums, 1990), p. 14.
25. Sir. C. Phillips, 'Art in Whitechapel: Twentieth Century Exhibition', *Daily Telegraph* (1914). TGA.
26. Marinetti to Severini, 16 May 1914. MART. This letter highlights a busy schedule in London, including four *conferenze* and the Coliseum show in June with the *intonarumori.*
27. *New Statesman* (2 May 1914), p. 115.
28. *Ibid.* (13 June 1914), p. 499.
29. *Daily Mirror* (6 May 1914), Cited in Wees, *Vorticism and the English Avant-Garde*, p. 103.
30. Wyndham Lewis, *New Weekly* (30 May 1914).
31. Apollinaire pointed out that the concept of words in freedom did not originate with Marinetti and pre-dated him to a poet called Jules Romain at least five years before.
32. R.W. Flint (ed.), *Marinetti: Selected Writings* (London, 1972), p. 147.
33. W.C. Wees, *Vorticism and the English Avant-Garde*, pp. 104–5.
34. Wyndham Lewis, *Blasting and Bombardiering: An Autobiography 1914–1926*, p. 33–5.
35. R. Cork, *Vorticism and Abstract Art in the First Machine Age: Vol. I*, p. 158
36. HWN Journals, e. 618/2, 4 April 1914.
37. *Ibid.*, e.618/2, 29 April 1914. 'Gould' is poet and journalist Gerald Gould.
38. C.R.W. Nevinson, *Paint and Prejudice*, p. 61.
39. W.C. Wees, *Vorticism and the English Avant-Garde*, p. 103.
40. R. Cork, *Art Beyond the Gallery* (New Haven and London, Yale University Press, 1985), p. 205.

41. HWN Journals, e.618/2, 3 May 1914.
42. H.W. Nevinson, *More Changes and More Chances* (London, Nisbet, 1925), p. 405.
43. '"Tum-tiddly-um-tum-pom-pom": A Futurist Masterpiece', *Western Mail* (15 May 1914).
44. It is believed that Ethelbert White RWS, NEAC, LG (1891–1972) also worked on this composition.
45. Nevinson to Carrington, 8 April 1912. HRHRC.
46. R. Cork, *Vorticism and Abstract Art in the First Machine Age*, p. 220.
47. T.E. Hulme, 'Modern Art III: The London Group', *New Age* (26 March 1914).
48. H. Gaudier-Brzeska, 'Allied Artists Associations Ltd', *Egoist* (15 June 1914).
49. G. Severini, *The Futurist Painter Severini Exhibits his latest works* (Marlborough Gallery, London, April, 1913).
50. *Ibid.*
51. *Ibid.*, p. 6.
52. 'Rebels in Art', *The Times* (16 June 1914).
53. C.R.W. Nevinson, letter to un-named newspaper (7 March 1914). TGA.
54. 'Art in its Weird Forms', *Aberdeen Journal* (11 June 1914). TGA.
55. See: D. Peters Corbett, *The Modernity of English Art 1914–1930* (Manchester University Press, 1997), p. 41 and also W.C. Wees, *Vorticism and the English Avant-Garde* (Manchester University Press, 1972), p. 106.
56. This is inaccurately recorded in M.W. Martin, *Futurist Art and Theory 1909–1915* (Oxford University Press, 1968), p. 182, when the author refers to a certain Charles Nevinson who was expelled from Lewis's Vorticist Group for being 'too Futurist'.
57. J. Rothenstein, *Modern English Painters* vol. 2 (London, Eyre & Spottiswoodie, 1956), p. 131.
58. R. Ingleby, 'Utterly Tired of Chaos' *C.R.W. Nevinson: The Twentieth Century* (London, Merrell Holberton, 1999), p. 16.
59. The others were Roberts, Aldington, Bomberg, Etchells, Pound, Wadsworth, Hamilton and Lewis.
60. HWN Journals, e.618/2, 4 April 1914.
61. *Ibid.*, e.618/2, 29 May 1914.
62. This is how it is recorded in *Paint and Prejudice.* The omission of the other artist's names and the problematic address is obvious.
63. 'Futurist Squabbles', *Daily Express* (11 June 1914).
64. L. Somigli, 'Towards a Theory of the Avant-garde Manifesto' (PhD diss., State University of New York at Stony Brook, 1996). Somigli elaborated on the question of the medical analogy throughout the section concerning all Futurist manifestos and in particular the English manifesto of 1914.
65. Charlotte Hallyday at the NEAC archive was very helpful in finding the documents pertaining to his proposal and acceptance.
66. The cricketers in particular bullied and abused Richard at Uppingham.
67. *Daily Express* (11 June 1914).
68. 'Between Stations', *Sketch* (24 June 1914).
69. 'The Asceticism of the Futurists', *T.P.'s Weekly* (4 June 1914).
70. G. Chesterton, 'The Futurists', chapter in: *The Uses of Diversity: A Book of Essays* (London, Methuen, 1920), p. 82.
71. Wyndham Lewis, *Blast: Review of the Great English Vortex* (London, John Lane,1914; Santa Barbara, The Black Sparrow Press, 1981), p. 143.
72. E. Pound, *Fortnightly* (1 September 1914).
73. 'Futurism', letter to the editor, *New Weekly* (June 1914).
74. W. Roberts, *Some Early Abstract and Cubist Work: 1913–1920* (London, Canale Publication of the Favil Press, 1957), p. 12.
75. H.W. Nevinson to Bliss, 28 January 1914. Cornell.
76. E. Wadsworth to W. Lewis, 25 February 1914. Cornell.
77. HWN Journals, e.618/2, 12 June 1914.
78. 'The Futurists Again', *Manchester Courier* (13 June 1914). George V.
79. *Atlantic Monthly* (November 1914), cited in H.W. Nevinson, *Visions and Memories* (Oxford University Press, 1944), pp. 81–2.
80. 'Futile-ism', *New Age* (18 June 1914).
81. Wyndham Lewis, *Blasting and Bombardiering*, p. 33.
82. This account of events was related in a lecture by J. Black at the Estorick Collection, London, in March, 1999, entitled 'The "Caffeine of Europe" Hits England: F.T. Marinetti (1876–1944) & The Futurists in England *c.* 1910–1914.'
83. 'Vorticism', *Manchester Guardian* (13 June 1914).
84. 'The Futurist Split', *Yorkshire Observer* (15 June 1914).
85. C.Tisdall and A. Bozzola, *Futurism* (London, 1996), p. 105.
86. C.R.W. Nevinson, *Paint and Prejudice*, p. 61.
87. Schonberg's *Five Pieces for Orchestra* was first performed in London in 1912 and so the concept of what Marinettti was doing, again, was not entirely new.
88. C.R.W. Nevinson, *Paint and Prejudice*, p.83.
89. Marinetti to Severini (30 June 1914). MART. In the same letter he acknowledges that Stravinsky had been impressed and that plans were well under way for an August show at the Dore Galleries.
90. *The Times* (16 June 1914). TGA.
91. HWN Journals, e.618/2, 19 June 1914.
92. *The Atlantic Monthly* (November 1914), cited in H.W. Nevinson, *Visions and Memories*, p. 85.
93. HWN Journals, e. 618/2, 22, 23, 24, 25 and 26 June – all writing on Futurism. On 28 June the entry reads 'Early to S. Place with four of Rich's pictures for lecture on Futurism. Quite a big congregation.' This is South Place Chapel, an ethical and radical centre.
94. C.R.W. Nevinson, *Paint and Prejudice*, p. 83.
95. 'The London Salon', *Observer* (21 June 1914). 'The Laughter Show' at the Holland Park Hall…is more likely to cause more saddness and depression than amusement'.
96. C.R.W. Nevinson, *Paint and Prejudice*, p. 83.
97. 'The London Salon', *Town Topics* (20 June 1914).
98. Cited in R. Cork, *Vorticism and Abstract Art in the First Machine Age*, p. 218.
99. *Ibid.*
100. 'The London Salon', *Observer* (21 June 1914). TGA.
101. 'The London Salon', *Standard* (15 June 1914). TGA.

102. *Ibid.*
103. A.J. Finberg, 'Allied Artists Association', *Star* (30 June 1914). TGA.
104. 'A Futurist's Conception of a London Street', *Manchester Guardian* (undated). TGA.
105. G.R.H., 'Mr. Bomberg's Futurist Bombshells', *Pall Mall Gazette* (25 June 1914). TGA.
106. Also exhibited as *My Arrival in Dunkirk* at the London Group, March 1915.
107. For reproduction of Delmarle's oils see P. Hulten, *Futurism and Futurisms* (New York, Abeville Press, 1986).
108. G. Agnese, *Vito di Boccioni* (Milano, Camunia, 1996). 'Nevinson was so struck by Severini's *Souvenir de Voyage* and by Russolo's *Ricordi Una Notte* that he poured the spirit of these two innovative paintings into his painting *The Arrival* of 1913, summary of the experiences, sensations and memories that arrive together with a boat in a port.'
109. *Le Vieux Port* is signed and dated, 1910, in the bottom right hand corner. This is highly unlikely considering the 1909 rendition of *The Port* from Richard's Slade days. It was presumably dated retrospectively to confuse critics or to pre-date his modernist leanings to a deceptively early period.
110. C. Harrison, *English Art and Modernism 1900–1939* (London, Allen Lane, 1981), p. 87.
111. T.M. Scheid, 'Experimentations in Temporal and Spiritual Techniques' (PhD diss., Ohio University, 1985).
112. 'Shocking Pictures Designed to Jolt the Senses: Cubist reproductions in regent Street', *Star* (undated). TGA.
113. G.K. Chesterton, *Illustarted London News* (11 July 1914). TGA.
114. Reproduction in *Daily Graphic* (11 September 1915). TGA. This work underwent many name changes including *Machine Slave* and *The Mechanic.*
115. G.K. Chesterton, *T.P.'s Weekly* (4 June 1914). TGA.
116. 'The London Show', *The Times of India* (28 July 1914). TGA.
117. Wyndham Lewis, 'Manifesto', *Blast*, pp. 39–41.
118. Wyndham Lewis, *Blasting and Bombardiering*, p. 35.
119. P. Hamilton, *The Role of Futurism, Dada and Surrealism in the Construction of British Modernism 1910-1940* (PhD diss., University of Oxford, 1987), p. 120.
120. Cited in W.C. Wees, *Vorticism and the English Avant-Garde*, p. 117.
121. *Nottingham Guardian* (10 June 1914). TGA.
122. *The New Weekly* (20 June 1914). TGA.
123. A letter from Marinetti to Francesco Cangiullo is reproduced in M.D. Gambillo & T. Fiori, *Archivi Del Futurismo: Vol. I* (Rome, 1986), p. 340.
124. 'Vorticism: The Latest Cult of the Rebel Artists', *New York Times* (9 August 1914), cited in:Wees, *Vorticism and the English Avant-Garde*, p. 193.
125. Ironically, Marinetti continued to overestimate the allegiance of the rebel English artists even after the war had begun when he claimed that Lewis, Wadsworth and Nevinson had all adapted Futurist techniques for the camouflaging of ships. Cited in R.W. Flint (ed.), *Marinetti: Selected Writings* (London, Secker & Warburg, 1971), p. 336. Also, as late as 1924 Marinetti was still listing Rodker, Newinson [*sic*], Windham Lewis [*sic*], Wadsworth, Aldington, Flint and Eliot as Futurists in 'Le Futurisme, revue synthetique illustree' (Milan, 11 January 1924). Cited in N. Laroni, *Il Passato al Futuro* (Bompiani, 1986), p. 33.
126. I have quoted the letter using Richard's use of capitals and underlining.
127. Nevinson to Lewis, 13 June 1914. Cornell.
128. Wyndham Lewis, 'Automibilism', *New Weekly* (20 June 1914).
129. C.R.W. Nevinson, letter to the editor of the *Observer.* TGA.
130. Richard's first draft of this letter, dated to the previous day, is in the TGA. The second draft is housed at Cornell University.
131. Nevinson to Lewis, 13 July 1914. Cornell.
132. C.R.W. Nevinson, *Paint and Prejudice*, p. 63.
133. 'Vital English Art – A lecture delivered by Mr. Nevinson at the Dore Galleries', *New Age* (18 June 1914).
134. *Ibid.*
135. 'The Futurists Again', *Manchester Guardian* (13 June 1914).
136. *Yorkshire Observer* (15 June 1914).
137. W. Sickert, 'The Thickest Painters in London', *New Age* (18 June 1914).
138. P. Hamilton, *The Role of Futurism, Dada and Surrealism in the Construction of British Modernism, 1910–1940* (PhD Diss., University of Oxford, 1987).
139. *Egoist* (1 April 1914), p. 140. TGA.
140. 'Blast', *Observer* (5 July 1914). TGA.
141. C. Farrell, 'Melodrama of Modernity', *University of Toronto Quarterly* (winter 1993–4).
142. E. Pound, *Fortnightly Review* (1 September 1914), p. 461.
143. C. Farrell, 'Melodrama of Modernity', p. 365.
144. C.R.W. Nevinson, 'New Art Movement', letter to the editor, *Observer* (undated). Published 12 July 1914. TGA.
145. Wyndham Lewis, 'Futurism and the Flesh', *T.P.'s Weekly* (11 July 1914). TGA.
146. W.C. Wees, *Vorticism and the English Avant-Garde*, p. 106.
147. *Yorkshire Observer* (15 June 1914). TGA
148. *English Review* (23 July 1914).
149. *Poetry Review* (July 1914).
150. *Illustrated London News* (4 August 1914). TGA.
151. G.K. Chesterton, *Illustrated London News* (11 July 1914). TGA.
152. Cited in W.C. Wees, *Vorticism and the English Avant-Garde*, p. 118.
153. A. Hewitt, *Fascist Modernism: Aesthetics, Politics and Avant-Garde* (Stanford, Stanford University Press, 1993), p. 18.
154. G. Severini to Soffici, letter dated 27 September 1913. Cited in M.W. Martin, *Futurist Art and Theory 1909–1915* (Oxford University Press, 1968), p. 138.
155. G. Severini, *The Futurist Painter Severini Exhibits his latest works* (Marlborough Gallery, London, April 1913).
156. A. Bozzola and C. Tisdall, *Futurism* (London, Thames & Hudson, 1977), p. 77.
157. *Daily Express*, (25 February 1915). TGA.

158. Cited in A. Bozzola and C. Tisdall, *Futurism*, p. 32.
159. Wyndham Lewis, cited in R.Cork, *Vorticism and Abstract Art in the First Machine Age. Vol. I*, p. 26.
160. Hamilton says that this unwittingly marked the end of the 'brief but heroic period of English Modernism…' P. Hamilton, *The Role of Futurism, Dada and Surrealism in the Construction of British Modernism*, p. 153.
161. L. Somigli, *Towards a Theory of the Avant-Garde Manifesto*, p. 143.
162. *Atlantic Monthly* (November 1914). Cited in H.W. Nevinson, *Visions and Memories* (Oxford Uuniversity Press, 1944), pp. 83–9.
163. C.R.W. Nevinson, *Paint and Prejudice*, p. 64.
164. H.W. Nevinson, *Visions and Memories*, p. 89.
165. *Ibid.*, p. 66.

CHAPTER SIX

1. J. Ruskin, 'War,' in *The Crown of Wild Olives. Three Lectures on Work, Traffic and War* (London, Smith & Elder, 1866), p. 143.
2. D. Lowe, 'Bourbon County', *Prose (*spring 1973), p. 155.
3. HWN Journals, e. 616/3, 25 October 1914.
4. *Ibid.*, e. 618/3, 27 October 1914.
5. *Ibid.*, e. 616/3, 7 November 1914.
6. C.R.W. Nevinson, *Paint and Prejudice*, p. 71.
7. *Ibid.*, p. 70.
8. *Ibid.*
9. C.R.W. Nevinson, 'When the Censor Censored 'Censored' *British Legion Journal* (October 1932).
10. C.R.W. Nevinson, *Paint and Prejudice*, p. 70.
11. Society of Friends, Friends House Library, London. (Temp. MSS 81-1-1-397).
12. C.R.W. Nevinson, *Paint and Prejudice*, p. 71.
13. HWN Journals, e. 618/3, 14 November 1914.
14. *Ibid.*, e. 618/4, 14 December 1914.
15. C.R.W. Nevinson to Miss K. M. Knowlmann, 24 November 1914. Artist's Estate.
16. HWN Journals, e. 618/3, 24 November 1914.
17. *Ibid.*, e. 618/ 3, 15 November 1914.
18. C.R.W. Nevinson, *Paint and Prejudice*, p. 99.
19. M. Tatham and J. E. Miles (eds), *Friends' Ambulance Unit, 1914–1919*, London, Swathmore, 1920, p. 7.
20. *Ibid.*
21. HWN Journals, e. 618/4, 19 December 1914. The fact that he was being used as an interpreter also substantiates, to some extent at least, the trilingual claim.
22. *Ibid.*, e. 618/4, 23 December 1914.
23. Paul Bond, in the 'Striking Visions of the First World War' *World Socialist Web Site* (January, 2000) described this painting as 'mawkish and unsuccessful' going on to say 'we know which buttons Nevinson was trying to press and he fails.'
24. C.R.W. Nevinson, *Paint and Prejudice*, p. 74.
25. *Ibid.*, p. 78.
26. HWN Journals, e. 618/4, 27 January 1915.
27. C.R.W. Nevinson, *Paint and Prejudice*, p. 78. HWN had stayed only until 23 December 1914. HWN Journals, e. 618/3.
28. Service Card, Society of Friends Archive, Friends House Library, London. (Temp. MSS 81-1-1-397).
29. It is interesting to note here that the newspapers that Richard wrote to were also the ones for which his father worked – i.e. the *Manchester Guardian, Daily Chronicle* and *Daily News*.
30. 'Painter of Smells at the Front. A Futurist's View of the War', *Daily Express* (25 February 1915).
31. C.R.W. Nevinson, 'A Futurist's Nerves', *Daily Express* (26 February 1915).
32. C.R.W. Nevinson, 'Red Cross Orderlies', *Manchester Guardian* (20 February 1915).
33. C.R.W. Nevinson, letter to the editor of *The Times*, unsent, TGA.
34. C.R.W. Nevinson. Letter, 'War Notes and Queries', *Daily Graphic* (11 March 1915).
35. 'Painter of Smells at the Front: A Futurist's View of the War', *Daily Express* (25 February 1915). TGA.
36. HWN Journals, e. 618/4, 6 February 1915.
37. The photographs were taken by a member of the Rebel Arts Centre called Malcolm Arbuthnot. They would have been produced in either late 1915 or early 1916 and can be seen in the October 1916 issue of *Vogue* and also in the September 1916 issue of *Graphic*.
38. D. Peters Corbett, *The Modernity of English Art 1914–1930* (Manchester University Press, 1997), p. 50.
39. C.R.W. Nevinson, *Paint and Prejudice*, p. 80.
40. Viscount Grey of Fallodon is said to have uttered this on 3 August 1914 on the eve of Britain's entry into the war.
41. E. Gosse, 'War and literature', *Edinburgh Review (*October 1914), p. 313.
42. S. Hynes, *A War Imagined* (London, Bodley Head, 1990), p. 13.
43. W.R. Colton, 'The Effects of War on Art', *Architect* (17 March 1916), p. 200.
44. C.S.H., 'After the War', *New Age* (29 October 1914), p. 635.
45. J. Ruskin, 'War' in *The Crown of Wild Olive. Three Lectures on Work, Traffic and War*, pp. 143–5.
46. S. Hynes, *A War Imagined: The First World War and English Culture*, p. 15.
47. The concept of purge was not unique to Britain. Hegel, Darwin and Bergson are cited as being believers in the regenerative power of war on society as seen in R. Stromberg, *Redemption by War: The Intellectuals and 1914* (Lawrence, Kansas), p. 5.
48. C.H. Collins Baker, 'Art and War', *Saturday Review* (22 August 1914).
49. A. Clutton-Brock, 'War and Poetry', *Times Literary Supplement* (8 October 1914).
50. R.H.C. [Orage], 'Readers and Writers', *New Age* (10 September 1914), p. 449.
51. W.S. Sparrow, 'Middle Articles: Is War Necessary to Social Progress', *Saturday Review* (17 April 1915), 397–9.
52. J.D. Symon, 'War and Creative Art', *English Review (*December 1915), p. 520.
53. L. Binyon, *The Art of Botticelli: An Essay in Pictorial Criticism* (London, 1913), p. 17.
54. C. Bell, 'Art and War', *International Journal of Ethics* (October 1915), pp. 1–10.
55. D. Sutton (ed.), *Letters of Roger Fry Vol. II* (London, Chatto and Windus, 1977), p. 386.

56. M. and S. Harries, *The War Artists* (London, Michael Joseph, 1983), p. 1–2.
57. C. Harrison, *English Art and Modernism 1900–1939* (London, Allen Lane, 1981), p. 119.
58. 'Studio Talk', *Studio* (September 1914).
59. O. Brown, *Exhibition: The Memoirs of Oliver Brown* (London, Evelyn Adams & Mackay, 1968), p. 47.
60. M. Hall, 'Modernism, Militarism and Masculinity' (PhD diss., State University of New York at Binghampton, 1994). The idea is expanded upon throughout chapter six.
61. J. Ferguson, *The Arts in Britain in World War I* (Open University, 1980), p. 26.
62. *Daily Graphic* (13 July 1915).
63. 'Art after Armageddon', *Athenaeum* (12 September 1914), p. 269.
64. H. Taylor, 'War and Art', *Colour* (September 1914), p. 46.
65. St John Ervine, 'The War and Literature', *North American Review* (July 1915), p. 98.
66. C.S.H., 'After the War', *New Age* (October 1914), p. 635.
67. D. Peters Corbett, *The Modernity of English Art 1914–1930* (Manchester University Press, 1997), p. 25.
68. *Ibid.*, p. 43.
69. F.T. Marinetti & C.R.W. Nevinson, *Vital English Art* (1914).
70. Jane Rye, *Futurism* (Studio Vista, 1972), p. 9.
71. W. Gaunt, *March of the Moderns* (London, Cape, 1949), p. 161.
72. M.W. Martin, *Futurist Art and Theory* (London, Oxford University Press, 1968), p. 203.
73. 'Art Notes', *Illustrated London News* (8 August 1914).
74. Paul Fussell, *The Great War and Modern Memory* (Oxford University Press, 1975), p. 21.
75. J.D. Symon, 'The Grotesque in Modern War', *Land and Water* (18 September 1915), p. 15.
76. *Ibid.*
77. 'The Passing of the Battle Painter: No Inspiration in the Trenches', *The Times*, (30 April 1915), p. 15.
78. L. Haward, *The Effect of War upon Art and Literature* (Manchester University Press, 1916).
79. The vandalism of the Germans is a reference to the shelling of Rheims Cathedral in the early stages of the war (22 September 1914), which led to outrage in intellectual and artistic circles throughout Europe. In the same letter Richard went on to proclaim that London should be made the new Mecca of art, eclipsing the previously fashionable centres of Munich and Berlin.
80. 'Painter of Smells at the Front. A Futurist's View on the War', *Daily Express* (25 February 1915). The view that the war was dull was shared by some of his ex-rebel peers also at the front. Roberts wrote 'One whose existence is so absolutely monotonous, repetition always, every day lived to order; the only excitement being to dodge and duck for your bloody miserable life'. Letter to Sarah Kramer, 11 November 1917. Cited in W. Roberts, *Howitzer Gunner, R.F.A. Memories of the War to End War 1914–1918* (privately printed, 1974), p. 42.
81. Wyndham Lewis, 'The Six Hundred, Verestchagin and Uccello', *Blast 2* (London, John Lane, July, 1915), p. 25.
82. Wyndham Lewis, 'A Super-Krupp – Or War's End', *Blast* (London, John Lane, 1914), p. 14.
83. Wyndham Lewis, *Blast No.2*, p. 25.
84. C.R.W. Nevinson, *Paint and Prejudice*, p. 107.
85. The following are known to have been exhibited at the Friday Club Exhibition, held at the Alpine Club Galleries: *Searchlights*, *Declaration of War*, *August Bank Holiday* and the sculpture *The Mechanic (The Automobilist)*.
86. The painting *Searchlights* was purchased and offered anonymously to the Tate Gallery, a gift that was declined.
87. I am not inclined to support this suggestion as the first recorded Zeppelin raids over Kings Lynn did not actually begin until January 1915. By then Richard would have been home form the Front.
88. Wyndham Lewis, *Evening News* (3 March 1915). TGA.
89. *Blast 2: The War Issue*, p. 77
90. *Athenaeum* (13 February 1915), p. 149.
91. P.G. Konody, 'Art & Artists. Futurism at the Friday Club', *Observer* (14 February 1914). TGA.
92. Konody, *Modern War: Paintings by C.R.W. Nevinson* (London, Grant Richards, 1917).
93. W.L.H., *Ploughshare* (December 1916), p. 353
94. *Ibid.*
95. *Ibid.* The Oxford English Dictionary defines mafficking as the behaviour of London crowds in celebrating events of national significance, originating after the Battle of Mafeking in May 1900. *Oxford English Dictionary* Vol.VI (1961), p. 21.
96. Wyndham Lewis, *Evening News*, (3 March 1915).
97. This painting, also known as *London Dockside War Devastation*, is actually of the Flemish town of Termonde. The destruction of the town was widely reported and photographed so this might be the source of Richard's composition. The *Illustrated London News* (19 September 1914, 26 September 1914, 3 October 1914) and the *Graphic* (12 September 1914) both carried the story and images.
98. E. Storer, 'The London Group', *The New Witness* (11 March 1915).
99. M. Hall, 'Modernism, Militarism and Masculinity' (PhD diss., State University of New York at Binghampton, 1 994). This argument is prevalent throughout chapter six.
100. 'Cubist Masters. Works of Art that Look Like Meaningless Daubs', *Star* (6 March 1915).
101. C.H. Collins-Baker, 'Dry Bones', *Saturday Review* (20 March 1915), pp. 304–5.
102. *Ibid.*
103. *Tatler*, (24 March 1915). TGA.
104. *Daily Express* (25 February 1915). TGA.
105. This comparison was championed by Clutton-Brock through the pages of *The Times*, most notably in an article called 'Junkerism in Art: The London Group at the Goupil Gallery' published on 10 March 1915.
106. P.G. Konody, 'Art and Artists: The London Group', *Observer* (14 March 1915). TGA.
107. 'War and the Post – Impressionists', *Manchester Guardian* (13 March 1915). 'There were some battle-pictures of the new kind – shell explosions, a trench under

water, and so on – which the sharper methods of the Futurist phases of art are specially fitted to express.'

108. P. G. Konody, 'Art and Artists: The London Group', *Observer* (14 March 1915). TGA.
109. 'Junkerism in Art: The London Group at the Goupil Gallery', *The Times* (10 March 1915).
110. S. Malvern compared the painting to Russolo's *La Revolta*, which had been exhibited at the Sackville Gallery Show in 1912. See S. Malvern, 'Art, Patronage and Propaganda: An History of the Employment of British War Artists 1916–1919' (PhD diss., Reading University, 1981).
111. R. Cork, *The Bitter Truth: Avant-Garde Art and the Great War* (New Haven & London, Yale University Press, 1994), p. 72.
112. J. Black, 'A Curious, Cold Intensity' *C.R.W. Nevinson: The Twentieth Century* (London, Merrell Holberton, 1999), p. 31.
113. Sir O. Sitwell, *Contemporary British Artists: C.R.W. Nevinson* (London, Ernest Benn Ltd, 1925), p. 24.
114. 'The Unconscious Humorists. The Art of Coloured Stripes and Mining Tolls', *Evening News*, (13 March 1915).
115. A Taube is a German monoplane, the name being derived, ironically, from the German word meaning 'Dove'.
116. Charles R. Samson (1883–1931) was one of the great pioneers in pre-war and war time aviation. His exploits took him to many of the theatres of operations in the first global conflict, including Ypres, Egypt, Gallipoli, and the Red Sea. It was reported that the Germans had a reward for him, dead or alive, of £500.
117. F. Rutter, 'Round the Galleries' *Sunday Times* (21 March 1915). TGA.
118. J.M., *Evening Standard and St. James Gazette* (16 March 1915). TGA.
119. 'The Unconscious Humorists. The Art of Coloured Stripes and Mining Tools', *Evening News* (13 March 1915).
120. The original manifesto of 1909 talked of 'trembling aeroplanes', as did the *Technical Manifesto of Futurist Literature* and in turn became the whole subject of the *Manifesto of Aeropainting*, 1929.
121. F. Denver, 'The London Group', *Egoist* (1 April 1915), p. 60. TGA.
122. 'Futurists and War', *Daily News and Leader* (6 March 1915). TGA.
123. C.R.W. Nevinson, 'War Notes and Queries. Comments and Suggestions in Brief from our readers', *Daily Graphic* (11 March 1915). TGA.
124. C.R.W. Nevinson, 'Dry Rot in Art', *Manchester Guardian* (20 April 1915). TGA.

CHAPTER SEVEN

1. E. Storer, 'London Groups', *The New Witness* (date unknown). TGA.
2. HWN Journals, e. 619/1, 20 May 1915. 'He determined to return to Quakers unit in June.'
3. *Ibid.*, e. 619/1, 27 May 1915.
4. *Ibid.*, e. 619/1, 28 May 1915.
5. C.R.W. Nevinson, *Paint and Prejudice*, p. 78.
6. On two occasions his father's journals record his anxiety at the very real prospect of being sent to Gallipoli. Both are dated to June 1915 (5 and 26 June).
7. HWN Journals, e. 619/1, 4 June 1915.
8. *Ibid.*, e. 619/1, 5 June 1915.
9. *Ibid.*, e. 619/1, 8, 14, 23, 29 June 1915.
10. C.R.W. Nevinson, *Paint and Prejudice*, p. 78.
11. *Ibid.*, p. 106
12. A positive result of his time at the hospital, and not recorded in his autobiography, is that he met, for the first time, his cousin from Australia who had fought and been wounded at Gallipoli. This was the son of Mervyn, Margaret's brother who had lived in Queensland.
13. C.R.W. Nevinson, *Paint and Prejudice*, p. 80.
14. F.T. Marinetti and C.R.W. Nevinson, *A Futurist Manifesto: Vital English Art* (June 1914)
15. K. Parkes, *Apollo* (November 1928), p. 259.
16. HWN Journals, e.619/1, 10 June 1915.
17. *Ibid.*, e. 619/1, 12 June 1916. He was showing it to E.S. – Evelyn Sharp.
18. There are two comments in *Paint and Prejudice* of this nature. The first is when he talks of his wedding and says 'My own father, of course, was in Gallipoli', p. 81, and also, later when he says 'My father was then with the forces in Egypt, and I don't think had even heard of my marriage.' p. 84. He did note, however, that Ward Muir attended the ceremony.
19. HWN Journals, e. 619/2, 11 October 1915.
20. *Ibid.*, e. 619/2, 19 and 21 October 1915.
21. *Ibid.*, e. 619/2, 30 October 1915.
22. M. Nevinson, *Life's Fitful Fever* (London, A. & C. Black, 1926), p. 246.
23. D. Holman-Hunt, *Latin Among Lions: Alvaro Guevara* (London, Michael Joseph, 1974), p. 83.
24. Richard suggests that it was his mother who extended the invitation to him and to his wife.
25. HWN Journals, e. 619/2, 5 November 1915. It is not clear if he meant to work or to recuperate from illness.
26. *Ibid.*, e. 619/3, 26 March 1916.
27. J. Black, 'A Curious Cold Intensity' *C.R.W. Nevinson: The Twentieth Century* (Merrell Holberton, 1999), p. 31.
28. M. Nevinson, *Life's Fitful Fever*, p. 247.
29. 'A Leeds Exhibition of Water – Colours', *Yorkshire Post* (7 May 1915). TGA.
30. W. Michel, *Wyndham Lewis: Paintings and Drawings* (London, 1971), pp. 432–3.
31. J.M.M., 'Vorticists and others', *Westminster Gazette* (18 June 1915). TGA.
32. 'Art of Yester-year', *Daily Graphic* (31 July 1915). TGA.
33. Entitled *On the Way to the Trenches.*
34. Wyndham Lewis, 'Artists and the War', *Blast 2*, p. 23.
35. This analogy is not my own. It was taken from M. Hall, 'Modernism, Militarism, and Masculinity' (PhD diss., State University of New York at Binghampton, 1994), p. 269.
36. F. Rutter, 'The Galleries: The Future of Painting and the Virtue of Vorticism', *Sunday Times* (19 August 1915).
37. 'Voticism and Others', *Westminster Gazette* (18 June 1915).

38. 'Vorticist Exhibition at the Dore Gallery', *Athenaeum* (19 June 1915).
39. C. Harrison, *English Art and Modernism: 1900–1939* (London, Allen Lane, 1981), p. 119.
40. Obvious exceptions were made for Queen Amelie of Portugal, H.R.H. Princess Louise, Duchess of Argyll (daughter of Queen Victoria and aunt of the reigning monarch, George V), Lady Randolph Churchill, and many more. Special guests were reported upon in *World* (14 September 1915).
41. 'Art and War', *British Architect* (24 September 1915).
42. The *Daily Graphic* published this photograph in the issue dated 11 September 1915 with the caption, 'Mr. Nevinson, the sculptor, who is doing duty with the R.A.M.C. orderly, explains to Private Smith wounded at Mons, the inner meaning of his Futurist sculpture.'
43. P.G. Konody, 'Art for the Wounded. Exhibition at 3rd London General Hospital: Futurism V War', *Observer* (12 September 1915).
44. C. Marriot, 'Soldier Artists', *Evening Standard* (9 September 1915). This feeling was echoed by the critic in *Queen* (18 September 1915).
45. 'Pictures and Sculptures at the Third London General Hospital', *Athenaeum* (11 September 1915).
46. 'Our Illustrators', *The Gazette of the Third London Hospital* (October 1915), p. 10. They included *Receiving Ward, 3rd, L.G.H.* and *New Hospital Wings (Huts).*
47. Other works, also in this category, might include: *The Observation Ward, Huts, Ambulance Driver, Receiving Ward; 3rd L.G.H., Dog Tired, Night Arrival of the Wounded* and *When Harry Tate Came Down.* Other compositions, such as *Temperature 102.4* may be said to fall half way between illustration and Futurism in its multi-faceted depiction of hallucinations and the mental trauma of some of the patients with whom he worked.
48. Also exhibiting were Gertler, the Nash brothers, Adeney, Allinson, Bevan, Gilman, Ginner, Godwin, Gosse and Schwabe.
49. Sir C. Phillips, 'The London Group', *Daily Telegraph* (27 November 1915). TGA.
50. P.G. Konody, 'Art and Artists: The London Group', *Observer* (28 November 1915). TGA.
51. *Ibid.*
52. *Ibid.*
53. F. Rutter, 'The Galleries. The London Group at the Goupil Galleries', *Sunday Times* (28 November 1915). TGA.
54. C. Marriott, 'London Group. Cubist Eccentricities Modified', *Standard* (3 December 1915).
55. 'Art and Artists. The London Group', *Observer* (28 November 1915).
56. C. Marriott, 'London Group. Cubist Eccentricities Modified', *Standard* (3 December 1915).
57. R. Davies, 'The London Group', *Queen* (11 December 1915).
58. O.R.D., 'The London Group', *Westminster Gazette* (1 December 1915). TGA.
59. M. Eksteins, *Rites of Spring: The Great War and the Birth of the Modern Age* (New York, Doubleday, 1989), p. 218.
60. R. Davies, 'The World of Art', *Queen* (11 December 1915). TGA.
61. 'The New English Art Club', *Westminster Gazette* (30 November 1915). TGA.
62. 'New English Art Club. Middle Aged but Active', *Daily Chronicle* (2 December 1915). TGA.
63. P.G. Konody, 'Art and Artists. The New English Art Club', *Observer* (12 December 1915).
64. E. Storer, 'London Groups', *New Witness* (date unknown). TGA.
65. C.R.W. Nevinson to Prof. Sadler, 23 December 1915. TGA. Correspondence.
66. D. Fox-Pitt, letter to the *Pall Mall Gazette* (3 June 1916). TGA.
67. D. Peters Corbett, *The Modernity of English Art 1914–1939* (Manchester University Press, 1997), p. 50.
68. *Ibid.*, p. 51.
69. C. Harrison, *English Art and Modernism 1900–1939*, p. 123.
70. *Ibid.*, p. 124.
71. A. Bozzola and C. Tisdall, *Futurism* (London, Thames & Hudson, 1977), p. 191.
72. Literally a re-call to order – a return to sanity and normality in response to the destruction of war; the end of polemicism and destruction in art and image-making.
73. S. Watney, *English Post-Impressionism* (London, 1980), p. 142.

CHAPTER EIGHT

1. C.R.W. Nevinson, *Paint and Prejudice*, p. 85.
2. The Eighth Annual Salon of the AAA held at the Grafton Galleries.
3. 'New Talent', *Daily Mail* (6 March 1916). TGA.
4. 'Allied Artists at Grafton Galleries', *Standard* (6 March 1916). TGA.
5. C. Lewis-Hind, 'Four Pictures', *Daily Chronicle* (9 March 1916). TGA.
6. The paintings were: *A Night Arrival of the Wounded, Portrait of an Ambulance Driver, Chasing a Taube, A Dawn, 1914, On the Ypres Road* and *Boesinghe Farm.*
7. P.G. Konody, 'Art and Artists: The Friday Club', *Observer* (26 March 1916).
8. *Ibid.*
9. 'The London Salon', *Truth* (5 April 1916). TGA.
10. The paintings were: *On the Road to Ypres, La Mitrailleuse* and *A Dawn, 1914.* Alternatively it could be argued that he would exhibit anywhere that would hang his paintings and expose him to the press. Whether this is an example of the NEAC moving close to him, or *vice versa*, is open to interpretation. Other members of the London Group, Gilman, Ginner and the Nash brothers, had also returned to the NEAC for exhibiting purposes, implying that he did not stand alone.
11. 'The Reward of the Patriot', *New Witness* (11 March 1916). TGA.
12. HWN Journals, e. 619/4, 3 May 1916.
13. *Ibid.*, e. 619/4, 5 May 1916.
14. *Ibid.*, e. 619/4, 11 May 1916 and e. 620/1, October 1916.
15. The paintings were: *Portrait of an Ambulance Driver,*

When Harry Tate Came Down and *La Patrie*.

16. *Paint and Prejudice* records that Richard was the secretary of the London Group from the outset. The exhibition catalogues for the Group list him as secretary for June and November 1916 only.
17. F. Rutter, *Art in my Time* (London, Rich & Cowan, 1933), p. 167.
18. 'The London Group', *Nottingham Guardian* (2 June 1916). TGA.
19. *Queen* (3 June 1916). TGA.
20. Perhaps to set a little distance between himself and Futurism he exhibited very early works, such as *Falmouth* and *Canal at Ghent* with the Decorative Arts Group, at the Modern Gallery, in early July 1916.
21. 'Why? Futurist Artist to Paint at the Front', *Daily Mirror* (30 May 1916). TGA. It was reported that he would be going out with John, Kennington, and McEvoy.
22. 'Lady Cunard's Views', *Pall Mall Gazette* (8 June 1916). TGA.
23. C. Lewis-Hind, *The Old World and the New: Exhibition of Paintings, Lithographs and Woodcuts by C.R.W. Nevinson of London, England* (Bourgeois Galleries, New York, 1920)
24. C.R.W. Nevinson, *Paint and Prejudice*, p. 85.
25. HWN Journals, *e.* 619/3, 14 April 1916.
26. *Ibid.*, e. 619/3, 17 April 1916.
27. *Ibid.*, e. 619/4, 27 May 1916.
28. *Ibid.*, e. 619/4, 1 June 1916.
29. *Ibid.*, e. 620/1, 31 August 1916.
30. *Ibid.*, e. 620/1, 1 Septmeber 1916.
31. *Ibid.*, e. 620/1, 4 November 1916.
32. C.R.W. Nevinson, *Paint and Prejudice*, p. 86.
33. *Catalogue of an Exhibition of Paintings and Drawings of War by C.R.W. Nevinson (Late Private R.A.M.C.)* (London, Leicester Galleries, September–October 1916).
34. His high diction and romantic descriptions based on mythology and the classics is hardly the imagery that Richard was trying to convey in his painting. In fact, they are diametrically opposed. John Salis, was quick to pick up on this point. See: J. Salis, 'The Poet of War', *New Witness* (28 September 1916).
35. *Catalogue of an Exhibition of Paintings and Drawings of War by C.R.W. Nevinson (Late Private R.A.M.C.)* (London, Leicester Galleries, September–October 1916).
36. 'Cubist Pictures of the War', *Yorkshire Evening Post* (23 September 1916). TGA.
37. O. Brown, *Exhibition: The Memoirs of Oliver Brown* (London, Evelyn Adams & Mackay, 1968), p. 49. Brown agreed that Sir Ian Hamilton's introduction seemed inappropriate. He also recorded that Richard would call for him for nights out at the Café Royal.
38. O. Sitwell, *C.R.W. Nevinson* Contemporary British Artists Series (London, Ernest Benn, 1925), p. 24.
39. 'Mr Nevinson as War Artist', *Observer* (24 September 1916). TGA.
40. F. Rutter, 'The Galleries', *Sunday Times* (24 September 1916). TGA.
41. Lenders included: Lord Henry Cavendish-Bentick, Michael Sadler, Douglas Fox-Pitt, The Leeds Arts Collection Fund, and the Contemporary Arts Society.
42. *Daily Mirror* (29 May 1916). TGA.
43. The story appeared in many newspapers in early August 1921 as to how the Louvre had been fooled by this and how Richard was the only exhibiting artist in that museum who was actually still living. His painting were subsequently removed.
44. Malcolm Arbuthnot (1874–1966) was associated with the Rebel Arts Centre and was a signatory of the Vorticist Manifesto. The images of Richard can be seen in *Vogue* (October 1916), and *Graphic* (September 1916).
45. C.R.W. Nevinson, *Paint and Prejudice*, p. 88.
46. 'War and the Artist', *Glasgow Herald* (15 February 1917). TGA.
47. C. Lewis-Hind, 'True War Pictures. Mr Nevinson's Moralities at the Leicester Galleries', *Daily Chronicle* (30 September 1916). TGA.
48. C. Lewis-Hind, 'Art After the War', *War Illustrated* (14 April 1917). TGA.
49. A. Clutton-Brock, 'Process or Person?', *Times Literary Supplement* (5 October 1916). TGA.
50. *Connoisseur* (March 1917) propounded the idea that modernism was associated with Prussianism and all that had led to war in the first place. It was in a minority by this late stage in the war. It claimed 'This is pure German pre-war doctrine…'
51. 'The Death of Futurism', *Egoist* (January 1917). TGA.
52. C. Lewis-Hind, 'Nevinson and his War Pictures', *Land and Water* (28 September 1916). TGA.
53. Louis Raemaekers and Bruce Bairnsfather were both artists doing precisely this. Raemaekers focused on atrocity and suffering, whilst Bairnsfather focused more on the mundane and uncomfortable conditions in the army.
54. 'London Diary', *Nation* (30 September 1916). TGA.
55. The catalogue introduction places him as a soldier, almost before an artist, and perpetuates the myth that he was 'attached' to the French army. It also suggests that Richard was in the ranks without a break from the outbreak of war through to January 1916.
56. C.M., 'War Pictures', *Evening Standard and St James' Gazette* (30 September 1916). TGA.
57. H.E., 'Mr Nevinson's Pictures', *Daily News* (6 October 1916). TGA.
58. This was the general consensus of opinion concerning Richard's painting, it was not however unanimous. Music critic, Huntley Carter, disagreed completely and argued that his paintings were just more of the same flag waving petitions to keep the war going. H.C., 'Mr. Shackleton's Pictures', *New Age* (26 November 1916).
59. 'War pictures', *The British Architect* (October 1916). TGA. Unsurprisingly they highlighted Elizabeth Butler's *The Roll Call* as a more suitable example of this genre of painting. Other articles, such as: C.H. Collins Baker, 'Middle articles', *Saturday Review* (7 October 1916), also criticizes his paintings on the same grounds by saying that his distrust and dislike of the old masters comes from the fact he had not the ability to paint like, let alone compete with them.
60. E. Pound, 'The War and Diverse Impressions', *Vogue* (October 1916). TGA.

61. H.M.T., 'War Pictures. Mr Nevinson's Work at the Leicester Galleries', *Star* (3 October 1916). TGA.
62. 'Over the Top', *Daily Mail* (22 December 1916). TGA.
63. Paul Nash had made this comment.
64. 'Warrior and Artist', *West Sussex Gazette* (26 October 1916). TGA.
65. 'Art and Artists', *Observer* (28 November 1915). TGA.
66. *La Guerre des Trous* is another depiction of the French army, something now of a recurring theme. The title itself is a play on words, translating literally to mean the 'War of Holes'. The word 'trou', however, can also be used as an integral part of several French expressions, all of which might usefully serve a purpose for the artist in his depiction of the front line. For example 'on l'a mis au trou' means to be imprisoned, while 'on l'a mis dans le trou' means to be buried and 'être dans le trou' metaphorically means to be dead and buried. Also in slang, 'un trou perdu' means a 'hell hole' or a dump. The references to holes may also suggest the animal nature that the men are reduced to at the front, amongst the destruction caused by the shells. Or one last interpretation may be the insulting vernacular 'trou du cul' which translates literally as arsehole – the reference being to the people running the war. These observations were made by C. Doherty, 'Nash, Nevinson and Roberts at War: A Catalogue Raisonne of First World War Paintings, Drawings and Prints by Paul Nash, C.R.W. Nevinson and William Roberts' (PhD diss., University of Wisconsin, Madison, 1989).
67. 'The War as Viewed by the Impressionists', *Daily Graphic* (26 November 1915). TGA.
68. 'The London Group Again', *Evening News* (26 November 1915). TGA.
69. F. Rutter, 'The Galleries. The London Group at the Goupil Galleries', *Sunday Times* (28 November 1915).
70. C. Lewis-Hind, 'More Untethered Art', *Daily Chronicle* (29 November 1915). TGA.
71. P.G. Konody, *Modern War by C.R.W. Nevinson* (London, Grant Richards, 1917), p. 28.
72. C. Lewis-Hind, 'Four Pictures. Developments in Modern Art', *Daily Chronicle* (9 March 1916). TGA.
73. C. Lewis-Hind, 'Man and His Machine', *Evening News* (16 March 1916). TGA.
74. P.G. Konody, 'Art and Artists. The Allied Artists Association', *Observer* (12 March 1916).
75. *Burlington Magazine* (April 1916), p. 35.
76. J. Salis, 'The Reward of the Patriot', *New Witness* (11 March 1916). TGA.
77. C. Doherty, 'Nash, Nevinson and Roberts at War: A Catalogue Raisonne of First World War Paintings, Drawings and Prints by Paul Nash, C.R.W. Nevinson and William Roberts' (PhD diss., University of Wisconsin, Madison, 1989).
78. H. W. Nevinson Journals, e. 619/4, 1 June 1916.
79. F. Rutter, 'The Galleries' *Sunday Times & Sunday Special* (4 June 1916). TGA.
80. C.L.H., 'Rebel Art', *Daily Chronicle* (13 June 1916). TGA.
81. C. Lewis-Hind, *Daily Chronicle* (30 September 1916). TGA.
82. Sir C. Phillips, 'Goupil Gallery', *Daily Telegraph* (2 June 1916). TGA.
83. M. and S. Harries, *The War Artists: British Official War Art of the Twentieth Century* (London, Michael Joseph, 1983),p. 40.
84. 'Futurism Finds the War', *Bystander* (7 June 1916). TGA.
85. C.R.W. Nevinson, *Paint and Prejudice*, pp. 71–2.
86. R. Cork, *A Bitter Truth: Avant-Garde Art and the Great War*, p. 131.
87. C. Lewis-Hind, 'True War Pictures. Mr Nevinson's Moralities at the Leicester Galleries', *Daily Chronicle* (30 September 1916). TGA.
88. 'The London Group', *Morning Post* (20 June 1916). TGA.
89. C.R.W. Nevinson, *Paint and Prejudice*, p. 107.
90. E. Pound, 'The War and Diverse Impressions', *Vogue* (October 1916). TGA.
91. C.A.P., 'The War from a New Angle: The Nevinson Pictures at the Leicester Galleries', *Graphic* (30 September 1916). TGA.
92. B.D.T., 'War in Art', *Manchester Guardian* (7 March 1917). TGA.
93. His father recorded that the opening night had seen 'a fair crowd, but not a cram.' He also recorded that Epstein was the only artist to attend the show. H.W. Nevinson Journals. e.620/1, 26 September 1916.
94. R. Ingleby, 'Utterly Tired of Chaos', *C.R.W. Nevinson: The Twentieth Century* (Merrell Holberton, 1999), p. 17.
95. P.G. Konody, *Modern War Paintings by C.R.W. Nevinson* (London, Grant Richards, 1917), p. 19.
96. *Ibid.*, p. 30. By the end of the exhibition he was involved in the production of some illustrations for Mrs H. Haden Guest (ed.), *Princess Marie-Jose's Children's Book* (London, Cassell & Co., 1916). Raising money for milk and clothes for children who had lost everything behind the firing lines of this war, Richard could now add the 'charitable' image to all those others so carefully crafted.
97. 'All Done', *Daily Mirror* (18 October 1916). TGA.
98. One composition, called *Music Hall*, was painted on a thick piece of wood, and had, stuck to the canvas, lace, tin foil, tinselled paper and silk. 'The London Group', *Glasgow Herald* (24 November 1916). TGA. This, while in place with the London Group, was certainly an odd choice to exhibit at the NEAC in the final weeks of 1916.
99. Tea, cakes and cigarettes were provided and Richard was reported to have been quite busy, explaining his ideas to groups, which on one occasion included his mother. 'Art At Homes', *Weekly Dispatch* (19 November 1916). TGA.
100. Nevinson to Rothenstein, 22 October 1916. Harvard.
101. 'Personality or Process. Mr Nevinson's Pictures of Men as War Machines', *The Times* (September 1916). TGA.
102. HWN Journals, e. 620/1, 17 October 1916.
103. *Ibid.*, e. 620/1, 9 November 1916.
104. *Ibid.*, e. 620/1, 15 November 1916.
105. *Ibid.*, e. 620/1, 23 November 1916.
106. *Ibid.*, e. 620/1, 1 December 1916.
107. *Ibid.*, e. 620/ 1, 11 December 1916.
108. H.W. Nevinson, *Visions and Memories* (Oxford University Press, 1944), p. 143.
109. HWN Journals, e. 620/1, 12 December 1916.

110. *Ibid.*, e. 620/1, 15 December 1916.
111. *Ibid.*, e. 620/1, 19 December 1916.
112. *Ibid.*, e. 620/1, 20 December 1916.
113. *Ibid.*, e. 620/1, 21 December 1916.
114. *Ibid.*, e. 620/1, 26 December 1916.
115. Severini to Nevinson, 18 December 1916. TGA.

CHAPTER NINE

1. Masterman to Buchan, 18 May 1917. IWM.
2. HWN Journals, e. 620/1, 11 January 1917.
3. *Ibid.*, e. 620/2, 17 March 1917.
4. *Ibid.*
5. *Ibid.*, e. 620/2, 18 March 1917.
6. *Ibid.*, e. 620/2, 29 March 1917.
7. C.F.G. Masterman was born at Rotherfield Hall in Sussex in 1873. He was educated at Christ's College, Cambridge, and later went on to write for the *Daily News*, *Athenaeum* and *Nation*. He became Liberal MP for West Ham in 1906. At the outbreak of war he was put in charge of the War Propaganda Bureau based at Wellington House, which would be responsible, amongst other things, for appointing war artists. By February 1917 he had been given the rank of lieutenant colonel within the Department of Information on a salary of £1,000 a year. He would have been pivotal in the selection of Richard as an official war artist.
8. The painting, it should be noted, shed all association with Futurism and the war modernism of the 1916 show. If anything it was an exercise in the conservative treatment of a dynamic new subject.
9. HWN Journals, e. 620/2, 5 April 1917.
10. Of course Henry did not 'serve' at Ladysmith he was there as a war correspondent.
11. Nevinson to Sir Edward Marsh, 1 April 1917. NYPL.
12. *Ibid.*, 17 April 1917. NYPL.
13. This is confirmed in *Paint and Prejudice* where Richard recorded 'I wrote to Eddie Marsh, who could do nothing for me.' C.R.W. Nevinson, *Paint and Prejudice*, p. 93.
14. HWN Journals, e. 620/2, 10 April 1917.
15. *Ibid.*, e. 620/2, 11 April 1917.
16. *Ibid.*, e. 620/2, 13 April 1917.
17. *Ibid.*, e. 620/2, 16 April 1917.
18. Nevinson to Mond, 30 April 1917. IWM.
19. Nevinson to Marsh, 24 April 1917. NYPL. In the previous letter dated 17 April he had added a p.s. to the bottom of his letter which had stated 'Some people have been trying to get me in as an Artist...but I have heard nothing of it so far & don't suppose I will!'
20. *Ibid.*, 26 April 1917. NYPL.
21. HWN to Masterman, 1 May 1917. IWM.
22. Masterman to Nevinson, 2 May 1917. IWM.
23. *T.P.'s and Cassell's Weekly* (19 June 1926).
24. Masterman to Charteris, 3 May 1917. IWM.
25. Masterman to Buchan, 18 May 1917. IWM.
26. C.R.W. Nevinson, *Paint and Prejudice*, p. 93.
27. *Ibid.*, p. 94.
28. *Ibid.*,p. 95.
29. The business of the uniform, which Richard wanted, was resolved by letting him wear his father's correspondents uniform. See Hutton-Wilson to Masterman, 19 June 1917. IWM, and also Nevinson to Derrick, 21 June 1917, IWM.
30. Basically, although he conceded that the government had all copyright on his work for the duration of the war, he wanted to be sure that he had the right to exhibit privately and that he could dispose of them at his own discretion.
31. Masterman to Nevinson, 2 July 1917. IWM.
32. Severini to Nevinson, 7 June 1917. TGA.
33. Air Vice-Marshall Sir William Sefton Brancker was Deputy Director of Military Aeronautics then later Major-General of the Air Force by the end of the war. Their paths had crossed in January 1917 when he had opened a show at the Grosvenor Galleries, organized by the Countess of Drogheda, which dealt with aviation and to which Richard had contributed four oil paintings.
34. C.R.W. Nevinson, *Paint and Prejudice*, p. 96. This was achieved, according to Richard, through the efforts of Elizabeth Asquith and Lady Parsons.
35. The 'Efforts and Ideals' series was a scheme sponsored by the Department of Information, commissioning lithographs from eighteen artists. Richard's contribution was six lithographs collectively entitled 'Building Aircraft'. The exhibition of these works first appeared at the Fine Arts Society in July 1917, and later toured Paris, New York and Los Angeles. The idea was to emphasize the efforts being made on the home front.
36. Nevinson to Masterman, 30 June 1917. IWM.
37. HWN Journals, e. 620/2, 3 July 1917.
38. S. Malvern, 'Art, Patronage and Propaganda: An History of the Employment of British War Artists 1916–1919' (PhD diss., Reading University, 1981), p. 99.
39. C.R.W. Nevinson, 'When the Censor Censored 'Censored.' Stories of a Strange Chateau in France and Other War Memories of C.R.W. Nevinson, the Famous War Artist' *British Legion Journal* (October 1932). He said that it had fake medieval turrets and drawbridge.
40. Nevinson to Derrick, 21 June 1917. IWM. He argued that this would reduce the chance of being thought of as a spy. He did however consider it a bastard affair and often used riding goggles to cover up the badge on his cap (or the lack of a badge).
41. Nevinson to Masterman, 24 July 1917. IWM.
42. HWN to W. Rothenstein, 26 July 1917. Harvard.
43. C.R.W. Nevinson, *Paint and Prejudice*, pp. 137–8.
44. C.R.W. Nevinson, 'When the Censor Censored 'Censored' *British Legion Journal*, p. 115.
45. This is a form of ground support for allied aircraft when anti-aircraft stations fire at enemy aircraft in pursuit. It often resulted in what we call today 'friendly fire'.
46. The term was coined by Rutter in the *Arts Gazette* (28 June 1917).
47. Nevinson to Masterman, undated. TGA.
48. *New York Evening Post* (31 May 1919).
49. HWN Journals, e. 620/2, 16 August 1917.
50. *Ibid.*, e. 620/2, 13 September 1917.
51. *Ibid.*, e. 620/2, 14 September 1917.
52. Hudson to Masterman, 26 October 1917. IWM.
53. Derrick to Masterman, 16 October 1917. IWM.
54. Cited in Malvern, 'Art, Patronage and Propaganda', p.

107.
55. *Ibid.*, p. 187.
56. HWN Journals, e. 620/3, 22 December 1918.
57. *Ibid.*, e. 620/3, 26 December 1917.
58. At which Richard would sell all his works, though how many that is, is not recorded.
59. This was Sir Henry Head, neurologist, lecturer, and editor of the neurological journal *Brain* from 1905 to 1921.
60. F. Rutter, 'The Galleries. New English Art Club', *Sunday Times* (13 January 1918). TGA.
61. B.H. Dias, [Ezra Pound] 'Art. The New English Art Club', *New Age* (22 January 1918). TGA.
62. In 1917 Richard had even veered away from the war subject completely, exhibiting works such as *From the Office Window*, *Cornish Landscape*, *Wind*, and *The Blue Wave*.
63. He even found himself omitted entirely from the *Exhibition of Works Representative of the Modern Movement* at the Mansard Gallery in October 1917, though this could be attributable to the fact that it was organized and chosen by Roger Fry.
64. F. Rutter, *Art in my Time* (London, Rich & Cowan, 1933), p. 168.
65. Michael Arthur Leeded, *The First Duce: D'Annunzio at Fuime* (Baltimore: John Hopkins University Press, 1977), pp. 1–2.
66. Nevinson to Masterman, 4 January 1918. IWM.
67. *Ibid.*, 9 January 1918. IWM.
68. HWN Journals, e. 620/3, 5 and 8 February 1918.
69. *Ibid.*, e. 620/3, 18 February 1918.
70. William Maxwell Aitken, born in Ontario, Canada, in 1879, moved to England in 1911 and became Conservative MP for Ashton-under-Lyne. He became Minister of Information in 1918 under Lloyd George who also gave him the title of Lord Beaverbrook.
71. HWN Journals, e. 620/3, 1 March 1918.
72. *Ibid.*, e. 620/3, 16 February 1918. HWN records 'The Friends Ambulance sent ribbons of the 1914 star for me and Richard, which was a welcome reward, though mine was cheaply won.' Richard, later in life was presented the Legion d'Honneur by the French Government.
73. Lee to Yockney, 3 March 1918. TGA.
74. C.R.W. Nevinson, *Paint and Prejudice*, p. 107.
75. *Ibid.*, p. 109.
76. *Catalogue of an Exhibition of Pictures of War by C.R.W. Nevinson (Official Artist on the Western Front)* (London, Leicester Galleries, March 1918).
77. *Ibid,*
78. General Sir Ian Hamilton bought *War Profiteers* whilst Lady Tradegar purchased *Bursting Shell.*
79. 'The War Pictures', *Westminster Gazette* (23 March 1918). TGA.
80. 'At the Leicesters', *Sketch* (13 March 1918). TGA.
81. 'The Khaki Cut', *Star* (8 March 1918). TGA.
82. The military aspect was not abandoned completely and stories continued to appear in the press about how he had been captured by his own men and nearly court-martialled as a spy, had more senior authorities not intervened. *Daily Mirror* (20 March 1918). TGA. Also, ironically, another reviewer said that it was precisely his unaffected appearance as an artist, and his appearance as a Philistine instead, which had lead to his success. L. McQuilland, 'The Man Who Paints Motion', *Lloyds Magazine* (undated). TGA.
83. 'British Artists at the Front', *Illustrated London News* (9 March 1918). TGA.
84. F. Maclean, 'Everyman's Pictures. The New Freedom in Art', *Everyman* (9 March 1918). TGA.
85. R. Cork, *A Bitter Truth: Avant-Garde Art and the Great War*, p. 168.
86. J. Ferguson, *The Arts in Britain in World War I* (London, Steiner & Bell, 1980), p. 112.
87. For example he exhibited with Severini and Epstein at the AAA show in June 1917.
88. As it had been when Lady Cunard had suggested it back in 1916.
89. 'As an Idealist Sees the War', *Everyweek and War Budget* (March 1918). TGA.
90. 'Mr Nevinson's Art', *Globe* (March 1918).
91. 'Duds for the Imperial War Museum', *Saturday Review* (16 March 1918). TGA. Clive Bell attacked this attack in the *New Age* (11 April 1918), saying that Richard was right for the job, so long as you believed that the job in hand was illustrating the war, for the general accolades of 'the people'.
92. 'Mr Nevinson on Himself', *Saturday Review* (13 April 1918). The editor didn't let it lie there either, adding a note at the bottom saying that if Richard hadn't been so out spoken about public schools etc there would have been no need for the attack. He therefore supported the 'well-merited rebuke of our reviewer.'
93. Campbell Dodgson, *British Artists at the Front I. C.R.W. Nevinson* (London, Country Life, 1918).
94. J. Turner, Lieut, letter, 'To the Editor of The Saturday Review', *Saturday Review* (25 May 1918).
95. J. Salis, 'Art of To-Day. Nevinson's Second War Exhibition', *New Witness* (undated). TGA.
96. 'An Aesthetic Contrast', *The Times* (4 March 1918). This was specifically said with reference to 'A Group of Soldiers'.
97. HWN Journals, e. 620/4, 25 February 1918.
98. Appropriately *The Bomber* was exhibited at the AAA at the Grafton Galleries in July 1918. It also may have provoked articles such as 'The Triumph of Futurism', *Bulletin*, Sydney, New South Wales, Australia (23 May 1918). TGA.
99. See also *Before the Storm*, 1916.
100. P.G. Konody, *Modern War Paintings by C.R.W. Nevinson* (London: Grant Richards, 1917), p. 24.
101. C. Dodgson, *British Artists at the Front I. C.R.W. Nevinson* (London: Country Life, 1918).
102. The sitter for which was the Sitwell's butler.
103. This method, or priority in depiction, was also apparent later when he exhibited *Squalor* and *The Triumph of Man* at the NEAC in June 1918. It is interesting to note that at this time Richard's mother had also published her own sketches of social issues and human suffering in the form of M. Nevinson, *Workhouse Characters* (London, George Allen and Unwin, 1918). The book is dedicated to her son.

104. C.E. Doherty, 'Nash, Nevinson and Roberts at War', p. 265
105. O.R.D., 'More War Pictures by Mr Nevinson', *The Westminster Gazette* (13 March 1918). TGA.
106. F. MacLean, 'The New Freedom in Art', *Everyman* (9 March 1918). TGA.
107. 'Art in London', *Architect* (16 March 1918). TGA.
108. Nevinson to Masterman, 10 and 17 March 1918. IWM.
109. O. Brown, *Exhibition: The Memoirs of Oliver Brown* (London: Evelyn Adams & Mackay, 1968), p. 50
110. J.E. Crawford-Flitch, *The Great War: Fourth Year* (London, Country Life, 1918), p. 8.
111. HWN Journals, e. 620/3, 5 October 1917.
112. J.E. Crawford-Flitch, *The Great War, Fourth Year: Paintings by C.R.W. Nevinson* (London, 1918), p. 15.
113. Major Lee, for example, had drawn Richard's attention to the fact that his traffic was on the wrong side of the road in *The Road from Arras to Bapaume.* Lee to Yockney, 27 October 1917. IWM.
114. Cited in S. and M. Harries, *The War Artists: British Official War Art of the Twentieth Century* (London, Michael Joseph, 1983), pp. 44–5. Richard rightly pointed out that his subjects were ordinary men asked to pose outside a tube station in London. They were not, therefore, idealized or stylized at all.
115. HWN Journals, e. 620/3, 22 November 1917.
116. Nevinson to Lee, undated. IWM.
117. Lee to Masterman, 13 December 1917. IWM and two letters from Lee to Yockney, 3 and 23 March 1917. TGA.
118. Major Lee had difficulty with other war artists too and commented on the work of Paul Nash by saying 'I cannot help thinking that Nash is having a huge joke with the British public, and lovers of "art" in particular. Is he?' Lee to Yockney, 2 May 1918. IWM.
119. Masterman to Nevinson, 26 November 1917. IWM.
120. Masterman to Lee, 27 October 1917. IWM.
121. C.H. Collins Baker, *Saturday Review* (16 March 1918).
122. C.R.W. Nevinson, *Paint and Prejudice*, p. 110.
123. Lee to Yockney, 29 November 1917. IWM.
124. Nevinson to Masterman, 3 December 1917. IWM. Later Richard reiterated the point that these were not portraits in the *Evening Post*, New York (31 May 1919).
125. *Daily Mirror* (22 November 1916).
126. Nevinson to Masterman, 3 December 1917. IWM.
127. *Evening Post*, New York (31 May 1919).
128. Nevinson to Masterman, 3 December 1917. IWM.
129. Yockney to Nevinson, 20 December 1917. IWM. This letter was seen as a 'formal' instruction not to exhibit or reproduce the painting.
130. HWN Journals, e. 620/ 3, 15 March 1918.
131. Gillian Forrester raised this whole question when she observed that the censorship question was unusual at a time when the government was actually looking for more 'savage' images from the artist. Cited in T. O'Shaughnessy, 'Gallery Displays Nevinson Images', *Sunday Republican* (27 February 2000).
132. Nevinson to Masterman, 17 March 1918. IWM.
133. *London Mail* (16 March 1918).
134. S. Malvern. 'War as it is: The Art of Muirhead Bone, C.R.W. Nevinson and Paul Nash, 1916–1917' *Art History* (December 1986), p. 507.
135. Nevinson to Masterman, 10 March 1918. IWM.
136. Nevinson to Masterman, 17 March 1918. IWM.
137. HWN Journals, e. 620/3, 3 April 1918.
138. *Ibid.*, e. 620/3, 10 March 1918.
139. *Ibid.*, e. 620/3, 3 April 1918.
140. *Ibid.*, e. 620/3, 8 April 1918.
141. *Ibid.*, e. 620/3, 13 April 1918.
142. Nevinson to Ross, 21 April 1918. IWM.
143. *Ibid.*, 7 April 1918. IWM.
144. *Ibid.*, 21 April 1918. IWM.
145. Louis J. McQuilland, 'The Man Who Paints Motion', *Lloyds Magazine* (1918).
146. HWN Journals, e. 620/3, 1 June 1918.
147. *Ibid.*, e. 620/3, 5 June 1918.
148. *Ibid.*, e. 620/4, 30 August 1918.
149. British Permanent Memorials Committee. Memorandum by Arnold Bennett. 9 March 1918. IWM: 486/12.
150. Ross to Bennett, 23 April 1918. IWM.
151. It was then thought that perhaps he could tackle a large depiction of the Royal Flying School at Gosport, or perhaps a tank.
152. C.R.W. Nevinson, *Paint and Prejudice*, p. 115.
153. Nevinson had said in *Paint and Prejudice* 'after the Armistice I did not do a stroke of painting which dealt with the war', p. 117.
154. Nevinson to Yockney, 8 July 1918 and 20 August 1918. IWM.
155. Arnold Bennett, British War Memorials Committee (9 March 1918). IWM.
156. 'Protective Mimicry', *Saturday Review* (16 November 1918). TGA.
157. Cited in M. Hall, *Modernism, Militarism and Masculinity*, p. 624.
158. D. Peters Corbett, *The Modernity of English Art 1914–1930* (Manchester University Press, 1997), p. 153.
159. F. Rutter, *Sunday Times* (5 January 1919). TGA.

CHAPTER TEN

1. K. Parkes, 'Nevinson', *Apollo* (November 1928), p. 259.
2. C.R.W. Nevinson, *Paint and Prejudice*, p. 117.
3. Sir John Lavery and Solomon J. Solomon were his seconds according to *Paint and Prejudice*, p. 117.
4. Richard contributed the *Roads of France* series, *War in the Air*, and nine other lithographs. This was not a Royal Academy show despite the address and as such some modern painting found its way into galleries previously out of reach to them. I allude here to the work of Lewis and Roberts. The previous December the R.A. had also lent its exhibition space for a show of official Australian war art. This was not the first post-war exhibition for Richard as the London Group show at Heal's Galleries actually straddled the war's end. Here he had exhibited the *Four Seasons*, which was the same landscape painted at four different times of the year. This drew comparisons with Claude Monet. He also exhibited a river scene of the Seine near Rouen. Likewise he had exhibited some of his etchings at the Leicester Galleries in November/ December, including *The Estuary.*
5. 'The Canadian War Memorials', *Canadian War*

Memorials Exhibition (London, Burlington House, January and February 1919).

6. *Sunday Times* (5 January 1919). TGA. There is a reference to this comment in the HWN Journals, e.621/1, 13 February 1919. A letter to the *Sunday Times* by F. Fitzgerald Price (15 January 1919), actually pointed out that Rutter's criticism was unjust for another reason, and that was that all the paintings bought by the Canadians were completed between November 1917 and June 1918. They had not purchased any from 1915 as stated.
7. C.R.W. Nevinson, 'Mr Nevinson's War Pictures', *Sunday Times* (26 January 1919). TGA.
8. Sir Claude Phillips, 'Royal Academy. Canadian War Memorials', *Daily Telegraph* (7 January 1919). TGA.
9. Though Richard did not necessarily remove himself from pre-war associations, writing the obituary for Guillaume Apollinaire in *Colour* (January 1919).
10. 'Canada in the War', *Daily News and Leader* (4 January 1919). TGA. Lewis, in this article, was also viewed as Futurist.
11. 'Rebels in the Fortress', *Daily Express* (3 January 1919). TGA.
12. 'Real War in Pictures', *Sheffield Daily Telegraph* (6 January 1919). TGA.
13. 'Are Futurists Mad?', *Illustrated Chronicle* (22 January 1919). The same article then appeared in other papers, such as the *Daily Express* (21 January 1919) and the *Westminster Gazette* (1 February 1919).
14. C.H. Moore, 'Mr Nevinson's War Pictures', *Sunday Times* (12 January 1919). TGA.
15. O.R.D., 'The Canadian War Memorials Exhibition', *Westminster Gazette* (29 January 1919). TGA.
16. Konody to Bomberg. Cited in R. Cork. *Vorticism and Abstract Art in the First Machine Age*, vol. 2 (Berkeley, University of California Press, 1976), p. 513.
17. *Manchester Guardian* (6 January 1919). TGA. This painting, *War in the Air*, actually came in for many positive reviews, and was reproduced in *The Bystander*, as an example of the quality work on display at the exhibition.
18. 'A Backslider', *Daily Mirror* (6 March 1919). TGA.
19. 'A Nevinson Dinner', *Daily Mirror* (15 March 1919). TGA.
20. 'As You Were', *Sunday Evening Telegram* (2 February 1919). TGA.
21. 'A Painter Among the Poets', *Daily Sketch* (27 February 1919). TGA.
22. 'A Celebrity Dances', *Sunday Pictorial* (23 February 1919). TGA.
23. Such was the interest in the celebrity couple that it was even reported in the *Empire News* (2 March 1919), TGA, that Richard had the flu.
24. Richard had told the reporter of the *Daily Express* (24 February 1919), TGA, that he would be leaving shortly for 'a tour in America'.
25. 'Bolshevism in Art: Catering for the Intellectual Snob', *Daily Express* (10 March 1919). TGA.
26. *Weekly Dispatch* (9 March 1919). TGA. Richard was also still exhibiting war pieces, for example at the 'War in the Air' (RAF) exhibition at the Grafton Galleries, throughout April and May, 1919.
27. O. Sitwell, *C.R.W. Nevinson* Contemporary British Artists Series (London, Ernest Benn, 1925), p. 8.
28. Even by 1921 Richard was still painting retrospective war scenes, by now tinged with bitterness and irony. One set of three paintings he called his 'Peace' series and they included *Yes, And They Still Have Their Hats Off*, *Success* and *A Memorial to Our Heroic Speakers* otherwise known as *Glittering Prizes*. The latter was a parody on a speech made by Lord Birkenhead, who had said, at Glasgow University on 7 November 1923 'The world continues to offer glittering prizes to those who have stout heart and sharp swords.' Cited in F.E.S. Birkenhead, *The Speeches of Lord Birkenhead* (London, Cassell, 1929). The painting in the catalogue was entitled *A Peace Memorial to Our Heroic (After Dinner) Speakers from a Few Unknown Soldiers*. Birkenhead threatened a lawsuit over Richard's comments, and Henry recorded in his journal that Richard painted out the cigars and champagne glass as a direct result. HWN Journal, e.623/3, 12 March 1924.
29. C.R.W. Nevinson, *Paint and Prejudice*, p. 125. Richard said that Matisse particularly admired *Clapham Common*, *Hampstead Heath*, *Adam and Eve* and *The Inexperienced Witch*, which, he conceded, displayed too much of the 'spirit of the immediate post-war days'.
30. The compositions exhibited with the Senefeld Club were reported, in the *Daily News and Leader* (25 January 1919), TGA, as *Le Post* and *A Wet Evening in Oxford Street*. The club was also reported as being called the Senefelder Club and was for 'the advancement of artistic lithography.'
31. Yockney to Nevinson, March 1919. IWM. The autumn show was 'The Nations War Pictures and Other Records' to be held at Burlington House.
32. Yockney to Central Press Photos, Ltd., 28 March 1919. IWM. Other photographs of the artist in his studio appeared at the same time; the *Daily Sketch* (29 March 1919), TGA, the *Daily Graphic* (31 March 1919), TGA, and the *Leeds Mercury* (1 April 1919), TGA. The latter two had the cropped version of *Harvest of Battle* in the background.
33. *Evening Standard & St. James Gazette* (9 April 1919), TGA, joked that he might also have provided information concerning taxi fares.
34. *Daily Express* (28 March 1919). TGA.
35. 'A great War Picture', *Glasgow Evening Citizen* (28 March 1919). TGA.
36. These 'facts' also widely reported that Richard had been at the Front for two entire years.
37. This painting became the focus of much more trouble for Richard, especially when he offered to buy it back from the government, which had intended it for the Hall of Remembrance. An angry letter to Yockney stated 'there are only two persons I wish to avoid in life one is artists & the other American crooks unfortunately through the IWM I have got mixed up with both – I want to free myself from both.' Nevinson to Yockney, 25

March 1920. IWM.

38. The dinner was arranged for 11 April at the Café Royal, for 7.15 p.m. On the committee were: the Right Hon. Lord Henry Cavendish-Bentick, MP, Mr H. Chadwick Moore (honorary secretary), Mr Grant Richards, Mr Walter Sickert (chairman) and Mr Charles Sims, RA (the latter did not attend).
39. H.W. N. Journals, e.621/1, 11 April 1919.
40. C.R.W. Nevinson, *Paint and Prejudice*, p. 128.
41. 'An Artist's War Cry', *Observer* (13 April 1919). TGA.
42. 'Hansoms, Pictures, Books, Plays', *Bristol Times & Mirror* (16 April 1919). TGA.
43. By which time the Friday Club show had opened at the Alpine Gallery in which Richard also exhibited *Demos, a Nightclub Decoration*, which apparently did harp back to his Futurist roots.
44. *New York Times Magazine* (25 May 1919), p. 13.
45. P.G. Konody, *Observer* (2 October 1921). TGA.
46. F. Rutter, *Art in my Time* (Rich & Cowan, 1933), p. 169.
47. C.R.W. Nevinson, *Paint and Prejudice*, p. 173.
48. This was reported on in the *Daily Express* (21 May 1919), and originated in an interview given in New York on 19 May.
49. *New York Times* (29 May 1919). TGA.
50. *American Art News* (29 October 1921).
51. C.R.W. Nevinson, 'The Arts Within this Bellicose Civilization', *The Seven Pillars of Fire: A Symposium by Dr Maude Royden, Dr L.P. Jacks, Prof. A.E. Richardson, the Marquis of Tavistock, C.R.W. Nevinson, Capt. Bernard Acwor and Sir E. Denison Ross* (London, Barrie Jenkins, 1936), p. 212.
52. 'Notes From New York', *Evening Standard & St. James Gazette* (3 July 1919). TGA.
53. *The Old World and the New*, exhibition catalogue (Bourgeois Galleries, 10 November – 4 December 1920).
54. C.R.W. Nevinson to Dr. Herman Theodore Radin. Smithsonian-Radin. In a further letter to Gallatin, dated 8 November 1930, and in the same collection, he described New York as 'the most beautiful city in the world'.
55. L.J. Price, 'New York Letter', *Leader*, 13 November 1920. TGA.
56. 'Some Famous Figures in the Foreign News', *Union*, Springfield, Mass (31 October 1920). TGA.
57. D. Cohen, 'The Rising City' *C.R.W. Nevinson: The Twentieth Century* (London, Merrell Holberton, 1999), p. 40.
58. Lisa Messinger has also suggested that Richard used other photographic compositions, especially those of Emil Otto Hoppe, and suggests that original compositional ideas, such as looking through Brooklyn Bridge, might have found their beginning there. 'Nevinson in New York' (unpublished, lecture at the Imperial War Museum, November 1999).
59. Though the Brooklyn Bridge was completed in 1883 it would still have been one of the tallest structures in New York, except perhaps for the steeple of Trinity Church, the 47-storey Singer Building, and the Woolworth Building.
60. Lisa Messinger turns to artists such as Max Weber as being the true pioneers of depicting the city, often in a kaleidoscopic way. She dates these experiments to 1913. 'Nevinson in New York', p. 3.
61. D. Cohen, 'The Rising City', *C.R.W. Nevinson: The Twentieth Century* (London, Merrell Holberton, 1999), p. 47.
62. Frederick Keppel & Co., 4 East 39th Street, New York City.
63. John Marin conducted experiments into Futurist images of New York City with watercolours prior to the outbreak of the Great War.
64. A.E. Gallatin, 'Introduction' *Etchings & Lithographs by C.R.W. Nevinson* (New York, Keppel & Co., 1919).
65. The literary reference is to a poem entitled 'Died of Wounds' by Siegfried Sassoon, which describes Delville Wood.
66. The latter would also be known as *Broadway in the Rain*.
67. C.R.W. Nevinson to Albert Eugene Gallatin. Smithsonian-Gallatin.
68. Richard suggested that the problem here lay with the ambiguity in the word 'pictures', which in America also means cinema reels. They were therefore signed away to be duplicated as a means of propaganda.
69. C.R.W. Nevinson to Albert Eugene Gallatin, 4 August 1919. Smithsonian-Gallatin. A further letter to Gallatin shows that the Worcester Art Msuem affair was still not resolved by the end of February 1920. Richard had tried to get the government to intervene, but to no avail. C.R.W. Nevinson to A.E. Gallatin, 29 February 1920. Smithsonain-Gallatin.
70. *Ibid.*
71. *Ibid.* Undated letter. Richard was part of a delegation sent to Prague in 1920 to take part in the Freedom Festival there. The delegation included H.G. Wells, Robert Nichols, Sir Edward Elgar, Mrs Patrick Campbell, Lord Dunsany, Ward Muir and P.G. Konody.
72. C.R.W. Nevinson to C. Lewis-Hind, 27 October 1920. Fitzwilliam Museum, Cambridge University. In the catalogue this point was added to, referring to 'the slimy productions of the Salon'.
73. C.R.W. Nevinson, 'My Art Creed', *The Old World and the New* (Bourgeois Galleries, 10 November – 4 December 1920).
74. C.R.W. Nevinson, *Paint and Prejudice*, p. 135.
75. H.W. N. Journals, e.621/1, 3 June 1919.
76. *Ibid.*, e. 621/1, 4 June 1919.
77. *Ibid.*, e. 621/1, 6 June 1919.
78. *Ibid.*, e. 621/1, 8 June 1919.
79. M. Nevinson, *Life's Fitful Fever* (London, A. & C. Black, 1926), p. 279.
80. C.R.W. Nevinson to A.E. Gallatin, 16 June 1919. Gallatin Papers. Reels 507, 508 & 1293. New-York Historical Society, Manuscripts Division. Copies at Archives of American Art, Smithsonian Institution, Washington, D.C.
81. C.R.W. Nevinson, *Paint and Prejudice*, p. 140.
82. HWN Journals, e. 621/1, 18 June 1919.
83. 'Movements in Art', *Sunday Evening Telegram* (29 June

1919). TGA.
84. C.R.W. Nevinson, 'Modern Art', *The World* (4 October 1919). TGA.
85. He was also reported to have bought to Matisse paintings at this show. See: 'Echoes of the Town', *Daily Sketch* (17 November 1919). TGA.
86. HWN Journals, e. 621/2, 7 September 1919.
87. *Ibid.*,e. 621/2, 19 October 1919.
88. *Daily Sketch* (25 October 1919). TGA.
89. *Catalogue of an Exhibition of New Works by C.R.W. Nevinson* (London, Leicester Galleries, October–November, 1919).
90. R. Ingleby, 'Utterly Tired of Chaos' *C.R.W. Nevinson: The Twentieth Century* (London, Merrell Holberton, 1999), p. 20.
91. '"Peace" by Nevinson', *Daily Herald* (27 October 1919). TGA.
92. Such was the diversity of his work, he exhibited *Lovers* at the 'Modern Masters of Etching' exhibition at the Leicester Galleries, also in October 1919. The image was described as the tenderest piece of work, youthful and full of the feeling which Mr Nevinson possesses in a superabundant degree.' *Truth* (15 October 1919). TGA. Nevinson also exhibited at the Society of Scottish Artists in Edinburgh in November 1919 and the Ceramic Society exhibition of modern painting at Stoke town hall.
93. D. Peters Corbett, *The Modernity of English Art 1914-1930* (Manchester University Press, 1997), p. 152.
94. C.R.W. Nevinson, *Paint and Prejudice*, p. 109.
95. Corisande, 'Comedy in Painting', *Evening Standard & St. James Gazette* (November 1919). TGA.
96. 'No Believer in "isms"', *Daily News* (27 October 1919). TGA.
97. 'Mr Nevinson's Return to Nature', *The Times* (28 October 1919). TGA.
98. 'A Painter of Modern Life', *Observer* (November 1919). TGA.
99. 'The Nevinson Palace of Varieties', *Westminster Gazette* (4 November 1919).
100. C. Marriott, 'Stunting in Art', *Outlook* (8 November 1919). TGA.
101. D. Peters Corbett, *The Modernity of English Art 1914–1930* (Manchester University Press, 1997), p. 157.
102. The father was also prepared to 'brawl' with Lord Birkenhead over the painting *Glittering Prizes*, which had provoked a threatened court action. He wrote 'I should have called Birkenhead's bluff. He would not have dared to bring an action.' HWN Journals. e. 620/3, 12 March 1924.
103. 'Off to Paris', *Pall Mall Gazette* (30 October 1919). TGA.
104. HWN Journals, e.621/2, 10 November 1919.
105. By the time of his return he was also exhibiting *The Power Station* and *Large War Picture* (catalogue description) at the Society of Scottish Artists in Edinburgh. Their return to England was reported in the *Bolton Evening News* (November 18 1919). TGA. Also exhibiting his work in and around this time was the Artist's Society, Aberdeen, and the Art Section of the Ceramic Society at Stoke town hall. He also clearly had got back into London nightlife and was reported widely at the opening of a new club called Desti's.
106. For a full history of this exhibition, the committees, priorities, aims and objectives see M. Hall, 'Modernism, Militarism and Masculinity', chapter fourteen.
107. Yockney to the President and Council of the Royal Academy, 25 January 1919. IWM.
108. 'Art and War', *Liverpool Courier* (12 December 1919). TGA.
109. 'Pictures of the War', *Daily News and Leader* (12 December 1919). TGA.
110. 'War Artists' Pictures: Triumph of Young Men in Realising Strife', *Daily Express* (15 December 1919). TGA.
111. 'Pictures of War', *Birmingham Post* (13 December 1919). TGA. Another source, *Building News* (19 December 1919), suggested that he had had sixteen selected (appendix C).
112. C.R.W. Nevinson to IWM, 15 December 1919. IWM.
113. 'War Paintings', *Yorkshire Evening Post* (18 December 1919). TGA.
114. C.R.W. Nevinson to Yockney, 11 June 1919. IWM.
115. 'Young Artists' Triumph', *Daily Mail* (12 December 1919). TGA.
116. B.H. Dias, [Ezra Pound] 'Art Notes', *New Age* (1 January 1920). TGA.
117. M. Chamot, *Painting in England* (London, Country Life, 1937), p. 67.
118. J. Ferguson, *The Arts in Britain in World War I*, p. 74.
119. P. Bond, 'Striking Visions of the First World War' *World Socialist Web Site* (January 2000), p. 8.
120. 'The Selfish Artist', *Sydney, N.S.W.* (10 November 1918). TGA.
121. 'The War Museum', *Evening Standard* (24 December 1919). TGA.
122. 'The Cost of War Pictures', *Evening Standard & St. James Gazette* (27 December 1919). TGA. It also seems that Nevinson did not give up on the aviation themes after the war. One exists entitled *Aerial View (From a Paris Plane)* and is dated to 1919–20.
123. HWN Journals, e. 621/2, 10 December 1919.
124. *Ibid.*, e. 621/2, 11 December 1919.
125. *Ibid.*, e. 621/2, 12 December 1919.
126. P.G. Konody, 'Art and Artists. War Paintings at the Royal Academy', *Observer* (14 December 1919). TGA.
127. This was led by Reginald Grundy in the *Daily Graphic* and *The Connoisseur*, as he labelled the paintings 'freaks' and despaired how they ever got to the walls of Burlington House at all. See *Daily Graphic* (21 January 1920) and *The Connoisseur* (February 1920).
128. C. Bell, 'Wilcoxism', *Atheneum* (5 March 1920). Lewis, on the other hand, gathered together Dismorr, Etchells, Ginner, Hamilton, McKnight Kauffer, Turnbull, Wadsworth and Dobson, under the monicker of 'Group X'. In the exhibition catalogue for the Mansard Gallery show of March 1919, he reiterated that the past ten years had seen important developments in painting that should not be dismissed, relaxed or let go. It was not, in his opin-

ion, sufficient to suggest that the moderation at Burlington House was now the avant-garde in England, nor was it acceptable to accept the NEAC, the London Group and the Slade as the centres for enlightened thought in post-war London.

129. J. Ferguson, *The Arts in Britain in World War One* (London, Steiner and Bell, 1980), p. 73.
130. C.R.W. Nevinson, *Paint and Prejudice*, p. 142.
131. HWN Journals, e.621/2, 10 December 1919.
132. C.R.W. Nevinson, *Paint and Prejudice*, p. 124.
133. HWN Journals, e. 621/2, 14 December 1919.
134. *Ibid.*, e. 621/2, 25 December 1919.
135. *Ibid.*, e. 621/2, 28 December 1919.
136. *Ibid.*, e. 621/2, 29 December 1919.
137. *Evening News* (13 June 1922).

BIBLIOGRAPHY

Archival Sources

Fitzwilliam Museum: Cambridge University
Letter from C.R.W. Nevinson to C. L. Hind. (cat. 'C.R.W. Nevinson').

Karl A. Kroch Library: Cornell University
Department of Rare Books. Wyndham Lewis Collection (no. 4612, box 128).

University of Delaware Library
Special Collections Department. Sir Gerald Barry Correspondence (box 3, folder F31).

Friends House Library: London
Service Records: (Temp. MSS 81-1-1-397).

Houghton Libraries: Harvard University
Sir William Rothenstein Collection (Bus. Eng 1148. 1080-27).

Imperial War Museum Archives: London
Nevinson, C.R.W., First World War, Correspondence, 1917–1918 (226A/6).
Nevinson, C.R.W., First World War, Correspondence, 1919–1963 (226B-6).
Nevinson, C.R.W., Second World War, Correspondence, 1940–1943 (GP/55/143).
Nevinson, C.R.W., First World War, Leicester Gallery Exhibition (470/10).
Nevinson, C.R.W., First World War, Roads of France (473/11).

Museo di Arti Moderna e Contemporanea di Trento e Rovereto: Italy
Wadsworth folder (MS 6590).
Fondo Gino Severini (Sev. 2.7, 4.4, 4.20, 4.34, 4.35, 4.62, 76.1, 76.13).
Fondo Fortunato Depero (MS 3223).
Archivi del Futurismo (Sev. 2.6, 2.7, 4.4).

New English Art Club, London
Minutes of the New English Art Club (uncatalogued).
Sales Records.

New York City Public Library: Albert A. Berg Collection
Artists' File: Nevinson, Christopher, Catalogues and Other Pamphlet Materials Relating to (MDGZ 316-05). Prints Division.
New York Public Library. World War I Collection
Marsh folder (7 A.L.S).
Firbank folder (2 A.L.S).

New-York Historical Society: Manuscripts Division
Gallatin Papers (Reels 507, 508 & 1293) (copies at the Archives of American Art, Smithsonian Institute, Washington, D.C.).

Bodleian Library: Oxford University
H.W. Nevinson. Journals (MSS Eng. Misc. e.610-628).

Archive: Slade School of Art
Archive Reader (MS ADD400 box 1+2).

Archive of American Art: Smithsonian Institution. Washington, D.C.
Herman T. Radin Letters (N.17 Frames 531-533).

Tate Archives: London
London Group press cuttings.
Nevinson,C.R.W., Correspondence (8812.1.2.4659/2).
Nevinson, C.R.W., Collection of Press Cutting Albums owned by C.R.W. Nevinson, 14 vols, 1910-1947. (T.G.A. 7311. 1-14).

Harry Ransome Humanities Research Center: University of Texas at Austin
Bennett, Arnold. Papers.
Carrington, Dora. Collection.
Cunard, Nancy. Papers.
Huddlestone, Sisley. Lake Collection.
Morrell, Lady Ottoline. Papers.
Sitwell, Edith. Papers.
Walpole, Sir Hugh. Papers.

Uppingham School Archive

Beinecke Rare Book and Manuscript Library: Yale University
Correspondence: (YCAL MSS 43, box 37, folder 1538).
MS Vault 'Lewis' (box 1).

Nevinson / Stein (YCAL. MSS 76, box 117, folder 2507).
McBride / Nevinson (YCAL. MSS 31, box 9, folder 243).
Exhibition Catalogue (YCAL. MSS 101, box 109, folder 2649).
(Uncat. MS Vault 727, box 14 & 15).

National Art Library: Victoria and Albert Museum, London
Nevinson, C.R.W. Press cutting and catalogue collection.

Secondary Sources

Agnese, G., *Marinetti: Una Vita Esplosiva*. Milan, Camunia, 1990.

———, *Vita di Boccioni*. Milan, Camunia, 1996.

Allied Artists Association, *Allied Artists Association. Fourth – Sixth Annual Salon*. London, Royal Albert Hall, 1911–13. Exhibition catalogue.

———, *Allied Artists Association Seventh Annual Salon*. London, Holland Park, 1914. Exhibition catalogue.

Anscombe, I., *Omega and After: Bloomsbury and the Decorative Arts*. London, Thames & Hudson, 1981.

Apollonio, U., *Futurist Manifestos*. London, Thames & Hudson, 1973.

Arts Council of Great Britain, *Decade 1910–1920*. Leeds City Art Gallery, 1965. Exhibition catalogue.

———, *Vorticism and its Allies*. London, Hayward Gallery, 1974. Exhibition catalogue.

Baldewitz, E.K., 'Les Camoufleurs: The Mobilisation of Art and Artists in Wartime France, 1914–1918'. PhD diss., University of California at Los Angeles, 1980.

Banham, R., *Theory and Design in the First Machine Age*. London, 1960.

Baron,W., *Sickert*. New York, Phaidon, 1973.

———, *The Camden Town Group*. London, Scolar Press, 1979.

Base Details: British Artists of the First World War. Nottingham, University Art Gallery, 1972. Exhibition catalogue.

Beechey, J., 'C.R.W. Nevinson: a controversial modernist', *The Lancet* (15 January 2000).

Bell, C., 'The English Group' *Catalogue of the Second Post Impressionist Exhibition*. London, Grafton Galleries, 1912. Exhibition catalogue.

———, *Art*. London, Chatto & Windus, 1914.

———, 'Art and War', *International Journal of Ethics* (October, 1915).

Binyon, L., *The Art of Botticelli: An Essay in Pictorial Criticism*. London, 1913.

Birkenhead, F., *The Speeches of Lord Birkenhead*. London, Cassell, 1929.

Blythe, R., *Just Friends: Paul and Bunty, John and Christine – and Carrington*. London, Viking, 1999.

Bond, P., 'Striking Visions of the First World War', *World Socialist Web Site* (January, 2000).

Bone, M., *The Western Front*. London, Country Life, 1917.

Borme, A., *The Academy and French Painting in the 19th Century*. New Haven, 1986.

Boulton, D., *Objection Overruled*. London, MacGibbon & Key, 1967.

Bourgeois Galleries, *The Old World and the New*. Bourgeois Galleries, New York, 1920. Exhibition catalogue.

Bozzola, A. and C. Tisdall, *Futurism*. London, Thames & Hudson, 1977.

Bradbury, M. and J. McFarlane (eds), *Modernism*. London, Penguin, 1976.

Braun, E. (ed.), *Italian Art in the Twentieth Century*. London and Munich, 1989.

Brown, O., *Exhibition: The Memoirs of Oliver Brown*. London, Evelyn Adams & Mackay, 1968.

Bullen, J.B., *Post-Impressionists in England*. London, Routledge, 1988.

Campbell, S., *The Enemy Opposite: The Outlaw Criticism of Wyndham Lewis*. Ohio University Press, 1988.

Canaan, G., *Mendel*. London, Lloyds, 1920.

Canaday, J., *Mainstreams in Modern Art*. New York, Rinehart & Winston, 1959.

Canadian War Memorials Fund, *Canadian War Memorials Exhibition*. London, Burlington House, January – February, 1919. Exhibition catalogue.

Carline, R., *Stanley Spencer at War*. London, Faber & Faber, 1978.

Carrington, N., *Carrington: Paintings, Drawings and Decorations*. Oxford, Oxford Polytechnic Press, 1978.

———, (ed.), *Mark Gertler - Selected Letters*. London, Rupert Hart-Davies, 1965.

Causey, A., *Paul Nash*. Oxford, Clarenden Press, 1980.

Caws, M., *Women of Bloomsbury: Virginia, Vanessa and Carrington*. New York, Routledge, 1990.

Chamot, M., *Modern Painting in England*. London, Country Life, 1937.

Chaplin, S., 'Slade School of Art'. University College London, 1998, (unpublished).

Chesterton, G., 'The Futurists' in *The Uses of Diversity: A Book of Essays*. London, Metheun, 1920.

Clark, Sir K., 'Foreword', *The War Artists*. Folkestone, New Metropole Art Centre, 1964.Exhibition catalogue.

Constantine, F., *C.R.W. Nevinson*. Sheffield, Graves Art Gallery, 1972. Exhibition catalogue.

Cork, R., *A Bitter Truth: Avant-Garde Art and the Great War*. New Haven and London, Yale University Press, 1994.

———, *Art Beyond the Gallery in Early 20th Century England*. New Haven and London, Yale University Press, 1985.

———, *David Bomberg*. New Haven and London, Yale University Press, 1987.

———, *Vorticism and Abstract Art in the First Machine Age*, 2 vols. Berkeley and Los Angeles, University of California Press, 1976.

Cournos, J., *Autobiography*. New York, G. P. Putnam's Sons, 1935.

Crawford-Flitch, J., *C.R.W. Nevinson: The Great War, Fourth Year*. London, Grant Richards, 1918.

Cummings, R., *Artists at War, 1914–1918*. Cambridge, Kettles Yard Gallery, 1974. Exhibition catalogue.

Curtis, P. (ed.), *Dynamism: The Art of Modern Life Before the Great War*. London, Tate Gallery, 1991.

Dangerfield, G., *Strange Death of Liberal England*. London, 1935.

Darracot, J. and B. Loftus, *First World War Posters*. London, 1972.

D'Harncourt, A., *Futurism and the International Avant-Garde*. Philadelphia Museum of Art, 1980.

Dodgson, C. and C.E. Montague, *British Artists at the Front, Vol I: C.R.W. Nevinson*. London, Country Life, 1918.

Doherty, C., 'Nash, Nevinson and Roberts at War. A Catalogue Raisonné of First World War Paintings, Drawings and Prints by Paul Nash, C.R.W. Nevinson and William Roberts'. PhD diss., University of Wisconsin, Madison, 1989.

Doherty, C.E., ' The War Art of C.R.W. Nevinson', *Imperial War Museum Bulletin* (1993).

Dore Galleries, *Exhibition of the Works of the Italian Futurist Painters and Sculptors*. London, Dore Galleries, April–May 1911. Exhibition catalogue.

———, *Post- Impressionist and Futurist Exhibition*. London, Dore Galleries, October 1913. Exhibition catalogue.

———, *Vorticist Exhibition*. London, Dore Galleries, June–July 1915. Exhibition catalogue.

Eddy, A., *Cubism and Post-Impressionsim*. Richards, 1914.

Edwards, P., *Wyndham Lewis: Art and War*. London, 1992.

Eksteins, M., *Rites of Spring: The Great War and the Birth of the Modern Age*. New York, Doubleday, 1989.

Epstein, J., *Epstein: An Autobiography*. London, Vista Books, 1963.

Eyre, A., *St. John's Wood: It's haunts, its houses and its celebrities*. London, Chapman & Hall, 1913.

Farr, D., *English Art 1870–1940*. Oxford, Clarendon Press, 1978.

———, *Gilbert Canaan: A Georgian Prodigy*. London, Chatto & Windus, 1978.

Farrell, C., 'Melodrama of Modernity', *University of Toronto Quarterly* vol. 63, no. 2 (winter 1993–4).

Ferguson, J., *The Arts in Britain in World War I*. London, Steiner & Bell, 1980.

Ferrall, C., 'The Politics of Reactionary Modernism before the Great War'. PhD diss., University of Toronto, 1991.

Fine Arts Society, *The Great War: Britain's Efforts and Ideals*. London, Fine Arts Society, 1917.

Flint, K., *The Impressionists in England: The Critical Reception*. London, 1984.

Flint, R.W. (ed.), *Marinetti: Selected Writings*. London, Secker & Warburg, 1971.

Foot, M.R.D., *Art and War. Twentieth Century Warfare as Depicted by War Artists*. London, Headline Book Publishing, 1990.

Ford, B. (ed.), *The Cambridge Guide to the Arts in Britain, Vol 8: The Edwardian Age and the Inter-War Years*. The Cambridge Guide to the Arts in Britain, Cambridge University Press, 1989.

Fraquelli, S., *Gino Severini: From Futurism to Classicism*. London, Estorick Collection, 1999.

Freeman, J., *Made at the Slade: A Survey of Mature Works by Ex-Students of the Slade School of Fine Art, 1892–1960*. Brighton, The Gallery, Brighton Polytechnic, 1979. Exhibition catalogue.

Friday Club, *Catalogue of an Exhibition of Pictures by Members of the Friday Club*. London, Alpine Club Galleries, 1911–19. Exhibition catalogue.

Fry, R., *Catalogue of the Second Post-Impressionist Exhibition*. London, Grafton Galleries, 1912. Exhibition catalogue.

Fuller, P., 'The Arts at War', *New Society* (June, 1982).

Fulleylove, J., *Pictures of Classic Greek Landscape and Architecture*. London, Dent, 1897.

Fussell, P., *The Great War and Modern Memory*. Oxford University Press, 1975.

Gambillo, M. and T. Fiori, *Archivi del Futurismo*. Rome, 1986.

Garnett, D. (ed.), *Carrington: Letters and Extracts from her Diaries*. Oxford University Press, 1979.

Gaunt, W., *March of the Moderns*. London, Cape, 1949.

Gerzina, G., *Carrington: A Life of Dora Carrington 1893–1932*. London, John Murray, 1989.

Golding, J. and Sir Roland Penrose (eds), *Picasso*. London, Paul Elek, 1973.

Grigson, G.E.H., *A Master of Our Time. A Study of Wyndham Lewis*. London, Methuen, 1951.

Guichard, K., *British Etchers 1850-1940*. London, Robin Garton, 1977.

Haden Guest, H., *Princess Maria-Jose's Children Book*. London, Cassell & Co., 1916.

Hall, M., 'Modernism, Militarism and Masculinity: British Modern Art Discourses and Official War Art During the First World War'. PhD diss., State University of New York at Binghampton, 1994.

Hamilton, P., 'The Role of Futurism, Dada and Surrealism in the Construction of British Modernism 1910–1940'. PhD diss., University of Oxford, 1987.

Hampton, C., *Carrington*. London, Faber & Faber, 1995.

Hanson, A., *Severini Futurista: 1912-1917*. London, 1995.

Harries, M. and S., *The War Artists: British Official War Art of the Twentieth Century*. London, Michael Joseph in association with the Imperial War Museum and the Tate Gallery, 1983.

Harrison, C., *English Art and Modernism 1900-1939*. Bloomington, Indiana University Press and London, Allen Lane, 1981.

HASTE, K., *Keep the Home Fires Burning: Propaganda in the First World War*. London, Allen Lane, 1977.

HAWARD, L., *The Effect of War Upon Art and Literature*. Manchester University Press, Longman, Green & Co., 1916.

HERTZ, R. and N. Klein, *Twentieth Century Art Theory: Urbanism, Politics and Mass Culture*. Englewood Cliffs, Prentice-Hall, 1990.

HEWITT, A., *Fascist Modernism: Aesthetics, Politics and the Avant-Garde*. Stanford University Press, 1993.

HILL, J., *The Art of Dora Carrington*. London, Herbert Press, 1994.

HOFFMAN, H., 'Days of a Futurist Past', *New Haven Advocate* (9 March 2000).

HOLROYD, M., *Augustus John*. London, 1974.

HONE, J., *The Life of Henry Tonks*. London, 1939.

HUGHES, G. (ed.), *Imagist Anthology*. London, Chatto & Windus, 1930.

HULTEN, P. (ed.), *Futurism and Futurisms*. New York, Abeville Press, 1986.

———, *Italian Art 1900-1945*. Milan, Bompiani, 1989.

HUNT, D., *Alvaro Guevara, Latin Among Lions*. London, 1974.

HYNES, S., *A War Imagined: The First World War and English Culture*. New York, Atheneum, 1991.

IMPERIAL WAR MUSEUM, *The Nations War Paintings and Other Records*. London, Burlington House, December 1919–January 1920. Exhibition catalogue.

———, *A Concise Catalogue of Paintings, Drawings, and Sculpture of the First World War 1914–1918*, 2nd ed. Introduction by Martin Conway. London, Imperial War Museum, 1963. Exhibition catalogue.

———, *War Pictures: Exhibition at the Royal Academy, Official Illustrated Record. Issued by Authority of the Imperial War Museum*. London, Walter Judd Ltd, 1920. Exhibition catalogue.

JEFFREY, I., 'C.R.W. Nevinson: Artist-Celebrity', *London Magazine* (February / March, 1989).

KAHN, E., *The Neglected Majority:* 'Les Camoufleurs', *Art History and World War I*. Lanham, New York and London, University Press of America, 1984.

KNOWLES, E., *C.R.W. Nevinson*. Cambridge, Kettle's Yard, 1988.

KONODY, P.G., *Modern War: Paintings by C.R.W. Nevinson*. London, Grant Richards 1917.

LARONI, N., *Il Passato al Futuro*. Milan, Bompiani, 1986.

LEGG, L. and E. Williams (eds), *Dictionary of National Biography*. London, Oxford University Press, 1959.

LEED, E., *No Man's Land: Combat and Identity in World War I*. Cambridge University Press, 1979.

LEEDED, M., *The First Duce: D'Annunzio at Fuime*. Baltimore, Johns Hopkins University Press, 1977.

LEWIS, P.W., *Blast: Review of the Great English Vortex*, No. 1. London, John Lane, 1914; Santa Barbara, The Black Sparrow Press, 1981.

———, *Blast: Review of the Great English Vortex*, No. 2. London, John Lane, 1915; Santa Barbara, The Black Sparrow Press, 1981.

———, *Blasting and Bombardiering*. London, Eyre & Spottiswoodie, 1937.

LEWIS-HIND, C., *The Post-Impressionists*. London, Methuen, 1911; Freeport, New York, Books for Libraries Press, 1969.

———, 'What Armageddon Did to Art', *Graphic* (12 January 1924).

LEWISON, J. (ed.), *A Genius of Industrial England: Edward Wadsworth 1889-1949*. Arkwright Arts Trust and Bradford Art Galleries & Museums, 1990.

LIPKE, W.C., 'Futurism and the Development of Vorticism', *Studio International* (April 1967).

LONDON GROUP, *London Group: First-Fifth Exhibition*. London, Goupil Galleries, 1914–16. Exhibition catalogue.

———, *London Group: Sixth-Eleventh Exhibition*. London, Mansard Galleries, 1917–19. Exhibition catalogue.

———, *The London Group Retrospective Exhibition*. Introduction by Roger Fry. London, New Burlington Galleries, 1928. Exhibition catalogue.

MACCOLL, D., *Nineteenth Century Art*. Glasgow, James Maclehose & Sons, 1902.

MCCONKEY, K., *British Impressionism*. New York, Harry N. Abrams, 1989.

MACDONALD, S., 'The Slade and its Concept of Drawing' in *The History and Philosophy of Art Education*. University of London Press, 1970.

MCNALLY, O., 'Images From the Front Lines', *The Hartford Courant* (24 February 2000).

MACEDO, A., 'Wyndham Lewis's Literary Work 1908–1928'. PhD diss., University of Sussex, 1990.

MALVERN, S., 'Art, Patronage and Propaganda: A History of the Employment of British War Artists 1916–1919'. PhD diss., Reading University, 1981.

MALVERN, S., 'War as it is: The Art of Muirhead Bone, C.R.W. Nevinson and Paul Nash, 1916–17', *Art History* (December 1986).

———, 'Memorising the Great War: Stanley Spencer at Burghclere', *Art History* (June 2000).

MARRIOTT, C., *Modern Movements in Painting*. London, Chapman and Hall, 1920.

MARTIN, M. W., *Futurist Art and Theory 1909–1915*. Oxford University Press, 1968.

MARTIN, C., 'C.R.W. Nevinson: The Artist and His Name' *Nevi(n)son News*, Issue 5 (2000).

MARTIN, C., *English Life in the First World War*. London, Wayland Publishers, 1974.

MARWICK, A., *The Deluge: British Society in the First World War*. New York, Norton, 1970.

MASTERMAN, L., *C.F.G. Masterman: A Biography*. London, Nicholson & Watson, 1939.

MAY, H., *Memories of the Artist's Rifles*. London, Howlett & Son, 1929.

MEYERS, J., *The Enemy: A Biography of Wyndham Lewis.* Routledge & Kegan Paul, 1980.

MICHEL, W., *Wyndham Lewis: Paintings and Drawings.* London, 1971.

MUIR, L.-Col. Ward, and Sergt Noel Irving (eds), *'Happy Though Wounded' The Book of the Third London General Hospital'.* London, Country Life, 1917.

NASH, P., *Outline. An Autobiography and Other Writings.* London, Faber & Faber, 1949.

Nash and Nevinson in War and Peace: The Graphic Work 1914–1920. London, The Leicester Galleries at the Alpine Club Gallery, 1977. Exhibition catalogue.

NEVE, C., 'An Artist Over Arras. C.R.W. Nevinson's Air Pictures', *Country Life* (28 September 1972).

NEVINSON, C.R.W. *Catalogue of an Exhibition of Paintings and Drawings of War by C.R.W. Nevinson (Late Private R.A.M.C.).* London, Leicester Galleries, September–October 1916. Exhibition catalogue.

———, *Catalogue of an Exhibition of Pictures of War by C.R.W. Nevinson (Official Artist on the Western Front).* London, Leicester Galleries, March 1918. Exhibition catalogue.

———, *Catalogue of an Exhibition of New Works by C.R.W. Nevinson.* London, Leicester Galleries, October–November 1919. Exhibition catalogue.

———, *Etchings and Lithographs by C.R.W. Nevinson,* with an introduction by A.E. Gallatin. New York, Frederick Keppel & Co., 1919. Exhibition catalogue.

———, *Nevinson Exhibition,* introduction by Lawrence Haward. Manchester, Manchester City Art Gallery, July–August 1920. Exhibition catalogue.

———, *Exhibition of Paintings, Etchings, Lithographs and Woodcuts by C.R.W. Nevinson, of London, England with an introduction by C.L. Hind.* New York, Bourgeois Galleries, November–December 1920. Exhibition catalogue.

———, 'When the Censor Censored "Censored." Stories of a strange Chateau in France and Other War Memories of C.R.W. Nevinson, The Famous War Artist', *British Legion Journal* (October 1932).

NEVINSON, C.R.W., *Paint and Prejudice.* London, Methuen, 1937; New York, Harcourt Brace & Co., 1938.

———, *Catalogue of the Memorial Exhibition of Pictures by C.R.W. Nevinson, A.R.A. (1889-1946),* introduction by Osbert Sitwell. London, Leicester Galleries, May–June 1947. Exhibition catalogue.

———, *C.R.W. Nevinson: War Painting 1914–1918.* Sheffield, Graves Art Gallery, 1972. Exhibition catalogue.

———, *C.R.W. Nevinson: The Great War and After.* London, Maclean Gallery, 1980. Exhibition catalogue.

———, *C.R.W. Nevinson, 1889–1946: Retrospective Exhibition of Paintings, Drawings and Prints.* Cambridge, Kettles Yard Gallery, 1988. Exhibition catalogue.

———, *C.R.W. Nevinson: The Twentieth Century.* Imperial War Museum, London, 1999–2000. Exhibition catalogue.

NEVINSON, H.W., *Changes and Chances.* Nisbet, London, 1923.

———, *Farewell to America.* London, John & Edward Bumpus, 1926.

———, *Last Changes and Last Chances.* Nisbet, London, 1928.

———, *More Changes and More Chances.* London, Nisbet, 1925.

———, *The Fire of Life.* Nisbet, London, 1935.

———, *Visions and Memories.* Oxford University Press, 1944.

NEVINSON, M., *Life's Fitful Fever.* London, A. & C. Black, 1926.

———, *Workhouse Characters.* London, George Allen & Unwin, 1918.

'C.R.W. Nevinson', *Antiques and Arts Weekly* (11 February 2000).

NEW ENGLISH ART CLUB. *Catalogues of the 48th–59th Exhibitions of Modern Pictures by the New English Art Club.* London, Galleries of the Royal Society of British Artists, 1912–18. Exhibition catalogue.

PERLOFF, M., *The Futurist Movement: Avant-Garde, Avant-Guerre, and the Language of Rupture.* Chicago University Press, 1986.

PETERS CORBETT, D., *The Modernity of English Art 1914-1930.* Manchester University Press, 1997.

——— (ed.), *Wyndham Lewis and the Art of Modern War.* Cambridge University Press, 1998.

PETRIE, Sir C., *The Edwardians.* London, 1965.

POPLE, K., *Stanley Spencer.* London, Collins, 1991.

ROBERTS, W., *Some Early Abstract and Cubist Work 1913–1920.* London, Canale Publication of the Favil Press, 1957.

ROSE, W. (ed.), *The Letters of Wyndham Lewis.* Norfolk, Virginia,1963.

ROSS, A., *Colours of War: War Art 1939–45.* London, Jonathan Cape, 1983.

ROSS, M. (ed.), *Robert Ross, Friend of Friends. Letters to Robert Ross, Art Critic and Writer, Together With Extracts From His Published Articles.* London, Jonathan Cape, 1952.

ROTHENSTEIN, J., *British Artists and the War.* London, Peter Davies, 1931.

———, *British Art Since 1900.* London, Phaidon, 1962.

———, ' C.R.W. Nevinson' in *Modern British Painters,* vol. II. London, Eyre & Spottiswoode, 1956.

———, *The Tate Gallery.* London, Thames & Hudson, 1962.

RUSKIN, J., 'War' in *The Crown of Wild Olive. Three Lectures on Work, Traffic and War.* London, Smith & Elder, 1866.

RUSSELL TAYLOR, J., 'The Big Show: C.R.W. Nevinson', *The Times* (30 October 1999).

RUTHERSTON, A. (ed.), *C.R.W. Nevinson.* Contemporary British Artist Series London, Ernest Benn, 1925.

RUTTER, F., *Revolution in Art.* London, Art News Press, 1910.

———, 'C.R.W. Nevinson' in *Some Contemporary Artists.* London, Edward Parsons, 1922.

———, 'The Influence of War on Art' in H.W. Wilson and J. A. Hammerton (eds), *The Great War: The Standard History of the All Europe Conflict,* vol. 12. London, The Amalgamated Press, 1919.

———, *Art in My Time.* London, Rich & Cowan Ltd., 1933.

Sackville Gallery. *Exhibition of the Works by the Italian Futurist Painters.* London, March 1912. Exhibition catalogue.

Salaman, M., *C.R.W. Nevinson*, Masters of Etching Series, No. 31. London, The Studio, 1932.

Sanders, M.L. and P. M. Taylor, *British Propaganda During the First World War, 1914–1918.* London, Macmillan, 1982.

Scheid, T.M., 'Experimentations in Temporal and Spiritual Techniques'. PhD diss., Ohio University, 1985.

Schneidau, H.N., *Ezra Pound. The Image and the Real.* London, 1969.

Severini, G., *The Painter Severini Exhibits his Latest Works.* Marlborough Gallery, London, April 1913. Exhibition catalogue.

Severini, G. (trans. F. Franchina), *The Life of a Painter.* Princeton University Press, 1995.

Sewell, B., 'Pictures that Pack a Punch', *Evening Standard* (19 November 1999).

Sharp, E., *Unfinished Adventure.* London, John Lane, The Bodley Head, 1933.

Sherry, V., *Ezra Pound, Wyndham Lewis and Radical Modernism.* Oxford University Press, 1993.

Shone, R., *The Century of Change: British Art Since 1900.* Oxford, Phaidon, 1977.

Sillars, S., *Art and Survival in First World War Britain.* Basingstoke and London, 1987.

Silver, K., *Esprit de Corps: The Art of the Parisian Avnat-Garde and the First World War, 1914–25.* Princeton University Press, 1989.

Sitwell, Sir O., Introduction: *Memorial Exhibition of Pictures by C.R.W. Nevinson, 1889–1946.* London, Leicester Galleries, 1947. Exhibition catalogue.

Skipworth, P., 'A Synthesis of War: The Painting of C.R.W. Nevinson, 1914–1916', *Connoisseur* (October 1972).

Somigli, L., 'Towards a Theory of the Avant-Garde Manifesto'. PhD diss., State University of New York at Stony Brook, 1996.

Spalding, F., *Roger Fry: Art and Life.* New York, Granada Publishing, 1980.

———, *British Art Since 1900.* London, Thames & Hudson, 1986.

Spencer, R., 'We Are Making a New World: Artists in the 1914–1918 War', *Studio* (December 1974).

Stromberg, R., *Redemption by War: The Intellectuals and 1914.* Kansas, Regents Press, 1982.

Sutton, D. (ed.), *Letters of Roger Fry: Vol. II.* London, Chatto & Windus, 1977.

Symons, J. (ed.), *The Essential Wyndham Lewis.* London, Vintage, 1989.

Tatham, M. and J.E. Miles (eds), *The Friends' Ambulance Unit, 1914–1919: A Record.* London, Swarthmore Press, 1920.

Taylor, J., *Futurism.* New York, Museum of Modern Art, 1961.

Terraine, J., *Impacts of War 1914–1918.* London, Hutchinson, 1970.

Thomas, D., *Battle Art: Images of War.* Oxford, Phaidon, 1977.

Tippett, M., *Art at the Service of War: Canada, Art and the Great War.* University of Toronto Press, 1984.

Trubetzkaya, Princess Mariya and C.R.W. Nevinson, *Exodus, A.D. A Warning to Civilians.* London, Hutchinson, 1934.

Turner, J. (ed.), *The Dictionary of Art.* London, Macmillan, 1996.

Viney, N., *Images of Wartime: British Art and Artists of World War I: Pictures from the Collection of the Imperial War Museum.* Newton Abbot, David & Charles, 1991.

Wadsworth, B., *Edward Wadsworth.* London, Michael Russell, 1989.

Watney, S., *English Post-Impressionism.* London, 1980.

Wees, W.C., *Vorticism and the English Avant-Garde.* University of Toronto Press, 1972.

Whistler, J., *The Gentle Art of Making Enemies.* London, Heinemann, 1890.

Whitechapel Art Gallery, *Twentieth Century Art: A Review of Modern Movements.* London, Whitechapel Art Gallery, May–June 1914. Exhibition catalogue.

Winter, J.M., *The Great War and the British People.* Cambridge, Mass., Harvard University Press, 1986.

Woodall, M., *The Early Years of the N.E.A.C.* London, 1952.

———, *The Experience of World War I* . Oxford University Press, 1989.

Woodson, J., *Mark Gertler.* London, Sidgwick & Jackson, 1972.

INDEX

Photographic Acknowledgements

While every effort has been made to trace copyright holders, any further information on their identity would be welcome. In most cases the illustrations have been made from the photographs or transparencies provided by the owners or custodians of the works. Those for which further credit is due are:
© Courtesy of the artist's estate/Bridgeman Art Library: 5, 7, 8, 9, 11, 16, 19, 21, 30, 31, 35, 37, 39, 42, 53, 54, 61, 62, 68, 69; © Birmingham Art Gallery: 39; © Tate Gallery, London/John Webb: 3, 23; © University Photographic Services, The Brynmor Jones Library: 54